S0-BNT-665

Food _and_ Beverage Cost Control

Second Edition

Jack E. Miller

David K. Hayes

Lea R. Dopson

John Wiley & Sons, Inc.

This book is printed on acid-free paper. ☺

Copyright © 2002 by Jack. E. Miller, David K. Hayes, and Lea R. Dopson. All rights reserved.

Published by John Wiley & Sons, Inc., New York.

Published simultaneously in Canada.

No part of this publication may be reproduced, stored in a retrieval system or transmitted in any form or by any means, electronic, mechanical, photocopying, recording, scanning or otherwise, except as permitted under Sections 107 or 108 of the 1976 United States Copyright Act, without either the prior written permission of the Publisher, or authorization through payment of the appropriate per-copy fee to the Copyright Clearance Center, 222 Rosewood Drive, Danvers, MA 01923, (978) 750-8400, fax (978) 750-4744. Requests to the Publisher for permission should be addressed to the Permissions Department, John Wiley & Sons, Inc., 605 Third Avenue, New York, NY 10158-0012, (212) 850-6011, fax (212) 850-6008, E-Mail: PERMREQ @ WILEY.COM.

This publication is designed to provide accurate and authoritative information in regard to the subject matter covered. It is sold with the understanding that the publisher is not engaged in rendering professional services. If professional advice or other expert assistance is required, the services of a competent professional person should be sought.

Contents

Preface

The authors of this text's second edition recognize, as did the first's, that all foodservice managers, regardless of the type of operation they are involved in, must understand and manage the costs associated with operating their business. The foodservice manager, whether in a commercial restaurant, hotel, or institutional setting, is faced with a variety of responsibilities, from accounting, marketing, human relations, facilities maintenance, and legal issues to sanitation, production, and service methods, to name but a few.

This text will focus, in a very clear way, on helping managers understand the logic and the systems involved with managing their costs. It is intended to be a primer, the first step, in what may be a lifelong and rewarding study of how to be a better manager in the important area of cost control.

The Integration of Technology

The first edition of this text met with great success, thanks in large measure to its easy to teach, easy to read, and easy to understand style. This has been painstakingly maintained in the new edition. The hospitality industry, however, has changed greatly in the years since the publication of the first edition. This change, especially in the area of technological advancements, was the determining factor in the decision to update the book. The authors were committed to producing a work that includes the most up-to-date material on technology and its impact on the critical area of cost control. We believe we have been successful.

Teachers using the text will now find that it allows easy integration of technology and that the teaching tools available to them have been greatly enhanced. The floppy diskette that now accompanies the purchase of each textbook is just one such new tool. There are many others. In adition, the ability to begin immediately to utilize now common tools such as manager-developed spreadsheets and Internet access in ways that were not readily available in the earlier edition are the defining characteristic of this new edition.

Students will quickly see how the skills they have previously acquired while learning to use a computer can be easily adapted to the study of cost control.

Practicing managers will find the book useful as a reference as well as a source of ready-to-use forms and formulas that can be easily applied to their own operations.

New in the Second Edition

New authors bring new vision, and that is certainly true in the case of this revision. In addition, those managers, students, and instructors who used the first edition were extremely helpful in guiding the direction of this revised work. As a result, significant changes in this edition include the following:

Technology Integration The primary driving force behind this revision was the commitment to fully utilize the computer and the Internet as teaching tools. This has been successfully achieved. As students have become more sophisticated in their use of technology, so, too, must those who write, publish, and use their learning tools. At the same time, those who teach from this text will find it remains purposefully teacher-friendly.

Expanded Coverage of Topics Practicing managers have access to computer technology never before available in the foodservice industry. The result is that they face a myriad of challenges as they select those technology tools that are right for their own operations. This new edition directly addresses this challenge of selecting technology tools appropriately with the inclusion of a chapter titled "Using Technology to Enhance Control Systems." Additional areas of expanded coverage include the *Uniform System of Accounts for Restaurants*, menu analysis, and cost/volume/profit analysis.

Chapter Reorganization This effort included the elimination of some topics not directly related to cost control, the inclusion of new topics, and the modification of chapters viewed by some as too long. The result is a 12-chapter, rather than 9-chapter book, with no loss of significant content. In addition, the shorter chapters make the book easier to teach from and understand. The authors' in-classroom testing of this new format shows excellent student acceptance.

Legal Information In those areas where knowledge of the law affects a manager's application of cost control techniques, the law's impact has been integrated.

Extensive Revision and Examination of Formulas Perhaps no area is more important in a book on cost control than the accuracy of the formulas and mathematical solutions used to demonstrate concepts. In addition to extensive reviewer analysis, the authors have conscientiously checked and rechecked to ensure that the formulas, examples, and answers provided are indeed accurate.

One thing that has not changed in the new edition, however, is that the authors continue to find the topic of cost management to be one of creativity, excitement, and, in many cases, outright fun. Contrary to the prevalent idea of cost control as drudgery, cost management in this text becomes an engaging challenge to be met by the foodservice manager.

It may be said that there are three kinds of managers: those who know what has happened in the past, those who know what is happening now, and those who know what is about to happen. Clearly, the manager who possesses all three traits is best prepared to manage effectively and efficiently.

This text will give the reader the tools required to maintain sales and cost histories (the past), develop systems for monitoring current activities (the present), and teach the techniques required to anticipate what is to come (the future).

Essential Elements of the Text

Overviews

Each chapter begins with a brief narrative overview. This is simply a quick and easy guide to the chapter's contents. Overviews make it easy for readers to see what the chapter is about and what they will learn by reading it.

Chapter Outline

The chapter outline that follows the overview helps teachers as well as students see how each topic follows the next and provides a simple way to quickly find material within the chapter.

Chapter Highlights

Each chapter's highlights tell the reader what to expect in that chapter. They are worded in such a way that the reader knows what he or she will be able to *do* at the conclusion of the chapter. These highlights are designed so that readers will be prepared for and excited about what they will be able to achieve when the chapter's material is successfully mastered.

Fun on the Web!

This new addition to the text adds to student learning by integrating the use of technology, in this case the Internet (World Wide Web), to the study of cost control. Students will quickly realize the power of the Web in assisting with the gathering of cost control–related information, as well as providing Web-based resources that help managers more effectively do their jobs.

Key Terms and Concepts

Students often need help in identifying key concepts that should be mastered after reading a section of a book. These are listed at the conclusion of each chapter and are invaluable as study aids.

Test Your Skills

This popular feature has been retained from the first edition, but expanded by using Microsoft Excel spreadsheets (the industry standard) in the solution of the exercise whenever applicable. These exercises are now presented in spreadsheet form via the inclusion of the student's computer diskette. Students can actually "test" their answers thus improving the Instructor's ability to evaluate mastery of the actual cost control concept rather than spreadsheet building ability. The Test Your Skills exercises allow the reader to conclusively determine if he or she has mastered the chapter's content. Again, the intent is to allow the reader to immediately practice the skill acquired in the chapter. Through these exercises, the authors seek to reinforce the concepts presented in the chapters.

Managerial Tools

It is the authors' hope that readers find the book as helpful to use as we found it exciting to develop. To that end, additional appendixes have been developed that will be of great value. *Appendix A: Spreadsheet Formulas* is designed to give readers the formulas that they will need to complete the Test Your Skills exercises at the end of each chapter.

As an easy reference guide, *Appendix B: Frequently Used Formulas for Managing Operations* is included in the back of the text.

This section allows the reader to quickly look up the mathematical formula for any of the computations presented in the text. We have intentionally chosen the simplest formulas that have the widest use.

Appendix C: Management Control Forms is a section devoted to providing simplified cost control–related forms. This popular appendix has been retained from the first edition. These forms can be used as guideposts in the development of property-specific forms. They may be implemented as is or modified as the manager sees fit.

Appendix D: Fun on the Web! Sites is designed to give readers the Internet addresses of those sites identified in the text as being helpful in learning more about cost control. In this appendix, the sites are listed as they appear in the chapters.

An expanded *Glossary* (larger by 50 percent than the glossary in the first edition) of industry terms will help the reader with the operational vocabulary necessary to understand the language of hospitality cost control management. This is included at the end of the text. Finally, a *Bibliography* is provided for the reader who wishes to pursue his or her study from a variety of excellent books.

Instructor's Materials

To help Instructors effectively manage their time and to enhance student learning opportunities, three significant educational tools have been developed specifically for this text. These are:

Student's Floppy Diskette   This diskette, included with the purchase of each text, introduces students to the important skill of spreadsheet development. The authors have selected the widely used Microsoft Excel spreadsheet program for this use. Using the supplied diskette, students can immediately see how their answers to "Test Your Skills" problems translate into cost control solutions via spreadsheet formula development and manipulation. These diskettes assist students in understanding the "how" and "why" of building spreadsheet solutions for the cost control related hospitality problems they will face in the classroom and in their careers. Instructors will find that the grading of problem sets becomes much easier when, with the aid of the diskette, all students use a consistent approach to classroom assignments.

Instructor's Manual   As an additional aid for Instructors, an Instructor's Manual (ISBN: 0-471-35738-3) has been painstakingly developed and classroom tested for this text. The manual includes:

Lecture outlines for each chapter
Answers to chapter ending "Test Your Skills" problems
A Test Bank including exam questions developed for each chapter

Wiley Web Site, (for <u>Food and Beverage Cost Control</u>) The segment of Wiley's Web Site devoted to this book (www.wiley.com/college) is significant. It includes two very important instructor aids that can immediately be used to enhance student learning. These are:

PowerPoint slides   These easy-to-read and graphically sophisticated teaching aids are excellent for use by instructors presenting their lectures via computer or for those who wish to download the graphics and present them as overhead transparencies.

Test Bank   Instructors utilizing the web site will find a password-protected bank of exam questions that include the question's correct, and classroom tested, answers.

NATIONAL RESTAURANT ASSOCIATION (NRA) Educational Foundation Student Workbook   The National Restaurant Association Educational Foundation, in consultation with the authors, has developed a Student Workbook for its ProMgmt. certificate program. The workbook contains exercises and a study outline for each chapter, and a practice test of 80 multiple-choice questions. This practice test will assist students in preparing for the certificate examination.

In addition, an Instructor's Guide (0-471-14992-6) is available to qualified instructors to complement and highlight the information in the textbook and Student Workbook.

As was true in the first edition, the authors hope that the study of cost management creates in the reader the same interest and excitement for the topic that the authors experience. If that is the case, we will have again been successful, and our readers will surely learn and be successful, too.

Acknowledgments

The impetus for the second edition of this book was due, as was the first, to the wisdom and insight of Jack Miller, a long-time hospitality educator at St. Louis Community College and a recognized leader of the hospitality education community. Jack was committed to an update of the material in the first edition that incorporated utilizing the computer applications so readily available today. Sadly, Jack passed away before the revision was complete.

Jack's vision was always to help students by giving them the most up-to-date material at hand, in a way that was easy to read, easy to understand, and easy to retain. We strove to achieve that vision. The final version of this edition would, we truly hope and believe, meet Jack's rigorous standards.

The first edition of this text was very popular, for which we are deeply grateful. Its success stemmed in large part from the testing of its concepts and materials in classes at Purdue University, Texas Tech University, the University of Houston, and, with the addition of a new author, the Collins School of Hospitality Management at California State Polytechnic University, Pomona, as well as those original St. Louis Community College students. Students today will indeed benefit from the insight and input of students in our past classes.

As with the first edition, we appreciate all the assistance and comments we have received in bringing this book to fruition. We are extremely grateful to those who contributed to the original concept and idea for the book as well as the book's continued support from the National Restaurant Association.

For comment, encouragement, and constructive criticism on the manuscript, we again thank our reviewers: Jane Boyland, Johnson & Wales University; Michael Brizek, Baltimore International College; Andrew Glidden, Mohawk Valley Community College; and Charlie Martin, Spokane Community College. They often reminded us of our original concept and kept us from straying from it.

We thank our editor, JoAnna Turtletaub, whose support and constant encouragement kept the book on track with the addition of a new author and, thus, a modified writing team. Thanks Coach!

We also want to thank those colleagues and loved ones who have been so supportive to us throughout our careers, Peggy, Joe,

Jack, Ray, Pauline, and MD. Thanks also to Loralei, Terry, Laurie, Lou, Billie, Trish, Ed, and Barb. A special thanks goes to Don St. Hilaire for the Web and Excel ideas and for testing the book in his class. The Collins School HRT 276 classes in Fall 2000 are also deeply appreciated for their input on the book. Also, thanks to Mike Meraz for assisting with the Excel spreadsheets early on, and thanks to Lucir Schlickmann for assisting with the Instructor's Manual. Also, thanks to Csilla Pomjanek for her brilliant computer assistance. We appreciate all of you.

Most important, we wish to thank Jack and Nita Miller. We hope this book demonstrates our love and gratitude to you and our commitment to hospitality education.

David K. Hayes

Lea R. Dopson

Chapter

1 MANAGING REVENUE AND EXPENSE

OVERVIEW   This chapter presents the relationship among foodservice revenue, expense, and profit. As a professional foodservice manager, you must understand the relationship that exists between controlling these three areas and the resulting overall success of your operation. In addition, the chapter presents the mathematical foundation you must know to express your operating results as a percentage of your revenue or budget, a method that is the standard within the hospitality industry.

CHAPTER OUTLINE

Professional Foodservice Manager
Profit: The Reward for Service
Getting Started
Understanding the Profit and Loss Statement
Understanding the Budget
Key Terms and Concepts, and Test Your Skills

HIGHLIGHTS   At the conclusion of this chapter, you will be able to:

○ Apply the basic formula used to determine profit.
○ Express both expenses and profit as a percentage of revenue.
○ Compare actual operating results with budgeted operating results.

Professional Foodservice Manager

There is no doubt that to be a successful foodservice manager you must be a talented individual. Consider, for a moment, your role in the operation of an ongoing profitable facility. As a foodservice manager, you are both a manufacturer and a retailer. A professional foodservice manager is unique because all the functions of product sales, from item conceptualization to product delivery, are in the hands of the same individual. As a manager, you are in charge of securing raw materials, producing a product, and selling it—all under the same roof. Few other managers are required to have the breadth of skills that effective foodservice operators must have. Because foodservice operators are in the service sector of business, many aspects of management are more difficult for them than for their manufacturing or retailing management counterparts.

A foodservice manager is one of the few types of managers who actually has contact with the ultimate customer. This is not true of the manager of a tire factory or automobile production line. These individuals produce a product, but do not sell it to the person who will actually use their product. In a like manner, grocery store or computer store managers will sell their product lines, but they have had no role in actually producing their goods. The face-to-face guest contact in the hospitality industry requires that you assume the responsibility of standing behind your own work and that of your staff, in a one-on-one situation with the ultimate consumer, or end-user of your products and services.

The management task checklist in Figure 1.1 shows just some of the areas in which foodservice, manufacturing, and retailing managers vary in responsibilities.

In addition to your role as a food factory supervisor, you must also serve as a cost control manager, because, without performing this vital role, your business might cease to exist. Foodservice management pro-

---

FIGURE **1.1** ●   Management Task Checklist

Task	Foodservice Manager	Manufacturing Manager	Retail Manager
1. Secure raw materials	Yes	Yes	No
2. Manufacture product	Yes	Yes	No·
3. Distribute to end-user	Yes	No	Yes
4. Market to end-user	Yes	No	Yes
5. Reconcile problems with end-user	Yes	No	Yes

vides the opportunity for creativity in a variety of settings. The control of revenue and expense is just one more area in which the effective foodservice operator can excel. In most areas of foodservice, excellence in operation is measured in terms of producing and delivering quality products in a way that assures an appropriate operating profit for the owners of the business.

Profit: The Reward for Service

There is an inherent problem in the study of cost control or, more accurately, cost management. The simple fact is that management's primary responsibility is to deliver a quality product or service to the guest, at a price mutually agreeable to both parties. In addition, the quality must be such that the consumer, or end-user of the product or service, feels that excellent value was received for the money spent on the transaction. When this level of service is achieved, the business will prosper. If management focuses on controlling costs more than servicing guests, problems will certainly surface.

It is important to remember that guests cause businesses to incur costs. You do not want to get yourself in the mind-set of reducing costs to the point where it is thought that "low" costs are good and "high" costs are bad. A restaurant with $5,000,000 in revenue per year will undoubtedly have higher costs than the same size restaurant with $200,000 in revenue per year. The reason is quite clear. The food products, labor, and equipment needed to serve $5,000,000 worth of food is likely to be greater than that required to produce a smaller amount of revenue. Remember, if there are fewer guests, there are likely to be fewer costs, but fewer profits as well! Because that is true, when management attempts to reduce costs, with no regard for the impact on the balance between managing costs and guest satisfaction, the business will surely suffer.

In addition, efforts to reduce costs that result in unsafe conditions for guests or employees are never wise. While some short-term savings may result, the expense of a lawsuit resulting from a guest or employee injury can be very high. Managers who, for example, neglect to spend the money to salt and shovel a snowy restaurant entrance area may find that they spend thousands more dollars defending themselves in a lawsuit brought by an individual who slipped and fell on the ice.

As an effective manager, the question to be considered is *not* whether costs are high or low. The question is whether costs are too high or too low, given management's view of the value it hopes to deliver to the guest and the needs of the foodservice operation's owners. Managers can eliminate nearly all costs by closing the operation's doors. Obviously, however, when you close the doors to expense, you close the doors to profits. Expenses, then, must be incurred, and they must be managed in a way that allows the operation to achieve its desired profit levels.

Some people assume that if a business purchases a product for $1.00 and sells it for $3.00, the profit generated equals $2.00. In fact, this is not true. As a business operator, you must realize that the difference between what you have paid for the goods you sell and the price at which you sell them does not represent your actual profit. Instead, all expenses, including advertising, the building housing your operation, management salaries, and the labor required to generate the sale, to name but a few, are expenses that must be subtracted before you can determine your profits accurately.

Every foodservice operator is faced with the following profit-oriented formula:

$$\text{Revenue} - \text{Expenses} = \text{Profit}$$

Thus, when you manage your facility, you will receive **revenue,** the term used to indicate the dollars you take in, and you will incur **expenses,** the cost of the items required to operate the business. The dollars that remain after all expenses have been paid represent your **profit.** For the purposes of this book, the authors will use the following terms interchangeably: revenues and sales; expenses and costs.

This formula holds even in the "nonprofit" sector of foodservice management. For example, consider the situation of Hector Bentevina. Hector is the foodservice manager at a business dining operation. Hector supplies the foodservice to a large group of office workers, each of whom is employed by the corporation that owns the facility Hector manages. In this situation, Hector's employer clearly does not have "profit" as its primary motive. In most business dining situations, food is provided as a service to employees and middle management either as a no-cost benefit or at a greatly reduced price. In some cases, executive dining rooms may be operated for the convenience of senior management. In all cases, however, some provision for profit must be made. Figure 1.2 shows the flow of business for the typical foodservice operation. Note that profit must be taken out at some point in the process, or management is in a position of simply trading cash for cash.

If you find that, in your own operation, revenue is less than or equal to real expense, with no reserve for the future, you will also find that there is no money for new equipment, needed equipment maintenance may not be performed, employee raises (as well as your own) may be few and far between, and, in general, the foodservice facility will become outdated due to a lack of funds needed to remodel and upgrade. One need look no further than to the facilities of many college and hospital feeding operations to see evidence of this type of situation in the nonprofit sector of the

FIGURE **1.2** ● Foodservice Business Flowchart

foodservice industry. The truth is, all foodservice operations need revenue in excess of expenses if they are to thrive. If you manage a foodservice operation in a nonprofit setting, it will be your responsibility to communicate this message.

Profit is the result of solid planning, sound management, and careful decision making. The purpose of this text is to give you the information and tools you need to make informed decisions with regard to managing your operation's revenue and expense. If these tools are utilized properly, the potential for achieving profits you desire is greatly enhanced.

Profit should not be viewed as what is left over after the bills are paid. In fact, careful planning is necessary to earn a profit. Obviously, investors will not invest in businesses that do not generate enough profit to make their investment worthwhile. Because that is true, a more appropriate formula, which recognizes and rewards the business owner for the risk associated with business ownership or investment, is as follows:

$$\text{Revenue} - \text{Desired Profit} = \text{Ideal Expense}$$

Ideal expense, in this case, is defined as management's view of the correct or appropriate amount of expense necessary to generate a given quantity of revenue. **Desired profit** is defined as the profit that the owner desires to achieve on that predicted quantity of revenue.

This formula clearly places profit as a reward for providing service, not a leftover. When foodservice managers deliver quality and value to their guests, anticipated revenue levels can be achieved and desired profit is attainable. Desired profit and ideal expense levels are not, however, easily achieved. In these competitive times, it takes an astute foodservice operator to consistently make decisions that will lead to maximizing revenue while holding expenses to the ideal or appropriate amount. This book will help you to do just that.

Revenue

To some degree, you can manage your revenue levels. Revenue dollars are the result of units sold. These units may consist of individual menu items, lunches, dinners, drinks, or any other item produced by your operation. Revenue varies with both the number of guests frequenting your business and the amount of money spent by each guest. You can increase revenue by increasing the number of guests you serve, by increasing the amount each guest spends, or by a combination of both approaches. Adding seating or drive-in windows, extending operating hours, and building additional foodservice units are all examples of management's efforts to increase the number of guests choosing to come to the restaurant or foodservice operation. Suggestive selling by service staff, creative menu pricing techniques such as bundling and upsizing, as well as guest discounts for very large purchases are all examples of efforts to increase the amount of money each guest spends.

It is the opinion of the authors that management's primary task is to take the steps necessary to deliver guests to the front door. This is true because the profit formula begins with revenue. Experienced foodservice operators know that increasing revenue through adding guests, suggestive selling, or possibly raising menu prices is an extremely effective way of increasing overall profitability, but only *if* effective cost management systems are in place.

The focus of this text is on managing and controlling expense, not generating revenue. While the two are clearly related, they are different. Marketing efforts, restaurant design and site selection, employee training and food preparation methods are all critical links in the revenue-producing chain. No amount of effective expense control can solve the profit problems caused by inadequate revenue resulting from inferior food quality or service levels. Effective cost control, when coupled with management's aggressive attitude toward meeting and exceeding guests' expectations, can result in outstanding revenue and profit performance.

FUN ON THE WEB!

www.restaurant.org Link to "Research," then "Pocket Factbook" to see the National Restaurant Association's revenue projections for the industry.

Expenses

There are four major foodservice expense categories that you must learn to control. They are:

1. Food costs
2. Beverage costs
3. Labor costs
4. Other expenses

Food Costs   **Food costs** are the costs associated with actually producing the menu items a guest selects. They include the expense of meats, dairy, fruits, vegetables, and other categories of food items produced by the food-service operation. When computing food costs, many operators include the cost of minor paper and plastic items, such as the paper wrappers used to wrap sandwiches. In most cases, food costs will make up the largest or second largest expense category you must learn to manage.

Beverage Costs   **Beverage costs** are those related to the sale of alcoholic beverages. It is interesting to note that it is common practice in the hospitality industry to consider beverage costs of a nonalcoholic nature as an expense in the food cost category. Thus, milk, tea, coffee, carbonated beverages, and other nonalcoholic beverage items are not generally considered a beverage cost.

   Alcoholic beverages accounted for in the beverage cost category include beer, wine, and liquor. This category may also include the costs of ingredients necessary to produce these drinks, such as cherries, lemons, olives, limes, mixers like carbonated beverages and juices, and other items commonly used in the production and service of alcoholic beverages.

Labor Costs   **Labor costs** include the cost of all employees necessary to run the business. This expense category would also include the amount of any taxes you are required to pay when you have employees on your payroll. Some operators find it helpful to include the cost of management in this category. Others prefer to place the cost of managers in the other expense category. In most operations, however, labor costs are second only to food costs in total dollars spent. If management is included as a labor cost rather than an other expense, then this category can well be even larger than the food cost category.

Other Expenses   **Other expenses** include all expenses that are neither food, nor beverage, nor labor. Examples include franchise fees, utilities, rent, linen, and such items as china, glassware, kitchen knives, and pots and pans. While this expense category is sometimes incorrectly referred to as "minor expenses," your ability to successfully control this expense area is critical to the overall profitability of your foodservice unit.

Getting Started

Good managers learn to understand, control, and manage their expenses. Consider the case of Tabreshia Larson, the food and beverage director of the 200-room Renaud Hotel, located in a college town and built near an interstate highway. Tabreshia has just received her end-of-the-year operating reports for the current year. She is interested in comparing these results to those of the prior year. The numbers she received are shown in Figure 1.3.

Tabreshia is concerned, but she is not sure why. Revenue is higher than last year, so she feels her guests must like the products and services they receive from her operation. In fact, repeat business from corporate meetings and special-events meals is really beginning to develop. Profits are greater than last year also, but Tabreshia has the uneasy feeling that things are not going so well. The kitchen appears to run smoothly. The staff, however, often runs out of needed items, and there seems to be a large amount of leftover food thrown away on a regular basis. Sometimes, there seem to be too many staff members on the property; at other times, guests have to wait too long to get served. Tabreshia also feels that employee theft may be occurring, but she certainly doesn't have the time to watch every storage area within her operation. Tabreshia also senses that the hotel general manager, Islah Richards, who is Tabreshia's boss, is less than pleased with her department's performance. She would really like to get a handle on the problem (if there is one), but how and where should she start?

FIGURE **1.3** ● Renaud Hotel Operating Results

	This Year	*Last Year*
Revenue	$1,106,040	$850,100
Expense	1,017,557	773,591
Profits	**88,483**	**76,509**

The answer for Tabreshia, and for you, if you want to develop a serious expense control system, is very simple. You start with basic mathematics skills that you must have to properly analyze your expenses. The mathematics used in this text consist only of addition, subtraction, multiplication, and division. These tools will be sufficient to build a cost control system that will help you manage effectively the expenses you incur.

What would it mean if a fellow foodservice manager told you that he spent $500 on food yesterday? Obviously, it means little unless you know more about his operation. Should he have spent $500 yesterday? Was that too much? Too little? Was it a "good" day? These questions raise a difficult problem. How can you compare expenses today with those of yesterday, or your foodservice unit with another, so that you can see how well you are doing?

We know that the value of dollars has changed over a period of time. A restaurant with revenue of $1,000 per day in 1954 is very different from the same restaurant with daily revenue of $1,000 today. The value of the dollar today is quite different from what it was in 1954. Generally, inflation causes the purchasing power of a dollar today to be less than that of a dollar from a previous time period. While this concept of changing value is useful in the area of finance, it is vexing when one wants to answer the simple question, "Am I doing as well today as I was doing five years ago?"

Alternatively, consider the problem of a multiunit manager. Two units sell tacos on either side of a large city. One uses $500 worth of food products each day; the other unit uses $600 worth of food products each day. Does the second unit use an additional $100 worth of food each day because it has more guests or because it is less efficient in utilizing the food?

The answer to all of the preceding questions, and more, can be determined if we use percentages to relate expenses incurred to revenue generated. Percentage calculations are important for at least two major reasons. First and foremost, percentages are the most common standard used for evaluating costs in the foodservice industry. Therefore, knowledge of what a percent is and how it is calculated is vital. Second, as a manager in the foodservice industry, you will be evaluated primarily on your ability to compute, analyze, and control these percent figures. Percent calculations are used extensively in this text and are a cornerstone of any effective cost control system.

Percent Review

Understanding percents and how they are mathematically computed is important. The following review may be helpful for some readers. If you thoroughly understand the percent concept, you may skip this section and the Computing Percent section and proceed directly to the Using Percent section.

Percent (%) means "out of each hundred." Thus, 10 percent would mean 10 out of each 100. If we asked how many guests would buy blueberry pie on a given day, and the answer is 10 percent, then 10 people out of each 100 we serve will select blueberry pie. If 52 percent of our employees are female, then 52 out of each 100 employees are female. If 15 percent of your employees will receive a raise this month, then 15 out of 100 employees will get their raise.

There are three ways to write a percent as shown in Figure 1.4.

Common Form   In its common form, the "%" sign is used to express the percentage. If we say 10%, then we mean "10 out of each 100" and no further explanation is necessary. The common form, the "%," is equivalent to the same amount expressed in either the fraction or the decimal form.

Fraction Form   In fraction form, the percent is expressed as the part, or a portion of 100. Thus, 10 percent is written as 10 over 100 (10/100). This is simply another way of expressing the relationship between the part (10) and the whole (100).

Decimal Form   A decimal is a number developed from the counting system we use. It is based on the fact that we count to 10 then start over again. In other words, each of our major units, 10s, 100s, 1,000s, and so on, are based on the use of 10s, and each number can easily be divided by 10. Instead of using the % sign, the decimal form uses the (.) or decimal point to express the percent relationship. Thus, 10% is expressed as 0.10 in decimal form. The numbers to the right of the decimal point express the percentage.

Each of these three methods of expressing percentages is used in the foodservice industry, and to be successful you must develop a clear understanding of how a percentage is computed. Once that is known, you can express the percentage in any form that is useful to you.

FIGURE **1.4** ● Forms for Expressing Percent

	Percent		
Form	1%	10%	100%
Common	1%	10%	100%
Fraction	1/100	10/100	100/100
Decimal	0.01	0.10	1.00

Computing Percent

To determine what percent one number is of another number, divide the number that is the part by the number that is the whole. Usually, but not always, this means dividing the smaller number by the larger number. For example, assume that 840 guests were served during a banquet at your hotel; 420 of them asked for coffee with their meal. To find what percent of your guests ordered coffee, divide the part (420) by the whole (840).

The process looks as follows:

$$\frac{\text{Part}}{\text{Whole}} = \text{Percent} \qquad or \qquad \frac{420}{840} = 0.50$$

Thus, 50% (common form), 50/100 (fraction form), or 0.50 (decimal form) represents the proportion of people at the banquet who ordered coffee. A large number of new foodservice managers have difficulty computing percent figures. It is easy to forget which number goes "on the top" and which number goes "on the bottom." In general, if you attempt to compute a percentage and get a whole number (a number larger than 1), either a mistake has been made or costs are extremely high!

Many people also become confused when converting from one form of percent to another. If that is a problem, remember the following conversion rules:

1. To convert from common form to decimal form, move the decimal two places to the left, that is, 50.00% = 0.50.
2. To convert from decimal form to common form, move the decimal two places to the right, that is, 0.40 = 40.00%.

In a commercial foodservice operation, the "whole" is usually a revenue figure. Expenses and profits are the "parts," which are usually expressed in terms of a percent. It is interesting to note that, in the United States, the same system in use for our numbers is in use for our money. Each dime contains 10 pennies, each dollar contains 10 dimes, and so on. Thus, it is true that a percent, when discussing money, refer to "cents out of each dollar" as well as "out of each 100 dollars." When we say 10% of a dollar, we mean 10 cents, or "10 cents out of each dollar." Likewise, 25% of a dollar represents 25 cents, 50% of a dollar represents 50 cents, and 100% of a dollar represents $1.00.

Sometimes, when using percent to express the relationship between portions of a dollar and the whole, we find that the part is, indeed, larger than the whole. Figure 1.5 demonstrates the three possibilities that exist when computing a percentage.

FIGURE **1.5** ● Percent Computation

Possibilities	Examples	Results
Part is smaller than the whole	$\frac{61}{100}$ = 61%	Always less than 100%
Part is equal to the whole	$\frac{35}{35}$ = 100%	Always equals 100%
Part is larger than the whole	$\frac{125}{50}$ = 250%	Always greater than 100%

Great care must always be taken when computing percents, so that the percent arrived at is of help to you in your work and does not represent an error in mathematics.

Using Percent

Consider a restaurant that you are operating. Imagine that your revenues for a week are in the amount of $1,600. Expenses for the same week are $1,200. Given these facts and the information presented earlier in this chapter, your profit formula for the week would look as follows:

> **Revenue − Expense = Profit**
>
> *or*
>
> **$1,600 − $1,200 = $400**

If you had planned for a $500 profit for the week, you would have been "short." Using the alternative profit formula presented earlier, you would find

> **Revenue − Desired Profit = Ideal Expense**
>
> *or*
>
> **$1,600 − $500 = $1,100**

Note that expense in this example ($1,200) exceeds ideal expense ($1,100) and, thus, too little profit was achieved.

These numbers can also be expressed in terms of percent. If we want to know what percent of our revenue went to expenses, we would compute it as follows:

$$\frac{\text{Expense}}{\text{Revenue}} = \text{Expense \%}$$

or

$$\frac{\$1,200}{\$1,600} = 0.75, \text{ or } 75\%$$

Another way to state this relationship is to say that each dollar of revenue costs 75 cents to produce. Also, each revenue dollar taken in results in 25 cents profit.

$$\$1.00 \text{ Revenue} - \$0.75 \text{ Expense} = \$0.25 \text{ Profit}$$

As long as expense is smaller than revenue, some profit will be generated, even if it is not as much as you had planned. You can compute profit % using the following formula:

$$\frac{\text{Profit}}{\text{Revenue}} = \text{Profit \%}$$

In our example:

$$\frac{\$400 \text{ Profit}}{\$1,600 \text{ Revenue}} = 25\% \text{ Profit}$$

We can compute what we had planned our profit % to be by dividing desired profit ($500) by revenue ($1,600):

$$\frac{\$500 \text{ Desired Profit}}{\$1,600 \text{ Revenue}} = 31.25\% \text{ Desired Profit}$$

In simple terms, we had hoped to make 31.25% profit, but made only 25% profit. Excess costs could account for the difference. If these costs could be identified and corrected, we could perhaps achieve the desired profit percentage. Most foodservice operators compute many cost percentages, not just one. The major cost divisions used in foodservice are as follows:

1. Food and beverage cost
2. Labor cost
3. Other expense

A modified profit formula, therefore, looks as follows:

Revenue − (Food and Beverage Cost + Labor Cost + Other Expenses) = Profit

Put in another format, the equation looks as follows:

> **Revenue (100%)**
>   − **Food and Beverage Cost %**
>   − **Labor Cost %**
>   − **Other Expense %**
>   = **Profit %**

Regardless of the approach used, foodservice managers must evaluate their expenses, and they will use percents to do so.

Understanding the Profit and Loss Statement

Consider Figure 1.6, an example from Pat's Steakhouse. All of Pat's expenses and profits can be computed as percents by using the revenue figure, $400,000, as the whole, with expenses and profit representing the parts as follows:

$$\frac{\text{Food and Beverage Cost}}{\text{Revenue}} = \text{Food and Beverage Cost \%}$$

or

$$\frac{\$150,000}{\$400,000} = 37.50\%$$

$$\frac{\text{Labor Cost}}{\text{Revenue}} = \text{Labor Cost \%}$$

or

$$\frac{\$175,000}{\$400,000} = 43.75\%$$

$$\frac{\text{Other Expense}}{\text{Revenue}} = \text{Other Expense \%}$$

or

$$\frac{\$25,000}{\$400,000} = 6.25\%$$

$$\frac{\text{Total Expense}}{\text{Revenue}} = \text{Total Expense \%}$$

or

$$\frac{\$350,000}{\$400,000} = 87.50\%$$

$$\frac{\text{Profit}}{\text{Revenue}} = \text{Profit \%}$$

or

$$\frac{\$50,000}{\$400,000} = 12.50\%$$

FIGURE **1.6** ● Pat's Steakhouse

Revenue		$400,000
Expenses		
Food and Beverage Cost	$150,000	
Labor Cost	175,000	
Other Expense	25,000	
Total Expense		$350,000
Profit		**$ 50,000**

A simplified statement that details revenue, expenses, and profit, for a given period of time, is called the **profit and loss statement (P&L).** It lists revenue, food and beverage cost, labor cost, and other expense. The P&L also identifies profits since, as you recall, profits are generated by the formula:

$$\text{Revenue} - \text{Expense} = \text{Profit}$$

Figure 1.7 is a simplified P&L statement for Pat's Steakhouse. Note the similarity to Figure 1.6. This time, however, expenses and profit are expressed in terms of both dollar amount and percent of revenue.

FIGURE **1.7** ● Pat's Steakhouse P&L

Revenue	**$400,000**	**100%**
Food and Beverage Cost	$150,000	37.50%
Labor Cost	175,000	43.75%
Other Expense	25,000	6.25%
Total Expense	**$350,000**	**87.50%**
Profit	**$ 50,000**	**12.50%**

Another way of looking at Pat's P&L is shown in Figure 1.8. The pieces of the pie represent Pat's cost and profit categories. Costs and profit total 100%, which is equal to Pat's total revenues. To put it in another way, out of every revenue dollar that Pat generates, 100% is used up as either costs or profit.

Pat knows from the P&L that revenues represent 100% of the total dollars available to cover expenses and provide for a profit. Food and beverage cost is 37.50%, and labor cost percentage in the steakhouse equals 43.75%. Other expense percentage equals 6.25%, and her total expense percent is 87.50% (37.50 + 43.75 + 6.25 = 87.50%). The steakhouse profit equals 12.50%. Thus, for each dollar in revenue, Pat earns a profit of 12.50 cents. Pat's revenue, expense, and profit information is contained in the steakhouse's P&L.

In many restaurants, food costs and beverage costs are separated into two categories in the P&L. Likewise, food revenues and beverage revenues are reported separately. This is done so that the food cost can be compared to food revenues, and the beverage cost can be compared to beverage revenues. Suppose, for example, that one manager is responsible for controlling food cost % in the restaurant and another manager is responsible for controlling beverage cost % in the bar. Separation of these two "departments," then, is especially helpful when evaluating the performance of these two managers. It also helps these managers to quickly identify and anticipate problems associated with their costs and identify ways to correct these problems.

FIGURE **1.8** ● Pat's Steakhouse Costs and Profit as a Percentage of Revenues

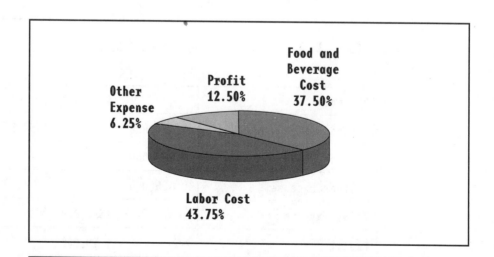

The P&L is important because it describes the efficiency and profitability of an operation. Because so many individuals and groups are interested in a food facility's performance, it is important that the P&L and other financial statements are prepared in a manner that is consistent with other facilities. If, for example, you own two Italian restaurants, it would be very confusing if one of your managers used a particular method for preparing his or her unit's P&L, while the other manager used an entirely different method. You, your investors, your accountant, governmental taxing entities, and your creditors may all be interested in your operational results, and unless you report and account for these in a manner they can easily understand, confusion may result.

To avoid such a set of circumstances, the Uniform System of Accounts is used to report financial results in most foodservice units. This system was created to ensure uniform reporting of financial results. The Uniform System of Accounts exists for restaurants, as well as one for hotels, and another for clubs. The Uniform System of Accounts will be discussed in greater detail in Chapter 9 of this text.

The primary purpose of preparing a P&L is to identify revenue, expenses, and profits for a given time period. As a manager, your efforts, more than any other factor, will influence your operation's profitability. Good managers provide excellent value to their guests, which increases revenue. In addition, good managers know how to analyze, manage, and control their costs. For these managers, expenses are held to the amount that was preplanned. The result is the desired profit level. Good managers influence the success of their units and their own employees. The results for them personally are promotions, added responsibilities, and salary increases. If you wish to succeed in the hospitality industry, it is important to remember that your performance will be evaluated primarily on your ability to achieve the profit levels your operation has planned for.

In addition to your own efforts, many factors influence profit dollars and profit percent, and you must be aware, and in control, of all of them. All of the factors that impact profit percent are discussed in later chapters of this text.

FUN ON THE WEB!

www.restaurant.org Link to "Research," then "Operating Ratios" to see industry averages for P&L's.

Understanding the Budget

Some foodservice managers do not generate revenue on a daily basis. Consider, for a moment, the foodservice manager at a summer camp run for children. In this case, parents pay a fixed fee to cover housing, activities, and meals for a set period of time. The foodservice director, in this situation, is just one of several managers who must share this revenue. If too many dollars are spent on providing housing or activities, too few dollars may be available to provide an adequate quantity or quality of food products. On the other hand, if too many dollars are spent on providing foodservice, there may not be enough left to cover other needed expense areas, such as housing and activities. In a case like this, foodservice operators usually prepare a budget. A **budget** is simply a forecast or estimate of projected revenue, expense, and profit. In some hospitality companies, the budget is known as the **plan,** referring to the fact that the budget details the operation's estimated, or planned for, revenue and expense for a given time period.

Both commercial and noncommercial foodservice operators may use budgets. They are most frequently used, however, by effective managers, whether in the commercial (for profit) or nonprofit sector. Budgeting is simply planning for revenue, expense, and profit. If these items are planned for, you can determine how close your actual performance is to your plan or budget.

In the summer camp example, the following information is known:

1. Number of campers, 180
2. Number of meals daily, 3
3. Length of campers' stay, 7 days

With 180 campers eating 3 meals each day for 7 days, 3,780 meals will be served (180 campers × 3 meals × 7 days = 3,780 meals).

Generally, in a case such as the summer camp, the foodservice director is given a dollar amount that represents the allowed expense for each meal to be served. For example, if $1.85 per meal is the amount budgeted for this director, the total revenue budget would equal $6,993 ($1.85 per meal × 3,780 meals = $6,993).

From this figure, an expense budget can begin to be developed. In this case, we are interested in the amount of expenses budgeted and the amount actually spent on expenses. Equally important, we would be interested in the percent of the budget actually used, a concept known as **performance to budget.**

A childhood example may help to firmly establish the idea of budget and performance to budget. Assume that a child has $0.50 per day to spend on candy. On Monday morning, the child's parents give the child $0.50 for each day of the week, or $3.50 total ($0.50 × 7 days = $3.50). If the child spends only $0.50 per day, he or she will be able to buy candy all week. If, however, too much is spent in any one day, there may not be any money left at the end of the week. A good spending pattern could be tabulated in Figure 1.9.

The % of Total column is computed by dividing $0.50 (the part) by $3.50 (the whole). Notice that we can determine the percent of total that

FIGURE **1.9** ● Candy Purchases

Weekday	Budgeted Amount	% of Total
Monday	$0.50	14.28%
Tuesday	$0.50	14.28%
Wednesday	$0.50	14.28%
Thursday	$0.50	14.28%
Friday	$0.50	14.28%
Saturday	$0.50	14.28%
Sunday	$0.50	14.28%
Total	$3.50	100.00%

should have been spent by any given day; that is, each day equals 14.28%, or 1/7 of the total.

This same logic applies to the foodservice operation. Figure 1.10 represents commonly used budget periods and their accompanying proportion amount.

Many foodservice operations are changing from "one month" budget periods to periods of 28 days. The **28-day-period approach** divides a year into 13 equal periods of 28 days each. Therefore, each period has four Mondays, four Tuesdays, four Wednesdays, and so on. This helps the manager compare performance from one period to the next without having to compensate for "extra days" in any one period. The downside of this approach is that you can no longer talk about the month of March, for example, because "period 3" would occur during part of February and part of March. Although using the 28-day-period approach takes a while to get used to, it is an effective way to measure performance and plan from period to period.

In the summer camp, after one week's camping was completed, we found the results shown in Figure 1.11. Assume that we used the expense records from last summer as well as our solid industry knowledge and experience to develop the expense budget figures for this summer.

In this case, we are interested in both the plan (budget) and our actual performance. Figure 1.12 shows a performance to budget summary

FIGURE **1.10** ● Common Foodservice Budget Periods

Budget Period	Portion	% of Total
One week	One day	1/7 or 0.143
Two-week period	One day One week	1/14 or 0.071 1/2 or 0.500

One month
  28 days
  30 days
  31 days
	One week
	One day
	One day
	One day
		1/4 or 0.250
		1/28 or 0.036
		1/30 or 0.033
		1/31 or 0.032

Six months	One month	1/6 or 0.167
One year	One day One week One month	1/365 or 0.003 1/52 or 0.019 1/12 or 0.083

with revenue and expenses presented in terms of both the budget amount and the actual amount. In all cases, percentages are used to compare actual expense with the budgeted amount, using the formula

$$\frac{\text{Actual}}{\text{Budget}} = \%\ \text{of Budget}$$

FIGURE **1.11** ● Camp Eureka One-Week Budget

Item	Budget	Actual
Meals Served	3,780	3,700
Revenue	$6,993	$6,993
Food Expense	$2,600	$2,400
Labor Expense	$2,800	$2,900
Other Expense	$ 700	$ 965
Profit	$ 893	$ 728

FIGURE **1.12** ● Camp Eureka Performance to Budget Summary

Item	Budget	Actual	% of Budget
Meals Served	3,780	3,700	97.9%
Revenue	$6,993	$6,993	100.0%
Food Expense	$2,600	$2,400	92.3%
Labor Expense	$2,800	$2,900	103.6%
Other Expense	$ 700	$ 965	137.9%
Total Expense	$6,100	$6,265	102.7%
Profit	$ 893	$ 728	81.5%

In this example, revenue remained the same although some campers skipped (or slept through!) some of their meals. This is often the case when one fee or price buys a number of meals, whether they are eaten or not. In some other cases, managers will only receive revenue for meals actually eaten. This, of course, is true in a traditional restaurant setting. In either case, budgeted amount, actual expense, and the concept of % of budget, or performance to budget, are important management tools. In looking at the Camp Eureka performance to budget summary, we can see that the manager served fewer meals than planned and, thus, spent less on food than estimated, but spent more on labor than originally thought necessary. In addition, much more was spent than estimated for other expenses (137.9% of the budgeted amount). As a result, the profit dollars were lower than planned. This manager has some problems, but they are not everywhere in the operation.

How do we know that? If our budget was accurate and we are within reasonable limits of our budget, we are said to be "in line," or in compliance, with our budget. If, as management, we decided that plus (more than) or minus (less than) 10% of budget in each category would be considered in line, or acceptable, we are in line with regard to meals served, food expense, labor expense, and total expense. We are not in line with other expenses because they were 137.9% of the amount originally planned. Thus, they exceed the 10% variation that was reasonably allowed. Profit also was outside the acceptable boundary we established because it was only 81.5% of the amount budgeted. Note that figures over 100% mean too much (other expense), while figures below 100% mean too little (profit).

Many operators use the concept of "significant" variation to determine whether a cost control problem exists. In this case, a significant variation is any variation in expected costs that management feels is an area of concern. This variation can be caused by costs that were either higher or lower than the amount originally budgeted or planned for.

When you manage a foodservice operation and you find that significant variations with your planned results occur, you must:

1. Define the problem.
2. Determine the cause.
3. Take corrective action.

It is crucial to know the kind of problem you have if you are to be an effective problem solver. Management's attention must be focused on the proper place. In this case, the proper areas for concern are other expense and profit. If, in the future, food expense became too low, it, too, would be an area of concern. Why? Remember that expenses create revenue; thus, it is not your goal to eliminate expense. In fact, those managers who focus too much on eliminating expense, instead of building revenue, often find that their expenses are completely eliminated when they are forced to close their operation's doors permanently! Control and management of revenue and expense are important. Elimination of either is not desired.

As you have seen, revenue and expense directly impact profit. Your role as a hospitality manager is to analyze, manage, and control your costs so that you achieve planned results. It can be done, and it can be fun.

The remainder of this text discusses how you can best manage and account for foodservice revenue and expense. With a good understanding of the relationship among revenue, expense, and profit, and your ability to analyze using percentages, you are ready to begin the cost control and cost management process.

Key Terms and Concepts

The following are terms and concepts discussed in the chapter that are important for you as a manager. To help you review, please define the terms below.

Revenue	Labor costs
Expense	Other expenses
Profit	Profit and loss statement (P&L)
Ideal expense	Budget/Plan
Desired profit	Performance to budget
Food costs	28-day-period approach
Beverage costs	

Test Your Skills

Throughout this book, all Test Your Skills exercises are available in Excel spreadsheets on your student disk. Although you will be able to calculate your answers by hand, the authors recommend that you use the spreadsheets for two main reasons: (1) you will be able to practice using the spreadsheets that you may use as a manager, and (2) you will be able to "play" with the numbers and create your own scenarios. These applications can be used with a variety of spreadsheet software packages; the authors chose Excel because it is widely available. It is assumed that you have basic knowledge of spreadsheets when using these applications. The dark bold outlined spaces in all of the Test Your Skills exercises indicate that answers are required in those spaces. Appendix A shows the kinds of Excel formulas you will need to solve the Test Your Skills exercises.

1. At the conclusion of her first month of operating Val's Donut Shop, Val computed the following revenue and expense figures:

Week	Revenue	Expense	Profit/Loss
1	$ 894.50	$ 761.80	
2	1,147.60	522.46	
3	1,261.80	879.14	
4	1,345.11	1,486.20	
Month			
To Receive $1,200.00 Profit for the Month			
Month			

Prepare both weekly and monthly profit formulas so that Val has a good idea about her current profit situation. Also, given her sales for the month, tell her how much her expenses should have been to realize the $1,200 profit she had hoped for.

2. Su Chan manages a Chinese restaurant called the Bungalow. Her P&L for the month of March is as follows.

The Bungalow's March P&L

Revenue		$100,000.00	100.0%
F&B Expense	34,000.00		34.0%
Labor Expense	40,000.00		40.0%
Other Expense	21,000.00		21.0%
Total Expense		95,000.00	95.0%
Profit		5,000.00	5.0%

Su has a meeting with the owner of the Bungalow next week, so she decided to create a pie chart showing the percentage of her costs in relation to her total sales (see the following diagram).

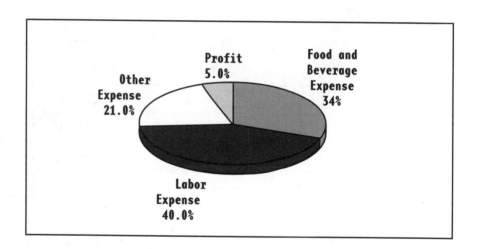

At the meeting with the owner, Su is asked to change the information on the pie chart to reflect next month's projections. The owner suggests that April revenues and costs should be as follows:

April revenues = $120,000.
Food and beverage costs = $44,000.
Labor and other expenses remain constant.

Using these numbers, is the owner's profit percentage going to be higher or lower than that in March? By how much?

After looking at the owner's projections, she thinks it might be too difficult (and not so good for her guests) if she cannot increase labor costs along with sales. She proposes a compromise and tells the owner that if he will agree to increased labor costs, she will try to decrease other expenses. So, Su proposes the following:

April revenues = $120,000.
Food and beverage costs = $44,000.
Labor costs = $50,000.
Other expenses = $19,000.

Using these numbers, is the owner's profit percentage going to be higher or lower than that in March? By how much?

Which set of projections has more reasonable goals?

Note: If you use the Excel spreadsheets on your student disk, the changes you make to the numbers should be reflected on the pie charts as well.

3. The dining room at the Roadrock Inn is extremely popular. Terry Ray, the food and beverage director, is pleased to see that his revenue is higher than last year. Of course, expenses are higher also. Express Terry's expenses and profit as a percentage of total revenue, both this year and last year (fill in all empty blanks).

	This Year	%	Last Year	%
Revenue	$965,971.00		$875,421.00	
F&B Expense	367,069.00		350,168.00	
Labor Expense	338,090.00		315,151.00	
Other Expense	144,896.00		140,068.00	
Total Expense				
Profit				

How is Terry doing in managing his expenses when comparing this year to last year? How do changes in revenue affect his performance?

4. Pamela Cantu operates a school foodservice department in a small, rural community. She feeds approximately 1,000 students per day in three different locations. She receives an average of $1.20 in revenues per meal. Her budget, set at the beginning of the school year by the superintendent, is developed in such a way that a small amount is to be reserved for future equipment purchases and dining room renovation. These funds are available, however, only if Pamela meets her budget.

She hopes to use this year's reserve to buy a $5,000 refrigerated salad bar for the high school. Since it is the midpoint of her school year, help her determine her "performance to budget" (fill in all empty blanks).

Item	Budget	Actual	% of Budget
Meals Served	300,000	149,800	
Revenue			
Food Expense	$170,000	$84,961	
Labor Expense	125,000	63,752	
Other Expense	60,000	31,460	
Total Expense	355,000		
Reserve	5,000		

Assuming that the year is 50% completed and Pamela continues doing what she is doing, is she likely to meet the reserve requirement and, thus, be able to purchase the salad bar by the end of the year? If not, what changes should she make over the next six months to ensure that she will have the $5,000 in reserve?

Sales = chic Avg X Customer
                              count
              ↑ Price

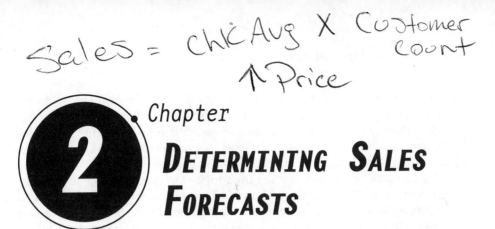

Chapter

2 DETERMINING SALES FORECASTS

OVERVIEW   This chapter presents the methods and procedures you must learn to create accurate histories of what you have sold in the past as well as projections of how much you will sell in the future. This includes the total revenue you will generate, the number of guests to be served, and the number of dollars each guest will spend. Knowledge of these techniques is critical if you are to analyze sales trends in the facility you manage and be prepared to serve your future guests well.

CHAPTER OUTLINE

Importance of Forecasting Sales
Sales History
Maintaining Sales Histories
Sales Variances
Predicting Future Sales
Key Terms and Concepts, and Test Your Skills

HIGHLIGHTS   At the conclusion of this chapter, you will be able to:

○ Develop a procedure to record current sales.
○ Compute percentage increases or decreases in sales over time.
○ Develop a procedure to estimate future sales.

Importance of Forecasting Sales

The first question operating managers must ask themselves is very simple: "How many guests will I serve today?–This week?–This year?" The answers to questions such as these are critical, since these guests will provide the revenue from which the operator will pay basic operating expenses. Simply put, if too few guests are served, total revenue may be insufficient to cover costs, even if these costs are well managed. In addition, purchasing decisions regarding the kind and quantity of food or beverage to buy are dependent on knowing the number of guests who will be coming to consume those products. Labor required to serve the guests is also determined based on the manager's "best guess" of the projected number of guests to be served and what these guests will buy. Forecasts of future sales are normally based on your sales history since what has happened in the past in your operation is usually the best predictor of what will happen in the future.

In the hospitality industry, we have many ways of counting or defining sales. In its simplest case, sales are the dollar amount of revenue collected during some predetermined time period. The time period may be an hour, shift, day, week, month, or year. When used in this manner, sales and revenue are interchangeable terms. When you predict the number of guests you will serve and the revenues they will generate in a given future time period, you have created a **sales forecast.**

You can determine your actual sales for a current time period by using a computerized system called a **point of sales (POS) system** that has been designed to provide specific sales information. Alternatively, a standard cash register or even manually produced guest checks or head counts will help you establish how many sales were completed. It is important to remember that a distinction is made in the hospitality industry between sales (revenue) and **sales volume,** which is the number of units sold. Consider Manuel, a bagel shop manager, whose Monday business consists of $2,000 in sales (revenue) because he actually sold 3,000 bagels (sales volume). Obviously, it is important for Manuel to know how much revenue is taken in, so he can evaluate the expenses required to generate his revenue *and* the number of units that have been sold. With this information, he can properly prepare to serve additional guests the next day.

In many areas of the hospitality industry, for example, in college dormitory foodservice, it is customary that no cash actually changes hands during a particular meal period. Of course, the manager of such a facility still created sales and would be interested in sales volume, that is, how much food was actually consumed by the students on that day. This is critical information because, as we have seen, a manager must be prepared to answer the question, "How many individuals did I serve today, and how many should I expect tomorrow?"

In some cases, your food and beverage operation may be a blend of cash and noncash sales. Consider Tonya Brown, a hospital foodservice director. It is very likely that Tonya will be involved in serving both cash guests (public cafeteria) and noncash patients (tray line). In addition, employee meals may be cash sales but at a reduced or subsidized rate. Clearly, Tonya's operation will create sales each day, and it will be im-

---

FIGURE **2.1** ● Advantages of Precise Sales Forecasts

1. Accurate revenue estimates
2. Improved ability to predict expenses
3. Greater efficiency in scheduling needed workers
4. Greater efficiency in scheduling menu item production schedules
5. Better accuracy in purchasing the correct amount of food for immediate use
6. Improved ability to maintain proper levels of nonperishable food inventories
7. Improved budgeting ability
8. Lower selling prices for guests because of increased operational efficiencies
9. Increased dollars available for current facility maintenance and future growth
10. Increased profit levels and stockholder value

---

portant to her and her staff to know, as accurately as possible, how many of each type guest she will serve.

An understanding of anticipated sales, in terms of revenue dollars or guest counts, will help you have the right number of workers, with the right amounts of product available, at the right time. In this way, you can begin to effectively manage your costs. In addition to the importance of accurate sales records for purchasing and staffing, sales records are valuable to the operator when developing labor standards. Consider, for example, a large restaurant with 400 seats. If an individual server can serve 25 guests at lunch, you would need 400/25, or 8, servers per lunch shift. If management keeps no accurate sales histories or forecasts, too few or too many servers could possibly be scheduled on any given lunch period. With accurate sales records, a sales history can be developed for each foodservice outlet you operate and better decisions will be reached with regard to planning for each unit's operation. Figure 2.1 lists some of the advantages that you gain when you can accurately predict the number of people you will serve in a future time period.

Sales History

A **sales history** is the systematic recording of all sales achieved during a predetermined time period. It is no less than an accurate record of what your operation has sold. Before you can develop a sales history, however, it is necessary for you to think about the definition of sales that is most helpful to you and your understanding of how the facility you manage functions. The simplest type of sales history records revenue only. The sales history format shown in Figure 2.2 is typical for recording sales revenue on a weekly basis.

Notice that, in this most basic of cases, you would determine daily sales either from your POS system, from sales revenue recorded on your cash register, or from adding the information recorded on your guest checks. You would then transfer that number, on a daily basis, to the sales history by entering the amount of your daily sales in the column titled Daily Sales. **Sales to date** is the cumulative total of sales reported in the unit. Sales to date is the number we get when we add today's sales to the sales of all prior days in the reporting period.

Sales to date on Tuesday, January 2, is computed by adding Tuesday's sales to those of the prior day ($851.90 + $974.37 = $1,826.27). The Sales to Date column is a running total of the sales achieved by Rae's Restaurant for the week. Should Rae's manager prefer it, the sales period could, of course, be defined in blocks other than one week. Common alternatives are meal periods, days, weeks, two-week periods, four-week periods, months, quarters (three-month periods), or any other unit of time that makes sense and is helpful to the manager.

FIGURE **2.2** ● Sales History

Rae's Restaurant			
Sales Period	Date	Daily Sales	Sales to Date
Monday	1/1	$ 851.90	$ 851.90
Tuesday	1/2	974.37	1,826.27
Wednesday	1/3	1,004.22	2,830.49
Thursday	1/4	976.01	3,806.50
Friday	1/5	856.54	4,663.04
Saturday	1/6	1,428.22	6,091.26
Sunday	1/7	1,241.70	7,332.96
Week's Total			7,332.96

Sometimes, you will not have the ability to consider sales in terms of revenue generated. Figure 2.3 is the type of sales history you can use when no cash sales are typically reported. Notice that, in this case, the manager is interested in recording sales based on meal periods rather than some alternative time frame such as a 24-hour (one-day) period. This approach is often used in such settings as nursing homes, college dormitories, prisons, hospitals, summer camps, or any other situation where a knowledge of the number of actual guests served during a given period is critical for planning purposes.

Given the data in Figure 2.3, the implications for staffing service personnel at the camp are very clear. Fewer service personnel are needed from 9:00 to 11:00 A.M. than from 7:00 to 9:00 A.M. The reason is obvious. Fewer campers eat between 9:00 and 11:00 A.M. (40) than between 7:00 and 9:00 A.M. (121). Notice that, as a knowledgeable manager, if you were operating this camp, you could either reduce staff during the slower service period or shift those workers to some other necessary task. Notice also that you might decide not to produce as many menu items for consumption during the 9:00 to 11:00 AM period. In that way, you could make more efficient use of both labor and food products. It is simply easier to manage well when you know the answer to the question, "How many guests will I serve?"

FIGURE **2.3** ● Sales History

Eureka Summer Camp								
	Guests Served							
Serving Period	Mon	Tues	Wed	Thurs	Fri	Sat	Sun	Total
7:00–9:00 A.M.	121							
9:00–11:00 A.M.	40							
11:00–1:00 P.M.	131							
1:00–3:00 P.M.	11							
3:00–5:00 P.M.	42							
5:00–7:00 P.M.	161							
Total Served	506							

Sales histories can be created to record revenue, guests served, or both. It is important, however, that you keep good records of how much you have sold because doing so is the key to accurately predicting the amount of sales you will achieve in the future.

Computing Averages for Sales Histories

In some cases, knowing the average number of revenue dollars generated in a time period, or the average number of guests served in that period, may be a real benefit to you. This is because it may be helpful to know, for example, the number of dollar sales achieved on a typical day last week or the number of guests served on that same typical day. Since future guest activity can often be expected to be very similar to the activities of guests in the past, using historical averages from your operation can be quite useful in helping you project future guest sales and counts.

An **average** is defined as the value arrived at by adding the quantities in a series and dividing the sum of the quantities by the number of items in the series. Thus, the average of 6 + 9 + 18 = 11. The sum of the quantities in this case equals 33 (6 + 9 + 18 = 33). The number of items in the series is *three,* that is, 6, 9, and 18. Thus, 33/3 = 11, the average of the numbers. Sometimes, an average is referred to as the **mean** in a series of quantities. The two major types of averages you are likely to encounter as a foodservice manager are as follows:

1. Fixed average
2. Rolling average

Fixed Average   A **fixed average** is an average in which you determine a specific time period, for example, the first 14 days of a given month, and then you compute the mean or average amount of sales or guest activity for that period. Note that this average is called fixed because the first 14 days of the month will always consist of the same days and, thus, the same revenue numbers, as shown in Figure 2.4, the sales activity of Dan's Take-Out Coffee for the first 14 days of this month.

This average (total revenue/number of days) is fixed or constant because Dan's management has identified 14 specific days that are used to make up the average. The number $427.14 may be very useful because it might, if management deems it so, be used as a good predictor of the revenue volume that should be expected for the first 14 days of next month.

Rolling Average   The **rolling average** is the average amount of sales or volume over a changing time period. Essentially, where a fixed average is computed using a specific or constant set of data, the rolling average is computed using data that will change regularly. To illustrate, consider the case of Ubalda Salas, who operates a sports bar in a university town in the Midwest. Ubalda is interested in knowing what the average revenue dol-

FIGURE **2.4** ● 14-Day Fixed Average

Dan's Take-Out Coffee	
Day	Daily Sales
1	$ 350.00
2	320.00
3	390.00
4	440.00
5	420.00
6	458.00
7	450.00
8	460.00
9	410.00
10	440.00
11	470.00
12	460.00
13	418.00
14	494.00
14-day total	$5,980.00

$$\frac{\$5,980}{14} = \$427.14 \text{ per day}$$

lars were in her operation for *each prior seven-day period.* Obviously, in this case, the prior seven-day period changes or rolls forward by one day, each day. It is important to note that Ubalda could have been interested in her average daily revenue last week (fixed average), but she prefers to know her average sales for the last seven days. This means that she will, at times, be using data from both last week *and* this week to compute the last seven-day average. Using the sales data recorded in Figure 2.5, the seven-day rolling average for Ubalda's Sports Bar would be computed as shown in Figure 2.6.

Note that each seven-day period is made up of a group of daily revenue numbers that changes over time. The first seven-day rolling average is computed by summing the seven days' revenue (revenue on days 1–7 = $2,828) and dividing that number by seven to arrive at a seven-day rolling average of $404.00 ($2,828/7 = $404.00). Each day, Ubalda would add her daily revenue to that of the prior seven-day total and drop the day that is now eight days past. This gives her the effect of continually rolling the most current seven days forward. The use of the rolling average, while

FIGURE **2.5** ● 14-Day Sales Levels

Ubalda's Sports Bar			
Date	Sales	Date	Sales
1	350	8	460
2	320	9	410
3	390	10	440
4	440	11	470
5	420	12	460
6	458	13	418
7	450	14	494

more complex and time consuming than that of a fixed average, can be extremely useful in recording data to help you make effective predictions about the sales levels you can expect in the future. This is true because, in many cases, rolling data are more current and, thus, more relevant than some fixed historical averages. You may choose to compute fixed averages for some time periods and rolling averages for others. For example, it may be helpful to know your average daily sales for the first 14 days of last month and your average sales for the last 14 days. If, for example, these two numbers were very different, you would know if the number of sales you can expect in the future is increasing or declining. Regardless of the type of average you feel is best for your operation, you should record your sales history because it is from your sales history that you will be better able to predict future sales levels.

Recording Revenue, Guest Counts, or Both?

As previously mentioned, some foodservice operations do not regularly record revenue as a measure of their sales activity. For them, developing sales histories by recording the number of individuals they serve each day makes the most sense. Thus, **guest counts,** the term used in the hospitality industry to indicate the number of people served, is recorded on a

FIGURE **2.6** ● Seven-Day Rolling Average

Ubalda's Sports Bar								
	Seven-Day Period							
Date	*1–7*	*2–8*	*3–9*	*4–10*	*5–11*	*6–12*	*7–13*	*8–14*
1	$350	–						
2	320	$320	–					
3	390	390	$390	–				
4	440	440	440	$440	–			
5	420	420	420	420	$420	–		
6	458	458	458	458	458	$458	–	
7	450	450	450	450	450	450	$450	–
8		460	460	460	460	460	460	$460
9			410	410	410	410	410	410
10				440	440	440	440	440
11					470	470	470	470
12						460	460	460
13							418	418
14								494
Total	2,828	2,938	3,028	3,078	3,108	3,148	3,108	3,152
7-Day Rolling Average	404.00	419.71	432.57	439.71	444.00	449.71	444.00	450.29

regular basis. For many other foodservice operations, sales are recorded in terms of sales revenue generated.

Not surprisingly, you may decide that your operation is best managed by tracking both revenue and guest counts. In fact, if you do decide to record both revenue and guest counts, you have the information you need to compute **average sales per guest**, a term also known as **check average.**

Average sales per guest is determined by the following formula:

$$\frac{\text{Total Sales}}{\text{Number of Guests Served}} = \text{Average Sales per Guest}$$

Consider the information in Figure 2.7 in which the manager of Brothers' Family Restaurant has decided to monitor and record the following:

1. Sales
2. Guests served
3. Average sales per guest

Most POS systems are designed to tell you the amount of revenue you have generated in a given time period, the number of guests you have served, and the average sales per guest. If the operation you manage does not have a POS system in place, the revenue generated may be determined by a cash register, and the number of guests served may be determined by

FIGURE **2.7** ● Sales History

Brothers' Family Restaurant				
Sales Period	Date	Sales	Guests Served	Average Sales per Guest
Monday	1/1	$1,365.00	190	$7.18
Tuesday	1/2	2,750.00	314	8.76
Two-Day Average		2,057.50	252	8.16

an actual guest head count, by a count of the number of utensils or trays issued, or by adding the number of individuals listed on the guest checks used. In the case of Brothers' Family Restaurant, Monday's revenue was $1,365, the number of guests served was 190, and the average sales per guest for Monday, January 1, was determined to be $7.18 ($1,365/190 = $7.18). On Tuesday, the average sales per guest was $8.76 ($2,750/314 = $8.76).

To compute his or her two-day revenue average, the Brothers' manager would add Monday's revenue and Tuesday's revenue and divide by 2, yielding a two-day revenue average of $2,057.50 [($1,365 + $2,750)/2 = $2,057.50]. In a like manner, the two-day guests-served average is computed by adding the number of guests served on Monday to the number served on Tuesday and dividing by 2, yielding a two-day average guests-served number of 252 [(190 + 314)/2 = 252].

It might be logical to think that the manager of Brothers' could compute the Monday and Tuesday combined average sales per guest by adding the averages from each day and dividing by 2. This *would not* be correct. A formula consisting of Monday's average sales per guest plus Tuesday's average sales per guest divided by 2 [($7.18 + $8.76)/2] yields $7.97. In fact, the two-day average sales per guest is $8.16 [($1,365 + $2,750)/(190 + 314) = ($4,115/504) = $8.16].

While the difference of $0.19 might, at first glance, appear to be an inconsequential amount, assume that you are the chief executive officer (CEO) of a restaurant chain with 4,000 units worldwide. If each unit served 1,000 guests per day and you miscalculated average sales per guest by $0.19, your daily revenue assumption would be "off" by $760,000 per day [(4,000 × 1,000 × $0.19) = $760,000].

Returning to the Brothers' Family Restaurant example, the correct procedure for computing the two-day sales per guest average is as follows:

$$\frac{\text{Monday Sales} + \text{Tuesday Sales}}{\text{Monday Guests} + \text{Tuesday Guests}}$$

or

$$\frac{\$1,365 + \$2,750}{190 + 314} = \$8.16$$

The correct computation is a **weighted average,** that is, an average that weights the number of guests with how much they spend in a given time period.

To demonstrate further, assume that you were to answer the question, "What is the combined average sales per guest?" using the data in

FIGURE **2.8** ● Weighted Average

	Sales	Guests Served	Average Sales per Guest
Day 1	$ 100	20	$ 5.00
Day 2	4,000	400	10.00
Two-Day Average	2,050	210	???

Figure 2.8. From the data in Figure 2.8, it is easy to "see" that the two-day average *would not* be $7.50 ($5.00 + $10.00/2) because many more guests were served at a $10.00 average than were served at the $5.00 average. Obviously, with so many guests spending an average of $10.00, and so few spending an average of $5.00, the overall average should be quite close to $10.00. In fact, the correct weighted average sales per guest would be $9.76, as follows:

$$\frac{\text{Day 1 Sales} + \text{Day 2 Sales}}{\text{Day 1 Guests} + \text{Day 2 Guests}}$$

or

$$\frac{\$100 + \$4,000}{20 + 400} = \$9.76$$

Maintaining Sales Histories

While a sales history may consist of revenue, number of guests served, and average sales per guest, you may want to use even more detailed information, such as the number of a particular menu item served, the number of guests served in a specific meal or time period, or the method of meal delivery (e.g., drive-through vs. counter sales). The important concept to remember is that you have the power to determine the information that best suits your operation. That information should be updated at least daily, and a cumulative total for the appropriate accounting period should also be maintained.

In most cases, your sales histories should be kept for a period of at least two years. This allows you to have a good sense of what has happened to your business in the recent past. Of course, if you are the manager of a new operation, or one that has recently undergone a major concept change, you may not have the advantage of reviewing meaningful sales histories. If you find yourself in such a situation, it is imperative that you begin to build and maintain your sales histories as soon as possible so you will have relevant data on which to base your future managerial decisions.

Sales Variances

Once an accurate sales history system has been established, you may begin to see that your operation, if it is like most, will experience some level of sales variation. These **sales variances,** or changes from previously experienced sales levels, will give you an indication of whether your sales are improving, declining, or staying the same. Because that information is so important to predicting future sales levels, many foodservice managers improve their sales history information by including sales variance as an additional component of the history.

Figure 2.9 details a portion of a sales history that has been modified to include a Variance column, which allows the manager to see how sales are different from a prior period. In this case, the manager of Quick Wok wants to compare sales for the first three months of this year to sales for the first three months of last year. Note, of course, that the manager would find this revenue information in the sales histories regularly maintained by the operation.

FIGURE **2.9** ● Sales History and Variance

Quick Wok			
Month	Sales This Year	Sales Last Year	Variance
January	$ 54,000	$ 51,200	$ 2,800
February	57,500	50,750	6,750
March	61,200	57,500	3,700
First-Quarter Total	172,700	159,450	13,250

The variance in Figure 2.9 is determined by subtracting sales last year from sales this year. In January, the variance figure is obtained as follows:

Sales This Year − Sales Last Year = Variance

or

$54,000 − $51,200 = $2,800

Thus, the manager of Quick Wok can see that sales are improving. All three months in the first quarter of the year showed revenue increases over the prior year. The total improvement for the first quarter was $13,250 ($172,700 − $159,450 = $13,250).

While the format used in Figure 2.9 does let a manager know the dollar value of revenue variance, good managers want to know even more. Simply knowing the dollar value of a variance has limitations. Consider two restaurant managers. One manager's restaurant had revenue of $1,000,000 last year. The second manager's restaurant generated one half as much revenue, or $500,000. This year both had sales increases of $50,000. It is clear that a $50,000 sales increase represents a much greater improvement in the second restaurant than in the first. Because that is true, effective managers are interested in the **percentage variance,** or percentage change, in their sales from one time period to the next.

Figure 2.10 shows how the sales history at Quick Wok can be expanded to include percentage variance as part of that operation's complete sales history. Percentage variance is obtained by subtracting sales last year from sales this year and dividing the resulting number by sales last year. Thus, in the month of January, the percentage variance is determined as follows:

$$\frac{\text{Sales This Year} - \text{Sales Last Year}}{\text{Sales Last Year}} = \text{Percentage Variance}$$

or

$$\frac{\$54,000 - \$51,200}{\$51,200} = 0.055$$
(in common form, 5.5%)

Note that the resulting decimal-form percentage can be converted to the more frequently used common form discussed in Chapter 1 by moving the decimal point two places to the right (or multiplying by 100).

FIGURE **2.10** ● Sales History, Variance, and Percentage Variance

Month	Sales This Year	Sales Last Year	Variance	Percentage Variance
Quick Wok				
January	$ 54,000	$ 51,200	$ 2,800	5.5%
February	57,500	50,750	6,750	13.3
March	61,200	57,500	3,700	6.4
First-Quarter Total	172,700	159,450	13,250	8.3

Of course, an alternative, and shorter formula for computing the percentage variance is as follows:

$$\frac{\text{Variance}}{\text{Sales Last Year}} = \text{Percentage Variance}$$

or

$$\$\frac{2,800}{\$51,200} = 0.055$$
(in common form, 5.5%)

Another way to compute the percentage variance is to use a math shortcut, as follows:

$$\frac{\text{Sales This Year}}{\text{Sales Last Year}} - 1 = \text{Percentage Variance}$$

or

$$\frac{\$54,000}{\$51,200} - 1 = 0.055$$
(in common form, 5.5%)

The computation of percentage variance is invaluable when you want to compare the operating results of two foodservice operations of different sizes. Return to our previous example of the two restaurant managers, each of whom achieved $50,000 revenue increases. Using the first percentage variance formula presented before, you will see that the restaurant with higher sales increased its revenue by 5.0%, [($1,050,000 − $1,000,000)/$1,000,000 = 5.0%], while the restaurant with lower revenue achieved a 10% increase [($550,000 − $500,000)/$500,000 = 10.0%]. As your level of expertise increases, you will find additional areas in which knowing the percentage variance in revenue, and later in this text, in expense areas, will be instrumental to your management decision making.

Predicting Future Sales

It has been pointed out that truly outstanding managers have an ability to see the future in regard to the revenue figures they can achieve and the number of guests they expect to serve. You, too, can learn to do this when you apply the knowledge of percentage variances you now have to estimating your own operation's future sales. Depending on the type of facility you manage, you may be interested in predicting, or forecasting, future revenues, guest counts, or average sales per guest levels. We will examine the procedures for all three of these in detail.

Future Revenues

Erica Tullstein is the manager of Rock's Pizza Pub on the campus of State College. Her guests consist of college students, most of whom come to the Rock to talk, listen to music, eat, and study. Erica has done a good job in maintaining sales histories in the two years she has managed the Rock. She records the revenue dollars she achieves on a daily basis, as well as the number of students frequenting the Rock. Revenue data for the last three months of the year are recorded in Figure 2.11.

As can easily be seen, fourth-quarter revenues for Erica's operation have increased from the previous year. Of course, there could be a variety of reasons for this. Erica may have extended her hours of operation to attract more students. She may have increased the size of pizzas and held her prices constant, thus creating more value for her guests. She may have raised the price of pizza, but kept the pizzas the same size. Or perhaps a competing pizza parlor was closed for renovation during this time period. Using all of her knowledge of her own operation and her market, Erica would like to predict the sales level she will experience in the first three months of next year. This sales forecast will be most helpful as she plans for next year's anticipated expenses, staffing levels, and profits.

The first question Erica must address is the amount her sales have actually increased. Revenue increases range from a low in October of 3.4%, to a high in December of 13.9%. The overall quarter average of 7.5%

FIGURE **2.11** ● Revenue History

Rock's Pizza Pub				
Month	Sales This Year	Sales Last Year	Variance	Percentage Variance
October	$ 75,000	$ 72,500	$ 2,500	3.4%
November	64,250	60,000	4,250	7.1
December	57,500	50,500	7,000	13.9
Fourth-Quarter Total	196,750	183,000	13,750	7.5

is the figure that Erica elects to use as she predicts her sales revenue for the first quarter of the coming year. She feels it is neither too conservative, as would be the case if she used the October percentage increase, nor too aggressive, as would be the case if she used the December figure.

If Erica were to use the 7.5% average increase from the fourth quarter of last year to predict her revenues for the first quarter of this year, a planning sheet for the first quarter of this year could be developed as presented in Figure 2.12.

FIGURE **2.12** ● First-Quarter Revenue Forecast

Rock's Pizza Pub				
Month	Sales Last Year	% Increase Estimate	Increase Amount	Revenue Forecast
January	$ 68,500	7.5%	$ 5,137.50	$ 73,637.50
February	72,000	7.5	5,400.00	77,400.00
March	77,000	7.5	5,775.00	82,775.00
First-Quarter Total	217,500	7.5	16,312.50	233,812.50

Revenue forecast for this time period is determined by multiplying sales last year by the % increase estimate and then adding sales last year. In the month of January, revenue forecast is calculated using the following formula:

Sales Last Year + (Sales Last Year × % Increase Estimate) = Revenue Forecast

or

$68,500 + ($68,500 × 0.075) = $73,637.50

An alternative way to compute the revenue forecast is to use a math shortcut, as follows:

Sales Last Year × (1 + % Increase Estimate) = Revenue Forecast

or

$68,500 × (1 + 0.075) = $73,637.50

Erica is using the increases she has experienced in the past to predict increases she may experience in the future. Monthly revenue figures from last year's sales history plus percent increase estimates based on those histories give Erica a good idea of the revenue levels she may achieve in January, February, and March of the coming year. Clearly, Erica will have a better idea of the sales dollars she may achieve than managers who did not have the advantage of sales histories to help guide their planning.

Future Guest Counts

Using the same techniques employed in estimating increases in sales, the noncash operator or any manager interested in guest counts can estimate increases or decreases in the number of guests served. Figure 2.13 shows how Erica, the manager of Rock's Pizza Pub, used a sales history to determine the percentage of guest count increases achieved in her facility in the fourth quarter of last year.

FIGURE **2.13** ● Guest Count History

Rock's Pizza Pub				
Month	Guests This Year	Guests Last Year	Variance	Percentage Variance
October	14,200	13,700	+ 500	3.6%
November	15,250	14,500	+ 750	5.2
December	16,900	15,500	+1,400	9.0
Fourth-Quarter Total	46,350	43,700	+2,650	6.1

If Erica were to use the 6.1% average increase from the fourth quarter of last year to predict her guest count for the first quarter of the coming year, a planning sheet could be developed as presented in Figure 2.14. It is important to note that Erica is not required to use the same percentage increase estimate for each month. Indeed, any forecasted increase management feels is appropriate can be used to predict future sales.

FIGURE **2.14** ● First-Quarter Guest Count Forecast

Rock's Pizza Pub				
Month	Guests Last Year	% Increase Estimate	Guest Increase Estimate	Guest Count Forecast
January	12,620	6.1%	770	13,390
February	13,120	6.1	800	13,920
March	13,241	6.1	808	14,049
First-Quarter Total	38,981	6.1	2,378	41,359

Notice that in January, for example, the guest increase estimate is rounded from 769.82 to 770. This is because you cannot serve "0.82" people!

The guest count forecast is determined by multiplying guest count last year by the % increase estimate and then adding the guest count last year. In the month of January, guest count forecast is calculated using the following formula:

> **Guest Count Last Year**
>   **+ (Guest Count Last Year × % Increase Estimate)**
>   **= Guest Count Forecast**
>
> *or*
>
> **12,620 + (12,620 × 0.061) = 13,390**

This process can be simplified if desired by using a math shortcut, as follows:

> **Guests Last Year × (1.00 + % Increase Estimate)**
>   **= Guest Count Forecast**
>
> *or*
>
> **12,620 × (1.00 + 0.061) = 13,390**

You should choose the formula you feel most comfortable with.

Future Average Sales per Guest

Recall that average sales per guest (check average) is simply the amount of money an average guest spends during a visit. The same formula is used to forecast average sales per guest as was used in forecasting total revenue and guest counts. Therefore, using data taken from the sales history, the following formula is employed:

> **Last Year's Average Sales per Guest**
>   **+ Estimated Increase in Sales per Guest**
>   **= Sales per Guest Forecast**

Alternatively, you can compute average sales per guest using the data collected from revenue forecasts (Figure 2.12) and combining that data with the guest count forecast (Figure 2.14). If that is done, the data presented in Figure 2.15 result.

Average sales per guest forecast is obtained by dividing the revenue forecast by the guest count forecast. Thus, in the month of January, the average sales per guest forecast is determined by the following formula:

$$\frac{\text{Revenue Forecast}}{\text{Guest Count Forecast}} = \text{Average Sales per Guest Forecast}$$

or

$$\frac{\$73,637.50}{13,390} = \$5.50$$

It is important to note that sales histories, regardless of how well they have been developed and maintained, are not sufficient alone to accurately predict future sales. Your knowledge of potential price changes, new competitors, facility renovations, and improved selling programs are just a few of the many factors that you must consider when predicting future sales. There is no question, however, that you must develop and monitor, daily, a sales history report appropriate for your operation. They are easily developed and will serve as the cornerstone of other management sys-

FIGURE **2.15** ● First-Quarter Average Sales per Guest Forecast

Rock's Pizza Pub			
Month	Revenue Forecast	Guest Count Forecast	Average Sales per Guest Forecast
January	$ 73,637.50	13,390	$5.50
February	77,400.00	13,920	5.56
March	82,775.00	14,049	5.89
First-Quarter Total	233,812.50	41,359	5.65

tems. Without accurate sales data, control systems, regardless of their so-phistication, are destined to fail.

When added to your knowledge of the factors that impact your unit, properly maintained histories will help you answer two important control questions, namely, "How many people are coming tomorrow?" and "How much is each person likely to spend?" The judgment of management is critical in forecasting answers to these questions. Since you can now an-swer those questions, you are ready to develop systems that will allow you to prepare an efficient and cost-effective way of serving those guests, be they guests in a hotel lounge, tourists visiting your restaurant as part of their overall travel experience, or any other foodservice guest. You want to be ready to provide them with quality food and beverage products and enough staff to serve them properly. You have done your homework with regard to the number of individuals who may be coming, and now you must prepare for their arrival!

FUN ON THE WEB!

Look up the following sites to see examples of point of sales sys-tems used to track sales information.

www.micros.com Link to "Products and Services" and continue link-ing from here to see product descriptions.

www.squirrelsystems.com Spend some time browsing this cool site.

www.datatrakpos.com Click on "Screen Shots" to see how sales are displayed on the system.

Key Terms and Concepts

The following are terms and concepts discussed in the chapter that are important for you as a manager. To help you review, please define the terms below.

Sales forecast	Rolling average
Point of sales (POS) system	Guest count
Sales volume	Average sales per guest (check
Sales history	average)
Sales to date	Weighted average
Average (mean)	Sales variance
Fixed average	Percentage variance

Test Your Skills

1. Laurie Fitsin owns a small sandwich shop called Laurie's Lunch Box. She has developed a sales history for the first week of March using to-tal sales and guests served. Help Laurie calculate her average sales per guest for each day of the week and calculate her totals.

Laurie's Lunch Box

Sales Period	Date	Sales	Guests Served	Average Sales per Guest
Monday	3/1	$1,248.44	200	
Tuesday	3/2	1,686.25	360	
Wednesday	3/3	1,700.00	350	
Thursday	3/4	1,555.65	300	
Friday	3/5	1,966.31	380	
Saturday	3/6	2,134.65	400	
Sunday	3/7	2,215.77	420	
Total				

Laurie has decided that she could take a shortcut and calculate the average sales per guest for the week by adding Monday through Sunday's average sales per guest and dividing by seven. Would this shortcut make a difference in her total average sales per guest for the week? If so, how much of a difference? Should she take this shortcut? Why or why not?

2. Peggy Richey operates Peggy's Pizza Place in southern California. She has maintained a sales history for January through June, and she wants to compare this year's sales with last year's sales. Calculate her sales variances and percentage variances for the first six months of the year.

Peggy's Pizza Place

Month	Sales This Year	Sales Last Year	Variance	Percentage Variance
January	$37,702.73	$34,861.51		
February	33,472.03	31,485.60		
March	36,492.98	33,707.79		
April	35,550.12	32,557.85		
May	36,890.12	37,852.42		
June	37,482.52	37,256.36		
6-Month Total				

3. Peggy (from preceding exercise) wants to use the sales and variance information from her first six months of the year to forecast her revenues for the last six months of the year. She decides to use her six-month total percentage variance of 4.75% to predict her changes in sales. Help her calculate the projected sales increases and revenue forecasts for the last six months of the year.

Peggy's Pizza Place

Month	Sales Last Year	Predicted Change	Projected Sales Increase	Revenue Forecast
July	$36,587.91	4.75%		
August	36,989.73	4.75%		
September	40,896.32	4.75%		
October	37,858.63	4.75%		
November	37,122.45	4.75%		
December	37,188.71	4.75%		
6-Month Total				

4. The Lopez brothers, Victor, Tony, and Soren, own the Lopez Cantina. Victor is in charge of marketing, and he is developing his sales forecast for next year. Because of his marketing efforts, he predicts a 5% increase in his monthly guest counts. Victor is not aware of any anticipated menu price increases and assumes, therefore, that his weighted check average will remain stable.

   a. Using last year's sales and guest counts, estimate Victor's weighted check average (average sales per guest) for the year.

Month	Sales Last Year	Guest Count Last Year	Check Average
January	$45,216.00	4,800	
February	48,538.00	5,120	
March	50,009.00	5,006	
April	45,979.00	4,960	
May	49,703.00	5,140	
June	48,813.00	5,300	
July	55,142.00	5,621	
August	59,119.00	6,002	
September	55,257.00	5,780	
October	50,900.00	5,341	
November	54,054.00	5,460	
December	50,998.00	5,400	
Total			

b. Using the weighted check average calculated in part a, determine Victor's projected sales assuming a 5% increase in guest counts.

Month	Guest Count Last Year	Guest Count Forecast	Weighted Check Average	Projected Sales
January	4,800			
February	5,120			
March	5,006			
April	4,960			
May	5,140			
June	5,300			
July	5,621			
August	6,002			
September	5,780			
October	5,341			
November	5,460			
December	5,400			
Total				

Chapter

3 MANAGING THE COST OF FOOD

OVERVIEW   In this chapter, you will learn the professional techniques and methods used to effectively purchase, receive, and store food products. You will also master the formulas used to compute the true cost of the food you provide your guests, as well as a process for estimating the value of food you have used on a daily or weekly basis, by applying the food cost percentage method, which is the standard in the hospitality industry.

CHAPTER OUTLINE

> Menu Item Forecasting
> Standardized Recipes
> Inventory Control
> Purchasing
> Receiving
> Storage
> Determining Actual Food Expense
> Key Terms and Concepts, and Test Your Skills

HIGHLIGHTS   At the conclusion of this chapter, you will be able to:

○ Use sales histories and standardized recipes to determine the amount of food products to buy in anticipation of forecasted sales.
○ Purchase, receive, and store food products in a cost-effective manner.
○ Compute the cost of food sold and food cost percentage.

Menu Item Forecasting

The menu determines the success of most foodservice operations. When selecting a restaurant, many guests start the process with the question,

"What do you feel like eating?" For many Americans, the answer to this question is the name of a restaurant, rather than a menu item. In 2000, the U.S. Bureau of Labor Statistics consumer expenditure surveys reported that sales of food consumed away from home grew an average of 5% per year in the 1990s, with annual expenditures for an average U.S. household exceeding $2,000. Projections for the decade from 2000 to 2010 call for continued growth at these rates or higher. The hospitality industry is the third largest retail industry in the United States, surpassed only by automobiles and food stores.

The restaurant industry generates sales revenues of over $350 billion a year. According to the National Restaurant Association's *2000 Restaurant Industry Forecast*, continued economic growth, gains in consumers' real disposable income, and changes in the lifestyles of today's busy American families are all spurring the sustained rise in hospitality-related services growth. The hospitality industry remains the nation's largest employer with 11 million-plus employees. In addition to lodging and restaurants, the industry includes country clubs, nightclubs, bars, private catering, meeting planners, and tourism-related destination points, such as theme parks, cruise ships, and casinos. This is good news for your career as a hospitality manager.

All this growth, activity, and consumer demand, however, will also create challenges for you. Consider the situation you would encounter if you used sales histories (Chapter 2) to project 300 guests for lunch today at the restaurant you manage. Your restaurant serves only three entrée items: roast chicken, roast pork, and roast beef. The question you would face is this, "How many servings of each item should we produce so that we do not run out of any one item?"

If you were to run out of one of your three menu items, guests who wanted that item would undoubtedly become upset. Producing too much of any one item would, on the other hand, cause costs to rise to unacceptable levels unless these items could be sold for their full price at a later time.

Clearly, in this situation, it would be unwise to produce 300 portions of each item. While you would never run out of any one item, that is, each of your 300 estimated guests could order the same item and you would still have enough, you would also have 600 leftovers at the end of your lunch period. What you would like to do, of course, is instruct your staff to make the "right" amount of each menu item. The right amount would be the number of servings that minimize your chances of running out of an item before lunch is over, while also minimizing your chance of having excessive leftovers.

The answer to the question of how many servings of roast chicken, pork, and beef you should prepare lies in accurate menu forecasting.

Let us return to the example cited previously. This time, however, assume that you were wise enough to have recorded last week's menu item sales on a form similar to the one presented in Figure 3.1.

FIGURE **3.1** ● Menu Item Sales History

Date: 1/1–1/5			Menu Items Sold				
Menu Item	Mon	Tues	Wed	Thurs	Fri	Total	Week's Average
Roast Chicken	70	72	61	85	77	365	73
Roast Pork	110	108	144	109	102	573	115
Roast Beef	100	140	95	121	106	562	112
Total	280	320	300	315	285	1,500	

As you can see, an estimate of 300 guests for next Monday makes sense because the weekly sales total last week of 1,500 guests served averages 300 guests per day (1,500/5 days = 300/day). You also know that, on an average day, you sold 73 roast chicken (365 sold/5 days = 73/day), 115 roast pork (573 sold/5 days = 115/day), and 112 roast pork (562 sold/5 days = 112/day).

Once you know the average number of people selecting a given menu item, and you know the total number of guests who made the selections, you can compute the **popularity index,** which is defined as the percentage of total guests choosing a given menu item from a list of alternatives. In this example, you can improve your "guess" about the quantity of each item to prepare if you use the sales history to help guide your decision. If you assume that future guests will select menu items much as past guests have done, given that the list of menu items remains the same, that information can be used to improve your predictions with the following formula:

$$\text{Popularity Index} = \frac{\text{Total Number of a Specific Menu Item Sold}}{\text{Total Number of All Menu Items Sold}}$$

In this example, the popularity index for roast chicken last week was 24.3% (365 roast chicken sold/1,500 total guests = 0.243, or 24.3%). Similarly, 38.2% (573 roast pork sold/1,500 total guests = 38.20%) prefer roast pork, while 37.50% (562 roast beef sold/1,500 total guests = 37.50%) select roast beef.

If we know, even in a general way, what we can expect our guests to select, we are better prepared to make good decisions about the quantity of each item that should be produced. In this example, Figure 3.2 illustrates your best guess of what your 300 guests are likely to order when they arrive.

The basic formula for individual menu item forecasting, based on an item's individual sales history, is as follows:

> **Number of Guests Expected × Item Popularity Index = Predicted Number of That Item to Be Sold**

The **predicted number to be sold** is simply the quantity of a specific menu item likely to be sold given an estimate of the total number of guests expected.

Once you know what your guests are likely to select, you can move to the next step, which is the determination of how many of each menu item your production staff should be instructed to prepare. It is important to note that foodservice managers face a great deal of uncertainty when attempting to determine the number of guests who will arrive on a given day. A variety of factors come together to influence the number of guests you can expect to serve on any specific day. Among these are the following:

FIGURE **3.2** ● Forecasting Item Sales

Menu Item	Guest Forecast	Popularity Index	Predicted Number to Be Sold
Roast Chicken	300	0.243	73
Roast Pork	300	0.382	115
Roast Beef	300	0.375	112
Total			300

1. Competition
2. Weather
3. Special events in your area
4. Hotel occupancy
5. Your own promotions
6. Your competitor's promotions
7. Quality of service
8. Operational consistency

The interplay of these, and other factors, which may affect sales volume, makes accurate guest count prediction very difficult.

In addition, remember that sales histories track only the general trends of an operation. They are not able to estimate precisely the number of guests who may arrive on any given day. Sales histories, then, are a guide to what might be expected. In our example, last week's guest counts range from a low of 280 (Monday) to a high of 320 (Tuesday). In addition, the percentage of people selecting each menu item changes somewhat on a daily basis.

As a professional foodservice manager, you must take into account possible increases or decreases in guest count and possible fluctuations in your predicted number to be sold computations when planning how many of each menu item you should prepare. The projection of guest counts and predicted number to be sold are tools to help you make better decisions about the kind and quantity of items to be produced. A more complete discussion of menu item forecasting as it relates to production planning is presented in Chapter 5.

In Chapter 2, we began to discuss the concept of sales forecasting. As you now know, forecasting can involve estimating the number of guests you expect, the dollar amount of sales you expect, or even what those guests may want to purchase. This forecasting is crucial if you are to effectively manage your food expenses. In addition, consistency in food production and guest service will greatly influence your overall success.

Standardized Recipes

While it is the menu that determines what is to be sold and at what price, the **standardized recipe** controls both the quantity and the quality of what your kitchen will produce. Simply put, a standardized recipe consists of the procedures to be used in preparing and serving each of your menu items. The standardized recipe ensures that each time a guest orders an item from your menu, he or she receives exactly what you intended the guest to receive.

Critical factors in a standardized recipe such as cooking times and serving size have been tested and retested and should remain constant.

Thus, the standardized recipe is the key to menu item consistency and, ultimately, operational success. It is always true that guests expect to get what they pay for. The standardized recipe helps you make sure that they do. Inconsistency is the enemy of any quality foodservice operation. It will make little difference to the unhappy guest, for instance, if you tell him or her that while the menu item he or she purchased today is not up to your normal standard, it will be tomorrow, or that it was the last time the guest visited your operation.

Standardized recipes must be appropriate for the operation using them. If they are not, they will simply not be used or followed. In general, standardized recipes contain the following information:

1. Item name
2. Total yield (number of servings)
3. Portion size
4. Ingredient list
5. Preparation/method section
6. Cooking time and temperature
7. Special instructions, if necessary
8. Recipe cost (optional)*

Figure 3.3 contains a standardized recipe for roast chicken.

If this standardized recipe represents the quality and quantity management wishes its guests to have and if it is followed carefully each time, then guests will indeed receive the value management intended.

Interestingly, despite their tremendous advantages, many managers refuse to take the time to develop standardized recipes. The excuses used are many, but the following list contains arguments often used against standardized recipes:

1. They take too long to use.
2. My people don't need recipes; they know how we do things here.
3. My chef refuses to reveal his or her secrets.
4. They take too long to write up.
5. We tried them but lost some, so we stopped using them.
6. They are too hard to read, or many of my people cannot read English.

Of the preceding arguments, only the last one, an inability to read English, has any validity. As one seasoned veteran in hospitality has

---

* This information is optional. If the recipe cost is *not* included in the standardized recipe, a standardized cost sheet must be developed for each recipe item (see Chapter 5).

FIGURE **3.3** ● Standardized Recipe

Roast Chicken

Special Instructions: <u>Serve with</u>	Recipe Yield: <u>48</u>	
<u>Crabapple Garnish (see Crabapple Garnish</u>	Portion Size: <u>¼ chicken</u>	
<u>Standardized Recipe).</u>	Portion Cost: <u>See cost sheet</u>	
<u>Serve on 10-in. plate.</u>		

Ingredients	Amount	Method
Chicken Quarters (twelve 3–3½ lb. chickens)	48 ea.	Step 1. Wash chicken; check for pinfeathers; tray on 24 in. × 20 in. baking pans.
Butter (melted)	1 lb. 4 oz.	Step 2. Clarify butter; brush liberally on chicken quarters; combine all seasonings; mix well; sprinkle all over chicken quarters.
Salt	¼ C	
Pepper	2 T	
Paprika	3 T	
Poultry Seasoning	2 t	
Ginger	1½ t	
Garlic Powder	1 T	Step 3. Roast at 325°F in oven for 2½ hours, to an internal temperature of at least 165°F.

stated, "When I don't want to do something, one excuse not to do it is as good as the next one!" Standardized recipes have far more advantages than disadvantages. Reasons for incorporating a system of standardized recipes include:

1. Accurate purchasing is impossible without the existence and use of standardized recipes.
2. Dietary concerns require some foodservice operators to know exactly the kinds of ingredients and the correct amount of nutrients in each serving of a menu item.

3. Accuracy in menu laws require that foodservice operators be able to tell guests about the type and amount of ingredients in their recipes.
4. Accurate recipe costing and menu pricing is impossible without standardized recipes.
5. Matching food used to cash sales is impossible to do without standardized recipes.
6. New employees cannot be trained without standardized recipes. If the chef quits, for instance, you are stuck!
7. The computerization of a foodservice operation is impossible unless the elements of standardized recipes are in place; thus, the advanced technological tools available to the operation are restricted or even eliminated.

In fact, standardized recipes are so important that they are the cornerstones of any serious effort to produce consistent, high-quality food products at an established cost. Without them, cost control efforts become nothing more than raising selling prices, reducing portion sizes, or lessening quality. This is not effective cost management. It is hardly management at all. Without established standardized recipes, however, this happens all too frequently.

The importance of standardized recipes should not be underestimated. The effective operator should have them printed in the language of his or her production people, or accept the responsibility of providing the training needed to learn to read them in their current form.

Any recipe can be standardized. The process can be quite complicated, however, especially in the areas of baking and sauce production. It is always best to begin with a recipe of proven quality. Frequently, you may have a recipe designed to serve 10 guests, but you want to expand it to serve 100 people. In cases like this, it may not be possible to simply multiply each ingredient used by 10. A great deal has been written regarding various techniques used to expand recipes. Computer software designed for that purpose is now on the market (see Chapter 12). As a general rule, however, any item that can be produced in quantity can be standardized in recipe form and can be adjusted, up or down, in quantity.

Recipe adjustment can be done in many ways. Some work better than others, but in all methods some principles must be remembered. The first principle is that the measurement standard must be consistent. Weighing with a pound or an ounce scale is the most accurate method of measuring any ingredient. The food item to be measured must be **recipe ready.** It must be cleaned, trimmed, cooked, and generally completed, save for its addition to the recipe. For liquid items, the measurement of volume, a cup, quart, or gallon, may be the preferred process. Of course, some operators prefer to weigh all ingredients, even liquids, for improved accuracy.

When adjusting recipes for quantity (total yield), two general methods may be employed. They are:

1. Factor method
2. Percentage technique

Factor Method

When using the factor method, you must use the following formula to arrive at a recipe conversion factor:

$$\frac{\text{Yield Desired}}{\text{Current Yield}} = \text{Conversion Factor}$$

If, for example, our current recipe makes 50 portions, and the number of portions we wish to make is 125, the formula would be as follows:

$$\frac{125}{50} = 2.5$$

Thus, 2.5 would be the conversion factor. To produce 125 portions, we would multiply each ingredient in the recipe by 2.5 to arrive at the proper amount of that ingredient.

Figure 3.4 illustrates the use of this method for a three-ingredient recipe.

Percentage Method

The percentage method deals with recipe weight, rather than with a conversion factor. In this regard, it is more accurate than using a conversion

FIGURE **3.4** ● Factor Method

Ingredient	Original Amount	Conversion Factor	New Amount
A	4 lb.	2.5	10 lb.
B	1 qt.	2.5	2$\frac{1}{2}$ qt.
C	1$\frac{1}{2}$ T	2.5	3$\frac{3}{4}$ T

factor alone. Essentially, the percentage method involves computing the percentage of each ingredient in relation to the total weight needed. In this method, the original recipe is used to determine the total weight of all ingredients used to prepare the item. A percentage is then established for each item ingredient.

To facilitate the computation, many operators convert pounds to ounces prior to making their percentage calculations. These can, of course, be converted back to standard pounds and ounces when the conversion is completed. To illustrate the use of the percentage method, let us assume that you have a recipe with a total weight of 10 pounds and 8 ounces, or 168 ounces. If the portion size is 4 ounces, the total recipe yield would be 168/4, or 42, servings. If you want your kitchen to prepare 75 servings, you would need to supply it with a standardized recipe consisting of the following total recipe weight:

$$\text{75 Servings} \times \text{4 oz./Serving} = \text{300 oz.}$$

You now have all the information necessary to use the percentage method of recipe conversion. Figure 3.5 details how the process would be accomplished. Note that % of total is computed as ingredient weight/total recipe weight. Thus, for example, ingredient A's % of total is computed as follows:

$$\text{Item A Ingredient Weight/Total Recipe Weight} = \text{\% of Total}$$

or

$$\text{104 oz./168 oz.} = 0.619 \ (61.9\%)$$

To compute the new recipe amount, we multiply the % of total figure times the total amount required. For example, with ingredient A, the process is

$$\text{Item A \% of Total} \times \text{Total Amount Required}$$
$$= \text{New Recipe Amount}$$

or

$$61.9\% \times \text{300 oz.} = \text{185.7 oz.}$$

FIGURE **3.5** ● Percentage Method

Ingredient	Original Amount	Ounces	% of Total	Total Amount Required	% of Total	New Recipe Amount
A	6 lb. 8 oz.	104 oz.	61.9%	300 oz.	61.9%	185.7 oz.
B	12 oz.	12	7.1	300 oz.	7.1	21.3 oz.
C	1 lb.	16	9.5	300 oz.	9.5	28.5 oz.
D	2 lb. 4 oz.	36	21.5	300 oz.	21.5	64.5 oz.
Total	10 lb. 8 oz.	168	100.0	300 oz.	100.0	300.0 oz.

The proper conversion of weights and measures is important in recipe expansion or reduction. The judgment of the recipe writer is critical, however, since such factors as cooking time, temperature, and utensil selection may vary as recipes are increased or decreased in size. In addition, some recipe ingredients such as spices or flavorings may not respond well to mathematical conversions. In the final analysis, it is your assessment of product taste that should ultimately determine ingredient ratios in standardized recipes. Recipes should be standardized and used as written. It is your responsibility to see that this is done.

Inventory Control

With a knowledge of what is likely to be purchased by your guests (sales forecast) and a firm idea of the ingredients necessary to produce these items (standardized recipes), you must make decisions about desired inventory levels. A desired inventory level is simply the answer to the question, "How much of each needed ingredient should I have on hand at any one time?"

It is clear that this question can only be answered if your sales forecast is of good quality and your standardized recipes are in place so you do not "forget" to stock an ingredient necessary for the production of your menu item. Inventory management seeks to provide appropriate **working stock,** which is the amount of an ingredient you anticipate using before purchasing that item again, and a minimal **safety stock,** the extra amount of that ingredient you decide to keep on hand to meet higher than anticipated demand. Demand for a given menu item can fluctuate greatly between delivery periods, even when the delivery occurs daily. With too little inventory, you will often run out of products and therefore reduce guest satisfaction. With too much inventory, food costs can become excessive. The ability to effectively manage the inventory process is one of the best skills a foodservice manager can acquire.

Determining Inventory Levels

Inventory levels are determined by a variety of factors. Some of the most important ones are as follows:

1. Storage capacity
2. Item perishability
3. Vendor delivery schedule
4. Potential savings from increased purchase size
5. Operating calendar
6. Relative importance of stock outages
7. Value of inventory dollars to the operator

Storage Capacity You cannot purchase inventory items in quantities that cannot be adequately stored and secured. Many times, kitchens lack adequate storage facilities. In some cases, they are short on space for frozen or refrigerated foods but have excess capacity in dry-storage areas. You must be careful not to determine inventory levels in a way that will overload your storage capacity. This may mean more frequent deliveries and holding less of each product on hand than would otherwise be desired. When storage space is too great, however, the tendency by some managers is to fill the space. It is important that this not be done as increased inventory of items generally leads to greater spoilage and loss due to theft. Moreover, large quantities of goods on the shelf tend to send a message to employees that there is "plenty" of everything. This may result in the careless use of valuable and expensive products. It is also unwise to overload refrigerators or freezers. This not only can result in difficulty in finding items, but may cause carryovers (those items produced for a meal period but not sold) to be "lost" in the storage process.

Item Perishability If all food products had the same **shelf life,** that is, the amount of time a food item retains its maximum freshness, flavor, and quality while in storage, you would have less difficulty in determining the quantity of each item you should keep on hand at any given time. Unfortunately, the shelf life of food products varies greatly.

Figure 3.6 demonstrates the difference in shelf life of some common foodservice items when properly stored in a dry storeroom or refrigerator.

FIGURE **3.6** ● Shelf Life

Item	Storage	Shelf Life
Milk	Refrigerator	5–7 days
Butter	Refrigerator	14 days
Ground Beef	Refrigerator	2–3 days
Steaks (fresh)	Refrigerator	14 days
Bacon	Refrigerator	30 days
Canned Vegetables	Dry Storeroom	12 months
Flour	Dry Storeroom	3 months
Sugar	Dry Storeroom	3 months
Lettuce	Refrigerator	3–5 days
Tomatoes	Refrigerator	5–7 days
Potatoes	Dry Storeroom	14–21 days

Figure 3.7 demonstrates the difference in shelf life of some common foodservice items when properly stored in a freezer.

Because food items have varying shelf lives, you must balance the need for a particular product with the optimal shelf life of that product. Serving items that are "too old" is a sure way to develop guest complaints. In fact, one of the quickest ways to determine the overall effectiveness of a foodservice manager is to "walk the boxes." This means to take a tour of a facility's storage area. If many products, particularly in the refrigerated area, are moldy, soft, overripe, or rotten, it is a good indication of a foodservice operation that does not have a feel for proper inventory levels based on the shelf lives of the items kept in inventory. It is also a sign that sales forecasting methods either are not in place or are not working well. Inventory rotation problems, which are examined in detail later in this chapter, may also exist in an operation such as this.

Vendor Delivery Schedule It is the fortunate foodservice operator who lives in a large city with many vendors, some of whom may offer the same

FIGURE **3.7** ● Recommended Freezer Storage Period Maximums

Food	Maximum Storage Period at −10 to 0°F (−2.23−−17.7°C)
Meat	
Beef, ground and stewing	3–4 months
Beef, roasts and steaks	6 months
Lamb, ground	3–5 months
Lamb, roasts and chops	6–8 months
Pork, ground	1–3 months
Pork, roasts and chops	4–8 months
Veal	8–12 months
Variety meats (liver, tongue)	3–4 months
Ham, frankfurters, bacon, luncheon meats	2 weeks (freezing not recommended)
Leftover cooked meats	2–3 months
Gravy, broth	2–3 months
Sandwiches with meat filling	1–2 months
Poultry	
Whole chicken, turkey, duck, goose	12 months
Giblets	3 months
Cut-up cooked poultry	4 months
Fish	
Fatty fish (mackerel, salmon)	3 months
Other fish	6 months
Shellfish	3–4 months
Baked Goods	
Cakes, prebaked	4–9 months
Cake batters	3–4 months
Cookies	6–12 months
Fruit pies, baked or unbaked	3–4 months
Pie shells, baked or unbaked	1 to 1½–2 months
Yeast breads and rolls, prebaked	3–9 months
Yeast breads and rolls, dough	½ month
Other	
French-fried potatoes	2–6 months
Fruit	8–12 months
Fruit juice	8–12 months
Precooked combination dishes	2–6 months
Vegetables	8 months

Source: HACCP Reference Book, SERVSAFE program of the Educational Foundation of the National Restaurant Association.

service and all of whom would like to have the operator's business. In many cases, however, you will not have the luxury of daily delivery. Your operation may be too small to warrant such frequent stops by a vendor, or the operation may be in such a remote location that daily delivery is simply not possible. Consider, for a moment, the difficulty you would face if you were the manager of a foodservice operation located on an offshore oil rig. Clearly, in a case like that, a vendor willing to provide daily doughnut delivery is going to be hard to find! In all cases, it is important to remember that the cost to the vendor for frequent deliveries will be reflected in the cost of the goods to you.

Vendors will readily let you know what their delivery schedule to a certain area or location can be. It is up to you to use this information to make good decisions regarding the quantity of that vendor's product you must buy to have both working stock and safety stock.

Potential Savings from Increased Purchase Size   Sometimes, you will find that you can realize substantial savings by purchasing large quantities and, thus, receive a lower price from your vendor. This certainly makes sense if the total savings actually outweigh the added costs of receiving and storing the larger quantity. For the large foodservice operator, who once a year buys canned green beans by the railroad car, the savings are real. For the smaller operator, who hopes to reduce costs by ordering two cases of green beans rather than one, the savings may be negligible. Generally, however, reduced packaging and shipping costs result in lower per unit costs when larger bags, boxes, or cartons of ingredients are purchased.

Remember, too, that there are costs associated with extraordinarily large purchases. These may include storage costs, spoilage, deterioration, insect or rodent infestation, or theft. As a general rule, you should determine your ideal product inventory levels and then maintain your stock within that need range. Only when the advantages of placing an extraordinarily large order are very clear should such a purchase be undertaken.

Operating Calendar   When an operation is involved in serving meals seven days a week to a relatively stable number of guests, the operating calendar makes little difference to inventory level decision making. If, however, the operation opens on Monday and closes on Friday for two days, as is the case in many school foodservice accounts, the operating calendar plays a large part in determining desired inventory levels. In general, it can be said that an operator who is closing down either for a weekend (as in school foodservice or a corporate dining situation) or for a season (as in the operation of a summer camp) should attempt to reduce overall inventory levels as the closing period approaches. This is especially true when it comes to perishable items. If this is not done, opening-day spoilage rates can be extensive. Many operators actually plan menus to steer clear of highly perishable items near their closing periods. They prefer to work highly perishable items such as fresh seafood and some meat items into the early or middle part of their operating calendar. This allows them to minimize the amount of perishable product that must be carried through the close-down period.

Relative Importance of Stock Outages In many foodservice operations, not having enough of a single food ingredient or menu item is simply not that important. In other operations, the shortage of even one menu item might spell disaster. While it may be all right for the local French restaurant to run out of one of the specials on Saturday night, it is not difficult to imagine the problem of the McDonald's restaurant manager who runs out of French fried potatoes on that same Saturday night!

For the small operator, a mistake in the inventory level of a minor ingredient that results in an outage can often be corrected by a quick run to the grocery store. For the larger facility, such an outage may well represent a substantial loss of sales or guest goodwill. Whether the operator is large or small, being out of a key ingredient or menu item is to be avoided, and planning inventory levels properly helps prevent it. In the restaurant industry, when an item is no longer available on the menu, you "86" the item, a reference to restaurant slang originating in the early 1920s (86 rhymed with "nix," a Cockney term meaning "to eliminate"). If you, as a manager, "86" too many items on any given night, the reputation of your restaurant as well as your ability to manage it will suffer.

A strong awareness and knowledge of how critical this outage factor is help determine the appropriate inventory level. A word of caution is, however, necessary. The foodservice operator who is determined never to run out of anything must be careful not to set inventory levels so high as to actually end up costing the operation more than if realistic levels were maintained.

Value of Inventory Dollars to the Operator In some cases, operators elect to remove dollars from their bank accounts and convert them to product inventory. When this is done, the operator is making the decision to value product more than dollars. When it is expected that the value of the inventory will rise faster than the value of the banked dollar, this is a good strategy. All too often, however, operators overbuy or "stockpile" inventory, causing too many dollars to be tied up in non-interest-bearing food products. When this is done, managers incur **opportunity costs.** An opportunity cost is the cost of foregoing the next best alternative when making a decision. For example, suppose you have two choices, A and B, both having potential benefits or returns for you. If you choose A, then you lose the potential benefits from choosing B (opportunity cost). In other words, you could choose to use your money to buy food inventory that will sit in your storeroom until it is sold, or you could choose *not* to stockpile food inventory and invest the money. If you stockpile the inventory, then the opportunity cost is the amount of money you would have made if you had invested rather than holding the excess inventory.

If the dollars used to purchase inventory must be borrowed from the bank, rather than being available from operating revenue, an even greater cost to carry the inventory is incurred since interest must be paid on the borrowed funds. In addition, a foodservice company of many units that invests too much of its money in inventory may find that funds for acquisition, renovation, or marketing are not readily available.

In contrast, a state institution that is given a one-year budget at the beginning of a **fiscal year,** that is, a year that is defined in terms that may or may not follow a standard calendar, may find it advantageous to use this purchasing power to acquire inventory at very low prices. Inventory represents real dollars waiting to be converted from products to sales revenue. Alternative uses of those dollars must be considered when establishing the correct inventory level of each product.

Setting the Purchase Point

A **purchase point,** as it relates to inventory levels, is simply that point in time when an item should be reordered. This point is typically designated by one of two methods:

1. As needed (just in time)
2. Par level

As Needed When you elect to use the **as-needed,** or just-in-time, method of determining inventory level, you are basically purchasing food based on your prediction of unit sales and the sum of the ingredients (from standardized recipes) necessary to produce those sales. Then, no more than the absolute minimum of needed inventory level is secured from the vendor. When this system is used, the purchasing agent, chef, or manager compiles a list of needed ingredients and submits it to management for approval to purchase. For example, in a hotel foodservice operation, the demand for 500 servings of a raspberries and cream torte dessert, to be served to a group in the hotel next week, would cause the responsible person to check the standardized recipe for this item and, thus, determine the amount of raspberries that should be ordered. Then, that amount, and no more, would be ordered from the produce vendor.

Par Level Foodservice operators may set predetermined purchase points, called **par levels,** for some items. In the case of the raspberries and cream torte dessert referred to previously, it is likely that the torte will require vanilla extract. It does not make sense, however, to expect your food production manager to order vanilla extract by the tablespoon! In fact, you are likely to find that you are restricted in the quantity you could buy due to the vendor's delivery minimum, namely, bottle or case, or the manufacturer's packaging methods. In cases such as this, or when demand for a product is relatively constant, you may decide to set needed inventory levels by determining purchase points based on appropriate par levels.

When determining par levels, you must establish both minimum and maximum amounts required. Many foodservice managers establish a minimum par level by computing working stock, then adding 25 to 50% more for safety stock. Then, an appropriate purchase point, or point at which additional stock is purchased, is determined. If, for example, you have decided that the inventory level for coffee should be based on a par system, the decision may be made that the minimum (given your usage) amount that should be on hand at all times is four cases. This would be the minimum par level. Assume that you set the maximum par level at ten cases. While the inventory level in this situation would vary from a low of four cases to a high of ten cases, you would be assured that you would never have too little or too much of this particular menu item.

If coffee were to be ordered under this system, you would always attempt to keep the number of cases between the minimum par level (four cases) and the maximum par level (ten cases). The purchase point in this example might be six cases; that is, when your operation had six cases of coffee on hand, an order would be placed with the coffee vendor. The intention would be to get the total stock up to ten cases before your supply got below four cases. Since delivery might take one or two days, six cases might be an appropriate purchase point.

Whether we use the as needed, par level, or, as in the case of most operators, a combination of both, each ingredient or menu item should have a management-designated inventory level. As a rule, highly perishable items should be ordered on an as-needed basis, while items with a longer shelf life can often have their inventory levels set using a par level system. The answer to the question "How much of each ingredient should I have on hand at any point in time?" must come from you. Many factors will impact this decision. The decision, however, must be made and compliance monitored on a regular basis.

Purchasing

Regardless of the method used to determine inventory levels, once the quantity needed on hand has been determined, you must then turn your attention to the extremely important area of purchasing. If the number of guests who will be coming is known from the sales forecast, you know what they are likely to select from your menu, and you have determined the proper product quantity to have on hand, you must purchase the ingredients your staff will need to service your guests. Purchasing is essentially a matter of determining the following:

1. What should be purchased?
2. What is the best price to pay?
3. How can a steady supply be assured?

What Should Be Purchased?

Just as it is not possible to determine inventory levels or items to be purchased without standardized recipes, it is not possible to manage costs where purchasing is concerned without the use of **product specifications,** or **"specs."** A product spec is simply a detailed description of an ingredient or menu item. A spec is a way for you to communicate in a very precise way with a vendor so that your operation receives the *exact* item requested, delivery after delivery. A foodservice specification generally consists of the following information:

1. Product name or specification number
2. Pricing unit
3. Standard or grade
4. Weight range/size
5. Processing and/or packaging
6. Container size
7. Intended use
8. Other information such as product yield

Of course, additional information may be included if it helps the vendor understand exactly what you have in mind when the order is placed. For extremely detailed specifications, it is also important that the person receiving the product apply good judgment about whether the product does or does not meet the specification before agreeing to accept it.

It is very important to note that the product specification determines neither the "best" product nor the product that costs the least. It is the product that you have determined to be the *most appropriate* product for its intended use in terms of both quality and cost.

A product specification that is written too loosely can be a problem because the needed level of item quality may not be delivered. On the other hand, if your product specifications are too tight, that is, they are overly and unnecessarily specific, too few vendors may be able to supply the product, resulting in your paying excessively high costs for that item.

The necessity of specifications will become clear if we listen in on a telephone call made by Louie, a manager who is about to place an order for bread with a new vendor, Sam's Uptown Bakery:

LOUIE: *"Sam, I need bread for sandwiches."*
SAM: *"Louie, you know I have the best in town!"*
LOUIE: *"Well, send me 50 loaves as soon as possible."*
SAM: *"No problem, Louie. We will deliver this afternoon!"*

Little does Louie know that Sam's definition of bread for sandwiches is *quite* different from his own. Louie is expecting 1¼-pound, white, split, thin-sliced, 45-slices-to-the-bag bread. From Sam's exotic shop, however, he may well receive a 2-pound, thick-sliced, sesame seed-topped Italian loaf. Even for a product as common as bread, a specification must be developed. Fortunately, the process is relatively simple because it depends mainly on your own view of appropriate product quality.

Figure 3.8 demonstrates a form used to develop product specifications. Each menu item or ingredient should have its own spec. In fact, management should make it a habit to ensure that only telephone conversations such as the following take place:

LOUIE: *"Sam, I need five loaves of my spec #617 as soon as possible."*
SAM: *"Spec #617? Let's see, I've got it right here. That's your bread for sandwiches spec, right?"*
LOUIE: *"That's right, Sam."*
SAM: *"No problem, Louie. We will deliver this afternoon!"*

Product Name This may seem self-explanatory, but, in reality, it is not. Mangos are a fruit to those in the southwestern United States, but may mean a bell pepper to those in the Midwest. Bell peppers do not just come

FIGURE **3.8** ● Product Specification

Product Name:	Bacon, sliced	Spec #: 117
Pricing Unit:	lb.	
Standard/Grade:	Select No. 1	
	Moderately thick slice	
	Oscar Mayer item 2040 or equal	
Weight Range:	14–16 slices per pound	
Packaging:	2/10 lb. Cryovac packed	
Container Size:	Not to exceed 20 lb.	
Intended Use:	Bacon, lettuce, and tomato sandwiches	
Other Information:	Flat packed on oven-proofed paper	
	Never frozen	
Product Yield:	60% Yield	

in green, their most common color, but can also be purchased in yellow and red forms. Thus, the product name must be specific enough to clearly and precisely identify the item you wish to buy.

Many canned hams are pear shaped, but a Pullman canned ham is square. You may know exactly what you mean when you use the word "syrup," but your vendor may not. For example, you may be referring to 100% maple syrup when you place an order, but your vendor assumes maple-"flavored" syrup is the item you desire. Purchasing food becomes even more difficult when you realize that, especially in the area of meats and seafood, different regions in the country may have different names for the same product.

When developing the product specification, you may find it helpful to assign a number to the item as well as its name. This can be useful when, for example, many forms of the same menu item may be purchased. A restaurant may use 10 to 20 different types of bread, depending on the intended use of the bread; thus, in our product specification example, bacon, which this operation uses in many forms, has both a name and a number assigned to the specification. The same may be true with a number of items such as cheese, which may come in a brick, sliced, shredded, or a variety of other forms.

Pricing Unit A pricing unit may be established in terms of pounds, quarts, gallons, cases, or any other commonly used unit. Parsley, for example, is typically sold in the United States by the bunch. Thus, it is also priced by the bunch. How much is a bunch? You must know. Grapes are sold by the "lug." Unless you are familiar with the term, you may not be able to buy that product in an effective way. Again, knowledge of the pricing unit, whether it is a gallon, pound, case, bunch, or lug, is critical when developing a product specification. Figure 3.9 lists some of the more common pricing units for produce in the United States. You should insist that your vendor supply you with definitions of each pricing unit upon which that vendor bases his or her selling price.

Standard or Grade Many food items are sold with varying degrees of quality or desirability. Because that is true, the U.S. Department of Agriculture, Bureau of Fisheries, and the Food and Drug Administration have developed standards for many food items. In addition, grading programs are in place for many commonly used foodservice items. Trade groups such as the National Association of Meat Purveyors publish item descriptions for many of these products. Consumers also are aware of many of these distinctions. Prime beef, in the consumer's mind, may be superior to choice beef. In a similar manner, you may wish to purchase and serve Coca-Cola rather than a lower cost generic fountain soda. When developing a specification, a specific brand name or product source (A-1 Steak Sauce, Maine lobster) may be included in this section. You should be cautious, however, about specifying a brand name unless it is actually critical

FIGURE **3.9** ● Selected Producer Container Net Weights

Items Purchased	Container	Approximate Net Weight (lb.)
Apples	Cartons, tray pack	40–45
Asparagus	Pyramid crates, loose pack	32
Beets, bunched	$\frac{1}{2}$ crate, 2 dozen bunches	36–40
Cabbage, green	Flat crates ($1\frac{3}{4}$ bushels)	50–60
Cantaloupe	$\frac{1}{2}$ wirebound crate	38–41
Corn, sweet	Cartons, packed 5 dozen ears	50
Cucumbers, field grown	Bushel cartons	47–55
Grapefruit, FL	$\frac{4}{5}$-bushel cartons and wirebound crates	$42\frac{1}{2}$
Grapes, table	Lugs and cartons, plain pack	23–24
Lettuce, loose leaf	$\frac{4}{5}$-bushel crates	8–10
Limes	Pony cartons	10
Onions, green	$\frac{4}{5}$-bushel crates (36 bunches)	11
Oranges, FL	$\frac{4}{5}$-bushel cartons	45
Parsley	Cartons, wax treated, 5 dozen bunches	21
Peaches	2-layer cartons and lugs, tray pack	22
Shallots	Bags	5
Squash	1-layer flats, place pack	16
Strawberries, CA	12 one-pint trays	11–14
Tangerines	$\frac{4}{5}$-bushel cartons	$47\frac{1}{2}$
Tomatoes, pink and ripe	3-layer lugs and cartons, place pack	24–33

to your operation. Unless several vendors are able to supply you with a product you need, the price you may pay to the vendor who does have the item may be too high.

Weight Range/Size   Weight range or size is important when referring to meats, fish, poultry, and some vegetables. In our standardized recipe example of roast chicken, the quarters were to have come from chickens in the 3- to 3½-pound range. This will make them very different than if they came from chickens in the 4- to 4½-pound range. In the case of products requiring specific trim or maximum fat covering, that should be designated also, such as 10-ounce strip steak, maximum tail 1 inch, fat covering ½ inch.

Four-ounce hamburger patties, 16-ounce T-bones, and ¼-pound hot dogs are additional examples of items of the type that require, not a weight range, but a high degree of accuracy. It is important to note that while the operator may specify such a specific weight, it is likely that he or she will pay a premium for such accuracy, especially in items such as steaks, where the supplier's ability to perfectly control product weight is somewhat limited.

Count, in the hospitality industry, is a term that is used to designate size. For example, 16- to 20-count shrimp refers to the fact that, for this size shrimp, 16 to 20 of the individual shrimp would be required to make 1 pound. In a like manner, 30- to 40-count shrimp means that it takes 30 to 40 of this size shrimp to make a pound. Many fruits and vegetables are also sold by count. For example, 48-count avocados means that 48 individual avocados will fit in a standard case. In general, the larger the count, the smaller the size of the individual food items.

Processing and/or Packaging   Processing and packaging refers to the product's state when you buy it. Apples, for example, may be purchased fresh, canned, or frozen. Each form will carry a price appropriate for its processed or packaged state. It is important to note that the term "fresh" is one with varying degrees of meaning. Fish that has been frozen and then thawed should be identified as such. Clearly, that product is not fresh in the sense of a fish that has never been frozen.

Packaging is also extremely important when determining product yield. For example, 3 pounds of canned corn will not yield the same number of 3-ounce servings as three pounds of fresh ear corn. Fresh fruits and vegetables may be of excellent quality and low in cost per pound, but the effective foodservice operator must consider actual usable product when computing the price per pound. Also, the labor cost of washing, trimming, and otherwise preparing fresh products must be considered when comparing their price to that of a canned or frozen product. The U.S. food supply is one of great variety and quality. Food can come packed in a large number of forms and styles, including slab packed, layered cell packed, fiberboard divided, shrink packed, individually wrapped, and bulk packed. While it is beyond the scope of this text to detail all of the many varieties of food processing and packing styles, it is important for you to know about them. Your vendors will be pleased to help explain to you all the types of item processing and packaging they offer. An excellent additional source of information is *Purchasing, Selection and Procurement for the Hospitality Industry* by John M. Stefanelli.

Container Size This term refers to the can size, number of cans per case, or weight of the container in which the product is delivered. Most operators know that a 50-pound bag of flour should contain 50 pounds. Many are not sure, however, what the appropriate weight for a "lug" of tomatoes would be.

Intended Use Different types of the same item are often used in the same foodservice operation, but in a variety of ways. Smart managers make sure this is the case. Consider, for example, the operator who uses strawberries in a variety of ways. Obviously, perfect, large berries are best for chocolate-dipped strawberries served on a buffet table. Less-than-perfect berries may cost less and be a perfectly acceptable form for sliced strawberries on strawberry shortcake. Frozen berries may make a good choice for a baked strawberry pie and would be much more cost effective. Breads, milk products, apples, and other fruits are additional examples of foods that come in a variety of forms; this requires you to know that the "best" form of a food product is not necessarily the most expensive.

A good knowledge of the products you intend to use is important, but it is not enough to make intelligent purchase decisions. You must also have a complete understanding of the concept of product yield.

Product Yield Most foodservice products are delivered in the **as-purchased (AP)** state. This refers to the weight or count of a product, as delivered to the foodservice operator. **Edible portion (EP)** refers to the weight of a product after it has been cleaned, trimmed, cooked, and portioned. Thus, AP refers to food products as the operator receives them; EP refers to food products as the guest receives them. If the purchasing agent attempts to fill required inventory levels and considers only AP weight, shortages are sure to occur. To demonstrate the reason for this, let's examine a typical foodservice occurrence. Assume that you wish to serve 40 guests each a 4-ounce portion of roast beef, for a total of 160 ounces.

40 Desired Servings × 4 oz. per portion = 160 oz. Required

Assume also that you began with a roast that had a 10-pound AP weight:

10-lb. Roast × 16 oz. per Pound = 160 oz.

To serve your guests properly, you must calculate the loss that will result from normal cooking, trimming, and portioning. This loss can be computed and, thus, forecasted.

Waste % is the percentage of product lost due to cooking, trimming, portioning, or cleaning. If past experience tells you that the type of roast you buy will lose 50 ounces during the preparation and cooking process, you can compute your waste % using the following formula:

$$\text{Waste \%} = \frac{\text{Product Loss}}{\text{AP Weight}}$$

In this example:

$$\text{Waste \%} = \frac{50 \text{ oz.}}{160 \text{ oz.}} = 0.3125$$

Once the waste % has been determined, it is possible to compute the yield %. **Yield %** is the percentage of product plus you will have remaining after cooking, trimming, portioning, or cleaning. Waste % + yield % = 1.00 as shown in the following formula:

$$\text{Yield \%} = 1.00 - \text{Waste \%}$$

In this example, our yield % is computed as follows:

$$\text{Yield \%} = 1.00 - 0.3125 = 0.6875$$

From the yield %, we can compute the **AP required** (AP weight required) to yield the appropriate EP weight required, by using the following formula:

$$\frac{\text{EP Required}}{\text{Yield \%}} = \text{AP Required}$$

In this example, with an EP required of 160 ounces and a yield % of 0.6875, the computation to determine the appropriate AP required is as follows:

$$\frac{160 \text{ oz.}}{0.6875} = 232.73 \text{ oz.}$$

$$= 232.73 \text{ oz.}/16 \text{ oz.}$$
$$= 14.55 \text{ lb. AP Required}$$

To check these figures to see if you should use the yield % of 0.6875 when purchasing this item, you can proceed as follows:

EP Required = AP Required × Yield %

In this example,

EP Required = 14.55 lb. × 0.6875 = 10.00 lb.

As you can see, with this product knowing that you will experience a yield % of 0.6875 will help you determine exactly the right amount of product to purchase. Obviously, yield % is important also in the area of recipe costing. This is true because a recipe cost must take into account the difference in price of products in their AP or EP state.

Waste % and yield % can be determined if records are kept on meat cookery, the cleaning and processing of vegetables and fruits, and the losses that occur during portioning. Since most recipes assume some consistency in these areas, the good foodservice manager takes the losses into account when making purchasing decisions. Good vendors are an excellent source for providing tabled information related to trim and loss rates for standard products they carry. Some operators go so far as to add a minimum or required yield % as an additional component of their product specifications (see Figure 3.8).

What Is the Best Price to Pay?

Once purchase specifications have been developed and quantities to be purchased have been established, your next step is to determine the best price. Many would say that determining the best price should be a simple matter of finding who has the lowest cost product and placing an order with that person. In fact, that is almost always a sure sign of a manager who lacks understanding of the way vendors operate. The **best price,** in fact, is more accurately stated as the lowest price that meets the requirements of both the foodservice operation and its vendor.

When you have a choice of vendors, each supplying the *same* product according to your product specifications, it is possible to engage in comparison shopping. The vehicle used to do this is called the **bid sheet** (see Figure 3.10). The bid sheet includes vendor information, buyer information, item description, unit of bid, bid price, salesperson's signature, and date. It also includes the dates that the bid prices will be "fixed," which means the dates that the supplier agrees to keep the bid price stable, usually one week. Using our example in Figure 3.10, the bid sheet would be sent to all meat vendors each week on Friday to be returned Monday for the weekly bid prices. Then you, as a manager, would compare the prices to see which vendor would get your bid on each item for the week.

After you have received bids from your suppliers, you can compare those bids on a **price comparison sheet** (Figure 3.11). A price comparison sheet typically has a place to list the category being bid, namely, produce, dairy products, meats, and so on, the name of the vendors available to bid, bid date, item description, unit of purchase, best bid price, best company quote, and last price paid. This information may then be used to select a vendor, based on the best price. Once the best price is determined for each item, then a purchase order (discussed later in this chapter) using the best prices can be developed for each vendor.

Bid sheets and price comparison sheets may be used to determine the specific vendor who can supply the lowest price, but they do not give enough information to determine the best price. This makes sense when you realize that your own guests do not necessarily go to the lowest priced restaurants for all of their meals. If they did, there would be no hope of success for the operator who tried to provide a better food product, in a better environment, with better service. In fact, most foodservice operators would resent guests who came into their operation and claimed they could get the *exact same* item for a lower price down the street.

It is a truism that any product can be sold a little cheaper if quality is allowed to vary. Even with the use of product specifications, vendor dependability, quality of vendor service, and accuracy in delivery can be determining factors when attempting to determine the "best price."

In Figure 3.11, Bill's Produce has the lowest price for iceberg lettuce, button mushrooms, and green bell peppers. Bill's Produce may be the preferred vendor for these items if price alone is the issue. If, however, Bill's Produce is frequently late in delivery, has questionable sanitary habits, and frequently is short or unable to deliver the promised product, the lower price may be no bargain. Davis Foods, on the other hand, may have a reputation for quality products and service that make it the vendor of choice. Any foodservice operator who uses price as the *only* criterion when shopping will find it very difficult to develop any meaningful relationship with a supplier.

For the smaller operation, the manager may be interested in comparing the *total* price from each supplier, rather than the price of individ-

FIGURE **3.10** ● Bid Sheet

Vendor: _____   Buyer: _____
Vendor's Address: _____   Buyer's Address: _____
Vendor's Telephone #: _____   Buyer's Telephone #: _____
Vendor's Fax #: _____   Buyer's Fax #: _____
Vendor's E-Mail: _____   Buyer's E-Mail: _____

Item Description	Unit	Bid Price
109 Rib, 19–22#, Choice	Pound	
110 Rib, 16–19#, Choice	Pound	
112A Ribeye Lip on 9–11#, Choice	Pound	
120 Brisket, 10–12# Deckle off, Choice	Pound	
164 Steamship Round, 60#, Square bottom, Choice	Pound	
168 Inside Round, 17–20#, Choice	Pound	
184 Top Butt, 9–11#, Choice	Pound	
189A Tender, 5# Avg.	Pound	
193 Flank Steak, 2# Avg., Choice	Pound	
1184b Top Butt Steak, 8 oz., Choice	Pound	
1190a Tenderloin Steak, 8 oz., Choice	Pound	
109 Rib, 19–22#, Certified Angus Beef, Choice	Pound	
123 Short Ribs, 10#	Pound	
180 Strip, 10–12#, Choice	Pound	

Bid Prices Fixed From: _____ to _____

Salesperson Signature: _____   Date: _____

FIGURE **3.11** ● Price Comparison Sheet

Vendors
  A. Bill's Produce
  B. Davis Foods
  C. Ready Boy

Category: Produce
Date Bid: 1/1

Price Comparison Sheet

Item Description	Unit	A	B	C	Best Bid ($)	Best Company	Last Price Paid
Lettuce, Iceberg, 24 ct.	case	9.70	10.20	9.95	9.70	A	9.50
Lettuce, Red Leaf, 24 ct.	case	10.50	10.25	10.75	10.25	B	10.10
Mushroom, Button, 10 lb.	bag	15.50	15.75	16.10	15.50	A	15.75
Mushroom, Portabello, 5 lb.	bag	19.00	19.80	18.90	18.90	C	19.00
Onion, White, Medium, 50 lb.	bag	20.25	20.00	20.50	20.00	B	19.80
Pepper, Green Bell, 85 ct.	case	28.90	29.50	30.10	28.90	A	27.00
Potato, Russet Idaho, 60 ct.	case	12.75	12.50	12.20	12.20	C	12.85

Reviewed By: *M. Hayes*

ual items. That is, each ordering day, the manager would multiply the quantity of an item needed by the best price. An approach such as this is used when buying strictly from the price comparison sheet may result in orders too small to meet a supplier's **minimum order requirement,** that is, the smallest order that can be placed with a vendor who delivers. If the minimum order requirement cannot be met using the lowest prices, then the manager may have to choose the supplier with the next highest price to fill a complete order.

In some cases, the vendor to be used by the foodservice operator has been determined in advance. This is often true in a large corporate organization or in a franchise situation. Contracts to provide goods may be established by the central purchasing department of these organizations. When that happens, the designated vendor may have a national or a long-term contract to supply products at a predetermined or fixed price. In all cases, however, products to be ordered must conform to predetermined specifications.

How Can a Steady Supply Be Assured?

Unfortunately, very little has been written in the field of foodservice about managing costs through cooperation with vendors. Your food salesperson can be one of your most important allies in controlling costs. Operators who determine their supplier only on the basis of cost will find that they receive only the product they have purchased, whereas their competitors are buying more than just food! Or, as one food salesperson said when asked why he should be selected as the primary food vendor, "With my products, you also get me!" And so it is; just as good foodservice operators know that guests respond to both products and personal service levels, so, too, do effective food suppliers. Assuring a steady supply of quality products at a fair price is extremely important to the long-term success of a foodservice operator, yet many operators treat their suppliers as if they were the enemy. In fact, suppliers can be of immense value in assuring a steady supply of quality products at a fair price if you remember the following points.

Suppliers Have Many Prices, Not Just One Unlike the restaurant business, which tends to hold its prices steady between menu reprints and generally charges the same price to all who come in the door, suppliers have a variety of prices based on the customer to whom they are quoting them. Therefore, when an operator gets a quote on a case of lettuce, the telephone conversation may sound like this:

FOODSERVICE OPERATOR:	*"Hello, is this Ready Boy Produce?"*
READY BOY:	*"Yes, how can I help you?"*
FOODSERVICE OPERATOR:	*"What is* your *price on lettuce?"*
READY BOY:	*"$28.50 per case."*

This conversation should really be interpreted, as follows:

FOODSERVICE OPERATOR:	*"Hello, is this Ready Boy produce?"*
READY BOY:	*"Yes, how can I help you?"*
FOODSERVICE OPERATOR:	*"What is* my *price on lettuce?"*
READY BOY:	*"Based on* our *relationship, it is $28.50 per case."*

Suppliers Reward Volume Guests It is simply in the best interest of a supplier to give a better price to a high-volume customer. The cost of delivering a $1,000 order is not that much different from the cost of delivering a $100 order. It still takes one truck and one driver. Those operators who decide to concentrate their business in the hands of fewer suppliers will, as a general rule, pay a lower price. Of course, the volume of products you must buy from a vendor to meet his or her minimum delivery requirement will vary. In addition, larger foodservice units certainly have a greater degree of flexibility in selecting multiple vendors because managers of these large units can more easily meet supplier requirements while still minimizing overall costs.

Cherry Pickers Are Serviced Last **Cherry pickers** is the term used by suppliers to describe the customer who gets bids from multiple vendors, then buys only those items each vendor has "on sale" or for the lowest price. If an operator buys only a vendor's low-end item, the vendor will usually respond by providing limited service. It is a natural reaction to the foodservice operator's failure to give credit for varying service levels, long-term relationships, dependability, or any other characteristic, except cheapest price. It is important to remember, however, that a foodservice manager who meets minimum delivery requirements and buys *regularly* from the same vendor is not seen as a cherry picker just because he or she buys each item from the vendor with the lowest price. The key concept here is to develop a history of regular buying and cooperation with your vendor.

Slow Pay Means High Pay Those operators who do not pay their bills in a timely manner would be surprised to know what their competitors are paying for similar products. In most cases, operators who are slow to pay will find that the vendor has decided to add the extra cost of carrying their account to the price the operator pays for his or her products.

Vendors Can Help Reduce Costs Vendors have a knowledge of the products they sell that exceeds that of the average foodservice operator. This skill can be used to help the competition, or it can be harnessed for your own good use. Vendors can be a great source of information related to new products, cooking techniques, trends, and alternative product usage.

One Vendor Versus Many Vendors

Every operator is faced with the decision of whether to buy from one vendor or many vendors. In general, the more vendors there are, the more time must be spent in ordering, receiving, and paying invoices. Many operators, however, fear that if they give all their business to one supplier, their costs may rise because of a lack of competition. In reality, the likelihood of this occurring is extremely small. Just as foodservice operators are unlikely to take advantage of their best guests (and, in fact, would tend to offer additional services not available to the occasional guest) so, too, does the vendor tend to behave in a manner that is preferential to the operator who does most of his or her buying from that vendor. In fact, it makes good business sense for the vendor to do so. It is never advisable, however, to be at the mercy of a particular vendor. A good business relationship can only occur among equals; thus, many operators strive to maintain both a primary and a secondary supplier of most products.

Using one or two vendors tends to bring the average delivery size up and should result in a lower per item price. On the other hand, giving one vendor all of the operation's business can be dangerous and costly if the items to be purchased vary widely in quality and price. Staples and non-perishables are best purchased in bulk from one vendor. Orders for meats, produce, and some bakery products are best split among several vendors, perhaps with a primary and a secondary vendor in each category so that you have a second alternative should the need arise. If you are using bid buying as a purchasing method, having three vendors is advisable so that you have an adequate choice of prices and services.

Purchasing Ethics

Purchasing food products is an area that can test the ethics of even the most conscientious manager. **Ethics** have been defined as the choices of proper conduct made by an individual in his or her relationships with others. Ethics come into play in purchasing products because of the tendency for some suppliers to seek an unfair advantage over the competition by providing "personal" favors to the buyer. These favors can range from small holiday gifts given in appreciation for another year's partnership to outright offers of cash "bribes"/kickbacks to the buyer in exchange for volume purchases. Some suppliers have been known to offer buyers computers, monthly cash payments, trips to Hawaii, and other such "big ticket" items to guarantee business. Although you, as a buyer, might personally benefit from these items, the foodservice operation, your employer, will ultimately "pay" for these kickbacks through higher product prices. Should you get caught accepting these items, it is likely that you will be fired. It is the wise manager who knows the boundaries of appropriate behavior with suppliers. Some large foodservice organizations have formal codes of conduct for their buyers. When these are in place, they should, of course, be carefully reviewed and followed. If your organization does not have a formal set of ethical guidelines for buying, the following self-tests can be helpful in determining whether a considered course of action with your supplier is indeed ethical.

Ethical Guidelines

1. **Is it legal?**
   Any course of action that violates written law or company policy and procedure is wrong.
2. **Does it hurt anyone?**
   Are benefits accruing to the buyer that rightfully belong to the owner of the business? Discounts, rebates, and free products are the property of the business, not the buyer.
3. **Am I being honest?**
   Is the activity one that you can comfortably say reflects well on your integrity as a professional, or will the activity actually diminish your reputation with other suppliers?
4. **Would I care if it happened to me?**
   If you owned the business, would you be in favor of your buyer behaving in the manner you are considering? If you owned multiple units, would it be good for the business if all of your buyers followed the considered course of action?
5. **Would I publicize my action?**
   A quick way to review the ethical merit of a situation is to consider whom you would tell about it. If you are comfortable telling your boss and your other suppliers about the considered course of action, it is likely ethical. If you would prefer that your actions go undetected, you are probably on shaky ethical ground.

Daily Inventory Sheet

Before you can place an order, you will need to find out what you need! The process is much like going through your house and making a shopping list of all items before you go to the store. Some managers say that they intuitively "know" what they need without looking at their storage areas. If you have ever gone grocery shopping without a list, however, you know that you will inevitably miss a few items. We have all been in a situation in which we went to the store, purchased what we thought we needed, only to find that we forgot the toilet paper!

You, as a foodservice manager, will want to have a detailed look at your inventory before you place an order. A good way to make sure that you have checked all your items in your storage areas is to use a **daily inventory sheet** (Figure 3.12). A daily inventory sheet will have the items listed in your storage areas, the unit of purchase, and the par value preprinted on the sheet. In addition, the form will have the following columns: on hand, special order, and order amount.

A preprinted list of all your items in storage and unit of purchase is important so that you will not have to write down the items every time you check the inventory. The list should be in the same order that you store the

FIGURE **3.12** ● Daily Inventory Sheet

Item	Description	Unit	Par Value	On Hand	Special Order	Order Amount
Hot Wings	15# IQF	Case	6	2	3	7
Babyback Ribs	2–2½#	Case	3	1.5	1	3
Sausage Links	96, 1 oz.	Case	5			
Drummies	2–5#	Case	4			
Bologna	10# avg.	Each	3			
Beef Pastrami	10# avg.	Each	4			
Slice Pepperoni	10# avg.	Each	6			
All-Beef Franks	8/1, 10#	Case	7			

items so that you can quickly and easily locate your products. The par value is listed so that you know how much inventory you *should* have in storage at any given time. You may also want to list the purchase point, if appropriate.

To use the daily inventory sheet, you would physically walk through your storage areas to determine what items (and amounts) you should order for the following day. Under the On-Hand column, you would list how many of each item you have on hand, that is, sitting on the shelf. You also need to list any "special order" amounts needed above the par level. An example of this would be extra cases of strawberries ordered for a banquet. Then you must calculate the order amount as follows:

Par Value − On Hand + Special Order = Order Amount

In Figure 3.12, the order amount for hot wings would be calculated as follows:

Order Amount for Hot Wings
6 − 2 + 3 = 7

or

Par Value − On Hand + Special Order = Order Amount

If you have less than a whole purchase unit on hand, for example, ½ case of babyback ribs as in Figure 3.12, you may want to round the order amount up to a full case as follows:

Order Amount for Babyback Ribs
3 − 1.5 + 1 = 2.5, round up to 3

Although the form in Figure 3.12 is called the *daily* inventory sheet, this does not mean that you have to check your inventory or place orders on a daily basis. You should make your "grocery lists" for your normal ordering days.

Preparing the Purchase Order

Some items will be purchased daily, others weekly, and some, perhaps, monthly. In addition, you may be able to choose from a variety of ways to communicate with your supplier. Of course, much purchasing is done face to face, but the technology available for placing orders today is significant and includes the fax machine, telephone keypad, e-mail, and direct access to the vendor's order system via modem on software supplied to you by that vendor. Some vendors will also come to your business and place orders for you on their laptop computers and then transfer your order electronically. In addition, more and more vendors are posting current prices on their Web pages, thus ensuring a rapid transfer of information to their customers.

Regardless of your communication method, however, it is critical that you prepare a written **purchase order,** or record of what you have decided to buy. The purchase order (PO) should be made out in triplicate (three copies). One copy goes to the receiving area for use by the receiving clerk. One copy is retained by management for the bookkeeping area. The original is, of course, sent to the vendor. If the purchase order is developed by telephone, management retains the original copy, with a notation in the Comments section, stating that the vendor has not seen the PO. In all cases, however, it is important to place *all* orders using a purchase order form. If this is not done, the receiving clerk will have no record of what is coming in on the delivery.

Purchase order preparation can be simple or complex, but, in all cases, the written purchase order form should contain space for the following information:

Purchase Order Information

1. Item name
2. Spec #, if appropriate
3. Quantity ordered
4. Quoted price
5. Extension price
6. Total price of order
7. Vendor information
8. Purchase order number
9. Date ordered
10. Delivery date
11. Ordered by _____
12. Received by _____
13. Delivery instructions
14. Comments

Figure 3.13 is an example of a simplified, yet effective purchase order form.

Each order you place should result in the preparation of a PO. This is true even if the vendor is delivering a standing order on a daily basis. The advantages of a written purchase order are many and include the following:

1. Written verification of quoted price
2. Written verification of quantity ordered
3. Written verification of the receipt of all goods ordered
4. Written and special instructions to the receiving clerk, as needed
5. Written verification of conformance to product specification
6. Written authorization to prepare vendor invoice for payment

FIGURE **3.13** ● Purchase Order

Vendor: _____   Purchase Order #: _____
Vendor's Address: _____   Delivery Date: _____
Vendor's Telephone #: _____
Vendor's Fax #: _____
Vendor's E-Mail: _____

Item Purchased	Spec #	Quantity Ordered	Quoted Price	Extended Price
1.				
2.				
3.				
4.				
5.				
6.				
7.				
8.				
9.				
10.				
11.				
12.				
13.				
14.				
15.				
16.				
Total				

Order Date: _____   Comments: _____
Ordered By: _____   _____
Received By: _____   _____
Delivery Instructions: _____   _____
_____   _____

Figure 3.14 shows the completed purchase order following a thorough inspection of a produce walk-in at the Ardmoor Hotel. The chef has used a sales forecast to determine the quantity of products needed for next Thursday's delivery. A check of the produce walk-in lets the chef know what is on hand and the quantity of each product required. This information allows for the accurate preparation of the PO. In this case, the order is then faxed to Scooter's Produce. The receiving clerk at the Ardmoor is now prepared with the information necessary to effectively receive the product from Scooter's.

You will learn even more about the process of developing the PO in Chapter 5.

FUN ON THE WEB!

Look up the following to see examples of sites that will help you learn more about food and nonfood products when purchasing.

www.produceonline.com Look up product news and search for your favorite fruit or vegetable.

www.namp.com North American Meat Processors Association. Look up information on beef, pork, lamb, veal, and poultry. Also, order the *Meat Buyer's Guide* and *Poultry Buyer's Guide* online.

www.seafood.com Search for your favorite seafood items. Buy wholesale or retail.

www.thomasregister.com Find listings of companies that carry nonfood items and equipment.

www.externalharddrive.com Click on "Food and Recipes" on the left-hand side. Then click on any major food manufacturing corporation. You can also get recipes of your favorite menu items.

www.usda.com United States Department of Agriculture. Look up government reports on food legislation and news.

Receiving

Once the PO has been prepared by the purchasing agent, it is time to prepare for the acceptance or receiving of the goods. This function is performed by the receiving clerk in a large operation or may be performed in a smaller operation by you, as the manager, or by a staff member you designate. In all cases, however, it is wise for you to establish the purchasing and receiving functions so that one individual places the order, while another individual is responsible for verifying delivery and acceptance of the product. When this is not done, the potential for fraud or theft is substantial. **Auditors,** those individuals responsible for reviewing and evaluating proper operational procedures, have frequently found that the purchasing agent in an operation ordered a product, signed for its acceptance, and

FIGURE **3.14** ● Purchase Order

Vendor: Scooter's Produce
Vendor's Address: 123 Anywhere
Vendor's Telephone #: 999-0000
Vendor's Fax #: 999-0001
Vendor's E-Mail: scootersproduce@isp.org

Purchase Order #: 56
Delivery Date: 1/3

Item Purchased	Spec #	Quantity Ordered	Quoted Price	Extended Price
1. Bananas	81	30 lb.	$0.24 lb.	$ 7.20
2. Parsley	107	4 bunches	0.80/bunch	3.20
3. Oranges	101	3 cases	31.50/case	94.50
4. Lemons	35	6 cases	29.20/case	175.20
5. Cabbages	85	2 bags	13.80/bag	27.60
6.				
7.				
8.				
9.				
10.				
11.				
12.				
13.				
14.				
15.				
16.				
Total				**$307.70**

Order Date: 1/1
Ordered By: Joshua David
Received By:
Delivery Instructions: After 1:00 p.m.

Comments:
Faxed on 1/1
Transmitted by Joshua David

thus authorized invoice payment when, in fact, no product was ever delivered! In this case, the purchasing agent could be getting cash payment from the purveyor or supplier without the manager's knowledge. This could happen unless there are additional individuals in the purchasing chain. Of course, it is possible that more than one individual can work together to defraud an operation. The likelihood of that happening, however, is greatly reduced when more than one individual is involved.

While it may not be possible to prevent all theft or fraud in the purchasing and receiving areas, proper control procedures will minimize this possibility. Again, it is imperative to remember that the purchasing agent and the receiving clerk should be two different individuals, or, if that is not possible, the work of the purchasing agent/receiving clerk must be carefully monitored by management to prevent fraud.

There is probably no area of the foodservice establishment more ignored than the area in which receiving takes place. This is truly unfortunate since this is the area where we are ensuring the quality of products we ordered. Proper receiving includes all of the following features:

1. Proper location
2. Proper tools and equipment
3. Proper delivery schedules
4. Proper training

Proper Location   The "back door," which is usually reserved for receiving, is often no more than that; just an entrance to the kitchen. In fact, the receiving area must be adequate to handle the job of receiving, or product loss and inconsistency will result.

First, the receiving area must be large enough to allow for checking products delivered against both the invoice, which is the supplier's record of products delivered and price charged, and the PO, which is the operation's record of the same thing. If physical space is insufficient to allow for this cross-check, receiving duties will not be performed adequately.

In addition to space required to allow for counting and weighing, accessibility to equipment required to move products to their proper storage area and to dispose of excess packaging is important. A location near refrigerated areas is helpful in maintaining refrigerated and frozen products at their desired temperatures. You should make sure the area stays free of trash and clutter, as these make it too easy to hide delivered food items that may be taken home at the end of the dishonest employee's shift. It is important to remember that the delivery person is also a potential thief. While most suppliers are extremely careful to screen their delivery personnel for honesty, it is a fact that a delivery person has access to products and has a truck available to *remove* as well as deliver goods. For this reason, it is important that the receiving clerk work in an area that has a clear view of both delivery personnel and their vehicles.

The receiving area should be kept extremely clean, since you do not want to contaminate incoming food, or provide a carrying vehicle for pests. Often, suppliers themselves are responsible for delivering goods that can harbor roach eggs or other insects. A clean receiving area makes it easier to both prevent and detect this type of problem. The area should be well lit and properly ventilated. Excessive heat in the receiving area can quickly damage delivered goods, especially if they are either refrigerated or frozen products. Too little light may cause product defects to go unnoticed; therefore, the receiving area should be well lit. Flooring should be light in color and of a type that is easily cleaned. In colder climates, it is important that the receiving area be warm enough to allow the receiving clerk to carefully inspect products. The outside dock area in February, if the temperature is below freezing, is no place for an employee to conduct a thorough inspection of incoming products!

Proper Tools and Equipment

While the tools and equipment needed for effective receiving vary by type and size of operation, some items are standard in any receiving operation. These include the following:

Scales Scales should be of two types: those accurate to the fraction of a pound and those accurate to the fraction of an ounce. The larger scale is used, of course, for large items. Fifty-pound sacks of onions, for example, would be weighed on the larger scale. The smaller scale, accurate to the fraction of an ounce, would be used to verify the proper weight of smaller items to ensure, for example, that the 10-ounce strip steaks are, in fact, 10 ounces. In both cases, you should have the scales checked regularly for accuracy.

Wheeled Equipment These items, whether hand trucks or carts, should be available so that goods can be moved quickly and efficiently to their proper storage areas.

Box Cutter This item, properly maintained and used, allows the receiving clerk to quickly remove excess packaging and thus accurately verify the quality of delivered products. Of course, care must be taken when using this tool, so proper training is essential.

Thermometer Foods must be delivered at their proper storage temperatures. The only way to make sure this is done is to provide receiving area employees a thermometer to check the temperature of incoming product. As the manager of the foodservice operation, you should establish the range of temperatures you deem acceptable for product delivery. For many operators, those temperatures would be the following:

Item	Acceptable Temperature Range	
	°F	°C
Frozen Foods	10°F or less	−12°C or less
Refrigerated Foods	30–45°F	−1–7°C

Calculator Vendor calculations should always be checked, especially when the invoice has been prepared by hand. It is especially useful if the calculator has a physical tape that can be used by the receiving clerk when needed. The calculator should also be available in case the original invoice is either increased or decreased in amount due to incorrect vendor pricing or because of items that were listed on the invoice but not delivered. In addition, invoice totals will change when all or a portion of the delivery was rejected because the items were of substandard quality.

Records Area This area should, in the best of cases, include a desk, telephone, computer/fax, copy machine, file cabinet, and ample office supplies such as pens, pencils, and a stapler. Obviously, larger operations are more likely to have such an area. In a smaller operation, however, the need for basic equipment still exists. Some managers solve this problem by supplying a clipboard with a pen or pencil attached to the wall! In any case, the records area should be appropriate to the size of the operation. In *all* cases, the records area should include a copy of all product specifications so there is no confusion about whether a delivered food or supply item meets the spec and, thus, should be accepted or rejected.

Proper Delivery Schedules

In an ideal world, you would accept delivery of products only during designated hours. These times would be scheduled during your slow periods, when there would be plenty of time for a thorough checking of the products delivered. In fact, some operators are able to demand that deliveries be made only at certain times, say between 9:00 A.M. and 10:30 A.M. These are called **acceptance hours.** In a case such as this, the operation may refuse to accept delivery at any other time. Some large operations prefer to establish times in which they will *not* accept deliveries, say between 11:00 A.M. and 1:00 P.M. These are called **refusal hours.** Since a busy lunchtime may make it inconvenient to accept deliveries at this time, some operators will simply not take deliveries then. In both cases, however, the assumption is that the operator is either a large enough or a good enough customer to make demands such as these.

You may find yourself in a situation, however, where the supplier will determine when goods are delivered. While this may seem inconvenient (and often is), remember that all foodservice units would like to have their deliveries made during the slow periods, between peak meal times. In many cases, it is simply not possible for the supplier to stop his or her trucks for several hours to wait for a good delivery time. In fact, in a remote location, some foodservice operators will be told only the day a delivery will be made, not a specific time!

The key to establishing a successful delivery schedule with suppliers is, quite simply, to work with them. If an operator is seen as especially difficult or costly to do business with, the supplier will pass those costs on, in the form of higher prices. On the other hand, the foodservice operator must make the supplier understand that there are certain times of the day when it is just not possible to accept delivery. While every relationship between operator and supplier is somewhat different, both sides, working together, can generally come to an acceptable solution on delivery hours. If you do decide to post either acceptance hours or refusal hours, these should be equally enforced with all vendors.

Proper Training

Receiving clerks should be properly trained to verify the following product characteristics:

1. Weight
2. Quantity
3. Quality
4. Price

Weight One of the most important items to verify when receiving food products is, of course, their weight. It is simply true that 14 pounds of ground beef in a box looks exactly like 15 pounds. There is no way to tell the difference without putting the product on the scale. Receiving clerks should be required to weigh all meat, fish, and poultry delivered. The only exception to this rule would be unopened Cryovac (sealed) packages containing items such as hot dogs, bacon, and the like. In this situation, the entire case should be weighed to detect shortages in content. Often, meat deliveries consist of several items, all of which are packaged together. When the receiving clerk or supplier is very busy, the temptation exists to weigh all of the products together. The following example shows why it is important to weigh each item rather than the entire group of items as a whole.

Assume that you ordered 40 pounds of product from Bruno's Meats. The PO that was prepared showed the information in Figure 3.15.

When the Bruno's delivery person arrived, all three items were in one box and the deliverer was in a hurry. He, therefore, suggested that your receiving clerk simply weigh the entire box. Your receiving clerk did just that and found that the contents weighed 40½ pounds. Since the box

FIGURE **3.15** ● Ordered

Item Ordered	Unit Price	Total Ordered	Total Price
Hamburger	$2.25/lb.	10 lb.	$ 22.50
New York Strip Steak	7.00/lb.	20 lb.	140.00
Corned Beef	8.60/lb.	10 lb.	86.00
Total		40 lb.	248.50

itself weighed about ½ pound, she signed for delivery. When she began to put the meat away, however, she weighed each item individually and found the information in Figure 3.16.

If you called the supplier to complain about the overcharge ($248.50 total price − $232.75 actual value = $15.75 overcharge), you would likely be told that the misdelivery was simply a mistake caused by human error. It may well have been, but the lesson here is to always instruct your receiving personnel to weigh delivered items individually, even if they are in a hurry.

When an item is ordered by weight, its delivery should be verified by weight. It is up to the operator to train the receiving clerk to *always* verify that the operation is charged only for the product weight delivered. Excess packaging, ice, or water in the case of produce can all serve to increase the

FIGURE **3.16** ● Delivered

Item Ordered	Unit Price	Total Delivered	Actual Value
Hamburger	$2.25/lb.	15 lb.	$ 33.75
New York Strip Steak	7.00/lb.	10 lb.	70.00
Corned Beef	8.60/lb.	15 lb.	129.00
Total		40 lb.	232.75

delivered weight. The effective receiving clerk must be aware of and be on guard against deceptive delivery practices as far as the delivery of the agreed-upon product is concerned. Verifying the weight of product alone, however, will not ensure that we have received all the goods we ordered.

Quantity The counting and weighing of product are equally important. It is a fact that suppliers make more mistakes in *not* delivering products than they do in excessive delivery. Products delivered but not charged for cost the supplier money. Products not delivered but charged for cost the foodservice operation money. If you order five cases of green beans, then, of course, you want to receive and pay for five cases. This is important for two reasons. First, you only want to pay for products that have been delivered. Second and just as important, if you have prepared your purchase order correctly, you truly need five cases of green beans. If only three are delivered, you may not be able to prepare the menu items that are necessary to service your guests. If this means you will run out of an item or have to make a substitute, you may be forced to deal with unhappy diners.

Shorting is the term used in the industry to indicate that an ordered item has not been delivered as promised. When a vendor shorts the delivery of an item you ordered, that item may or may not appear on the invoice. If it does not appear, note must be taken so that management knows that the item is missing and appropriate action can be taken. If the item is listed on the invoice, the delivery driver should sign a **credit memo.** The credit memo should be filled out in triplicate (three copies). One copy goes to the receiving area to be filed. One copy is retained by management for the bookkeeping area. The original is, of course, sent to the vendor. Figure 3.17 is an example of such a form that, in this case, documents the shortage of two cases of green beans from a delivery invoice. Note that the credit memo has a place for the signature of a representative from your operation, as well as that of the vendor. It must be signed by both. The credit memo is simply a formal way of notifying the vendor that an item listed on the original invoice is missing, and, thus, the value of that item should be reduced from the invoice total. If a supplier consistently shorts your operation, that supplier is suspect in terms of both honesty and lack of concern for your operation's long-term success.

The counting of boxes, cases, sacks, barrels, and the like must be routine behavior for the receiving clerk. Counting items, such as the number of lemons or oranges in a box, should be done on a periodic basis, but the value of counting items such as these on a regular basis is questionable. While an unscrupulous supplier might be able to remove one or two lemons from each box delivered, the time it would take for an employee to detect such behavior is hardly worth the effort expended. It is preferable to do a periodic check and to work with reputable vendors.

The direct delivery of products to a foodservice operator's storeroom or holding area is another cause for concern. The delivery person may deliver some items, such as bread, milk, and soda, directly to the storage

FIGURE **3.17** ● Credit Memo

CREDIT MEMO

Unit Name: _____

Vendor: _____   Delivery Date: _____

Invoice #: _____   Credit Memo #: _____

Correction

Item	Quantity	Short	Refused	Price	Credit Amount
Total					

Original Invoice Total: _____

Less: Credit Memo Total: _____

Adjusted Invoice Total: _____

Additional Information: _____

_____

_____

Vendor Representative: _____

Vendor Representative Telephone #: _____

Operation Representative: _____

Operation Representative Telephone #: _____

area, thus bypassing the receiving clerk. This should not be allowed, if possible. After such an activity, it is simply impossible to verify the accurate quantity of items delivered. If this process must be used, product dates on each item can help assure that all products listed on the invoice were indeed delivered.

Quality No area of your operation should be of greater concern to you than that of the appropriate quality of product delivered. If you go to the trouble of developing product specifications, but then accept delivery of products that do not match these specifications, you are simply wasting time and effort. Without product specifications, verification of quality is difficult because management itself is unsure of the quality level that is desired. Many foodservice operators think that all food items are basically alike. Nothing could be further from the truth. Suppliers know their products. They also know their customers. Some customers will accept only those items they have specified. Others will accept anything that comes in the back door because they do not take the time to verify a product's quality when it is delivered. If you were a supplier and you had a sack of onions that was getting a bit old, which customer would you deliver it to?

Unscrupulous suppliers can cost your operation guests because of both overcharging and shortchanging. Imagine, for example, a restaurant manager who requests a ¼-inch fat cover on all New York strip steaks ordered. Instead, the meat company delivers steaks with a ½-inch fat cover. The operation will, of course, pay too much for the product since steaks with a ¼-inch fat covering sell at a higher price per pound than those with a ½-inch covering. Guests, however, will hold the operator responsible for steaks that suddenly seem to be a little "fatter" than they used to be. Coincidentally, the guests who eat the fatter steaks may tend to be a bit fatter themselves in the future!

Checking for quality means checking the entire shipment for conformance to specifications. If only the top row of tomatoes in the box conforms to spec, it is up to the receiving clerk or manager to point that out to the vendor. If the balance of the box does not meet the specification, it should be refused. The credit memo can then be used to reduce the total on the invoice to the proper amount.

Sometimes, quality deficiencies are not discovered until after a delivery driver has left your establishment. When that is the case, you should notify the vendor that a thorough inspection has uncovered substandard product. The vendor is then instructed to pick up the nonconforming items. Many managers use the same Additional Information section of the credit memo form shown in Figure 3.17 to record this requested pickup. When the product is picked up, the pickup information is recorded. Alternatively, a separate memo to the vendor requesting a product pickup could be produced. It is best, however, to keep the number of cost control forms to a minimum whenever possible, especially when minor modifications of one form will allow that form to serve two purposes.

Vendors are sometimes out of a product, just as you may sometimes run out of a menu item. In cases such as these, the receiving clerk must know whether it is management's preference to accept a product of higher quality, lower quality, or no product at all, as a substitute. If this information is not known, one can expect that suppliers will be able to downgrade quality simply by saying that they were "out" of the requested product and did not want the operator to be "shorted" on the delivery.

Training to assess and evaluate quality products is a continuous process. The effective receiving clerk should develop a keen eye for quality. This is done not merely to protect the operation and ensure that it gets what it pays for, but also to ensure that guests get what they pay for. The receiving clerk might accept a lower quality. Your guests, however, may not. In fact, accepting a lower quality substitute merely because it costs less is almost always a sure sign that management is unclear about the concept of establishing quality standards and sticking to them.

Price In the area of training for price, two major concerns are to be addressed. They are:

1. Matching PO unit price to invoice unit price
2. Verifying price extensions and total

Matching Purchase Order Unit Price to Invoice Unit Price
When the person responsible for purchasing food for the operation places an order, the confirmed quoted price should be written on the purchase order. There can then be no mistake about the cost of an item when it is delivered. It is never safe to assume, however, that the delivered price will match the price on the purchase order. While most suppliers are honest, it is amazing how often the price quoted on the telephone or in person ends up being lower than the price the operation is charged at delivery time. Often, this variation is said to be "computer error" or a "clerical mistake." It is interesting to note, however, that the errors most often result in the food-service operator being overcharged and rarely result in an undercharge.

As an ethical manager, you should not be happy with either an overcharge or an undercharge for a purchased product. Just as you would hope that a guest would inform you if a waiter forgot to add the price of a bottle of wine to the dinner check, a good receiving clerk works with the supplier to ensure that the operation is fairly charged for all items delivered. The acceptance of products puts the integrity of both supplier and operator on the line. Honesty and fair play must govern the actions of both parties in this area.

If the receiving clerk has a copy of the purchase order, it is a simple matter to verify the quoted price and the delivered price. If these two do not match, management should be notified immediately. If management notification is not possible, both the driver and the receiving clerk should initial the Comments section of the purchase order, showing the difference in the two prices, and a credit memo should be prepared. Obviously, if the receiving clerk has no record of the quoted price, from either a purchase order or an equivalent document, price verification of this type is not possible. An inability to verify the quoted price and the delivered price *at the time of delivery* is a sure indication that all is not well in the food cost control system.

Some operators deal with suppliers in such a way that a contract price is established. A **contract price** is simply an agreement between buyer and seller to hold the price of a product constant over a defined period of time. For example, Bernardo uses Dairy O Milk. Dairy O agrees to supply Bernardo with milk at the price of $2.15 per gallon for three months from January 1 through March 31. Bernardo is free to buy as much or as little as he needs. The milk will always be billed at $2.15 per gallon; $2.15, then, is the contract price. The advantage to Bernardo is that he knows exactly what his per-gallon milk cost will be for the three-month period. The advantage to Dairy O is that it can offer a lower price in the hope of securing all of Bernardo's milk business. Even in the case of a contract price, however, management must insist that the receiving clerk verify the invoice delivery price against the established contract price.

Verifying Price Extensions and Total   Price extension is just as important for you to monitor as is the ordered/delivered price. Price extension is the process by which you compute **extended price.** Extended price is simply the unit price multiplied by the number of units delivered. If the price for a case of lettuce is $18.00 and the number of cases delivered is six, the price extension becomes

Price Extension
Unit Price × Number of Units = Extended Price
$18.00 × 6 = $108.00

Price extension verification is extremely important. Consider, for a moment, the case of Loralei, the foodservice director for the Downtown Society Club, a private dining club in the heart of a major city. Loralei is receiving the produce order for the day. She has been well trained to check for product weight, quantity, and quality. She also has a copy of the purchase order used to place the day's order with Larson's Produce. The Larson invoice contains the following information:

Item	Unit Price	Number Delivered	Extended Price
Tomatoes	$18.50	3	$55.50
Potatoes	12.90	6	83.40
Carrots	18.29	4	82.30

Loralei has verified that the unit price matches the purchase order and that the number of items delivered is correct. That is, there are three boxes of tomatoes, six sacks of potatoes, and four bags of carrots. Should Loralei sign the invoice verifying acceptance of the product? *No!* The extended price of both potatoes and carrots is wrong. The potatoes should be $77.40 ($12.90 × 6 = $77.40, *not* $83.40) and the carrot extended price should be $73.16 ($18.29 × 4 = $73.16, *not* $82.30). If Loralei does not check the extended price, the operation will pay more (in this case, $15.14) than it should for the products delivered.

There seem to be two major reasons why operators do not always insist that the receiving clerk verify the extended price. The most common reason is the belief that there is not enough time to do so. The driver may be in a hurry and the operation may be very busy. If that is the case, the process of verifying the extended price can be moved to a slower time. Why? Because there is a written record provided by the vendor of both the unit price and the number of units delivered. Remember that verification of price extensions is a part of the receiving verification process that need not be done at the time of delivery. Extension errors are vendor errors, in the vendor's own handwriting! Or, more accurately, today they are in the vendor's own computer.

The second reason operators sometimes ignore price extensions is related to these same computers. Some operators believe that if an invoice is computer generated, the mathematics of price extension must be correct. Nothing could be further from the truth. Anyone familiar with the process of using computers knows that there are many possible entry errors that can result in extension errors.

Once all extensions have been verified, it is always a good idea to check the invoice total against the sum of the individual, correct price extensions. Returning to the example of Loralei, she may find the following situation:

Item	Unit Price	Number Delivered	Extended Price
Tomatoes	$18.50	3	$ 55.50
Potatoes	12.90	6	83.40
Carrots	18.29	4	82.30
Total Due		13	216.06

In fact, the total due is *not* $216.06, but rather $206.06. The important fact for you to remember is that verification of price extension is only half of the invoice pricing verification requirement. Ensuring that stated totals are, in fact, correct is equally important.

For the effective manager, the conclusion is to verify both extension prices and invoice totals. If this cannot be done at the time of delivery, it must be done as soon thereafter as possible. Errors are made, and they can cost your operation greatly if they go undetected.

Receiving Record or Daily Receiving Sheet

Some large operations use a receiving record when receiving food. This method, while taking administrative time to both prepare and monitor, does have some advantages.

A receiving record generally contains the following information:

1. Name of supplier
2. Invoice number
3. Item description
4. Unit price
5. Number of units delivered
6. Total cost
7. Storage area (unit distribution)
8. Date of activity

Figure 3.18 is an example of a receiving record, specifically designed for the receiving area of a large hotel.

Note that some items are placed directly into production areas (direct use), while others may be used in specific units or sent to the storeroom. Sundry items, such as paper products, ashtrays, matches, and cleaning supplies, may be stored in specific nonfood areas. Note also that subtotals for storage areas can be determined in terms of both units or dollars, as the operator prefers. In all cases, the sums for each distribution area should equal the total for all items received during the day.

Receiving reports can be useful to management if it is important to record where items are to be delivered or where they have been delivered. While some foodservice operators will find the receiving report useful, many will not since most of the information it contains is also included in the receiving clerk's copy of the purchase order.

Storage

The ideal situation for you and your operation would be for you to store only the food you will use between the time of a vendor's delivery and the time of that vendor's next delivery. This is true because storage costs money, both in terms of providing the storage space for inventory items and in terms of money that is tied up in inventory items and, thus, unavailable for use elsewhere. It is always best, whenever possible, to order only the products that are absolutely needed by the operation. In that way,

FIGURE **3.18** ● Hotel Pennycuff

Receiving Report Date: <u>1/1</u>

Supplier	Invoice #	Item	Unit Price	No. of Units	Total Cost	Distribution A	B	C	D	E
Dairy O	T-16841	½ pt. milk	$ 0.24	800	$192.00	75	600	125	–	
Tom's Rice	12785	Rice (bags)	12.00	3	36.00	–	1	–	2	–
Barry's Bread	J-165	Rye	0.62	25	15.50	–	25	–	–	–
		Wheat	0.51	40	20.40	20	–	20	–	–
		White	0.48	90	43.20	40	10	–	40	–
Total units				958		135	636	145	42	0
Total cost					$307.10					

Distribution Key:
A = Coffee Shop   D = Storeroom
B = Banquet Kitchen   E = Sundry (nonfood items)
C = Direct Use

Comments: _____
_____
_____
_____

the vendor's storeroom actually becomes your storeroom. The vendor then absorbs the costs of storing your needed products. In all cases, however, you must have an adequate supply of products on hand to service your guests. They are your main concern. If you are doing your job well, you will have many guests and will need many items in storage!

Once the receiving clerk has properly accepted the food products you have purchased, the next step in the control of food costs is that of storing those items. The storage process, in most foodservice establishments, consists of essentially four main parts:

1. Placing products in storage
2. Maintaining product quality and safety
3. Maintaining product security
4. Determining inventory value

Placing Products in Storage

Food products are highly perishable items. As such, they must be moved quickly from your receiving area to the area selected for storage. This is especially true for refrigerated and frozen items. An item such as ice cream, for example, can deteriorate substantially if it is at room temperature for only a few minutes. Most often, in foodservice, this high perishability dictates that the same individual responsible for receiving the items is the individual responsible for their storage.

Consider the situation of Kathryn, the receiving clerk at the Speedway Hotel. She has just taken delivery of seven boxes of coffee creamers. They were delivered in accordance with the purchase order and now must be put away. While Kathryn has many decisions to make as she stores her items, the first decision is whether management requires her to use the **LIFO** (last in, first out) or **FIFO** (first in, first out) method of storage.

LIFO System When using the LIFO storage system, the storeroom operator intends to use the most recently delivered product (last in) before he or she uses any part of *that same product* previously on hand. If Kathryn decides, for example, to use the seven *new* boxes of creamers before she uses the product already on hand, she would be electing the LIFO system. Her use of the new boxes (last in) before the use of the product already on hand would assure her guests of the freshest possible product. Unfortunately, it might also assure the operation, at some point, of spoiled creamers, since our old product will now be used only if we run out of fresh product.

While most authorities on food cost control do *not* recommend the use of the LIFO system, there are areas where its use does make sense. Imagine, for a moment, a truck stop restaurant that sells doughnuts and pastries. These are delivered daily. It makes no sense, in this case, to sell yesterday's few remaining doughnuts before starting to sell today's fresh product. It would be better to sell all of today's delivery first and, thus, ensure a quality product, since doughnuts left over from yesterday will not have the same desirability as today's delivery. The older doughnuts should be rotated out of stock and back to an area where they can be used as a carryover or discarded. Some operators would say that the few remaining doughnuts from yesterday should be sold *before* selling the new product. This would not be in the best interest of the operation or its guests. If we expect to gain repeat business, we must set our quality standards and stay with them. If our quality standard is "fresh today doughnuts," each and every guest deserves that standard. If our standard is "fresh yesterday's doughnuts," you should buy Tuesday's doughnuts on Monday so you could meet the standard. Obviously, you would not.

In all cases, you must strive to maintain a consistent product standard. In the case of *some* bread, pastry, dairy, fruit, and vegetable items, the storeroom clerk could practice the LIFO system, if these items have been designated as LIFO items by management.

To be successful, you will need to take great care to order only the quantity of product needed between deliveries. If too much product is ordered, loss rates will be very high. Costs can rise dramatically when LIFO items must eventually be discarded or used in a way that reduces their revenue-producing ability. For most items you buy, the best storage system to use is the FIFO system.

FIFO System First in, first out (FIFO) means that you intend to rotate your stock in such a way that product already on hand is sold prior to the sale of more recently delivered product. If this is the case, the storeroom clerk must take great care to place new stock behind or at the bottom of old stock. It is the tendency of employees not to do this. Consider, for example, the storeroom clerk who must put away six cases of tomato sauce. The cases weigh about 40 pounds. The FIFO method dictates that these six cases be placed *under* the five cases already in the storeroom. Will the clerk place the six newly delivered cases underneath the five older cases? In many instances, the answer is no. Unless management strictly enforces the FIFO rule, employees may be tempted to take the easy way out. Figure 3.19 demonstrates the difference between LIFO and FIFO when dealing with cases of food products.

FIFO is the preferred storage technique for most perishable and nonperishable items. This is because it is generally a good idea to sell the oldest stock first. Failure to implement a FIFO system of storage management can result in excessive product loss due to spoilage, shrinkage, and deterioration of quality. All of these must be avoided if you are to effectively manage food expenses.

Decisions about storing food items according to the LIFO or FIFO method are your decisions. Once these decisions have been made, they should be communicated to the storeroom clerk and monitored on a reg-

FIGURE **3.19** ● FIFO and LIFO Storage Systems

Oldest
Oldest
Oldest
Newest
Newest
Newest
FIFO

Newest
Newest
Newest
Oldest
Oldest
Oldest
LIFO

ular basis to ensure compliance. To ensure that this is so, some foodservice managers require the storeroom clerk to mark or tag each delivered item with the date of delivery. These markings provide a visual aid in determining which product should be used first. This is especially critical in the area of highly perishable and greater cost items such as fresh meats and seafood. Special meat and seafood date tags will be available from your vendor. These tags contain a space for writing in the item name, quantity, and delivery date. The use of these tags or an alternative date tracking system is strongly recommended. If the supplier has computerized his or her delivery, the box or case may already bear a strip identifying both the product and the delivery date. When this is not the case, however, the storeroom clerk should assume this function.

Figure 3.20 demonstrates the visual aspect of products in a dry-storage area when management requires that the storeroom clerk mark each item with its date of delivery.

Storage Areas

The food and related products you buy will generally be placed in one of the following three major storage areas within your facility:

1. Dry storage
2. Refrigerated storage
3. Frozen storage

FIGURE **3.20** ● FIFO Stacking System

Apples	2/10	Onions	2/10	Lettuce	2/18
Apples	2/18	Onions	2/10	Lettuce	2/18
Apples	2/18	Onions	2/18	Lettuce	2/22
Apples	2/22	Onions	2/22	Lettuce	2/22

Dry Storage Dry-storage areas should generally be maintained at a temperature ranging between 65°F and 75°F. Temperatures lower than those recommended can be harmful to food products. More often, however, dry-storage temperatures can get very high, exceeding by far the upper limit of temperature acceptability. This is because storage areas are frequently in poorly ventilated closed-in areas of the building. Excessive temperatures damage dry-storage products. Many dry-storage areas are not air conditioned, so it may be necessary to monitor the temperature of these areas with a thermometer.

Shelving in dry-storage areas must be easily cleaned and sturdy enough to hold the weight of dry products. Local health codes can vary, but shelving should generally be placed at least 6 inches above the ground to allow for proper cleaning beneath the shelving and to ensure proper ventilation. Slotted shelving is generally preferred over solid shelving when storing food, because slotted shelving allows better air circulation around the product. Regardless of the type of shelving used, all products should be stored on it. Dry-goods products should never be stored directly on the ground and it is a violation of all local health codes to do so.

Can labels should face out for easy identification. For those bulk items stored in bins or large containers, wheels on these items should be used whenever possible so that heavy lifting and resulting employee injuries can be avoided. Most important, dry-storage space must be sufficient in size to handle your operation's needs. Cramped and cluttered dry-storage areas tend to increase costs because inventory cannot be easily rotated, maintained, and counted. Theft can go undetected, and you may find yourself accidentally using the FIST (first in, still there!) method of inventory storage because products get "lost" in the storeroom.

Refrigerated Storage Refrigerator temperatures should generally be maintained between 32°F (0°C) and 36°F (2°C). In fact, the refrigerator itself will vary as much as four degrees between its coldest spot (near the bottom) and its warmest spot. The bottom tends to be coldest in a refrigerator because warm air rises and cold air falls. Refrigerators actually work by removing heat from the contents, rather than "making" food cold. This is an important point to remember when refrigerating food. Foods that are boiling hot should be precooled to 160°F before placing them in the refrigerator. This results in lower operating costs for the refrigerator, but is still well above the potentially hazardous food danger zone, which most food experts place at 40°F to 140°F (4°C to 60°C).

Refrigerators should have easily cleaned shelving units that are at least 6 inches off the floor and are slotted to allow for good air circulation. They should be properly cleaned on a regular basis and be opened and closed quickly, both to lower operational costs and to ensure that the items in the refrigerator stay at their peak of freshness. Carryover items should be properly labeled, wrapped, and rotated so that items can be found easily, resulting in both greater employee efficiency and reduced energy costs because refrigerator doors will be opened for shorter periods of time. Many managers find that requiring foods to be stored in clear plastic containers also helps in this regard.

Freezer Storage Freezer temperatures should be maintained between 0°F and −10°F (−18°C and −23°C). What is usually called a freezer, however, is more properly a "frozen-food storage unit." The distinction is an important one. To be frozen at its peak of freshness, a food item must be frozen very quickly. This involves temperatures of −20°F (−29°C) lower. Freezer units in a foodservice operation do not generally operate at these temperatures; thus, they really are best at "holding" foods that are already frozen, rather than freezing food.

Frozen foods comprise an increasingly large portion of the foods you are likely to buy. It is anticipated that, in the future, more and more foodservice storage space will be devoted to frozen food. Therefore, the conversion of dry or refrigerated space to frozen-food storage is highly recommended. Most foodservice operators also find that their carryover items will, in many cases, have a longer shelf life when held frozen rather than in refrigeration. Frozen foods should be wrapped securely to reduce moisture loss, and newly delivered products should be carefully checked with a thermometer when received to ensure that they are at the proper temperature. In addition, these items should be carefully inspected to ensure that they have not been thawed and refrozen.

Frozen-food holding units must be regularly maintained, a process that includes cleaning inside and out and constant temperature monitoring to detect possible improper operation. A thermometer permanently placed in the unit or read from outside the unit, as is the case with digital displays, is highly recommended. It is also a good idea to periodically check that gaskets on freezers, as well as refrigerators, tightly seal the food cabinet. This will not only reduce operating costs, but will also maintain food quality for a longer period of time.

Storage Basics

Regardless of the storage type, food and related products should be stored neatly in some logical order. This makes them easier to find and to count when the need arises. You may decide, for example, to arrange your stored products on the basis of how often your staff uses them. That is, frequently used items are placed near the front of the storage area. When a few items constitute a majority of the sales volume in your unit, this can be an effective storage technique. No matter what type of storage system you choose, make sure your inventory sheet matches the physical order of items in storage. This saves time in taking inventory, and it results in fewer errors. It is also important to note that the objective of a neat storage area is to both maximize storage space and minimize the time it takes to locate the item in storage. When possible, the storage area should be in close proximity to the area in which the product will be used. This reduces unnecessary time lost in traveling to remote storage areas to secure needed products.

In this regard, proper storage techniques, while assisting in lowering the cost of food products, also help in reducing costs associated with labor. It is sometimes amazing how long it can take an employee to go to the storeroom for a can of beans! In an improperly maintained storage area, employees can claim that it took a long time to "find" the desired product. When a storage area is well located, properly labeled, kept clean, and monitored regularly, problems such as this will not occur.

Maintaining Product Quality and Safety

It is important that your storeroom clerk understand his or her role in maintaining product quality. It is a fact that food product quality rarely improves with increased storage time. In most cases, the quality of ingredients you buy is at its peak when the product you ordered is delivered to you. From then on, the products can only decline in freshness, quality, and nutrition. The only exception to this might be the gourmet restaurant that elects to age some of its own products. The general case, however, is that your storeroom clerk must make every effort to maintain food quality in all of your storage areas, since food quality tends to diminish during the storage process.

The primary method for ensuring product quality while in storage is through proper product rotation and high standards of storeroom sanitation. Storage areas are excellent breeding grounds for insects, some bacteria, and also rodents. To protect against these potentially damaging hazards, you should insist on a regular cleaning of all storage areas. Compressor units on refrigerators and frozen-food holding units should be checked regularly for the buildup of dust and dirt. Interior storage racks should be kept free of spills and soil. Since refrigerators and frozen-food holding units actually remove heat, rather than "add" cold, they also remove product moisture, thus causing shrinkage in meats and produce and freezer burn in poorly wrapped or stored items kept at freezing temperatures. Unless they are built in, refrigerators and frozen-food holding units should be high enough off the ground to allow for easy cleaning around and under them to prevent cockroaches and other insects from living beneath them. Both refrigerators and frozen-food holding units should be kept 6 to 10 inches from walls to allow for the free circulation of air around, and efficient operation of, the units. Drainage systems in refrigerators should be checked at least weekly. Ideally, frozen-food holding units and refrigerators should have *externally visible* internal thermometers, whether they are read as a digital display or in the more traditional temperature scale.

In larger storage areas, hallways should be kept clear and empty of storage materials or boxes. This helps both in finding items in the storage area and in reducing the number of hiding places for insects and rodents.

Maintaining Product Security

Food products are the same as money to you. In fact, you should think of food inventory items in exactly that way. The apple in a produce walk-in is not just an apple. It represents, at a selling price of $2.00, that amount in revenue to the airport foodservice director, who hopes to sell a crisp, fresh apple to a weary traveler. If the apple disappears, revenue of $2.00 will disappear also. When you think of inventory items in terms of their sales value, it becomes clear why product security is of the utmost importance. As such, systems must be in place to reduce employee, vendor, and guest theft to the lowest possible level.

All foodservice establishments will experience some amount of theft, in its strictest sense. The reason is very simple. Some employee theft is impossible to detect. Even the most sophisticated, computerized control system is not able to determine if an employee or vendor's employee walked into the produce walk-in and ate one green grape. Similarly, an employee who takes home two sugar packets per night will likely go undetected for a great length of time. In neither of these cases, however, is the amount of loss significant, and certainly not enough to install security cameras in the walk-in or to frisk your employees as they leave for home at the end of their shifts. What you do want to do, however, is to make it difficult to remove food from storage without authorization, so that you can know when that food has been removed. Good cost control systems must be in place if you are to achieve this goal.

It is amazing how large the impact of theft can be on profitability. Consider the following example. Jesse is the receiving clerk at the Hole in the Wall sports bar. On a daily basis, Jesse takes home $2.00 worth of food products. How much, then, does Jesse cost the bar in one year? The answer is a surprising $14,600 in sales revenue! If Jesse steals $2.00 per day for 365 days, the total theft amount is $730 (365 days × $2.00 per day = $730). If the bar makes an after-tax profit of 5% on each dollar of food products sold, the operation must sell

$$\frac{\$1.00}{0.05} \times \$730 = \$14,600$$

to recover the lost $730.

In order to recover the dollar amount of Jesse's theft, the sports bar must sell $14,600 of food per year and make 5 cents per dollar sold on these sales. In the case of a smaller bar, $14,600 may well represent several days' sales revenue. Clearly, small thefts can add up to large dollar losses!

Most foodservice operators attempt to control access to the location of stored products. This may be done, in some areas, by a process as simple as keeping the dry-storage area locked and requiring employees to "get the keys" from the manager or supervisor. In other situations, cameras may be mounted in both storage areas and employee exit areas. It is generally a good idea to limit access to storage areas. While the physical layout of the foodservice operation may prevent management from being able to effectively lock and secure all storage areas, too much traffic is sure to cause theft problems. This is not because employees are basically dishonest. Most are not. Theft problems develop because of the few employees who feel either that management will not miss a few of whatever is being stolen or that they "deserve" to take a few things because they work so hard and are paid so little!

It is your responsibility to see to it that the storeroom clerk maintains good habits in securing product inventory. As a general rule, if storerooms are to be locked, only one individual should have the key during any shift. The temptation sometimes exists for management to hang the key by the door, that is, to have the storeroom locked, but give the key to any employee who says that he or she needs it. This obviously defeats the purpose of the locked system. In reality, it is simply not possible to keep all inventory items under lock and key. Some items must be received and immediately sent to the kitchen for processing or use. Also, what would happen if you or another designated "key holder" were gone from the operation for a few minutes? Most operators find that it is impossible to operate under a system where *all* food products are locked away from the employees. Storage areas should, however, not be accessible to guests or vendor employees. Unlocked storage areas near exits are extremely tempting to the dishonest individual. If proper control procedures are in place, employees will know that you can determine if theft has occurred. Without such control, employees are aware that theft can go undetected. This must, and can, be avoided.

Determining Inventory Value

It is the responsibility of the storeroom clerk, or other person you select, to maintain the inventory in a way that makes it easy to count and to determine its monetary value. Both, the concepts of inventory management and product issuing, are discussed more fully in Chapter 5. This is because **issuing,** the process of placing products into the production system, impacts inventory levels and must be carefully accounted for. Issuing, in fact, begins the food production process.

Regardless of the inventory system or issuing system in place, you must be able to answer this fundamental question, "What is the value of the products I currently have on hand?" The answer to this question is important for many reasons. Foremost among them is the following one. It is not possible to know your actual food expense without an accurate inventory. Indeed, the mathematical formula used to determine the cost of food sold (food expense) is driven primarily by knowing the dollar value of all food products in inventory. The process of determining inventory value is quite simple, even if the actual task is time consuming.

Valuing, or establishing a dollar value for your entire inventory, is done by using the following inventory valuation formula:

$$\text{Item Amount} \times \text{Item Value} = \text{Item Inventory Value}$$

Item Amount Item amount may be determined by counting the item, as in the case of cans, or by weighing items, as in the case of meats. Volume, that is, gallons, quarts, and the like, is another method of establishing product amounts. If an item is purchased by the pound, it is generally weighed to determine item amount. If it is purchased by the piece or case, the appropriate unit to determine the item amount may be either pieces or cases. If, for example, canned pears are purchased by the case, with six cans per case, management might decide to consider the item either as case or as can. That is, three cases of the canned pears might be considered as three items (by the case) or as 18 items (by the can). Any method you use to accurately establish the amount of product you have on hand is acceptable. If product is undercounted, your expenses will appear higher than they actually are. If, on the other hand, inventory amounts are overstated, or **padded inventory,** costs will appear artificially low until the proper inventory values are determined.

Item Value An item's actual value can be more complicated to determine than its amount. This is because the price you pay for an item may vary slightly each time you buy it. Assume, for example, that you bought curly endive for $2.20 per pound on Monday, but the same item was $2.50 per pound on Wednesday. On Friday, you see that you have one pound of the curly endive in your refrigerated walk-in. Is the value of the item $2.20 or $2.50?

Item value is, generally speaking, determined by using either the LIFO or the FIFO method. When the LIFO method is in use, the item's value is said to be the price paid for the least recent (oldest) addition to item amount. If the FIFO method is in use, the item value is said to be the price paid for the most recent (newest) product on hand. In the hospitality industry, most operators value inventory at its most recently known value; thus, FIFO is the more common method. A simple illustration may help. Peggy purchased grapes on Monday and paid $30.00 per lug. On Friday, she again purchased grapes, but paid $40.00 per lug. On Saturday morning, she took inventory and found that she had 11/2 lugs of grapes. What is their inventory value? The LIFO system says that Peggy's grapes have an inventory value of $45.00 ($30.00 LIFO price × 1.5 lugs = $45.00). The FIFO method places a value of $60.00 on the grapes ($40.00 FIFO price × 1.5 lugs = $60.00). Because it is closest to the actual replacement cost of the inventory item, choosing to value inventory at the most recently paid price (FIFO) is the best method for establishing item value for the majority of hospitality operators.

Inventory value is determined using a form similar to the **inventory valuation sheet** shown in Figure 3.21. This inventory valuation sheet has a place for all inventory items, the quantity on hand, and the unit value of each item. There is also a place for the date the inventory was taken, a spot for the name of the person who counted the product, and another space for the person who extends or establishes the value of the inventory. It is recommended that these two be different individuals to reduce the risk of inventory valuation fraud.

The inventory valuation sheet should be completed each time the inventory is counted. It can be preprinted from a computerized list of items, a process that saves much in the way of staff time and effort. Regardless of the form used, the item's inventory value is determined as described earlier. Thus, if we have five cases of fresh beets in our inventory, and each case has a value of $20.00, the inventory value of our beets is

$$5 \times \$20 = \$100$$

Item Amount × Item Value = Inventory Value

The process of determining inventory value requires that you or a member of your staff count all food products on hand and multiply the value of the item by the number of units on hand. The process becomes

FIGURE **3.21** ● Inventory Valuation Sheet

Unit Name: _____   Inventory Date: _____

Counted By: _____   Extended By: _____

Item	Unit	Item Amount	Item Value	Inventory Value
			Page Total	

Page _____ **of** _____

more difficult when one realizes that the average foodservice operation has hundreds of items in inventory. Thus, "taking the inventory" can be a very time consuming task. A **physical inventory,** one in which the food products are actually counted, must, however, be taken to determine your actual food usage. Some operators take this inventory monthly, others weekly or even daily! Some, unfortunately, feel that there is no need to ever take inventory. These operators cannot effectively control their costs because they do not know what their costs are. Without taking inventory, it is not possible for you to determine your actual food cost.

Determining Actual Food Expense

Assume that you own and manage a small ice cream store that makes its own products. You have reviewed your records for the past month and found the following:

January Revenue and Expense

Ice Cream Sales = $98,000

Food Expense = $39,000

You have determined your revenue figure from the sales history you maintained (see Chapter 2). You have determined your food expense by adding the dollar value of all the properly corrected delivery invoices that you accumulated for the month. That is, you totaled the value of all food purchased and delivered between the first day of the month and the last. Would it be correct to say that your food expense for the month of January is $39,000? The answer is *No.* Why not? Because you may have more, or less, of the food products required to make your ice cream in inventory on the last day of January than you had on the first day. If you have more food products in inventory on January 31 than you had on January 1, your food expense is less than $39,000. If you have fewer products in inventory on January 31 than you had on January 1, your food expense is higher than $39,000. To understand why this is so, you must understand the formula for computing your actual food expense. The correct formula is shown in Figure 3.22.

Cost of food sold is the dollar amount of all food actually sold, thrown away, wasted, or stolen.

FIGURE **3.22** ● Formula for Cost of Food Sold

Beginning Inventory

PLUS

Purchases
= Goods Available for Sale

LESS

Ending Inventory
= Cost of Food Consumed

LESS

Employee Meals

= Cost of Food Sold

Beginning Inventory

Beginning inventory is the dollar value of all food on hand at the beginning of the accounting period. It is determined by completing an actual count and valuation of the products on hand.

Purchases

Purchases are the sum cost of all food purchased during the accounting period. It is determined by adding all properly tabulated invoices for the accounting period.

Goods Available for Sale

Goods available for sale is the sum of the beginning inventory and purchases. It represents the value of all food that was available for sale during the accounting period.

Ending Inventory

Ending inventory refers to the dollar value of all food on hand at the end of the accounting period. It also is determined by completing a physical inventory.

Cost of Food Consumed

The **cost of food consumed** is the actual dollar value of all food used, or consumed, by the operation. Again, it is important to note that this is not merely the value of all food sold, but rather the value of all food no longer in the establishment and includes the value of any meals eaten by employees.

Employee Meals

Employee meal cost is a labor-related, *not* food-related cost. Free or reduced-cost employee meals are a benefit much in the same manner as medical insurance or paid vacation. Therefore, the value of this benefit, if provided, should be transferred and charged as an employee benefit. The dollar value of food eaten by employees is subtracted from the cost of food consumed to yield the cost of food sold.

Cost of Food Sold

As stated earlier, the cost of food sold is the actual dollar value of all food expense incurred by the operation except for those related to employee meals. It is not possible to determine this number unless a beginning inventory has been taken at the start of the month, followed by another inventory taken at the end of the month. Without these two numbers, it is impossible to accurately determine the cost of food sold. Figure 3.23 illustrates a recap sheet used to determine the cost of food sold.

In the ice cream store example, had you completed such a form, you would have known your actual cost of food sold. Every manager should, on a regular basis, compute the actual cost of food sold because it is not possible to improve your cost picture unless you first know what your costs are.

Variations on the Basic Cost of Food Consumed Formula

While Figure 3.23 demonstrates the format most commonly used to determine cost of food sold, some operators prefer slightly different formulas, depending on the unique aspects of their units. The important point to remember, however, is that all of these formulas should seek to accurately reflect actual cost of food sold by the operation for a given time period. Two variations of the formula follow.

FIGURE **3.23** ● Recap Sheet

Cost of Food Sold

Accounting Period: _____ to _____
Unit Name: _____

Beginning Inventory $ _____

PLUS

Purchases $ _____

Goods Available for Sale $ _____

LESS

Ending Inventory $ _____

Cost of Food Consumed $ _____

LESS

Employee Meals $ _____

Cost of Food Sold $ _____

No Employee Meals Are Provided When an operation has no employee meals at all, the computation of cost of food sold is as follows:

Beginning Inventory $ _____
PLUS
Purchases $ _____
Goods Available for Sale $ _____
LESS
Ending Inventory $ _____
Cost of Food Sold $ _____

Food or Beverage Products Are Transferred from One Foodservice Unit to Another This is the case when, for example, an operator seeks to compute one cost of food sold figure for a bar and another for the bar's companion restaurant. In this situation, it is likely that fruit juice, vegetables, and similar items are taken from the kitchen for use in the bar, while wine, sherry, and similar items may be taken from the bar for use in the kitchen. This concept of transferability is covered in detail in Chapter 4. The formula for cost of food sold in this situation would be as follows:

Beginning Inventory	$ _____	
PLUS		
Purchases	$ _____	
Goods Available for Sale		$ _____
LESS		
Ending Inventory		$ _____
LESS		
Value of Transfers Out		$ _____
PLUS		
Value of Transfers In		$ _____
Cost of Food Sold		$ _____

It is important for you to know exactly which formula or variation is in use when analyzing cost of food sold. The variations, while slight, can make big differences in the interpretation of your cost information. In all cases, it is critical that accurate beginning and ending inventory figures be maintained if accurate cost data are to be computed.

In the following example following, both beginning inventory and ending inventory figures are known, thus enabling you to determine your actual cost of food sold.

Beginning Inventory	$22,500
Purchases	$39,000
Ending Inventory	$27,500
Employee Meals	$ 725

You are now able to complete your recap sheet as illustrated in Figure 3.24.

FIGURE **3.24** ● Recap Sheet

Cost of Food Sold		
Accounting Period: 1/1 to 1/31		
Unit Name: Your Ice Cream Store		
Beginning Inventory	$22,500	
PLUS		
Purchases	$39,000	
Goods Available for Sale		$61,500
LESS		
Ending Inventory		$27,500
Cost of Food Consumed		$34,000
LESS		
Employee Meals		$ 725
Cost of Food Sold		$33,275

In this example, employee meals were determined by assigning a food value of $1.00 per employee ice cream treat consumed. It is important to note that food products do not have to be consumed as a meal in order to be valued as an employee benefit. Soft drinks, snacks, and other food items consumed by employees are all considered employee meals for the purpose of computing cost of food sold.

If records are kept on the number of employees eating per day, monthly employee meal costs are easily determined. Some operators prefer to estimate the dollar value of employee meals each month rather than record actual employee meals. This is not a good practice, both from a control point of view and in terms of developing accurate cost data.

It is important to note that ending inventory for one accounting period becomes the beginning inventory figure for the next period. For example, in the case of your ice cream store, the January 31 ending inventory figure of $27,500 will become the February 1 beginning inventory figure. In this manner, it is clear that physical inventory need only be taken one time per accounting period, not twice. Again, while the physical inventory process can be time consuming, it must be performed in order to determine actual food expense.

While there is no reliable method for replacing the actual counting of inventory items on hand, there are many computer programs on the market programmed to allow an individual to scan the bar codes on products using a handheld scanning device and, thus, perform both the counting and the price extension process necessary to develop actual inventory valuations. Using technology in this manner can make a time-consuming task much less tedious and more efficient.

Food Cost Percentage

You know from Chapter 1 that food expense is often expressed as a percentage of total revenue or sales. Since you can now determine your actual cost of food sold, you can also learn to compute and evaluate your operation's food cost percentage. Again, this is both the traditional way of looking at food expense and generally the method used by most operators when preparing the profit and loss statement.

The formula used to compute actual food cost percentage is as follows:

$$\frac{\text{Cost of Food Sold}}{\text{Food Sales}} = \text{Food Cost \%}$$

Food cost % represents that portion of food sales that was spent on food expenses.

In the case of the ice cream store example discussed previously, you know that cost of food sold equals $33,275 (Figure 3.24). If the store experienced $98,000 in food sales for the period of January 1 to January 31, the food cost percentage for the period would be

$$\frac{\$33,275}{\$98,000} \quad \frac{\text{Cost of Food Sold}}{\text{Food Sales}} = 34\% \text{ Food Cost}$$

Thus, 34% of the dollars in sales revenue taken in was needed to buy the food used to generate that revenue. Put another way, 34 cents of each dollar in sales were used to buy the products needed to make the ice cream.

Estimating Daily Cost of Food Sold

Many operators would like to know their food usage on a much more regular basis than once per month. When this is the case, the physical inventory may be taken as often as desired. Again, however, physical inventories are time consuming.

It would be convenient if you could have a close estimate of your food usage on a weekly or daily basis without the effort of a daily inventory count. Fortunately, such an approximation exists. Figure 3.25 illustrates a six-column form, which you can use for a variety of purposes. One of them is to estimate food cost % on a daily or weekly basis.

As an example, assume that you own an Italian restaurant that serves no liquor and caters to a family-oriented clientele. You would like to monitor your food cost percentage on a more regular basis than once a month, which is your regular accounting period. You have decided to use a six-column form to estimate your food cost percentage. Since you keep track of both daily sales and purchases, you can easily do so. In the space above the first two columns, write the word "Sales." Above the middle two columns, write "Purchases," and above the last two columns, enter the words "Cost %."

You then proceed each day to enter your daily sales revenue in the column labeled Sales Today. Your invoices for food deliveries are totaled daily and entered in the column titled Purchases Today. Dividing the Purchases Today column by the Sales Today column yields the figure that is placed in the Cost % Today column. Purchases to Date (the cumulative purchases amount) is divided by Sales to Date (the cumulative sales amount) to yield the Cost % to Date figure. A quick summary is as follows:

Six-Column Food Cost % Estimate

1. $\dfrac{\text{Purchases Today}}{\text{Sales Today}} = \text{Cost \% Today}$

2. $\dfrac{\text{Purchases to Date}}{\text{Sales to Date}} = \text{Cost \% to Date}$

Figure 3.26 shows this information for your operation for the time period January 1 to January 7.

As can be seen, you buy most of your food at the beginning of the week, while sales are strongest in the later part of the week. This is a common occurrence at many foodservice establishments. As can also be seen, your daily cost percent ranges from a high of 130 (Monday) to a low of 0% (Sunday), when no deliveries are made. In the Cost % to Date column, however, the range is only from a high of 130% (Monday) to a low of 39.20% (Sunday).

FIGURE **3.25** ● Six-Column Form

Date: _____

_____   _____   _____

Weekday	Today	To Date	Today	To Date	Today	To Date

FIGURE **3.26** ● Six-Column Food Cost Estimate

Date: <u>1/1–1/7</u>

	Sales		Purchases		Cost %	
Weekday	**Today**	**To Date**	**Today**	**To Date**	**Today**	**To Date**
Monday	$ 850.40	$ 850.40	$1,106.20	$1,106.20	130.00%	130.00%
Tuesday	920.63	1,771.03	841.40	1,947.60	91.40	110.00
Wednesday	1,185.00	2,956.03	519.60	2,467.20	43.80	83.50
Thursday	971.20	3,927.23	488.50	2,955.70	50.30	75.30
Friday	1,947.58	5,874.81	792.31	3,748.01	40.70	63.80
Saturday	2,006.41	7,881.22	286.20	4,034.21	14.30	51.20
Sunday	2,404.20	10,285.42	0	4,034.21	0	39.20
Total	10,285.42		4,034.21		39.20	

What is your best estimate about what your food cost % actually is as of Sunday? The answer is that it will be slightly less than 39.20%. Why? Let us go back to the formula for cost of food sold. Before we do, we must make one important assumption that, for any time period we are evaluating, the beginning inventory and ending inventory amounts are the same. In other words, over any given time period, you will have approximately the same amount of food on hand at all times. If this assumption is correct, the six-column food cost estimate is, in fact, a good indicator of your food usage. The reason is very simple. The formula for cost of food sold asks you to *add* beginning inventory and then later *subtract* ending inventory (see Figure 3.22). If these two numbers are assumed to be the same, they can be ignored, since adding and subtracting the same number will result in no effect at all. For example, if we start with $10, add $50, and subtract $10, we are left with $50. In terms of the cost of food sold formula, when beginning inventory and ending inventory are assumed to be the same figure, it is the mathematical equivalent of adding a zero and subtracting a zero. To continue our example, if we start with $0, add $50, and subtract 0, we are left, again, with $50. Thus, when beginning inventory and ending inventory are equal, or assumed to be equal, the cost of food sold formula would look, as follows:

	Beginning Inventory	$0
+	**Purchases**	
=	**Purchases**	
−	**Ending Inventory**	$0
=	**Purchases**	
−	**Employee Meals**	
=	**Cost of Food Sold**	

Therefore, as stated earlier, if you assume that your inventory is constant, your cost of food sold for the one-week period is a little less than $4,034.21, or 39.20% of sales. Why a little less? Because we must still subtract the value of employee meals, if any are provided, since they are an employee benefit and not a food expense. How accurate is the six-column form? For most operators, it is quite accurate and has the following advantages:

1. It is very simple to compute, requiring 10 minutes or less per day for most operations.
2. It records both sales history and purchasing patterns.
3. It identifies problems before the end of the monthly accounting period.

4. By the ninth or tenth day, the degree of accuracy in the To Date column is very high.

5. It is a daily reminder to both management and employees that there is a very definite relationship between sales and expenses.

   The use of a six-column food cost estimator is highly recommended for the operator who elects to conduct a physical inventory less often than every two weeks.

   The control of food expense is critical to all foodservice operations. From the purchase of the raw ingredient to its receiving and storage, the effective foodservice operator strives to have the proper quality and quantity of product on hand at all times. Food represents a large part of your overall expense budget. Protecting this product and accounting for its usage are extremely important in helping to manage overall costs.

Key Terms and Concepts

The following are terms and concepts discussed in the chapter that are important for you as a manager. To help you review, please define the terms below.

Popularity index	Waste %	Extended price
Predicted number to be sold	Yield %	LIFO
	Best AP required price	FIFO
Standardized recipe	Bid sheet	Issuing
Recipe ready	Price comparison sheet	Padded inventory
Working stock		Inventory valuation sheet
Safety stock	Minimum order requirement	Physical inventory
Shelf life		Cost of food sold
Opportunity cost	Cherry picker	Beginning inventory
Fiscal year	Ethics	Purchases
Purchase point	Daily inventory sheet	Ending inventory
As needed/just in time	Purchase order	Goods available for sale
Par level	Auditors	Ending inventory
Product specification/spec	Acceptance hours	Cost of food consumed
	Refusal hours	
Count	Shorting	Employee meals
As purchased (AP)	Credit memo	Food cost %
Edible portion (EP)	Contract price	

Test Your Skills

1. Liza operates a lunch room in a large, exclusive health club. The members demand high-quality service and are especially concerned about

reducing fat in their diets. They like high-protein items for their lunches, which are light and generally consumed prior to or immediately after a workout. The menu in Liza's restaurant consists of five main lunch specials. Each meat, poultry, or fish item is purchased by the pound (using product specifications), then prepared and served in a 4-ounce portion (EP), according to the standardized recipe. Liza keeps excellent sales records and, thus, knows her % selecting figures, which are tabulated as follows. She also carefully monitors waste % data, which are tabulated for each item. How much of each item should Liza order for next week, given that she expects 500 customers for lunch next week, each of whom will order one of her five menu items?

What should the total of Liza's purchases for these items be next week, if she buys at the purchase prices listed.

Do you think Liza should buy these items on a par or as-needed basis? Why?

Item	Percent Selecting	Waste	Purchase Price/lb.
Beef	0.21	0.30	$3.20
Pork	0.18	0.25	1.70
Chicken	0.15	0.10	0.89
Sole	0.30	0.10	3.20
Tuna	0.16	0.05	4.10

Item	Total Served	Percent Selected	Number of Servings	Ounces per serving	Serving Weight	Yield	Purchase Weight (oz.)	Ounces Per Pound	Purchase Weight (lb.)	Purchase Price	Total Purchases
Beef	500	21%	105	4 oz	420 oz	70%	600	16 oz	38	3.20	121.60
Pork	500	18%	90	4 oz	360 oz	75%	480	16 oz	30	1.70	51.00
Chicken	500	15%	75	4 oz	300 oz	90%	333.3	16 oz	21	.89	18.69
Sole	500	30%	150	4 oz	600 oz	90%	666.7	16 oz	42	3.20	134.40
Tuna	500	16%	80	4 oz	320 oz	95%	336.6	16 oz	22	4.1	90.20

2. Saint John's Hospital foodservice director, Herman Zindu, has a problem. He has the following information about his operation for the month of April, but has forgotten how to compute cost of food sold for the month. Use Herman's figures to compute actual cost of food sold for his operation.

Inventory on March 31		$22,184.50
April Purchases		
Meats	$11,501.00	
Dairy	$ 6,300.00	
Fruits and Vegetables	$ 9,641.00	
All Other Foods	$32,384.00	
Number of Employees Eating Daily	85	
Cost per Employee for Employee Meals	$1.25	
Inventory on April 30		$23,942.06

Could Herman have computed this figure if he had not taken a physical inventory on April 30? Why or why not?

3. "Fast Eddie" Green operates a restaurant in the casino town of Taloona. He is checking over the work of his assistant manager who has been newly hired. One of the jobs of the assistant manager is to complete daily the six column food cost estimate. "Fast Eddie" finds that, while the data are there for the first 10 days of the accounting period, the form has not been completed. Complete the form for "Fast Eddie" so that he can go home.

Six-Column Form

Date: 1/1–1/10

Weekday	Sales		Purchases		Cost %	
	Today	To Date	Today	To Date	Today	To Date
1/1	$3,842.50		$1,645.80			
1/2	2,970.05		2,006.40			
1/3	2,855.20		1,107.20			
1/4	3,001.45		986.24			
1/5	3,645.20		1,245.60			
1/6	4,850.22		2,006.40			
1/7	6,701.55		0.00			
1/8	3,609.20		1,799.90			
1/9	2,966.60		851.95			
1/10	3,105.25		924.50			
Total						

4. Billie Mendoza is the purchasing manager for a medium-sized suite hotel with a restaurant and a banquet hall. She needs to create the food purchase orders for tomorrow, and she wants to make sure that she is getting the best price for the best quality and service. At the beginning of this week, Billie received bids on produce items from Village Produce, City Produce, and Country Produce. She has listed these prices in the following price comparison sheet.

a. Identify the best bid price and best company for each of Billie's produce items.

Price Comparison Sheet

Item	Description	Unit	Village Produce	City Produce	Country Produce	Best Bid $	Best Company Quote	Last Price Paid
Avocados	48 ct.	Case	$61.80	$60.30	$59.46			$57.94
Cauliflower	12 ct.	Case	12.80	12.90	13.27			13.26
Cucumbers	Medium	Case	11.10	11.52	10.91			11.34
Grapes	Red Seedless	Lug	19.32	19.50	19.14			18.72
Lettuce	Green Leaf, 24 ct.	Case	9.53	9.84	10.27			10.02
Lettuce	Romaine, 24 ct.	Case	17.75	17.82	18.22			18.10
Pears	D'Anjou	Case	20.82	20.58	20.64			20.62
Peppers	Green Bell, Med.	Case	8.30	8.38	9.28			9.02
Pineapples	7 ct.	Case	10.50	10.38	10.68			10.08
Potatoes	B Reds	50# Bag	15.06	14.82	14.88			14.98
Potatoes	Peeled, Large	25# Bag	17.52	17.22	17.28			17.18
Squash	Yellow #2	30# Case	8.55	8.71	8.98			9.10
Strawberries	Driscoll	Flat	18.29	18.06	17.10			18.30

b.1. Now that Billie knows which vendors have the best prices, she decides to take the daily inventory to find out what she needs to order for tomorrow. Her par value, on-hand, and special-order requirements are as follows. Help Billie determine the amount of each item she needs to order.

Item	Description	Unit	Par Value	On Hand	Special Order	Order Amount
Avocados	48 ct.	Case	6	2	3	
Cauliflower	12 ct.	Case	5	1		
Cucumbers	Medium	Case	3	0		
Grapes	Red Seedless	Lug	4	1		
Lettuce	Green Leaf, 24 ct.	Case	5	2	4	
Lettuce	Romaine, 24 ct.	Case	3	0.5		
Pears	D'Anjou	Case	3	1		
Peppers	Green Bell, Med.	Case	7	2	5	
Pineapples	7 ct.	Case	4	0		
Potatoes	B Reds	50# Bag	3	0.5		
Potatoes	Peeled, Large	25# Bag	4	1	4	
Squash	Yellow #2	30# Case	5	2	2	
Strawberries	Driscoll	Flat	3	1.5		

b.2. Next, Billie needs to create the purchase order for tomorrow. Help her create the correct purchase order for Village Produce based on her inventory needs (part b.1.) and the bid prices for Village Produce located on the price comparison worksheet (part a).

Purchase Order

Supplier				Purchase Order	
Company Name:	Village Produce			P.O. Number	456
Street Address:	123 Somewhere			Order Date:	1/1
City, State, Zip:	Village, CA 12345			Delivery Date:	1/2
Supplier				Purchase Order	
Phone Number:	555-5555			Phone Number:	555-5557
Fax Number:	555-5556			Fax Number:	555-5558
E-Mail:	village@isp.org			E-Mail:	Billie@isp.org
Contact:	Mr. Green			Buyer:	Ms. Mendoza
Item	Description	Unit	Quantity	Unit Price $	Extention
Total					

Chapter

4 Managing the Cost of Beverages

OVERVIEW   This chapter begins with an overview of the special responsibilities you assume when your operation serves alcoholic beverages. It then details the various types of beverage products you might sell and the techniques used to purchase them, as well as the specific knowledge you must have to store them properly. Important topics in this chapter include the use of standardized drink recipes and the procedures used to monitor and forecast beverage sales. Lastly, the chapter explains how your guest's beverage choices influence the beverage cost percentages that you will compute as you evaluate the cost efficiency of your beverage unit.

CHAPTER OUTLINE

Serving Alcoholic Beverages
Forecasting Beverage Sales
Standardized Drink Recipes and Portions
Purchasing Beverage Products
Receiving Beverage Products
Storing Beverage Products
Bar Transfers
Computing Cost of Beverages
Special Features of Liquor Inventory
Sales Mix
Key Terms and Concepts, and Test Your Skills

HIGHLIGHTS   At the conclusion of this chapter, you will be able to:

○ Use sales histories in conjunction with standardized drink recipes to develop a beverage purchase order.
○ Compute the dollar value of bar transfers both to and from the kitchen.
○ Compute an accurate cost of goods sold percentage for beer, wine, and spirits.

Serving Alcoholic Beverages

It might seem unusual that a book about cost management would have to separate the study of cost control into a segment dealing with food and another one dealing with alcoholic beverage products. In fact, it might seem unusual that the very term "beverages" in this chapter will always refer to those beverages with an alcoholic content. In fact, if you have the skill to serve alcoholic beverages responsibly and can properly account for the cost of serving these beverages, you are better prepared to manage a variety of foodservice operations than those managers who do not have those skills. The reason is simple. Many operations include alcohol as a major component of the products they offer to guests. There are three types of operations that serve alcoholic beverages. These can be grouped as:

1. Beverage only
2. Beverage and food
3. Beverage and entertainment/activity

Beverage Only

The beverage-only operation has been in existence in the United States for a little more than a hundred years. Prior to that, alcohol was generally sold only in conjunction with food and lodging services. Actually, in these facilities, snacks such as pretzels, chips, and nuts are often served, but beverage service is clearly most important. Beverage-only bars are often neighborhood gathering places. Some are frequented by businesspeople who work in the vicinity, while travelers may drop in when they are in the area. Decor can be anything from comfortably casual to upscale. When provided, entertainment may include television, recorded music, a pool table, or pinball and video games. In some cases, an outdoor setting may be an attractive customer draw.

Beverage-only bars usually have a predictable traffic flow. Because they deal only in beverages, these are usually the easiest service operations to manage. Beverage-only operations can include:

1. Neighborhood bars
2. Taverns
3. Hotel bars
4. Airport bars
5. Bus terminal bars
6. Breweries
7. Wineries

Beverage and Food

Beverage and food operations are the predominant type of beverage operation in the United States and a major industry in the world today. Restaurants serving wine, beer, and liquor as well as bars that serve light meals are examples of this type of service.

It is important to remember that the profit margins on alcoholic beverages are generally much higher than that of food; thus, it just makes good business sense to add the service of alcoholic beverages to the service of providing food whenever possible. While it is impossible to state the appropriate profit levels for alcoholic beverages, profits are generally two to five times greater for beverage products than for food products. Thus, it is highly likely that the profit in the pitcher of beer that you may sell in a pizza restaurant you own will exceed that of its accompanying pizza by a great deal, even though the beer may be sold for half the price of the pizza.

Many alcoholic beverages were created because they are enjoyed most when combined with food; thus, it is only natural for professional food and beverage managers to seek out and promote these combinations. Beverage and food operations can include:

1. Quick-service restaurants
2. Full-service restaurants
3. Self-service and cafeterias
4. Airport bars
5. Sports complexes
6. Grocery store carryout
7. Brew pubs
8. Hotel room service
9. Banquet halls
10. Country clubs

Beverage and Entertainment/Activity

Beverage and entertainment/activity operations exist because many people want to do something while they consume their favorite alcoholic beverage. As discussed earlier, eating is one of those favorite activities. This segment of the beverage business, however, can offer even more.

There is enormous variety in the types of entertainment and activities that can accompany beverage service, ranging from dartboards and pool tables, to elaborate stage shows in nightclubs and cabarets. Dance clubs can provide live or recorded music while your guests enjoy dancing. Piano bars and small clubs provide quiet, intimate places to enjoy music and conversation. There are high-tech clubs where the entertainment comes from giant video screens and computerized toys, and old-fashioned ballparks where your guests can enjoy a ballgame. Beverage and entertainment/activity operations can include:

1. Comedy clubs
2. Taverns
3. Entertainment clubs
4. Full-service restaurants

5. Sports complexes
6. Brew pubs
7. Nightclubs
8. Country clubs
9. Dance clubs
10. Music clubs
11. Bowling alleys

Classifications of Alcoholic Beverages

Alcoholic beverages are simply those products that are meant for consumption as a beverage and that contain a significant amount of ethyl alcohol. These products are generally classified as:

1. **Beer:** a fermented beverage made from grain and flavored with hops
2. **Wine:** a fermented beverage made from grapes, fruits, or berries
3. **Spirits:** fermented beverages that are distilled to increase the alcohol content of the product

When you combine the sale of food products with that of beverages or if you manage a facility that sells beverages exclusively, you face a set of challenges that deserve special attention. In many ways, you will treat beverage products in a manner similar to that of food products. The beverage products you buy will be specified, ordered, received, and stored in a fashion that is very close to that of food products. In other ways, however, when you are the one responsible for the sale and service of alcohol, you take on a responsibility that society views as extremely critical.

Responsible Alcoholic Beverage Service

People have long been fond of alcoholic beverages regardless of where they are consumed for they add greatly to the enjoyment of food and friends. In moderate doses, ethyl alcohol, the type found in beverage products, acts as a mild tranquilizer. In excessive doses, it can become toxic, causing impaired judgment and, in some cases, death. Clearly, a foodservice manager whose establishment serves alcoholic beverages must take great care in the serving and monitoring of guests' alcohol intake.

Many states have now enacted third-party liability legislation, which, under certain conditions, holds your business and, in some cases, you, personally, responsible for the actions of your guests who consume excessive amounts of alcoholic beverages. This series of legislative acts, commonly called **dramshop laws,** shifts the liability for acts committed by an individual under the influence of alcohol from that individual to the server or operation that supplied the intoxicating beverage.

Dramshop is derived from the word *dram,* which refers to a small drink, and *shop,* where such a drink was sold. Because of these laws, managers are becoming increasingly concerned about alcohol awareness and the importance of safely serving their guests. This means training employees to serve alcoholic beverages properly and to notice telltale signs of guest intoxication.

Through passage of dramshop and related laws, it is very clear that society holds the seller of alcoholic beverages to a very high standard. In all states, the sale of these products is regulated either by the licensing of establishments that are allowed to sell alcoholic beverages **(license states)** or by direct control and sale of the products by the state **(control states).**

While the special requirements involved in serving alcoholic beverages are many, including licensing, age restrictions, promotional limitations, drinking and driving issues, and social responsibility, to name just a few, the control of beverage costs is similar, in many respects, to the control of food-related costs.

This chapter details the unique aspects of sales forecasting, purchasing, receiving, and storage of beverage products. In some areas, beverage control is no different from that of nonalcoholic food products. In others, the differences are pronounced.

FUN ON THE WEB!

Do a Web search! Search for "Alcoholic Beverage Commission" to find regulations on the sale and service of alcohol. When you get a list of sites, just pick a state. Yours might be one of them! (Recommended search engine: MSN.)

Forecasting Beverage Sales

The number of possible "menu items" in the average bar or lounge is staggering. Human imagination has few limits; thus, the number of different mixtures a skilled bartender can concoct makes forecasting guest item selection a difficult process, indeed. Of course, you now know how to track the number of guests served and the items these guests will buy. This is done exactly as previously discussed (Chapter 2). Percent selecting—the proportion of people who will buy a particular drink, given a choice of many different drink types—must be modified somewhat if it is to be applied to forecasting beverage sales. In fact, beverage sales forecasting varies also by the type of beverage sold.

Forecasting Beer Sales

Forecasting beer sales is essentially the same as forecasting any regular menu item. That is, given a choice of beverage products, some percentage of your guests will likely choose beer. However, the questions you must answer to effectively manage your costs are, "What percentage of my guests will choose beer?" *and* "Which kind of beer?" *and* "In what packaging format will they choose?"

Assume that you are the owner of LeRae, a small bar in a trendy section of a large West Coast city. Your clientele generally consists of upscale office and managerial professionals. For the time period 1/1 to 1/8, you served an alcoholic beverage to a total of 1,600 guests: 400, or 25%, selected a beer product; 160, or 10%, selected a wine product; and 1,040, or 65%, selected some type of spirit-based drink.

Using your sales history, you have a good idea of how many people will be coming to your bar on any given day. You have monitored your percent selecting data and found that one out of four guests coming to LeRae's will order beer. You need to determine, however, which *specific* brand of beer your guests will buy, given the several brands of beer that you carry. In addition, it is very likely that at least some of the beer you serve will come packaged in more than one form. That is, a specific beer brand might be sold in individual cans or bottles or in kegs. **Keg beer** is also known as **draft beer,** or beer in a form of packaging in which the beer is shipped to you in multigallon units for bulk sale. By charting current beer sales, you can know what your guests' beer preferences are. Figure 4.1

FIGURE **4.1** ● LeRae's Bar

Beverage Sales		Date: <u>1/1–1/8</u>
Product: Beer	**Number Sold**	**Percentage Sold**
Budweiser Bottles	45	11.25%
Coors Bottles	18	4.50
Miller Cans	61	15.25
Coors Cans	68	17.00
Budweiser Draft	115	28.75
Harp's Draft	93	23.25
Total	400	100.00

demonstrates that, for the period 1/1 to 1/8, LeRae's served 400 beers to guests. It also details which specific beer your guests ordered.

If you are to build the information database necessary to accurately develop purchase orders based on projected sales, you must know both what percentage of your guests select beer and which kind of beer they will select.

By either manual tracking or the use of your point of sales (POS) system, you will know exactly which beers, by brand and packaging form, you have sold in the bar on a daily basis. A tally of guest checks would also furnish you with the same information, but such a system is labor intensive, time consuming, and subject to inaccuracy.

Regardless of the tracking method used, the goal is the same as that of tracking a food item sale. That is, with a good idea of what guests have purchased in the past, we are better prepared to order the products we believe they will purchase in the future. When that product is beer, it is especially important that you consider both the brand and the packaging preferred by your guests.

Forecasting Wine Sales

The forecasting of wine sales is similar to that of beer sales in that it must be divided into more than one part. For most managers, forecasting wine sales is a process that must be divided into two main parts:

1. Forecasting bottled-wine sales
2. Forecasting wine-by-the-glass sales

Forecasting Bottled-Wine Sales When forecasting wine sales by the bottle, you treat an individual type of bottled wine exactly as you would treat a menu item. A wine list or wine menu detailing the selections of wines available can be presented to the guest, who then makes a choice. Percent selecting figures are computed exactly as they would be when analyzing food item sales. You may find, however, that it is possible and quite desirable to offer wines with very small percent selecting figures because wines in a bottle are not highly perishable. Thus, many operators develop extensive wine lists consisting of a large number of wines, many of which sell only rarely. While this selling strategy has its place because some restaurants consider an extensive wine list as an integral part of their marketing strategy, it must be remembered that excessive product inventory, whether food or beverage, must be avoided. Dollars invested in extravagant inventory are not available for use in other areas of the foodservice organization. While bottled wine is not highly perishable, all wine products are perishable to some degree; thus, excessive inventory of some wine types can result in increased product loss through oxidation (deterioration), theft, or both.

FIGURE **4.2** ● LeRae's Bar

Beverage Sales		Date: 1/1–1/8
Product: Wine by the Glass	Number Sold	Percentage Sold
Chardonnay	30	18.75%
Merlot	16	10.00
Zinfandel	62	38.75
House Zinfandel	52	32.50
Total	160	100.00

Forecasting Wine-by-the-Glass Sales Generally, forecasting the sale of **house wines,** the wine served to a guest who does not stipulate a specific brand when ordering, or any wine sold by the glass is done in a manner similar to that used in forecasting beer sales. Once you have estimated the number of guests who will select wine, the type of wine they will select can be forecasted.

Figure 4.2 details the by-the-glass sales of wine at LeRae's for the period 1/1 to 1/8. From the data, you know that one out of ten guests will buy wine by the glass. Thus, 160 (from a total of 1,600 guests) will select this beverage.

If your guests remain consistent in their buying habits, you will have a good idea of the total demand for your wine-by-the-glass products and will be better able to ascertain the amount that must be on hand on any given day.

Forecasting Spirit Sales

Like beer and wine, the number of guests who order a mixed drink can be tracked. Unlike beer and wine, however, the exact item the guests will request is very difficult to determine. When ordering spirits, tracking sales can become somewhat complicated. For example, assume that two guests order bourbon and soda; one guest specifies Jack Daniel's brand of bourbon, whereas the other one prefers Heaven Hill brand. From the guests' point of view, they both ordered bourbon and soda. From the operator's point of view, two distinct items were selected. To make matters a bit more complicated, a third guest comes in and orders bourbon and soda without preference as to the type of bourbon used. Obviously, a different method of sales forecasting is necessary in a situation such as this, and, in fact, several are available. One method requires that the operator view guest selection not in terms of the drink requested, such as bourbon and water, gin and tonic, Sea Breeze, and so on, but rather in terms of the particular spirit that forms the base of the drink. Consider a table of four guests who order the following:

1. Kahlua on the rocks
2. Kahlua and coffee
3. Kahlua and cream
4. Kahlua and Coke

Each guest could be considered as having ordered the same item: a drink in which Kahlua, a coffee-flavored liqueur from Mexico, forms the base of the drink. The purpose of this method is, of course, to simplify the process of recording guests' preferences.

Depending on the degree of accuracy desired by the operator, tracking spirit sales can be done by any of the following methods:

1. Generic product name:
   a. Coffee liqueur
   b. Bourbon
   c. Vodka
   d. Gin
2. Specific product name:
   a. Kahlua
   b. Jack Daniel's Black Label
   c. Absolut
   d. Bombay
3. Specific drink requested:
   a. Kahlua on the rocks
   b. Kahlua and coffee
   c. Kahlua and cream
   d. Kahlua and Coke

Figure 4.3 demonstrates the system you would use to track spirit sales using the generic product method illustrated previously. It also is an excellent example of the power of an effective beverage POS system to help track sales in a manner that is far more effective than can be done manually. The number of different spirit drinks that can be made numbers in the hundreds. A POS system programmed specifically for your operation can be a great asset in helping you develop the sales histories you

FIGURE **4.3** ● LeRae's Bar

Beverage Sales		Date: 1/1–1/8
Product: Spirits	Number Sold	Percentage Sold
Scotch	210	13.1%
Bourbon	175	10.9
Vodka	580	36.3
Gin	375	23.4
Kahlua	175	10.9
Tequila	85	5.3
Total	1,600	100.0

need to purchase spirit products effectively because it can easily track this large number of drink combinations.

As the amount of time and effort required to track specific drink sales increases, so does accuracy. Each operator must determine the level of control appropriate for his or her own operation. This is due to the simple fact that there must be a relationship between the time, money, and effort required to maintain a control system and the cost effectiveness of such an endeavor.

Standardized Drink Recipes and Portions

If a beverage operation is even moderately busy, it is simply unrealistic to assume that the bartender can stop each time an order comes in, consult a written standardized recipe as discussed in Chapter 3, and then prepare the drink requested. Imagine the resulting confusion, chaos, and time delay if such a system were in place! The demand for control in the bar, however, is even greater than that required in the kitchen. The reason is simple. The potential for employee theft and waste is greater in the bar than in the kitchen. Also, the AP price of beverages is, in most cases, higher than that of food. Consider, for a moment, just a few of the unique aspects of beverage operations that require strict adherence to control procedures:

1. Beverage operations are subject to tax audits to verify sales revenue. In some states, these audits can be unannounced.
2. Beverage operations can be closed down "on the spot" for violation of law.
3. Employees in a bar may attempt to become operational "partners" by bringing in their own products to sell and keeping sales revenue.
4. Detecting the disappearance of small amounts of beverage products is extremely difficult, as, for example, the loss of 8 ounces of beer from a multigallon keg.

For these reasons and others, using standardized recipes is an absolute must for the beverage operation, even if using written standardized recipes for each drink is not a viable option. Consider the case of Paul, the bar manager at a full-service restaurant. He knows that each bourbon and water he produces should consist of 95 cents in product cost. His selling price is $4.75. He uses the beverage cost % formula to determine his beverage cost percentage. The following beverage cost % formula, as you can easily see, is nearly identical to the food cost % formula presented in Chapter 3:

$$\frac{\text{Cost of Beverage Sold}}{\text{Beverage Sales}} = \text{Beverage Cost \%}$$

Thus, Paul's beverage cost % should be as follows:

$$\frac{\$0.95}{\$4.75} = 20.0\%$$

Yet, his actual beverage cost % on this item is much higher. How can this be, on an item as uncomplicated as bourbon and water? The answer is simple. The bartender did not follow the standardized recipe. Even on an item as ordinary as bourbon and water, the bartender must know exactly the amount of product to use. It is not simply a matter of bourbon and water, but rather a matter of *how much* bourbon with how much water. Figure 4.4 shows the beverage cost that would be achieved with different drink sizes and a standard 1-liter bottle of spirits.

As shown, the difference in the drink recipe can make a big difference in total beverage cost percent. For purposes of accuracy, assume approximately a 0.8-ounce-per-liter evaporation loss, thus leaving Paul with 33 ounces of usable product from this liter of bourbon. Also, assume a

FIGURE **4.4** ● Beverage Cost Comparison

Beverage: <u>Bourbon</u> Container Size: <u>One liter (33.8 oz.)</u>
Product Cost: <u>$24.80/liter</u>

Portion Size	Number of Portions	Liter Cost	Portion Cost	Selling Price	Total Beverage Sales	Beverage Cost %
1.00 oz.	33	$24.80	$0.75	$4.75	$156.75	15.8%
1.25 oz.	26	24.80	0.95	4.75	123.50	20.1
1.50 oz.	22	24.80	1.13	4.75	104.50	23.7
1.75 oz.	19	24.80	1.31	4.75	90.25	27.5

product cost of $24.80 per liter, with a $4.75 per drink selling price and a normal portion size of 1 ounce of bourbon. Obviously, the quantity of alcohol actually used makes the liquor cost percent vary greatly.

Stated in another way, assume that you manage a large convention hotel that has a beverage sales volume in spirit drinks of $2,000,000 per year. If your bartenders consistently pour 1½-ounce drinks rather than 1-ounce drinks, and you assume average costs and selling prices as related in Figure 4.4, then beverage costs will be 23.7% rather than the planned 15.8%. The difference is 7.9% (23.7 − 15.8 = 7.9). The loss represents $2,000,000 × 0.079 = $158,000 for this one operation in just one year! A loss as sizable as this is certainly career threatening for any manager!

While standardized recipes, which include step-by-step methods of preparation, may be necessary for only a few types of drinks, standardized recipes that detail the quantity of product management has predetermined as appropriate should be strictly adhered to. That is, if management has determined that bourbon and water should be a 1-ounce portion of bourbon and a 2-ounce portion of water, then *both* items should be measured by a proper **jigger,** a tool for measuring liquid, or an automated device. Some mechanized/computerized bar systems on the market today will premeasure both items simultaneously. The capabilities of such a system are many, and are outlined in Chapter 12 of this text. Regardless of method of measurement, both bourbon and water, in this case, must be delivered to the guest in the proper ratio if product quality is to be maintained. Thus, standardized portion size is critical.

Consider, for a moment, the case of a manager who determines that a particular blend of bourbon, while expensive, can be sold at a premium price. The manager sets the drink price and instructs the bartender that the portion size is to be 1 ounce of spirit with 2 ounces of water. Consider the following guest reactions when the bartender varies the quantity of water added to the bourbon:

Drink Ratio	Possible Guest Response
A. 1 oz. bourbon 1 oz. water	1. Gee, the drinks sure are small here! 2. Gee, this sure is strong! Can you add a splash of water?
B. 1 oz. bourbon 2 oz. water	1. Gee, this sure tastes good! Just right!
C. 1 oz. bourbon 3 oz. water	1. Gee, this tastes watered down. Can you add a splash of bourbon? 2. Gee, these drinks cost a lot for such a small amount of alcohol!

Remember that the quantity of spirit used and, thus, the product cost percentage, did not change under scenario A, B, or C. In this case, the bartender was very careful not to use more product than he or she had been instructed to do. In effect, the bartender put the profitability of the operation before guest satisfaction. It is important to remember that happy guests provide profits; profits do not provide happy guests. The manager of this operation might be pleased with the bartender's precise product control, since the cost of 1 ounce versus 3 ounces of water is minuscule. Guests, however, will react to sloppy drink preparation in the same way they do to sloppy food preparation.

In summary, each drink in the bar must have a standardized recipe or, if the preparation of the drink is simple, a standardized portion size. These recipes will affect the planned profitability of the operation as well as guest satisfaction.

Since it is necessary to cost beverage recipes just as it necessary to cost food item recipes, a standardized recipe sheet (see Chapter 3) should be prepared for each drink item to be sold. A notebook of these recipes should be available at each beverage outlet. If questions about portion size or preparation arise, the standardized recipe sheet should be referred to.

Purchasing Beverage Products

Most foodservice operators select only one quality level for food products. Once a determination on necessary quality level has been made and a product specification written, then only *that* quality of egg, lettuce, milk, bread, and so on is selected. In the area of alcoholic beverage products, however, several levels of quality are generally chosen. This ensures that a beverage product is available for those guests who wish to purchase the very best, while a product is also offered for those guests who prefer to spend less. Thus, the beverage manager is faced with deciding not only whether to carry wine on the menu, but also how many different kinds of wine and their quality levels. The same process is necessary for spirits and, to a lesser degree, for beers.

Determining Beer Products to Carry

Beer is the most highly perishable of beverage products. The **pull date,** or expiration date, on these products can be as short as a few months. Because of this, it is important that the beverage operator only stock those items that will sell relatively well. This generally means selecting both brand and packaging methods.

Brand Selection   Beverage operators typically carry between three and ten types of beer. Some operations, however, stock as many as 50 or more! Generally speaking, geographic location, clientele, ambiance, and menu help determine the beer product that will be selected. Obviously, we would not expect to see the same beer products at Hunan Gardens Chinese Restaurant that we would at Three Pesos Mexican Restaurant. Most foodservice operators find that one or two brands of light beer, two or three national domestic brands, and one or two quality import beers meet the great majority of their guests' demand. One must be very careful in this area not to stock excessive amounts of products that sell poorly. Again, beer is perishable, and great care must be taken to ensure proper product movement. It is important, however, to train bartenders to make a notation on a **product request log** (see Figure 4.5) so that guest requests that cannot be filled are noted and monitored by management. This log should be easily accessible to service personnel. Its purpose is to maintain a record of guest product requests that are not currently available. In the case of beverages, those items that guests wish to purchase that are *not* available are nearly as important to track as the sales of the items that are available.

If you were running the operation that generated the requests documented in Figure 4.5, you might, for example, wish to investigate the possibility of stocking Lowenbrau beer.

FIGURE **4.5** ● Beverage Product Request Log

Date	Item Requested	Entry By
1/1	Lowenbrau Beer	P. J.
1/1	Cherry Schnapps	L. T.
1/2	Rolling Rock Beer on Draft	T. R.
1/4	Lowenbrau Beer	P. J.
1/5	Soave Wine	L. D.
1/6	Any Texas Wine	S. H.
1/6	Lowenbrau Beer	T. R.

Packaging Beer typically is sold to foodservice operators in cans, bottles, or kegs. While each of these containers has its advantages and disadvantages, most foodservice operators with active beverage operations will select some of each of these packaging methods. It makes little sense to carry the same beer product in both bottles and cans; however, many operators choose to serve some brands of their bottled or canned beer in draft form as well.

Many beer drinkers prefer draft beer (beer from kegs) over bottled or canned beer, and the cost to you per glass served is lower with beer from a keg. Special equipment and serving techniques are, however, required if quality draft beer is to be sold to guests. Also, the shelf life of keg beer is the shortest of all packaging types, ranging from 30 to 45 days for an untapped keg, that is, one that has not yet been opened by the bartender, and even fewer days for a keg that has been **tapped** (opened). Kegs can be difficult to handle because of their weight, and it is hard to keep an exact count of the product served without special metering equipment. Despite these drawbacks, many operators serve draft beer. Draft beer is sold in a variety of keg and barrel sizes as listed in Figure 4.6.

FIGURE **4.6** ● Draft Beer Containers

Container	Ounces	Liters
Barrel	3,968	117.33
1/2 Barrel (keg)	1,984	58.67
1/4 Barrel (1/2 keg)	992	29.33
1/8 Barrel (1/4 keg)	496	14.67

FUN ON THE WEB!

Look up the following to see examples of sites that will help you learn more about beers and breweries.

www.beerweek.com This site is a beer "news" site. Instead of *Newsweek*, explore *Beerweek*. Also, play a beer game for fun!

www.alestreetnews.com This is another beer "news" site. It prides itself on being a "brewspaper."

www.beerhistory.com Explore the history of beer and breweries. This site includes brewer profiles and a beer library.

www.allaboutbeer.com *All About Beer* is a beer magazine in print. This Web site is its dot.com venue.

www.celebrator.com *Celebrator Beer News* is a bimonthly magazine. Go on this site to see the e-version of this magazine.

Determining Wine Products to Carry

Determining which wines to carry is, like beer, a matter of your selecting both product and packaging. Typically, you must determine if you will sell wine by the:

1. Glass
2. Split or half-bottle
3. Carafe
4. Bottle

Wines sold by the glass or carafe can be served from bottles opened specifically for that purpose or they can be drawn from specially boxed wine containers. Wines in a box typically are house wines sold to the beverage manager in multiliter-sized boxes to ease handling, speed, and service and to reduce packaging costs. Bottled wines of many sizes and varieties can, of course, also be purchased.

In addition, you may find that wine for cooking must also be purchased. In general, these products will be secured from your beverage wholesaler rather than the grocery wholesaler. It makes little sense to use extraordinarily fine wine in cooking. Again, the guiding principle for you should be to select the appropriate quality food or beverage product for its intended use. Some operators add salt to their cooking wines in an effort to discourage the kitchen staff from drinking them. This method, if used, should be clearly communicated to kitchen personnel if the operator is to avoid possible liability.

Wine Lists   As a good manager, you will build a **wine list,** the term used to describe your menu of wine offerings, that fits your own particular operation and guest expectations. Figure 4.7 is an example of a wine list that might be used at a mid-priced restaurant.

At Toliver's Terrace, the wine list is first divided by types of wines/grape varietals: Sparkling Wine and Champagne, Chardonnay, Other White Wines, Cabernet Sauvignon, Merlot, and Pinot Noir. Each category of wines is then numbered as follows: 100s for sparkling wine and champagne, 200s for white wines (Chardonnay and other white wines), and 300s for red wines (Cabernet Sauvignon, Merlot, and Pinot Noir). The numbering system is used to assist the guest in ordering and to help the server identify the correct wine in storage. Guests may feel intimidated by the French, Italian, or German names of wines and, thus, might not order them for fear of pronouncing the words incorrectly. A numbering system allows guests to choose a number rather than a name, and so reduces the amount of anxiety they may have in ordering.

The second column in Figure 4.7 lists the name and place of the **vintner,** or wine producer. The third column lists the price by the glass and/or the price per bottle. Usually, it is the less expensive wines that are available by the glass because more people are likely to order the less expensive wines than the most expensive wines, especially at a mid-priced restaurant. It is much more cost effective to offer wine by the glass from a $20.00 bottle of wine than from an $80.00 bottle of wine because, once the bottle is opened, it has a relatively short shelf life.

In wine list development, several points must be kept in mind. First, you must seek to provide alternatives for the guest who wants the best, as well as for those who prefer to spend less. Second, wines that either complement the food or, in the case of a bar, are popular with the guests must be available. Tastes in wines change, and you must keep up with these changes. Subscribing to at least one wine journal in the hospitality field is a good way to do so. You must also avoid the temptation to offer too many wines on a wine list. Excess inventory and use of valuable storage space

FIGURE **4.7** ● Sample Wine List

	Toliver's Terrace	
	Sparkling Wine and Champagne	**Dollars per Glass/ Dollars per Bottle**
101	Gloria Ferrer, Brut, Sonoma County	$7.00/$26.00
102	Pommery, Reims, France	$43.00
103	Jordan "J", Sonoma	$48.00
104	Moët Chandon, Epernay, France	$55.00
105	Dom Perignon, Epernay, France	$125.00
	Chardonnay	
201	Kendall-Jackson, California	$5.00/$20.00
202	Camelot, California	$6.00/$22.00
203	St. Francis, Sonoma	$7.00/$26.00
204	Cartlidge & Browne, California	$30.00
205	Stag's Leap, Napa Valley	$52.00
	Other White Wines	
206	Fall Creek, Chenin Blanc, Texas	$5.00/$18.00
207	Max Richter, Riesling, Germany	$6.00/$22.00
208	Honig, Sauvignon Blanc, Napa Valley	$7.00/$25.00
209	Tommasi, Pinot Grigio, Italy	$7.00/$25.00
210	Santa Margherita, Pinot Grigio, Italy	$34.00
	Cabernet Sauvignon	
301	Tessera, California	$5.00/$20.00
302	Guenoc, California	$7.00/$27.00
303	Sebastiani Cask, Sonoma	$35.00
304	Franciscan, Napa Valley	$38.00
305	Chateau Ste. Michelle, Cold Creek, Washington	$45.00

Toliver's Terrace		
	Merlot	
306	Talus, California	$5.00/$20.00
307	Tapiz, Argentina	$6.00/$22.00
308	Ironstone, Sierra Foothills	$7.00/$26.00
309	Solis, Santa Clara County	$35.00
	Pinot Noir	
310	Firesteed, Oregon	$6.00/$23.00
311	Carneros Creek, Carneros	$31.00
312	Iron Horse, Sonoma	$39.00
313	Domain Drouhin, Willamette Valley, Oregon	$55.00

make this a poor idea. In addition, when selling wine by the glass, those items that sell poorly can lose quality and flavor rapidly. Third, wine sales can be diminished due to the complexity of the product itself. You should strive to make the purchase of wine by the bottle a pleasant, nonthreatening experience. Waitstaff, who help in selling wine, should be knowledgeable but not pretentious.

In general, when foodservice managers have trouble selling wine (the world's most popular beverage), the difficulty lies in the delivery of the product rather than with the product selected. It would almost appear as if some operators go out of their way to make the ordering, presentation, and service of wine so pretentious as to intimidate many guests into not purchasing wine at all. This is unfortunate since wine is perceived as a beverage of moderation and is enjoyed the world over by so many guests. You can enlist the aid of your own wine supplier to help you train your staff in the effective marketing of wine, either by the bottle or by the glass. Far too few operators use this valuable resource to their advantage.

FUN ON THE WEB!

Look up the following to see examples of sites that will help you learn more about wines.

www.wine.com Learn about wine and maybe buy a bottle! Click on "Learn More About Wine" to get in-depth information about this tasty beverage.

www.winespectator.com Have you read the *Wine Spectator* lately? It is a publication all about wines. This is the online version of the magazine.

www.wineculture.com This site will help you with everything from selecting, purchasing, and storing wines to serving them at the table. You can also find out some fun things about food and wine pairings.

www.wino.net Although a tongue-in-cheek name, this site is helpful in linking you to a collection of sites about wines. Click on "Web of Wine" Favorite Links to get to many interesting wine sites.

www.vine2wine.com This site is a convenient way to search through a wine directory of the wine industry. Cool sites and cool wineries.

Determining Spirit Products to Carry

Distilled spirits have an extremely long shelf life. Thus, you can make a "mistake" and purchase the wrong spirit product without disastrous results, if that product can be sold over a reasonable period of time. Guest preference will dictate the types of liquors that are appropriate for a given operation, but it is your responsibility to determine product quality levels in the beverage area. Nowhere is this more important than in the area of distilled spirits.

Consumer preferences concerning alcoholic beverages can change rapidly. The wise beverage manager stays abreast of changing consumption trends by reading professional journals and staying active in his or her professional associations. These associations can be major providers of information related to changes in consumer buying behavior as far as beer, wine, and spirits are concerned. What is hot one year may be out of fashion the next! It is important to spot these trends and respond to them quickly.

Packaging is not a particular issue, as it is for beer and wine, in the selection of spirits for an establishment's use. In the United States, as in most parts of the world, bottle sizes for spirits are standard. Since the early 1980s, the bottle sizes shown in Figure 4.8 represent those most commonly offered for sale to the hospitality market.

The mini-bottle (50 ml) is typically offered for sale on airlines and in some situations, such as in-room mini-bars and room service, in the hotel segment of the hospitality industry. In some areas of the country, it can even be purchased singularly in bars. By far the most common bottle size used in the hospitality industry is the 1-liter size.

While packaging is not a major concern of the operator selecting a spirit product, brand quality is crucial. As a comparison, consider a prod-

FIGURE **4.8** ● Bottle Sizes of Common Spirits

Bottle Type	Capacity
Mini (50 ml)	1.7 oz.
750 ml	25.4 oz.
1 liter	33.8 oz.
1.75 liter	59.2 oz.

uct such as Budweiser Light beer, a standard product, which tastes the same from coast to coast. An operator who chooses to carry *that* beer need only decide whether it will be sold in bottles, cans, or on draft. Should that same operator elect to carry scotch, however, an extremely wide selection of products at widely varying prices is available for purchase. In general, restaurant operators will select spirits in two major categories. These are well liquors and call liquors.

Well Liquors **Well liquors** are those spirits that are poured when the guest does not specify a particular brand name when ordering. The name stems from the concept of "well," or the bottle holding area in the bar. The wise operator will choose well liquors very carefully. By electing to buy spirits that are very low in cost, such as well items, the operator may find that the quality is accordingly low. Make no mistake, guests who order well liquors may be price conscious, but that does not mean they are not quality conscious also. It is fairly easy to tell the difference between a well liquor of average quality and one of very poor quality. Managers who shop for well liquors considering only price as a criterion for selection will find that guest reaction is extremely negative. Conversely, if exceptionally high quality products are chosen as well items, liquor costs may be excessive unless an adequate price structure is maintained.

Call Liquors **Call liquors** are those spirits that are requested by name, such as Jack Daniel's, Kahlua, and Chivas Regal. Extremely expensive call liquors are sometimes referred to as **premium liquors.**

You will generally charge a higher price for those drinks prepared with call or premium liquors. Guests understand this and, in fact, by specifying call liquors indicate their preference to pay the price required for these special products.

Figures 4.9 and 4.10 illustrate the effect of changes in the selection of well liquors. In Figure 4.9, 50 well drinks and 50 call drinks are sold. Total beverage cost percentage, in this example, equals 19.1%.

In Figure 4.10, the portion cost of our well brand is reduced from 45 cents to 30 cents, due to a reduction in the quality of product selected for

FIGURE **4.9** ● Spirit Cost Percentage

Original Portion Cost						
Spirit	Number Sold	Portion Cost	Total Cost	Selling Price	Total Sales	Beverage Cost %
Well	50	$0.90	$ 45	$5	$250	18.0%
Call	50	1.20	60	6	300	20.0
Total	100		105		550	19.1

this purpose. This results in a decrease in beverage cost percentage to 16.4%.

While the decision to lower the quality of well liquor used did, in this case, reduce overall liquor cost percentage, the question of the long-term effect on guest satisfaction and loyalty is not addressed. In fact, changes in guest behavior may seem negligible in the short run. Successful foodservice operators, however, remember that you cannot fool all of the people all of the time. *Quality products at fair prices build guest loyalty.* Because that is true, you are wise to select well products that are in keeping with your clientele, price structure, and desired image. Anything less cheats both you and your guests.

FIGURE **4.10** ● Spirit Cost Percentage

Reduced Portion Cost						
Spirit	Number Sold	Portion Cost	Total Cost	Selling Price	Total Sales	Beverage Cost %
Well	50	$0.60	$30	$5	$250	12.0%
Call	50	1.20	60	6	300	20.0
Total	100		90		550	16.4

FUN ON THE WEB!

Look up the following to see examples of sites that will help you learn more about spirits and cocktails.

www.cocktails.about.com Go to this site to learn about bartending, cocktail recipes, cocktail culture, and much more!

www.food.epicurious.com This site approaches food, wine, and liquor from an epicurean perspective. Click on "Drinking" to find out more about cocktails.

If you are 21 or over, you can explore numerous sites developed by liquor companies. Go to the MSN search engine, and click on "Liquor & Spirits." From there, you will be launched into a world of spirits companies.

Beverage Purchase Orders

The form in Figure 3.13 can be used to document the beverage purchase order in the same way it is used for food purchases. Special laws, depending on the state and county, may influence how beverage purchases are to be made or paid for. One of the first responsibilities you have is to become familiar with all applicable state and local laws regarding beverage purchases. As with food, the goal in purchasing is to have an adequate, but not excessive amount of product on hand at all times. Unlike most food products, however, beverage distributors will sometimes sell products in less than one-case lots. This is called a **broken case** and occurs when several different brands or products are used to completely fill the case. Take, for example, the operator who orders a case of scotch, consisting of 12 bottles. The case, however, might contain four bottles of Scotch Brand A, four bottles of Brand B, and four bottles of Brand C.

As a general rule, wine, beer, and spirits are purchased by the case. Beer, of course, may also be bought by full- or reduced-size kegs. As with food products, smaller container size usually results in higher cost per ounce. It is important to remember that both product quality and container size are critical when determining what to buy.

Receiving Beverage Products

The skill required to receive beverage products is somewhat less than what is needed for receiving food. The reason is that beverage products do not vary in quality in the same manner food products do. As with food, the receiving clerk needs a proper location, tools, and equipment. In addition, proper delivery schedules must be maintained. The training required in beverage receiving, however, is reduced due to the consistent nature of the product received. A case of freshly produced Coors beer, for example, will be consistent in quality regardless of the vendor. And if the product is **fresh dated,** that is, a date is stamped on the product to indicate its freshness, very little inspection is required to ensure that the product is exactly what was ordered. In fact, when matching the purchase order to the vendor invoice, only quantity ordered and price must be verified, unlike food deliveries that require the verification of weight, quantity, quality, and price. It is possible, however, that the goods delivered will not match those ordered. Or, in fact, the goods delivered are defective in some manner. Thus, appropriate receiving procedures must be in place.

When receiving beverage products, the following items are of concern and should be verified:

Key Beverage Receiving Checkpoints

1. Correct brand
2. Correct bottle size
3. No broken bottles or bottle seals
4. Freshness dates (beer)
5. Correct vintage, or year produced (wine)
6. Refrigerated state (if appropriate)
7. Correct unit price
8. Correct price extension
9. Correct invoice total

If errors are detected, a credit memo should be filled out and signed by both the delivery person and the receiving clerk.

Credit Memo

A credit memo is an addendum to the delivery invoice. As discussed in Chapter 3, its purpose is to correct any differences between the purchase order (PO) prepared by the foodservice establishment and the delivery slip or invoice that is signed at the time the ordered goods are delivered. If, for example, ten cases of Tanqueray gin have been ordered on a given day, but only five cases of Tanqueray and, erroneously, five cases of Beefeater gin are delivered, the vendor's delivery invoice will not match the purchase order. In this situation, you may want to instruct your delivery clerk to refuse delivery of the five cases of Beefeater, while accepting the five cases of Tanqueray. A credit memo deleting the charge for the five cases of Beefeater would be filled out and signed by both your beverage receiving clerk and the liquor delivery person. This would ensure that you received and paid for the proper merchandise. Figure 4.11 shows the method for completing a credit memo such as this. Credit memos are as useful for receiving food and paper products as they are for receiving beverages. The documents may be numbered, if so desired, but for good control they should be made in triplicate so that one copy can be returned to

FIGURE **4.11** ● Credit Memo

Credit Memo #: 322 Unit Name: LeRae's Date: 1/9
Vendor: Hagen's Liquors Vendor Invoice Number: 307J571

Correction

Item	Quantity	Short	Refused	Price	Credit Amount
Beefeater Gin	5 cases		X	$137.09	$685.45
Total					$685.45

Explanation: _Ordered 10 cases Tanqueray Gin. Received 5 Cases Beefeater Gin by mistake._
Vendor Representative: _T. Ride_
Operation Representative: _I. M. Thinkin_

the purchasing agent, one attached to the invoice itself and sent to accounting, and one for the driver to take back to the vendor.

Storing Beverage Products

While the shelf life of most beverage products is relatively long, alcoholic beverages, especially wine, must be treated in a very careful manner. Beverage storage rooms should be easily secured since beverages are often expensive items and are a favorite target for both employee and guest theft. These storage areas should, of course, be kept clean and free of insect or rodent infestations, and they should be large enough to allow for easy rotation of stock. Many beverage managers use a **two-key system** to control access to beverage storage areas. In this system, one key is in the possession of the individual responsible for the beverage area. The other key, used when the beverage manager is not readily available, is kept in a sealed envelope in the safe or other secured area of the operation. Should this key be needed, management will be aware of its use since the envelope will be opened. Of course, it is up to management to ascertain the validity of the use of this key should the envelope be opened.

Liquor Storage

Spirits should be stored in a relatively dry storage area between 70 and 80°F (21 to 27°C). Since these products do not generally require refrigeration, they may be stored along with food products, if necessary. An organized, well-maintained area for spirits will also ensure that purchasing decisions will be simplified since no product is likely to be overlooked or lost. In addition, care should be taken that access to liquor storage areas is strictly limited.

Beer Storage

Beer in kegs should be stored at refrigeration temperatures of 36 to 38°F (2–3°C) because keg beer is unpasteurized and, thus, must be handled carefully to avoid excessive bacteria. When receiving and storing canned and bottled beer, it is also important to examine freshness dates. If these dates are not easily discernible, you should demand that the vendor explain to you the coding system that is being used. Pasteurized beer in either cans or bottles should be stored in a cool, dark room at 50 to 70°F (10–21°C) but does not, of course, require refrigeration.

Storage areas should be kept clean and dust free. Canned beer, especially, should be covered when stored to eliminate the chance of dust or dirt settling on the rims of the cans. Nothing is quite as disturbing to a beer drinker than to find the top of a cold beer can covered with dirt or foreign material that cannot be removed. Because that is true, it is a good idea for the individual issuing canned beer to the bar to rinse beer can tops prior to delivering these products for use in the bar.

Product rotation is critical if beer is to be served at its maximum freshness, and it is important that you and your team devise a system to ensure that this happens. The best method is to date each case or six-pack as it comes in. In this manner, you can, at a glance, determine whether proper product rotation has occurred.

Wine Storage

Wine storage is the most complex and time-consuming activity required of beverage storeroom personnel. Depending on the type and volume of the restaurant, extremely large quantities of wine may be stored. In general, the finer wines in the United States are sold in bottles of 750 ml. Foreign wines are generally sold in bottles of approximately this size, but the contents may vary by a few milliliters more or less. Sometimes, larger bottle sizes may be sold, especially of sparkling wine, such as champagne. A tremendously underutilized bottle size that may also be purchased and stored is the **half-bottle or split,** which is about half the size of the 750-ml bottle. If you find that large numbers of couples or two-person groups are coming to your restaurant, it is simply unrealistic to assume that they will have before-dinner drinks, a full 750-ml bottle of wine with dinner, and then finish the meal with coffee and after-dinner drinks. In today's age of caution about drinking and driving, the trend is away from this kind of consumption, and if wine sales are to maintain their current levels, operators would do well to provide the option of the half-bottle to their guests.

Regardless of bottle size stored, the techniques for proper wine storage must be followed in all cases if the quality of the product is to be maintained and product losses are to be kept at a minimum. Despite the mystery associated with wine storage, the effective manager will find that proper wine storage can be achieved if the following factors are monitored:

1. Temperature
2. Light
3. Cork condition

Temperature A great deal of debate has centered around the proper temperature at which to store wine. All can agree that red wine should be served at cellar temperature. There is, however, less agreement about what exactly is meant by "cellar temperature." When serving white wine by the glass, we may find that the proper storage temperature, at least for the containers currently being used, is refrigerator temperature. Obviously, this would not do for a case of fine red wine. But, generally speaking, most experts would agree that wines should be stored at a temperature of 50 to 65°F (10–18°C). If you find, however, that wines must be stored at higher temperatures than this, the wine storage area should be as cool as can reasonably be achieved, and it is important to remember that, while wine may improve with age, it improves only if it is properly stored. Heat is an enemy of effective wine storage.

Light Just as wine must be protected from excess heat, it must also be protected from direct sunlight. In olden times, this was achieved by storing wines in underground cellars or caves. In your own foodservice establishment, this means using a storage area where sunlight cannot penetrate and where the wine will not be subject to excessive fluorescent or incandescent lighting. With regard to light, the rule of thumb for storing wine is that it should be exposed only to the minimum amount necessary.

Cork Condition   It is the wine's cork that protects it from oxygen, its greatest enemy, and from the effects of **oxidation.** Oxidation occurs when oxygen comes in contact with bottled wine; you can detect a wine that has been overly oxidized because it smells somewhat like vinegar. Oxidation deteriorates the quality of bottled wines; thus, keeping oxygen out of the wine is a prime consideration of the vintner and should be important to you as well.

Cork has proven, over the years, to be the bottle sealer of choice for most wine producers. Quality wines demand quality corks, and the best wines are fitted with cork sealers that should last many years *if* they are not allowed to dry out. This is the reason wine should be stored in such a manner that the cork remains in contact with the wine and, thus, stays moist. In an effort to accomplish this, most foodservice managers store wines on their sides, usually on specially built wine racks. Corks should be inspected at the time the wine is received and periodically thereafter to ensure that there are no leaks resulting in oxidation and, thus, damaged products. If a leak is discovered, the wine should be refused; if the leak occurs during storage, the wine should be examined for quality and then either consumed or discarded, as appropriate.

In general, you can effectively manage the storage of wines if you think about how you should treat the cork protecting the wine. If the cork is always kept

1. Cool
2. In the dark
3. Moist

then the wine the cork is protecting is likely to be properly stored.

Proper beverage storage techniques are important if you hope to have the desired amount of product ready and available for service during the beverage production process. In most instances, wine and beer will be consumed directly from their original containers. With spirits, on the other hand, the bartender will probably find that the guest prefers the spirit mixed with some other product to make the beverage fit his or her personal preference. While this presents no particular problem in making the drink, it does raise a unique costing and control issue for you.

Bar Transfers

While the great majority of product cost related to bar operations is in the area of beverages, you must also manage the cost of those items associated with the preparation and service of beverage products. In the case of wine and beer, there are, in general, no additions to the beverage prior to serving and, thus, no additional product costs. As far as spirits are concerned, however, a great number of nonalcoholic food products may be served as a part of the drink order. To illustrate this, assume that a guest in your bar orders Irish coffee. This popular drink has as its two primary ingredients, Irish whiskey and brewed coffee. The cost of the spirit itself should clearly be charged to the cost of operating the bar. A question arises, however, on how to account for the coffee. In this case, coffee is as central to the preparation of the drink as the whiskey itself. If your operation is a standalone bar, accounting for the cost of purchasing the coffee is not complex. If the bar is, however, operated as part of a larger foodservice operation, the ground coffee used to make the brewed coffee in the bar may have to come from the general foods storeroom. When that is the case, the transfer of the product, and its associated costs, from the kitchen *to* the bar must be controlled and recorded. If this is not done, the food cost percentage in the restaurant will be artificially inflated, while the total cost of beverage sold percentage in the bar will be understated. This same issue exists with products like cherries, limes, lemons, cream, coffee, sugar, and a host of other items, which may be ordered as regular food products for the kitchen but are needed by and transferred to the bar area. Similarly, many foodservice operators use items from the bar when preparing menu items for service in the dining room. Using a bottle of beer from the bar to prepare bratwurst in the kitchen would be an example of a transfer of products from the bar *to* the kitchen. Wines may frequently be used by the kitchen to produce some items. In fact, a close working relationship between kitchen and bar management is helpful as both areas attempt to assist each other to the best of their ability in providing needed ingredients and in helping to utilize any carryover products.

The control procedure for kitchen and bar transfers is quite simple. To be effective, it requires nothing but consistency. Assume that you manage the Surfside Bar, on the beach in Florida. Figure 4.12 is an example of what your transfer record for the first week of January might be. It is the type of form that you can use to monitor product flow either to or from the bar. Should you prefer it, a separate form can be used for each transfer area, but, for most operators, Figure 4.12 would be sufficient. Note that the form requires the initials of both the person receiving and the person issuing the product. In addition, space is available to compute the sum total of all product values at the end of the accounting period. These figures

FIGURE **4.12** ● Transfer Record

Location: Surfside Bar   Month/Date: 1/1–1/7

Product Value

Date	Item	Quantity	To Bar	From Bar	Issued By	Received By
1/1	Lemons	6	$ 0.72		T. S.	B. H.
	Limes	2	0.28		T. S.	B. H.
	Cream	2 qt.	4.62		T. S.	B. H.
1/2	Chablis	1 gal.		$11.10	B. H.	T. S.
1/3	Coffee	2 lb.	10.70		T. S.	B. H.
1/4	Cherries	½ gal.	12.94		T. S.	B. H.
1/4	Lemons	4	0.48		T. S.	B. H.
	Limes	2	0.28		T. S.	B. H.
	Ice Cream (vanilla)	1 gal.	13.32		T. S.	B. H.
1/5	Pineapple Juice	½ gal.	3.00		T. S.	B. H.
1/6	Tomato Juice	1 case	20.00		T. S.	B. H.
1/6	Sherry	750 ml		6.70	B. H.	T. S.
1/7	Celery	1 bunch	0.54		T. S.	B. H.
Total Product Value			66.88	17.80		

would then be used to adjust, as needed, either cost of food sold data or cost of beverage sold data. This procedure will be discussed in detail later in this chapter. In either case, the principle is that all product costs should be assigned to the area of the operation that is reporting the sale of that product.

Computing Cost of Beverages

The proper computation of beverage cost percentage is identical to that of food cost percentage with one important difference. Typically, there is no equivalent for employee meals since the consumption of alcoholic beverage products by employees who are working should be strictly prohibited. Thus, "employee drinks" would never be considered as a reduction from overall beverage cost.

Consider the situation you would face as manager of Rio Lobo's, a popular Tex-Mex-style restaurant that does a high volume of alcoholic beverage sales. To prepare your drinks, your bartenders use limes, lemons, and fruit juices from the kitchen. You would, of course, like your beverage cost percentage to reflect all the costs associated with the actual ingredients used in drink preparation. You keep excellent daily records of the number of food products transferred from the kitchen to the bar, as well as the dollar value of these transfers. In this operation, there are no transfers from the bar to the kitchen as there might be, for instance, in a French restaurant that uses wine extensively in its recipes. Figure 4.13 details how you would compute your actual cost of beverage sold for a month where the following data represent your operating results:

Operating Data
Rio Lobo's

1. Beverage sales   = $100,000
2. Beginning inventory = $ 24,405
3. Ending inventory   = $ 18,741.25
4. Purchases   = $ 21,986.40
5. Transfers to bar   = $ 2,140
6. Transfers from bar   = $ 0

Note, again, that beginning inventory for this accounting period is the ending inventory figure from the prior accounting period.

FIGURE **4.13** ● Cost of Beverage Sold

	Accounting Period: 1/1 to 2/1	
	Unit Name: Rio Lobo's	
Beginning Inventory	$24,405.00	
PLUS		
Purchases	21,986.40	
Goods Available for Sale		$46,391.40
LESS		
Ending Inventory		18,741.25
		27,650.15
LESS		
Transfers from Bar		0
		27,650.15
PLUS		
Transfers to Bar		2,140.00
Cost of Beverage Sold		$29,790.15

Special Features of Liquor Inventory

Determining beginning and ending inventory levels for beverage products is generally more difficult than determining these same levels for food. Food items can most often be weighed, counted, or measured for inventory purposes. Of course, any of these methods may be used for liquor inventory, should you choose to do so. Unopened containers of beer, wine, and spirits can, of course, be counted. Opened containers, however, must be valued also. It is the process of valuing these opened containers that will present a challenge to you. Three inventory methods are commonly in use to accomplish this goal. They are:

1. Weight
2. Count
3. Measure

Liquor Inventory by Weight

The weight method uses a scale to weigh open bottles of liquor. This system is effective if you remember to subtract the weight of the empty bottle itself from the total product weight and if you remember that each liquor, due to its unique specific gravity (density), must be weighed separately. Because some liquors are heavier than others, 3 fluid ounces of each, for example, would not weigh the same amount. Figure 4.14 lists the specific gravity of some common products used to make the colorful pousse-café, a layered drink that relies on the fact that differing spirit products have different weights (the more dense liquids will fall to the bottom of the glass). Just as your bartender will use his or her knowledge of specific gravity to create drinks, you can use that same knowledge to weigh the amount of product in an opened bottle and, thus, establish its inventory value.

FIGURE **4.14** ● Specific Gravity of Selected Liqueurs

Liqueur or Cordial	Color	Specific Gravity
Kirsch	Clear	0.940
Sloe Gin	Red	1.040
Rock and Rye	Amber	1.065
Triple Sec	Clear	1.075
Peach Brandy	Peach	1.085
Blue Curaçao	Blue	1.120
Crème de Cacao	Brown	1.150
Crème de Cassis	Purple	1.170
Crème de Banana	Yellow	1.180

Liquor Inventory by Count

Counting full bottles is easy; counting the value of partial bottles is more difficult. You can do it rather quickly and fairly accurately, however, if you use the tenths system. This system requires that the inventory taker assign a value of 10/10 to a full bottle, 5/10 to a half bottle, and so on. Then, when inventory is taken, the partial bottle is examined and the appropriate "tenth" is assigned, based on the amount left in the bottle. While this system results in an approximation of the actual amount in a bottle, many managers feel the tenths system is accurate enough for their purposes. It does have the advantage of being a rather quick method of determining inventory levels of open bottles.

Liquor Inventory by Measure

Some beverage managers determine product levels of open bottles by using a ruler to determine the amount the bottle contains. Dollar values are then assigned to each inch or portion of an inch for inventory evaluation purposes. This method has a high degree of accuracy and is favored by many.

In general, it is important to take liquor inventories at a time when the operation is closed so that product quantities on hand do not change when the inventory is being taken. It is also important that product contained in the lines of mechanical drink-dispensing systems be counted if the quantity of product in these lines is deemed to be significant.

Returning to the Rio Lobo example, regardless of the method used to determine the actual value of ending inventory, with sales of $100,000 and a cost of beverage sold of $29,790.15, you would apply the beverage cost percentage formula as follows:

$$\frac{\text{Cost of Beverage Sold}}{\text{Beverage Sales}} = \text{Beverage Cost \%}$$

$$or$$

$$\frac{\$29,790.15}{\$100,000.00} = 29.79\%$$

Again, it is important to note that transfers both to and from the bar must be accounted for, if and when they occur. These adjustments will affect the overall product cost percentages in the kitchen and the bar. In addition, computing transfers to the bar will help your bar staff remember that the use of fruit juices, milk, cherries, lemons, limes, and the like do impact the total cost effectiveness of the bar.

There are a large number of factors that can influence the actual beverage cost percentage you achieve. Many of these factors are discussed in Chapter 5. Note, however, that *guests themselves* can contribute to relatively major changes in food or beverage cost percentages, both on the plus and on the minus side of the ledger. This is due to the concept that food and beverage operators call the sales mix or product mix. Our preferred term is the former.

Sales Mix

Sales mix is defined as the series of guest purchasing decisions that result in a specific food or beverage cost percentage. Sales mix affects overall product cost percentage anytime guests have a choice among several menu selections, each one having its own unique product cost percentage.

To illustrate the effect of sales mix on beverage cost percentage, assume that you are the food and beverage director at the Raider Resort, a 400-room beachfront property on the Gulf Coast of Texas. In addition to your regular restaurant, you serve beverages in three basic locations. They are as follows:

1. Banquet beverages for receptions prior to meal events, typically served in your grand ballroom, foyer, or outdoors; banquet beverages are also served during meal functions.
2. The Starlight Bar, an upscale bar with soft piano music that appeals to the 50+ guest.
3. Harry O's, a bar with indoor and poolside seating. Contemporary Top 40 music in the evenings draws a younger crowd interested in dancing.

You compute a separate beverage cost percentage for each of these beverage outlets. Figure 4.15 details the separate operating results for each outlet and an overall percentage for the three units using the standard beverage cost percentage formula.

You know that each beverage location uses the same portion size for all standard drinks. Well and call liquors, as well as wine-by-the-glass brands, are constant in all three locations. Since, in this resort setting, you dislike the difficulty associated with serving draft beer, beer is sold in cans or bottles only. In addition, bartenders are typically rotated on a regular basis through every serving location. Should you be concerned that your beverage cost percentage varies so greatly by service location? The answer, in this case, is that you have no cause for concern. In this situation, it is sales mix not poor control that governs your overall beverage cost percentage in each individual location. A close examination of Figure 4.16, #1, #2, and #3, will reveal how this can happen.

Although product cost percentages are constant in each location for beer, wine, and spirits, the *overall* beverage cost percentage is not. The rea-

FIGURE **4.15** ● Raider Resort

Monthly Beverage Percentage Report			
Location	Cost of Beverages	Beverage Sales	Beverage Cost %
Banquets	$20,500	$ 80,000	25.6%
Starlight Bar	10,350	45,500	22.7
Harry O's	16,350	67,000	24.4
Total	47,200	192,500	24.5

son that each unit varies in total beverage cost percentage is due to sales mix, or the guests' selection of product. In other words, guests, and not management alone, have helped to determine your final beverage cost %. While you can certainly help shape guest selection by such techniques as cost controls, effective pricing, menu design, and marketing, to some degree it is the guest who will determine overall cost percentage through sales mix. This is true in both the beverage and the food areas. In the case of the Raider Resort, it is easy to analyze the sales mix by examining Figure 4.17, a detailing of the beverage products guests selected in each beverage outlet.

Each sales percent in Figure 4.17 was computed using the formula:

$$\frac{\text{Item Dollar Sales}}{\text{Total Beverage Sales}} = \text{Item \% of Total Beverage Sales}$$

Therefore, in the case of beer sales in the banquet area using the data from Figure 4.16:

$$\frac{\text{Banquet Beer Sales}}{\text{Total Banquet Beverage Sales}} = \text{\% Banquet Beer Sales}$$

or

$$\frac{\$10,000}{\$80,000} = 12.5\%$$

FIGURE **4.16** ● Raider Beverage Outlets

Monthly Beverage Percentage Recap			
#1 Outlet Name: Banquets		Month: January	
Product	Cost of Beverages	Beverage Sales	Beverage Cost %
Beer	$ 2,500	$10,000	25.0%
Wine	12,000	40,000	30.0
Spirits	6,000	30,000	20.0
Total	20,500	80,000	25.6
#2 Outlet Name: Starlight Bar			
Product	Cost of Beverages	Beverage Sales	Beverage Cost %
Beer	$ 3,750	$15,000	25.0%
Wine	1,500	5,000	30.0
Spirits	5,100	25,500	20.0
Total	10,350	45,500	22.7
#3 Outlet Name: Harry O's			
Product	Cost of Beverages	Beverage Sales	Beverage Cost %
Beer	$11,250	$45,000	25.0%
Wine	2,100	7,000	30.0
Spirits	3,000	15,000	20.0
Total	16,350	67,000	24.4

As indicated, each beverage outlet operates with a unique sales mix. Figure 4.17 shows that, in the banquet area, the mix is heavy in wines and spirits, the choice of many guests when they are at a reception or dining out. The Starlight Bar clientele is older, and their preferred drink tends to be spirits. Harry O's, on the other hand, caters to a younger crowd that

FIGURE **4.17** ● Raider Resort

Beverage Sales Percentage Recap				
Unit	Beer	Wine	Spirits	Total Sales
Banquets	12.5%	50.0%	37.5%	100%
Starlight Bar	33.0%	11.0%	56.0%	100%
Harry O's	67.0%	10.5%	22.5%	100%

prefers beer. Thus, you may rest assured that, despite controls that are in place, costs that are in line, and effective management policies, variations in beverage cost percentages can still occur due to sales mix, rather than other confounding factors.

Beverages are, and will remain, an important part of the hospitality industry. Marketed and consumed properly, they enhance many an occasion and in the hands of the thoughtful and conscientious manager, they are a powerful profit center.

Now that we know who is coming (Chapter 2), and we have enough food (Chapter 3) and beverages (Chapter 4) available to be served, we turn into one of the most challenging aspects of foodservice management, namely managing the food and beverage production process.

Key Terms and Concepts

The following are terms and concepts discussed in the chapter that are important for you as a manager. To help you review, please define the terms below.

Alcoholic beverages	House wine	Premium liquors
Beer	Jigger	Broken case
Wine	Product request log	Fresh dated
Spirits	Tapped keg	Two-key system
Dramshop laws	Wine list	Half-bottle or split
License states	Vintner	Oxidation
Control states	Well liquors	Sales mix
Keg beer/Draft beer	Call liquors	

Test Your Skills

1. Gil Bloom is planning for the wedding of the mayor's daughter in his hotel. The reception, to be held in the grand ballroom, will be attended by 1,000 people. From his sales histories of similar events, Gil knows that the average drinking habits of those attending receptions of this type are as follows:

   25% select champagne
   50% select white wine
   25% select spirits

   Assuming three drinks per person and a portion size of 3 ounces for champagne, 4 ounces for wine, and 1 ounce for spirits, how much of each product, in 750-ml bottles, should Gil order? (Multiply fluid ounces by 29.57 to convert to milliliters.) If you were Gil, would you order more than you think you would need? Why or why not? If so, how much more would you order?

Beverage Selection	Percent Selecting	Total Guests	# of Guests Selecting	# of Drinks per Guest	# of Portions	Portion Size (oz.)	Amount Needed (oz.)	Total Milliliters	Total Bottles (750 ml)
Champagne	0.25								
Wine	0.50								
Spirits	0.25								

2. Jim Heeb operates a magical restaurant called Shazam! In it, he features both excellent food and magic shows. The lounge is popular since that is where the magic is viewed. Help Jim first calculate his transfers to and from the bar and then help him compute his cost of beverage sold percentage using the following data for the month of January:

Sales	$15,000
Beginning inventory	5,000
Purchases	1,000
Ending inventory	3,500

			Product Value			
Date	Item	Quantity	To Bar	From Bar	Issued By	Received By
1/1	Lemons	40	$ 2.40		T. A.	B. P.
1/2	Coffee	12 lb.	25.20		T. A.	B. P.
	Cream	2 qt.	1.60		T. A.	B. P.
1/3	Chablis	1 gal.		$ 5.20	B. P.	T. A.
	Ice Cream	½ gal.	3.33		T. A.	B. P.
1/4	Pineapple Juice	1 gal.	3.00		T. A.	B. P.
	Sherry	½ gal.		7.10	B. P.	T. A.
1/5	Celery	1 cs.	9.72		T. A.	B. P.
1/6	Olives	1 gal.	8.50		T. A.	B. P.
1/7	Brandy	750 ml.		10.00	B. P.	T. A.
Total						

Beginning Inventory	Purchases	Ending Inventory	Transfers to Bar	Transfers from Bar	Cost of Beverage Sold	Beverage Cost %

3. Mary Louise operates a popular French restaurant in a large midwestern city of the United States. Her establishment is a favorite both for its cozy cocktail area and for its superb cuisine, patterned after that of the

Nantes area of France. Mary Louise keeps excellent records on all of her product usage. She wishes to compute, for the month of January, cost of goods sold in the food, beer, wine, and spirits areas. In effect, she desires a separate product cost percentage for each of these four areas. In addition, she has determined that the value of all transfers from the kitchen to the bar will be assigned to the "spirits" area for cost purposes.

a. Given the following data, compute these four cost percentages.

Sales

Food	$175,000
Beer	$ 12,000
Wine	$ 45,000
Spirits	$ 51,000

Employee Meals $ 3,500

Transfers from Bar

Beer	$ 125
Wine	$ 1,800
Spirits	$ 425

Transfers to Bar $ 960

Beginning Inventory

Food	$ 45,800
Beer	$ 4,500
Wine	$ 65,000
Spirits	$ 6,400

Ending Inventory

Food	$ 41,200
Beer	$ 4,400
Wine	$ 66,900
Spirits	$ 8,050

Purchases

Food	$ 65,400
Beer	$ 2,900
Wine	$ 15,400
Spirits	$ 11,850

	Beginning Inventory	Purhcases	Ending Inventory	Employee Meals	Transfers from Bar	Transfers to Bar	Cost of Goods Sold	Cost %
Food								
Beer								
Wine								
Spirits								
Total Beverage								

b. Calculate Mary Louise's Sales Mix (sales percentages) for beer, wine, and spirits. Then create, either manually or electronically, a pie chart like the following that shows these percentages.

Beverage Sales Mix

Chapter

5 MANAGING THE FOOD AND BEVERAGE PRODUCTION PROCESS

OVERVIEW   In this chapter, you will learn the methods used to issue and prepare food and beverage products in a cost-effective manner, including steps you can take to minimize theft and spoilage. You will also discover how to estimate the costs you will incur in producing the menu items you sell. In addition, you will learn how to compare the cost results you actually achieve with those you planned to achieve, and discover methods to reduce your costs if they begin to get too high.

CHAPTER OUTLINE

Managing the Food and Beverage Production Process
Product Issuing
Inventory Control
Managing the Food Production Area
Managing the Beverage Production Area
Employee Theft
Determining Actual and Attainable Product Costs
Reducing Overall Product Cost Percentage
Key Terms and Concepts, and Test Your Skills

HIGHLIGHTS   At the conclusion of this chapter, you will be able to:

○ Use management techniques to control the costs associated with preparing food and beverages for guests.
○ Compute the actual cost of producing a menu item and compare that cost against the cost you should have achieved.
○ Apply various methods to reduce the cost of goods sold percentage.

Managing the Food and Beverage Production Process

Once you have ordered and received the food and beverage products you believe will be purchased by your guests, your concern turns toward the most important function of all, controlling the food and beverage production process. If any activity were at the heart of foodservice management and control, it would be this. To study this process, assume that you are the manager of Scotto's Supper Club. Scotto's is a high-volume, business/upscale-clientele steakhouse. Business is good both during the lunch period and in the evenings. Volume is especially heavy on Friday and Saturday nights, as well as Sunday brunch. As you prepare for another week of business, you would review your sales history, forecasts, purchase orders, and menu specials. You would do these things to take the first step in the production process: developing your kitchen production schedules.

Production Schedules

Fundamentally, each foodservice manager is in charge of kitchen production. How much of each item to prepare may be a joint decision between you and your chef or production manager, but it is you who must ultimately take the responsibility for proper production decisions. The complete production process involves the following steps:

1. Maintain sales histories.
2. Forecast future sales levels.
3. Purchase and store needed food and beverage supplies.
4. Plan daily production schedules.
5. Issue needed products to production areas.
6. Manage the food and beverage production process.

Planning daily production schedules is important because you will want to have both the products and the staff needed to properly service your guests. If, for example, you forecast that 50 chocolate cakes will be needed on a given day for the college residence hall you manage, then you must have both the products and the staff necessary to produce the cakes. In a similar manner, if you know that 500 pounds of ground beef must be cooked for your burger restaurant, then the ground beef and the staff to prepare it must be secured. In this chapter, we will examine the food and beverage production process; in Chapter 7, we will consider the planning required to secure the labor needed to produce these products.

Ideally, the process of determining how much of each menu item to prepare on a given day would look as follows:

**Prior-Day Carryover + Today's Production
= Today's Sales Forecast ± Margin of Error**

The margin of error amount should be small; however, since projecting sales and guest counts is an imprecise science at best, most foodservice managers will find that they must produce a small amount more than they anticipate selling each day. This is to minimize the chances of running out of an important menu item. Of course, with some menu items, preparation does not begin until the sale is made. A New York strip steak, for example, will not be cooked until it is ordered. An order for coconut cream pie, however, cannot be filled in the same manner. It is because of items like coconut cream pie that production sheets are necessary. Figure 5.1 demonstrates the production sheet in use at Scotto's.

Reviewing Figure 5.1, you can see that you had 15 servings of prime rib left over from the prior day's operation. You would know that by looking at the carryover section of the *prior* day's production sheet. Since you anticipate sales of 85 servings of prime rib, it might seem that only 70 servings should be prepared (70 new servings + 15 carryovers from prior day = 85). In fact, you would prepare a number of new servings that is slightly higher than anticipated demand. The reason is simple: if you have more guests come in than anticipated or if more of the guests that you did forecast select prime rib, you do not want to run out of the item. There is no standard percentage that should be overproduced for a given item. The amount you plan to make will depend on a variety of factors, including your own knowledge of your guests and the importance or nonimportance of running out of a given item. Standard overages tend to run 5 to 10% above normal forecasts. For purposes of this example, assume that five extra servings of prime rib is the amount of overproduction you deem appropriate for this item.

In the case of broccoli, you make the decision not to carry over any broccoli that was not sold on the prior day. If any such product exists, it could be used to make soup or, if there is no appropriate use for it, discarded because the quality of precooked broccoli is not at the same high level as that of freshly cooked broccoli. Regardless of the type of operation you manage, you will likely find that some of your menu items simply do not retain their quality well when they are carried over. Again, in the case of broccoli, proposed production exceeds anticipated demand by a small margin (10 servings). In the case of the coconut cream pie, you make the decision to produce none on this particular day. This is because this item is made in large quantities, but not each day. With 70 servings available and an anticipated demand of 41, you have enough to carry your operation through this day and, perhaps, the next as well.

At the end of the evening service period, you would enter the number sold in the appropriate column and make a determination on how much, if any, of each product you will carry over to the next day. Some foodservice managers preprint their production sheets listing all menu items and, thus, ensure that production levels for each major menu item are considered on a daily basis. Others prefer to use the production sheet on an "as needed" basis. When this is the case, it is used daily, but only for the items to be prepared that day. Either method is acceptable, but pro-

FIGURE **5.1** ● Production Schedule

Unit Name: <u>Scotto's Supper Club</u>   Date: <u>1/1</u>

	Menu Item	Sales Forecast	Prior-Day Carryover	New Production	Total Available	Number Sold	Carryover
1.	Prime Rib	85	15	75	90		
2.	Broccoli	160	0	170	170		
3.	Coconut Cream Pie	41	70	0	70		
4.							
5.							
6.							
7.							
8.							
9.							
10.							
11.							
12.							
13.							
14.							
15.							
16.							
17.							
18.							

Special Instructions: <u>Thaw turkeys for Sunday preparation</u>

Production Manager: <u>S. Antony</u>

duction schedules in and of themselves are critical to operational efficiency.

When your kitchen production staff knows what you want them to produce for a given meal period, they can move to the next logical step, which is to **requisition,** or request, the inventory items they must have to produce the menu items indicated by your production schedule. These inventory items are then **issued,** that is, taken from storage and placed into the food and beverage production areas. In both the food and the beverage production process, the issuing of products from the storage area is a critical part of the control process.

Product Issuing

Getting necessary beverage, food, and supply products from the storage area in smaller properties may be as simple as entering the locked storeroom, selecting the product, and locking the door behind you. In a more complex operation, especially one that serves alcoholic beverages, this method is simply inadequate to achieve appropriate control.

The act of requisitioning products from the storage area need not be unduly complex. Often, however, foodservice managers create difficulties for their workers by developing a requisition system that is far too time consuming and complicated. The difficulty in such an approach usually arises because management hopes to equate products *issued* with products *sold* without taking a physical inventory. In reality, this process is difficult, if not impossible, to carry out.

Consider, for example, the bar area of Scotto's Supper Club. If, on a given night, you attempt to match liquor issued to liquor sold, you would need to assume that all liquor issued today is sold today *and* that no liquor issued on a prior day was sold on this day. This will, generally, not be the case. In the kitchen, some items issued today, for example, coconut cream pie, will be sold over several days; thus, in the same way as for liquor, food products issued will not relate exactly to products sold. It is simply good management to see an issuing system as one of providing basic product security, and an inventory control/cost system as a separate entity entirely. Given that approach, let us observe how Scotto's issuing system can be designed to protect the security of food and beverage products, and then move to the process of inventory control, with a view toward achieving effective cost control and purchasing.

The process of requisitioning and issuing food, beverages, and supplies to employees need not be tremendously complicated. Remember that employees should requisition food and beverage items based on management-approved production schedules. While special care must be taken to ensure that employees use the products for their intended purpose, maintaining product security can be achieved with relative ease if a few principles are observed:

1. Food, beverages, and supplies should be requisitioned only as needed based on approved production schedules.
2. Required items (issues) should be issued only with management approval.
3. If a written record of issues is to be kept, each person removing food, beverages, or supplies from the storage area must sign, acknowledging receipt of the products.
4. Products that do not ultimately get used should be returned to the storage area, and their return recorded.

Some foodservice operators who employ a full-time storeroom person prefer to operate with advance requisition schedules. This process can sometimes be helpful because requisition schedules for tomorrow's food, for instance, can be submitted today, thus allowing storeroom personnel the time to gather these items prior to delivering them to the kitchen. Occasionally, products are even weighed and measured for kitchen personnel, according to the standardized recipes to be prepared. When this system is in place, the storeroom is often called an **ingredient room.** Figure 5.2 illustrates the kind of food and supplies requisition form you might use at Scotto's.

Note that the requested amounts and issued amounts may vary somewhat. In the case of rice, it is relatively easy to issue exactly the amount requisitioned because the rice can be weighed. In the cases of broccoli and rib roast, however, the nature of the product itself may make it impossible to exactly match the amount issued with the amount requisitioned. In other cases, the storeroom may be out of a requested item completely.

Note also that the total cost is arrived at by computing the value of the issued amount, not the requisitioned amount. This is so because it is the value of the issued amount that has actually been removed from inventory and, thus, will ultimately be reflected in the cost of food sold computations.

If you wish to do so, the Unit Cost and Total Cost columns may be omitted. If they are to be included, it is important to remember that their primary role is to remind employees that *all food items have a cost.* It is not recommended that these dollar amounts be considered as being equal to the cost of goods sold. That system might work in a manufacturing or shipping company but is not sufficiently accurate for use in foodservice.

It is vital that a copy of the storeroom requisition form be sent to the purchasing agent after it has been used so that this individual will have a sense of the movement of product in and out of the storage areas. The form in Figure 5.2, or one similar to it, could also be used by your bar manager at Scotto's to serve as a record of the product requisitions and issues to the bar from the kitchen. As we have seen, you must know the dollar value of these transfers to accurately compute the cost of beverage sold.

FIGURE **5.2** ● Storeroom Requisition

Unit Name: <u>Scotto's Supper Club</u>   Requisition #: <u>0221</u>

Date: <u>1/15</u>

Item	Storage Unit	Requested Amount	Issued Amount	Unit Cost	Total Cost
Rice	1 lb.	5 lb.	5 lb.	$0.25/lb.	$ 1.25
Broccoli	1 lb.	30 lb.	28.5 lb.	$0.90/lb.	$ 25.65
Rib Roast	1 lb.	100 lb.	103.5 lb.	$6.40/lb.	$662.40
Total					$689.30

To: Kitchen   X   Requisition Approved By: <u>S.A.R.</u>
     Bar _____   Requisition Filled By: <u>T.A.P.</u>

Product Issuing: Special Concerns for Beverages

The basic principles of product issuing that apply to food and supplies also apply to beverages. There are, however, special concerns that must be addressed when issuing beverage products. Assume that, as the manager of

Scotto's, you have developed a system whereby beverage issues routinely are one of two types:

1. Liquor storeroom issues
2. Wine cellar issues

Liquor Storeroom Issues   While several methods of liquor issues could be in place, one choice you would have as a manager, and the system favored by the authors, is to implement the **empty for full system** of liquor replacement. In this system, each bartender is required to hold empty liquor bottles in the bar or a closely adjacent area. At the conclusion of the shift, or at the start of the next shift, each empty liquor bottle is replaced with a full one. The empty bottles are then either broken or disposed of, as local beverage law requires.

Figure 5.3 illustrates the requisition form you would use to issue liquor products with the empty for full system. Note that this requisition form does not include unit or total price on product issued since monitoring those costs should be a function of the liquor storeroom personnel or management and not the bartender. You could, of course, elect to include the unit and total costs on the requisition should you so desire.

It is important to note that all liquor issued from the liquor storage area should be marked in a manner that is not easily duplicated. This allows management to ensure, at a glance, that all liquor sold is the property of the foodservice operation and not that of a bartender who has produced his or her own bottle for the purpose of going into an illicit partnership with the operation. In a partnership of this type, the operation supplies the guest, while the bartender provides the liquor and then pockets the product sales and profit! While bottle marking will not prevent dishonest bartenders from bringing in their own liquor, it will force them to pour their product into the operation's bottles and to dispose of their own empties, which does make the process more difficult.

Occasionally, it may be necessary for a bartender or supervisor to enter the liquor storeroom area during a shift. Typically, when this need arises, you or your management designee will be available to meet the bartenders' product needs. There may be occasions, however, when the bartenders themselves must enter the beverage storage area. In preparation for this possibility, management should have a key, sealed in an envelope, and then signed over the seal so that it cannot be opened without detection. This key should only be used if the manager or supervisor is not immediately available. When it is used, management should be notified immediately of its use. If the key is used, it should be made clear that an adequate explanation of this occurrence will be expected. It is wrong not to give employees controlled access to the products desired by your guests, but it is equally wrong to allow employees this access without your knowledge.

FIGURE 5.3 ● Liquor Requisition

Unit Name: <u>Scotto's Supper Club</u>

Shift: <u>P.M.</u>

Date: _____ <u>1/15</u>
Service Area: <u>Cocktail Lounge</u>

_____ Verified by Management

Product	Number of Empties	Bottle Size	Bartender	Management
Old Crow	6	750 ml	P.O.F.	S.A.R.
Tanqueray	4	750 ml	P.O.F.	S.A.R.
Peach Schnapps	2	1,000 ml	P.O.F.	S.A.R.
Seagrams 7	3	750 ml	P.O.F.	S.A.R.
Jack Daniel's	2	750 ml	P.O.F.	S.A.R.
Absolut Vodka	8	1,000 ml	P.O.F.	S.A.R.
Total Empties	25			

Wine Cellar Issues The issuing of wine from a wine cellar is a special case of product issuing because these sales cannot be predicted as accurately as sales of other alcoholic beverage products. That is, you may know that a given percentage of your guests are likely to select wine, but you may not know the specific wine they will select. This is especially true in an operation where a large number of valuable wines are routinely stored. If the wine storage area contains products valuable enough to remain locked, it is reasonable to assume that each bottled wine issued should be noted. You can use Figure 5.4 to record your operation's wine-issuing activity.

This form may be used to secure wine for either the bar or the kitchen, as well as for dining room sales. In the case of transfers to the kitchen or the bar, it should be noted that the product has been directed to one of these two locations, rather than having been assigned to a guest check number. Forcing servers to identify a guest check number when requesting wine will ensure that, at the conclusion of the shift, wine issues will match wine sales. If the wine is to be sent to a guest as "complimentary," or "comp," that can be noted as well, along with the initials of the management personnel authorizing the "comp." In the case of the wine cellar issue, the form itself should remain in the wine cellar for use by the wine-purchasing agent, while a copy should be sent to management for review.

Estimating Daily Costs Using the Issues System

For operations that prefer to use a strict issue and requisition system, it is still possible to estimate product usage on a daily basis. This is done using the six-column estimate, but not by using "purchases" as discussed in Chapter 3. Rather, in an issues system, the dollar amount of "issues" is used to form the basis of the estimate.

In Chapter 3, the rationale for estimating cost of food sold on a regular basis was presented using a six-column format. This same technique can be used to estimate other product costs also. Consider the case of Shondra Jackson. Shondra operates a busy Irish pub in a large hotel and would like to have a daily estimate of her beverage costs. She completes her physical inventory on the last day of each month, yet, because of the time it takes for her corporate office to produce and distribute a final month-end profit and loss statement, it is after the seventh or eighth day of the next month before she is informed of the prior month's beverage cost percentage. At that point, of course, the previous month has come and gone. Shondra has been "surprised" by high costs in this process more than she can bear! In an effort to generate more current data about her operation, Shondra analyzes her daily beverage issues and finds them to be as shown in Figure 5.5 for the first 10 days of January.

Shondra determines her daily issues amount by simply adding the total of all beverage requisitions she has filled during the day. That is, she reviews all requisition/issue forms that resulted in product going into the bar and determines their total dollar value. At the end of each day, Shondra records total operational sales and, using her beverage issues totals, fills in the six-column beverage estimate form shown in Figure 5.6. Data for the period 1/1 to 1/10 have been entered.

FIGURE **5.4** ● Wine Cellar Issues

Unit Name: <u>Scotto's Supper Club</u>

Date: <u>1/1</u>

	Product	Vintage	Number of Bottles	Guest Check #	Removed By
1.	Bolla Soave	1998	2	60485 L	T. A.
2.	Glen Ellen Cabernet Sauvignon	1991	1	60486 L	S. J.
3.	Barton & Guestier Medoc	1994	1	Manager's "comp"	S.A.R.
4.	Copperridge Cabernet	Current Stock	1	Kitchen	S.A.R.
5.	Bolla Soave	1998	1	60500 M	S. J.
6.	Copperridge Cabernet	Current Stock	1	Bar stock	S.A.R.
7.					
8.					
9.					
10.					
11.					
12.					

Remarks: #4 Requested by Chef 1/1

#6 House Wine Sent to Bar Area 1/1

FIGURE **5.5** ● Beverage Issues Recap

The Irish Pub	Date: 1/1–1/10
Date	**Total Issues**
1/1	$ 945.00
1/2	785.00
1/3	816.50
1/4	975.40
1/5	1,595.50
1/6	1,100.20
1/7	18.40
1/8	906.50
1/9	1,145.25
1/10	546.25
Total	**$8,834.00**

As can be seen, the six-column form requires only that you divide to-day's issues by today's sales to arrive at the today estimate. The formula for day 1/1 is as follows:

$$\frac{\text{Issues Today}}{\text{Sales Today}} = \text{Beverage Cost Estimate Today}$$

or

$$\frac{\$945.00}{\$1,450.22} = 65.2\%$$

FIGURE **5.6** ● Six-Column Beverage Cost Estimate

Unit Name: **The Irish Pub**   Date: 1/1–1/31

	Issues		Sales		Beverage Cost Estimate	
Date	**Today**	**To Date**	**Today**	**To Date**	**Today**	**To Date**
1/1	$ 945.00	$ 945.00	$1,450.22	$ 1,450.22	65.2%	65.2%
1/2	785.00	1,730.00	1,688.40	3,138.62	46.5%	55.1%
1/3	816.50	2,546.50	2,003.45	5,142.07	40.8%	49.5%
1/4	975.40	3,521.90	1,920.41	7,062.48	50.8%	49.9%
1/5	1,595.50	5,117.40	5,546.50	12,608.98	28.8%	40.6%
1/6	1,100.20	6,217.60	5,921.27	18,530.25	18.6%	33.6%
1/7	18.40	6,236.00	495.20	19,025.45	3.7%	32.8%
1/8	906.50	7,142.50	1,292.20	20,317.65	70.2%	35.2%
1/9	1,145.25	8,287.75	1,381.51	21,699.16	82.9%	38.2%
1/10	546.25	8,834.00	1,548.21	23,247.37	35.3%	38.0%
Subtotal		**$8,834.00**		**$23,247.37**		**38.0%**
+/−		**−$1,000.00**				
Total		**$7,834.00**		**$23,247.37**		**33.7%**

The To Date columns represent cumulative totals of both issues and sales. Therefore, Shondra adds today's issues to the issues total of the prior day. She does the same with the sales figure. Thus, on 1/2, the to date estimate would be as follows:

$$\frac{\text{Issues to Date}}{\text{Sales to Date}} = \text{Beverage Cost Estimate to Date}$$

or

$$\frac{\$1,750.00}{\$3,138.62} = 55.1\%$$

Shondra's 10-day beverage cost estimate is 38%. Notice that her *daily* cost estimate varies greatly. Notice also, however, that the To Date column is beginning to settle in the mid- to high-30 range and that it remains there, despite rather major changes in the daily cost estimates. This is because each passing day adds to both the issues and the sales cumulative total. By the 10th or 11th day, it is unlikely that normal changes in daily issues activity will move the to date figure in a substantial way.

It is important to note that Shondra does not know, at this point, what her actual cost of beverage sold really is for this 10-day period. That, of course, can only be determined by a physical inventory and the application of the cost of beverage sold formula presented in Chapter 4 of this text. Shondra's estimate, however, will be *extremely* close to her actual cost of goods sold percentage, if one assumption she makes is either true or nearly true. That assumption is, if you remember, that Shondra's bar inventory remains constant or nearly constant in total dollar value from month to month. If this assumption is true, then Shondra's estimate will be quite accurate.

Of course, it is unlikely that bar inventory levels are *exactly* the same from month to month or from accounting period to accounting period. It is true, however, that these values should not change a great deal. In fact, if changes are slight, the monthly estimate will be extremely close to the actual cost of beverage sold figure. Note that Figure 5.6 has, at the bottom, an entry point to adjust issues back to actual inventory levels at the end of the accounting period. If, for example, ending inventory is lower than beginning inventory, the difference between the two numbers is *added* to the issues total. If ending inventory is higher than beginning inventory, the difference between these two numbers will be *subtracted* from the issues total. In this way, management can determine actual cost of beverage sold if all issues have been accounted for and an ending physical inventory has been taken.

In this example, Shondra's ending inventory is $1,000 higher than her beginning inventory. Thus, this amount is subtracted from the issues to date total to arrive at her true cost of beverage sold. As can be seen in Figure 5.6, when the $1,000 is subtracted from issues to date, Shondra's cost can be computed as

$$\frac{\text{Issues to Date} - \text{Inventory Adjustment}}{\text{Sales to Date}} = \text{Cost of Beverage Sold}$$

or

$$\frac{\$8,834.00 - \$1,000.00}{\$23,247.37} = 33.7\%$$

Inventory levels can vary based on the delivery days of vendors, the day of the week inventory is taken, and even the seasonality of some businesses. Because of this variability, it is critical that you perform the month-end inventory adjustment. Because it keeps costs uppermost in the minds of managers and employees alike, it is recommended that the issues cost estimate be posted where all employees can see it. It daily communicates both sales and the costs required to generate those sales to employees and lets them see the importance of controlling product usage.

Inventory Control

Regardless of the methods used by employees to requisition food and beverage products, or management to issue these, inventory levels will be affected. It will be your responsibility and that of your purchasing agent to monitor this movement and purchase additional products, as needed. Restocking the inventory is critical if product shortages are to be avoided and if product necessary for menu item preparation is to be available. Nothing is quite as traumatic for the foodservice manager than to be in the middle of a busy meal period and to find that the operation is "out" of a necessary ingredient or frequently requested menu item. Therefore, you must carefully monitor inventory levels. It would obviously be very expensive and time consuming to monitor each ingredient, food product, and all supplies on an individual daily basis. The average foodservice operation stocks hundreds of items, each of which may or may not be used every day. The task could be overwhelming.

Imagine, for example, the difficulty associated with monitoring, on a daily basis, the use of each sugar packet or cube in a high-volume restaurant. Taking a daily inventory of the use of such a product would be akin to spending $10 to watch a penny! The effective foodservice manager knows that proper control involves spending time and effort where it is most needed and can do the most good. It is for this reason that many operators practice the ABC method of inventory control.

ABC Inventory Control

To fully understand the principles of ABC inventory control, you first must be very familiar with the concepts of physical inventory and perpetual inventory.

A **physical inventory** is one in which an actual physical count and valuation of all inventory on hand is taken at the close of each accounting period. A **perpetual inventory** system is one in which the entire inventory is counted and recorded, then additions to and deletions from total inventory are recorded as they occur. Both physical and perpetual inventories have advantages and disadvantages for the foodservice operator. The physical inventory, properly taken, is the most accurate of all since each item is actually counted and then valued. It is the physical inventory, taken at the end of the accounting period (ending inventory), that is used in conjunction with the beginning inventory (the ending inventory value from the prior accounting period) to compute the cost of food sold. In turn, the cost of food sold determines actual product usage and is used to compute the food cost percentage (see Chapter 3). Despite its accuracy, the physical inventory suffers from being extremely time consuming. Even with the use of software programs that can extend inventory (multiply number of units by unit cost) or handheld bar scanners that assist in the process, counting each food and beverage item in storage can be a cumbersome task. It is important that the individuals who actually count the inventory be well trained in the process. Guessing at the weights of products, such as prime ribs and roasts, must not be allowed. If you are to control overall costs, accuracy in taking the physical inventory is critical.

Perpetual inventory seeks to eliminate the need for frequent counting by adding to the inventory when appropriate (receiving slips) and subtracting from inventory when appropriate (requisitions or issues). Perpetual inventory is especially popular in the area of liquor and wine, where each product may have its own inventory sheet or, in some cases, a **bin card.** A bin card is simply an index card or other record that details additions to and deletions from a given product's inventory level. Figure 5.7 illustrates the use of such a card.

Bin cards are especially useful for food products, such as staples and dry goods. Of course, the accurate use of a perpetual inventory system requires that each change in product quantity be noted. In the ideal situation, perpetual inventory systems, regardless of the form they take, could be verified by the physical inventory for costing purposes.

Some managers prefer to use the same form for recording both the quantity and the price of an inventory item. This can be done by using a

FIGURE **5.7** ● Bin Card

| Product Name: Canadian Club | | Bottle Size: 750 ml | |
| Balance Brought Forward: 24 | | Date: 12/31 | |

Date	In	Out	Total on Hand
1/1	4		28
1/2		6	22
1/3		5	17
1/4	12		29

perpetual inventory card. Perpetual inventory cards are simply bin cards, similar to the one in Figure 5.7, but they include the product's price at the top of the card. A new perpetual inventory card is created each time the product's purchase price changes, with the quantity of product on hand entered on the new card. Perpetual inventory cards should be kept in an index file in chronological order. This system allows for continual tracking of the quantity of items on hand and their prices. At month's end, a physical inventory can be taken and the *actual* prices of items can be applied to the inventory value. For example, if six cases of corn are sitting on the shelf at the end of the month, three cases purchased this week at $10.00 per case (3 × $10 = $30) and three cases purchased last week at $11.00 per case (3 × $11 = $33), then the inventory value would equal $30 + $33 = $63. By using perpetual inventory cards, the manager can determine the *actual* value of the inventory rather than only using the last price paid for the month, which is often done with physical inventories.

Today, many managers use computer spreadsheets and spreadsheet programs to set up bin cards and perpetual inventory cards electronically. In addition, some POS systems include inventory components that can be as simple as maintaining an electronic perpetual inventory system with accurate prices or as complex as a scanner system that is used to electronically record additions to and subtractions from inventory.

Of course, the accurate use of a perpetual inventory system requires that each change in product quantity be noted. In the ideal situation, the perpetual inventory, whether using bin cards, perpetual inventory cards, or a scanner, needs to be verified by the physical inventory when taken for costing purposes. Again, in the ideal situation, perpetual inventory quantities would match actual product counts. The reasons for discrepancies in quantity are many, not the least of which is that employees, when in a hurry, simply forget to update the perpetual system. For example, products, such as canned green beans, may be removed from inventory in the morning but may not be used and, thus, will be returned in the afternoon. Knowing this, the employee may elect to wait and adjust the perpetual inventory just once, at the end of the day. Obviously, shortcuts like these begin to wear at the accuracy of the perpetual inventory.

In the foodservice industry, it is not wise to depend solely on a perpetual inventory system. While a lone perpetual inventory system may make sense for some businesses, the foodservice industry, because of its complexity, does not appear to be one of them. There are, however, advantages to the perpetual inventory system that must be acknowledged, among them the ability of the purchasing agent to quickly note quantity of product on hand, without resorting to a daily physical inventory count.

Physical or Perpetual Inventory

When making the decision about whether to use a physical or perpetual inventory system, the question is, "Which of the two systems is best?" The answer is, "Neither is best, so use the best of both." This is exactly what the ABC inventory system attempts to do. It separates inventory items into three main categories:

Category A items are those that require tight control and the most accurate record keeping. These are typically high-value items, which can make up 70 to 80% of the total inventory value.
Category B items are those that make up 10 to 15% of the inventory value and require only routine control and record keeping.
Category C items make up only 5 to 10% of the inventory value. These items require only the simplest of inventory control systems.

Returning to the hypothetical example of Scotto's Supper Club, assume that the following 10 items are routinely held in your inventory:

1. Precut New York strip steak
2. Prepared horseradish
3. Eight-ounce chicken breasts (fresh)

4. Garlic salt
5. Onion rings
6. Crushed red pepper
7. Dried parsley
8. Lime juice
9. Fresh tomatoes
10. Rosemary sprigs

As can be seen, even with this short list, you have a variety of items in inventory. Some, like the New York strip steak, are very valuable, highly perishable, and critical for the execution of your menu. Others, like the crushed red pepper, are much less costly, not highly perishable, and may not dramatically affect the operation if you ran out between deliveries. Clearly, these two example items should not be treated the same for inventory purposes. The simple fact is that they are not equally critical to the operation's success. The ABC system helps you determine which items deserve special, perhaps daily attention, and those you may spend less time managing.

To develop the A, B, and C categories, you simply follow these steps:

1. Calculate monthly usage in units (pounds, gallons, cases, etc.) for each inventory item.
2. Multiply total unit usage times purchase price to arrive at the total monthly dollar value of product usage.
3. Rank items from highest dollar usage to lowest.

In a typical ABC analysis, 20% of the items will represent about 70 to 80% of the total monthly product cost. This represents the A product category. It is not critical that the line between A, B, and C products be drawn at any given point. Many operators use the following guide, but it can be adapted, as you see fit:

Category A–Top 20% of items
Category B–Next 30% of items
Category C–Next 50% of items

It is important to note that, while the percentage of items in category A is small, the percentage of total monthly product cost the items account for is large. Conversely, while the number of items in category C is large, the total dollar value of product cost the items account for is small. It is important to note that the ABC inventory system is concerned with monetary value of products, not count. Returning to the Scotto's example may help make the distinction of the ABC system clear. One item on your menu is New York strip steak. The preparation of this item is simple. Your cook sprinkles the steak with garlic salt and cooks it to the guest's specification. The steak is then garnished with one large onion ring, which you buy frozen. In this example, these inventory items would likely be grouped as follows:

Scotto's Strip Steak	
Ingredient	**Inventory Category**
New York Strip Steak	A
Onion Ring	B
Garlic Salt	C

Figure 5.8 shows the complete result of performing an ABC analysis on the 10 menu items listed previously and then ranking those items in terms of their inventory value.

FIGURE **5.8** ● ABC Inventory Analysis on Selected Items

Item	Monthly Usage	Purchase Price	Monthly Value	Category
Precut New York Strip Steak	300 lb.	$ 7.50/lb.	$2,250.00	A
8-Ounce Chicken Breasts (Fresh)	450 lb.	2.10/lb.	945.00	A
Fresh Tomatoes	115 lb.	0.95/lb.	109.25	B
Onion Rings	30 lb.	2.20/lb.	66.00	B
Rosemary Sprigs	10 lb.	4.50/lb.	45.00	B
Prepared Horseradish	4 lb.	2.85/lb.	11.40	C
Lime Juice	2 qt.	4.10/qt.	8.20	C
Garlic Salt	2 lb.	2.95/lb.	5.90	C
Crushed Red Pepper	1 oz.	16.00/lb.	1.00	C
Dried Parsley	4 oz.	4.00/lb.	1.00	C

The ABC inventory system specifically directs your attention to the areas it is most needed. Reducing product costs, especially for category A items, is extremely important and is discussed more fully later in this chapter. Figure 5.9 details the differences in handling items in the A, B, and C categories.

The ABC system attempts to focus management's attention on the essential few items in inventory, while focusing less attention on the many low-cost, slow-moving items. Again, it is important to note that management's time is best spent on the items of most importance. In the case of inventory management, these are the category A and, to a lesser degree, category B items.

The ABC system can be used to arrange storerooms or to determine which items should be stored in the most secure area. Regardless of the inventory management system used, however, whether it is the physical,

FIGURE **5.9** ● Guide to Managing ABC Inventory Items

Category	Inventory Management Techniques
A	1. Order only on an as-needed basis. 2. Conduct perpetual inventory on a daily or, at least, weekly basis. 3. Have clear idea of purchase point and estimated delivery time. 4. Conduct monthly physical inventory.
B	1. Maintain normal control systems; order predetermined inventory (par) levels. 2. Monitor more closely if sale of this item is tied to sale of an item in category A. 3. Review status quarterly for movement to category A or C. 4. Conduct monthly physical inventory.
C	1. Order in large quantity to take advantage of discounts if item is not perishable. 2. Stock constant levels of product. 3. Conduct monthly physical inventory.

perpetual, or ABC inventory, management must be strict in monitoring both withdrawals from inventory and the process by which inventory is replenished. The reasoning behind this is quite simple. While it is critical that you know how to compute your cost of goods sold and, thus, your food cost percentage, accurate inventory records allow you to know much more about your operation. To illustrate, consider Figure 5.10, which details Scotto's food usage in five major inventory categories. In this case, you have decided to categorize your product usage in terms of broad categories of food. In other words, while you are interested in your overall food cost percentage, you are also interested in your meat cost percentage, produce cost percentage, and so on. When the storeroom inventory is set up as a series of mini-inventories, this approach is possible. It simply requires you to determine desired subcategories and then use inventory valuation sheets that match these groups.

FIGURE **5.10** ● Inventory Recap

Unit Name: <u>Scotto's Supper Club</u> Date: <u>January 31</u>

	Meat	Seafood	Dairy	Produce	Other	Total
Beginning Inventory	$26,500	$ 4,600	$ 7,300	$ 2,250	$23,000	$ 63,650
Purchases	33,800	17,700	4,400	15,550	1,800	73,250
Goods Available	60,300	22,300	11,700	17,800	24,800	136,900
Ending Inventory	28,000	10,900	6,000	4,500	21,000	70,400
Cost of Food Consumed	32,300	11,400	5,700	13,300	3,800	66,500
Employee Meals	900	200	100	250	50	1,500
Cost of Food Sold	31,400	11,200	5,600	13,050	3,750	65,000

These groups may be determined in any manner management feels is appropriate. At Scotto's, meat, seafood, dairy, produce, and "other" items comprise the five major categories. Figure 5.10 details food usage at Scotto's when monthly food sales are $190,000 and total cost of food sold equals $65,000, yielding a food cost percentage for the month of $65,000/$190,000 = 34.2%.

Given sales of $190,000 for the month of January, you can now determine both food cost percentages by category and product usage ratios. You compute your **category food cost %,** that is, a food cost percentage computed on a portion of total food usage, by using the cost of food sold/sales formula. This is illustrated in Figure 5.11.

In each category group, including the total, you would use $190,000 as the denominator in your food cost percentage equation and the cost of food sold in each category as the numerator. The proportion of total cost percentages is developed by the formula:

$$\frac{\text{Cost in Product Category}}{\text{Total Cost in All Categories}} = \text{Proportion of Total Product Cost}$$

FIGURE **5.11** ● Food Cost Category %/Proportion

	Scotto's		Sales: $190,000
Category	Cost of Food Sold	Food Cost %	Proportion of Total Cost
Meat	$31,400	16.53%	48.31%
Seafood	11,200	5.89	17.23
Dairy	5,600	2.95	8.62
Produce	13,050	6.87	20.08
Other	3,750	1.97	5.77
Total	65,000	34.21	100.00

Thus:

$$\frac{\text{Cost in Meat Category}}{\text{Total Cost in All Categories}} = \text{Meat Cost Proportion of Total Cost}$$

In this example:

$$\frac{\$31,400}{\$65,000} = 48.31\%$$

By using the categories listed in Figure 5.11, you are better able to determine when your costs are above those you would expect. Using the category food cost percentage, you know, for example, that meats accounted for 48.31% of your total food usage in the month of January. You can compare this figure to the meat expense of prior months to determine whether your meat cost percentage is rising, declining, or staying constant. If your category or overall percentages are higher than you anticipated, you must find out why. One possible reason for costs that are higher than you expect is the food and beverage production process itself. The food and beverage production process is also one of the most complex and difficult to manage unless you truly understand how it influences your total operation and your costs.

Managing the Food Production Area

Often, those individuals who manage restaurants do so because they relish managing the **back of the house,** or kitchen production area, of the food facility. Managing food production to produce tasty, nutritious, and cost-effective meals is one of the most challenging and enjoyable aspects of foodservice management. Managing the food production process entails control of the following five areas:

1. Waste
2. Overcooking
3. Overserving
4. Improper carryover utilization
5. Inappropriate make or buy decisions

Waste

Food losses through simple product waste can play a large role in overall excessive cost situations. This waste may be simple to observe, as when an employee does not use a rubber spatula to get all of the salad dressing out of a 1-gallon jar, or as difficult to detect as the shoddy work of the salad preparation person who trims the lettuce just a bit more than management would prefer. This would, of course, reduce the amount of usable lettuce available to make salads and result in higher costs. Management must show its concern for the value of products on a daily basis. Each employee should be made to realize that wasting food affects the profitability of the operation and, thus, their own economic well-being. In general, food waste is the result of poor training or management inattentiveness. Unfortunately, some managers and employees feel that *small* amounts of food waste are unimportant. Your primary goal in reducing waste in the food production area should be to maximize product utilization and minimize the "it's only a few pennies worth" syndrome.

Overcooking

It is a truism that prolonged cooking reduces product volume, whether the item cooked is roast beef or vegetable soup! Cooking times on standardized recipes must be carefully calculated and meticulously followed. It is important to remember that, in many ways, heat is the enemy of well-prepared foods. Too much time on the steam table line or in the holding oven extracts moisture from products and, thus, fewer portions are available for service. Figure 5.12 details the change in portion cost when yield is reduced in a roast prime rib of beef due to overcooking.

If we assume that a properly cooked pan of roast beef yields 50 pounds EP and costs $6.00 per EP pound, the total product cost equals $300.00 (50 pounds × $6.00/pound = $300.00). In its properly cooked state, the roast beef would yield 100 eight-ounce portions, for a cost of $3.00 per portion. As you can see, increased cooking time or temperature can cause product shrinkage, which increases average portion cost.

While the difference between a portion cost of $3.00 and $3.53 may seem small, it is the control of this type of production issue that separates the good foodservice manager from the outstanding one.

In attempting to control loss due to overcooking, you must strictly enforce standardized recipe cooking times. This is especially true for meats, soups, stews, baked goods, and the like. Moreover, extended cooking times can result in total product loss if items are placed in an oven, fryer, steam equipment, or broiler and then "forgotten." It is, therefore, advisable to supply kitchen production personnel with small, easily cleanable timers for which they are responsible. This can help, substantially, in reducing product loss due to overcooking.

FIGURE **5.12** ● Prime Ribs

Effect of Overcooking on Portion Cost of 50 Pounds (800 Ounces) of Roast Beef			
			50# EP Cost = $300
Preparation State	Ending Weight (oz.)	Number of 8-Ounce Portions	Portion Cost
Properly prepared	800	100	$3.00
Overcooked 15 min.	775	97	3.09
Overcooked 30 min.	750	94	3.19
Overcooked 45 min.	735	92	3.26
Overcooked 60 min.	720	90	3.33
Overcooked 90 min.	700	88	3.41
Overcooked 120 min.	680	85	3.53

Overserving

No other area of food and beverage cost control has been analyzed and described as fully through articles, speeches, and even books as the control of portion size. There are two reasons for this. First, overportioning on the part of service personnel has the effect of increasing operational costs and may cause the operation to mismatch its production schedule with anticipated demand. For example, assume that 100 guests are expected and 100 products are produced, yet overportioning causes us to be out of product after only 80 guests have been served. The remaining 20 guests will be left clamoring for "their" portions, which, of course, have already been served to others. Also, overportioning must be avoided because guests want to feel that they have received fair value for their money. If portions are large one day and small the next, guests may feel that they have been cheated on the second day. Consistency is a key to operational success in foodservice. Guests want to know exactly what they will get for their money.

It is not possible, of course, to set one standard portion size for all foodservice operations. The proper portion size of an entrée in a college dormitory feeding male athletes will clearly be different from that of an extended-care facility whose residents might be, on average, 85 years old. It is important for you to consider clientele, ambiance, pricing structure, and quality prior to establishing an appropriate portion size for your own operation.

Once portion size has been established, it is up to you to strictly enforce it. Often, employees resist management's efforts. When this is the case, it is a clear indication that management has failed in its mission to provide employees with a basic understanding that underlines the foodservice industry. Employees must be made to see that strict adherence to predetermined portion size is a benefit both to the guest and to the operation. Management must be sensitive, also, to the fact that it is the line, or dining room, server who must deal with the guest who complains about the inadequacy of portion size. Therefore, servers must be made to feel comfortable about predetermined portion sizes so that management, along with the employees, will want to maintain them.

In most cases, tools are available that will help employees determine proper portion size. Whether these are scales, scoops, ladles, dishes, or spoons, employees must have an adequate number of easily accessible portion control devices, if they are to use them. Scoops, for example, are sized based on the number of servings per guest. Thus, a #12 scoop will yield 12 servings per quart, or 48 servings per gallon; a #20 scoop, 20 servings per quart, and so on.

Many portion sizes are closely tied to the purchasing function. In order to serve a ¼-pound hot dog, for instance, one must begin with ¼-pound hot dogs. In a similar vein, if one banana is sliced for addition to breakfast cereals, the purchasing agent must have been diligent in ordering and accepting only the banana size for which management has developed a specification.

Constant checking of portion size is an essential task of management. When incorrect portion sizes are noticed, they must be promptly corrected. If not, considerable cost increases can be incurred. Returning again to our example of Scotto's Supper Club, consider that you purchase, on occasion, and in accordance with your menu plan, 3-pound boxes of frozen yellow corn to be served as your vegetable of the day. Each box costs $2.80. With a total of 48 ounces (3 pounds × 16 ounces = 48 ounces) and an established portion size of 3 ounces, you know that you should average 48 ounces/3 ounces = 16 servings per box. Figure 5.13 demonstrates the effect on total portion cost if one, two, or three servings are lost to overportioning.

As Figure 5.13 demonstrates, a small amount of overportioning on an item as inexpensive as corn costs the operation only a few cents per serving. Those few cents per serving, however, multiplied time after time can mean the difference between a profitable operation and one that is only marginally successful. If your portion cost for corn should have been 17.5

FIGURE **5.13** ● Scotto's

Corn Portion Cost Chart @ $2.80 per 3-lb. Box		
Number of Portions per 3-lb. Box	Portion Size (oz.)	Portion Cost (cents)
16	3.0	17.5
15	3.2	18.7
14	3.4	20.0
13	3.7	21.5

cents ($2.80/16 = 17.5 cents) but, due to overportioning, rises to 21.5 cents ($2.80/13 = 21.5 cents) your costs are 4.0 cents higher than they should be, on this item. If Scotto's is open seven days a week and serves an average of 200 portions of corn per day, your total "loss" for a year would be 365 × 200 × 0.04 = $2,920, enough to buy your operation proper portioning tools. It is also an amount worthy of your attention and correction.

Improper Carryover Utilization

As was discussed earlier in this text, predicting guest counts is an inexact science at best. Because this is true, and because most foodservice operators want to offer the same broad menu to the evening's last diner, as well as its first, it is inevitable that some food that has been prepared will remain unsold at the end of the operational day. In some areas of the hospitality industry, this is a particular problem; in others, it is less of a concern. Consider, for a moment, the operation of a shaved ice or snow cone facility. At the end of the day, any unsold ice is simply held until the next day with no measurable loss of either product quantity or quality. Contrast that situation, however, with a full-service cafeteria. If closing time is 8:00 P.M., management wishes to have a full product line, or at least some of each item, available to the guest who walks in the door at 7:55 P.M. Obviously, in five more minutes a large number of items will become carryover items. Indeed, your ability to effectively integrate carryover items on subsequent days can make the difference between profits and losses. In almost every case, food products are at their peak of quality when they are delivered to the back door. From then on, storage, temperature, and handling work against product quality. These forces are especially at work in the area of carryovers. It is for this reason that production schedules must note carryover items on a daily basis. If this is not done, these items tend to get stored and lost in walk-in refrigerators or freezer units.

You need to have a clear use in mind for each menu item that may have to be carried over. Broiled or sautéed fish may become seafood chowder or bisque. Today's prime rib roast may be the key ingredient in tomorrow's beef stroganoff, and so on. This process can be creative and, if you involve your staff, quite effective.

It is important to understand that carryover foods seldom can be sold for their original value. Today's beef stew made from yesterday's prime rib will not likely be sold at prime rib price. Thus, it is critical that you strive for a minimal carryover. Carryovers generally mean reduced income relative to product value and, thus, reduced profit levels.

There are very few items that do not have some value in their carryover state. Akin to the idea of carryover usage is that of using products that were intended for sale but for which sales did not materialize. Consider the case of a hotel that has been made inaccessible due to a severe snowstorm. A banquet function, planned for the evening, had to be canceled. The items intended to be sold must be used, and quickly! Menu specials, substitutions, and employee meals can be sources of utilization for products like these.

Inappropriate Make or Buy Decisions

Many foodservice operators elect to buy some food products that are preprepared in some fashion. These items, called convenience or ready foods, can be of great value to your operation. Often, they can save dollars spent on labor, equipment, and hard-to-secure food products. They can also add menu variety beyond the skill level of the average kitchen crew. A disadvantage, however, is that these items tend to cost more on a per-portion basis. This is to be expected since these items include a charge for labor and packaging, as well as for the food itself.

Convenience items are not, of course, an all-or-nothing operational decision. Nearly all foodservice operations today use canned products, sliced bread, precut produce, and the like–items that would have been considered convenience items years ago. Therefore, the question is not whether to use convenience items but, rather, how many of a certain kind of convenience item to use. In general, the following guidelines may be of value when determining whether to adopt the use of a convenience product:

1. **Is the quality acceptable?**
   This question must be answered from the point of view of the guest, not management alone.

2. **Will the product save labor?**
   Identifiable labor savings must be discovered if management is to agree that the convenience item will indeed save labor costs.
3. **Would it matter if the guest knew?**
   If an operation has built its image on made-on-premise items, guests may react negatively to "boil in a bag" or microwave-type products.
4. **Does the product come in an acceptable package size?**
   If convenience items are not sold in a size that complements the operation, excessive waste can result.
5. **Is storage space adequate?**
   Many convenience items are delivered to be stored in a refrigerated or frozen form. Your facility must have the needed storage capacity for these items or product quality can be diminished.

Managing the Beverage Production Area

Control in the beverage area is just as important as control in the food production area. In some regards, beverage production is easier than that of food because the variability of product in the beverage area is so much less than that of food. On the other hand, controlling the amount of the product that actually is served to the guest is more complex with alcoholic beverages than with food. As a beverage manager, you will generally have several choices to consider when you decide exactly how you will control your beverage production area.

In its simplest, but least desired form, beverage production can consist of a bartender **free-pouring,** that is, pouring liquor from a bottle without measuring the poured amount. In a situation such as this, it is very difficult to control product costs. At the other end of the control spectrum, some automated beverage-dispensing systems are extremely sophisticated control devices. The following are various beverage control systems that you can use based on the amount of control you feel is appropriate in a specific operation or physical setting.

Free-Pour

As previously mentioned, the lack of control resulting from free-pouring alcohol is significant. It should never be allowed in the preparation of the majority of drinks your bartenders will serve. It is appropriate in some settings, however, for example, in wine-by-the-glass sales. In this situation, the wine glass itself serves as a control device. Also, it is necessary for a bartender to free-pour when he or she must add extremely small amounts of a product as an ingredient in a drink recipe. An example would be a bartender who must add a very small amount of vermouth to a larger martini recipe.

Jigger Pour

A **jigger** is a device (like a small cup) used to measure alcoholic beverages, typically in ounces and portion of ounce quantities. Because jiggers are inexpensive, this control approach is inexpensive. It is also quite portable. In other words, it is a good system to use in remote serving locations such as a pool area, beach, guest suite, or reception hall. The disadvantage, of course, is that there is still room for employee overpouring error and the potential for fraud.

Metered Bottle/Dispenser

In some situations, you may determine that a metered bottle or other metered dispensing unit makes sense. In this case, a predetermined portion of product is dispensed whenever the bartender is called upon to serve that product. A metered draft beer system, for example, may be preset to dispense 12 ounces of beer whenever the bartender uses the draft system to serve a beer. In a like manner, a bottle of vodka may have a metering device (spout) attached to it so that, upon pouring, a preset amount of the product is dispensed.

Beverage Gun

In some large operations, beverage "guns" are connected directly to liquor products. The gun may be activated by pushing a mechanical or electronic button built into the gun. In either case, the bartender may find, for example, that pushing a "gin and tonic" button on a gun device will result in the dispensing of a predetermined amount of both gin and tonic. While the control inherent in such a system is great, the cost, lack of portability, and possible negative guest reaction are limiting factors in its selection.

Total Bar System

The most expensive, but also the most complete, the total bar system combines sales information with product dispensing information to create a complete revenue and product management system. Depending on the level of sophistication and cost, the total bar system can perform one or all of the following tasks:

1. Record beverage sale by brand.
2. Record who made the sale.
3. Post sale to room folio (in hotel).
4. Measure liquor.
5. Add predetermined mixes to drink.

6. Reduce liquor from inventory.
7. Prepare liquor requisition.
8. Compute liquor cost by brand sold.
9. Calculate gratuity on check.
10. Identify payment method, that is, cash, check, credit card.
11. Record guest check number.
12. Record date and time of sale.

You must establish in each location that sells alcohol exactly how much control over the production process you desire. At a supper club like Scotto's, you may elect to use a relatively simple beverage production control system. In the bar area, metering devices used on liquor bottles will allow the bartender only to pour a predetermined amount of liquor, yet give each guest the sense of a drink made to order by the bartender. Larger beverage operations that serve greater amounts of product may find that investing in more sophisticated and costly production control systems can be beneficial. The point to remember here is that you should establish and enforce the level of control you feel is appropriate.

While the control of product cost is critical, it is also very important to designate a proper glass size and ice quantity for each drink. This ensures that the portion size of the drink is consistent with the guest's visual perception of a full glass. The type of ice used is also important. You should select an ice machine that makes ice in a form that you feel best fits your view of proper spacing in the glass and that possesses desirable melting characteristics.

It is also important to remember that not all alcohol sales take place in a traditional, designated bar area. This creates special issues of beverage production management that will be of concern to you. Some of these issues include:

1. In-room mini-bars
2. Bottle sales
3. Open bars
4. Banquet operations

Mini-Bars

Mini-bars, serving 50-ml bottles, have become popular in hotels that cater to the upscale business traveler. The control issue here is one of matching requests by housekeeping for replenishment bottles with guest usage of product. Some large hotels deal with this issue by having a single individual or department charged with the responsibility of filling the mini-bars. If this is not practical, it is critical that bottles be issued only after consumption has been determined. While this will necessitate two trips to the guests' rooms per day, the control features inherent in such a system make it preferable to issuing bottles prior to determining guest usage.

Bottle Sales

When liquor sales are made by the bottle, either through room service, in the case of a hotel, or at a reception area, the control issue is one of verifying bottle count. The guest and the operation must be treated fairly in such a transaction. In the case of full-bottle sales to a guestroom, the guest must be required to sign a receipt accepting the product. It is the only way to avoid potential misunderstandings about cost. In the case of receptions or banquets, guests should be charged only for empty bottles, or, in the case of a purchase of a specified number of bottles, should be shown both full and empty bottles equal to the number used and charged for the event. In an effort to protect both the establishment and the guest from employee theft, the thoughtful beverage manager will mark the bottles for that reception or banquet in a way that is not easily duplicated, thus preventing employees from bringing in their own empty bottles and then removing full ones at the guest's expense.

Open Bars

Open bars, or hosted bars, are those in which no charge is made for the individual drinks at the time they are served because, when the open bar is closed, one total bar charge is assessed against the host of the open bar. Unfortunately, because the individual drinker is not paying for each drink, the open-bar situation can, unless you are vigilant, create an "all you can drink" environment. Open bars are common, especially in cases such as weddings, special-occasion parties, and cocktail receptions.

The production control issues associated with open bars fall into one of two main categories, namely, portion size and accountability. In this environment, guests can cajole bartenders into pouring larger than normal portion drinks. This must, of course, be resisted through management's strict enforcement of the use of jiggers, metered devices, or alternative systems you have put in place. Bartenders, as well as guests, must understand that, while it may be an open bar, someone will be paying the bill at the end of the event. The hosts have the right to expect reasonable portion control if they are paying on a per-drink or per-bottle-used basis. If the foodservice operation has established a per-person charge for the open bar, overportioning costs will have to be absorbed by the operation. This, obviously, necessitates strict control of portion size and total liquor consumption per guest.

As great an issue as overportioning is, accountability looms larger and larger on the horizon as an area of legitimate cost control concern for the effective beverage manager. With states holding liquor sellers responsible for the actions of their patrons through the enactment of dramshop legislation, the entire concept of reasonable and prudent care in beverage operations is called into question. Bartenders who work open bars should be specially trained to spot signs of guest intoxication. As difficult as it may sometimes be, guests should be made aware that it is illegal, in all states, to serve an intoxicated guest. To do so puts the entire food and beverage operation at risk. Some managers have virtually eliminated the open-bar concept, preferring to go to a coupon system where each coupon issued is good for one drink, and the number of coupons issued, rather than the number of drinks, can be controlled. While the possibility exists that coupons can be shared and thus given to an intoxicated guest, the coupon system does demonstrate an attempt by you to exercise reasonable care, an effort that may prove vital in your defense in the event of litigation.

Banquet Operations

The sale of alcoholic beverages during a seated banquet usually takes the form of bottled-wine sales. Guests usually are provided with a set number of bottles on the table, to be shared by those seated at the table. Alternatively, as they consume their wine, they can be served by the waitstaff. It is the latter method that presents cost control problems as the host of the event will be charged by either the number of bottles served or the number of guests served. If the payment is based on the number of bottles served, the bottles should be marked and the empties made available for inspection by either the guest or the banquet captain. If the sale is based on the number of glasses poured, then both the host of the event and the beverage operation must be in agreement as to the desired portion size and the total number of portions to be served.

Employee Theft

Loss of product can happen when systems of control are too slack to prevent employee theft. While all kitchens and beverage operations can expect to experience small amounts of product slippage, such as an apple eaten in secret or a carrot nibbled where the supervisor cannot see it, extensive loss of product is, of course, to be avoided. Product theft can occur in either the bar or the kitchen production areas yet is probably more prevalent in the bar areas.

Reducing Bar-Related Theft

Experienced food and beverage managers seem to have an endless supply of stories related to theft in bar operations. Indeed, bar theft is one of the most frequent types of thefts in the foodservice industry. While it may well be impossible to halt all kinds of bar theft, the following are areas that you should check periodically to ensure proper safeguards.

Order Filled But Not Rung Up   In this case, the bartender delivers the drink as requested by the guest or server, but the drink is never rung up on the POS system, and the bartender simply pockets the sale. All drinks should be recorded by the POS system to prevent this type of theft. Management's vigilance is critical to ensure that no drink is prepared until *after* the ticket is rung up.

Bringing in Extra Product   In this scenario, mentioned earlier in this text, the bartender sells products that he or she has brought in and, of course, pockets the sales. Bottle stamps or markings help prevent this type of theft since nonmarked bottles can be easily detected.

Over- and Underpouring   When bartenders overpour, they are stealing from the operation; when they underpour, they are stealing from the guest. Remember that your bartenders will pour the appropriate amount if you insist that they do so. When bartenders underpour, they may be making up for drinks they have given away or sold but have not rung up. When they overpour, they may be doing so for their friends or for the extra tips this activity may yield. In either case, management must prevent such behavior.

Proper portion size in the spirits area is preserved through the enforced use of jiggers, metered devices, or other mechanical or electronic equipment. In the case of draft beer, **head size,** that is, the amount of foam on top of the glass, directly affects portion size and portion cost and, thus, must be controlled.

Incorrect Change Making   If a bar is extremely busy, and if guests are paying little attention, bartenders may be greatly tempted to give incorrect change for drinks that are sold. This can be as simple as "forgetting" that a guest paid with a $20 bill, and returning change from a $10 bill, or as clever as maintaining that the change was returned to an inattentive guest, when, in fact, no change was returned at all!

Dilution of Product   Often called "watering down the drinks," this method of bar or storeroom theft involves adding water to the product in order to make up for spirits that have either been stolen or given away. It is especially easy to water down products such as gin, vodka, rum, or tequila since these clear spirits will not change color with the addition of water. Detection of this type of theft is rather difficult. Periodic sampling of a known-proof alcohol against bar stock by a knowledgeable food and beverage director is one of the few defenses against such bartender fraud. Since each alcohol product has a particular specific gravity or weight associated with it, you may also check for product dilution through the use of a **hydrometer,** which identifies specific gravity. If water has been added to the bottle of liquor, the specific gravity will change from the value originally associated with that liquor.

Product Theft   Alcohol is a highly desirable product; therefore, its theft is always a possibility. This is especially true in a beverage service area that is secluded or in which the bartender has access to both product inventory and ease of exit. Proper controls as well as strict rules limiting the access of employees to beer, wine, and liquor storage areas should help deter and detect this sort of theft.

Product Substitution   If a call brand liquor has been ordered and paid for, it should, of course, be served. If the bartender, however, substitutes a less expensive well liquor for the call brand, he or she may pocket the difference in price between the two items. This has the effect of shortchanging the guest, who has paid a premium for something he or she did not receive. Conversely, if the guest has ordered a well drink, but the bartender serves from the premium or super premium stock, the guest has received more value than he or she has paid for, and the operation is shortchanged.

While it is impossible to list all types of bar thefts, it is important to note that they can and do occur. Conscientious managers should hire honest bartenders, train them well, and demand that they follow all house policies. Perhaps the best advice of all is simply to be vigilant. Watch the bar area carefully, or enlist the aid of a **spotter,** a professional who, for a fee, will observe the bar operation with an eye toward reporting any unusual or inappropriate behavior by the bartender.

While theft may occur during the normal operation of the bar, it may also occur in the area of receptions and special events. Consider, for a moment, the case of a bride and groom who wish to serve champagne to their guests at the wedding reception, to be held in a local hotel. It is estimated that 10 cases of champagne will be used. The food and beverage director orders 12 cases since it would not be appropriate to run out of champagne. The newlyweds will pay for each bottle used. Potential difficulties loom in two areas, neither of which bode well for the couple. In one scenario, more champagne is used than should have been because the bartenders use larger than normal glasses or pour larger than normal portions. Obviously, this could also happen when serving spirits. In the second scenario, 10 cases are served, as predicted, yet one case ends up in the bartender's automobile trunk. The result is that 11 cases are gone. The bartender maintains that all 11 cases were used. Management, trusting the integrity of the bartender, calls upon the guests to pay for one extra case. Imagine, however, the embarrassment if management is asked by the bride and groom to produce the empty bottles from 11 cases!

While bartenders suffer from a poor reputation in many parts of the foodservice industry, it is important for you to remember that anytime the same individual is responsible for both the preparation of a product and the collection of money for its sale, the opportunity for theft is greatly increased. In a small beverage operation, this situation is common. When you manage an operation such as this, your vigilance is critical and the quality of your control system is crucial.

Reducing Kitchen-Related Theft

Most kitchen-related theft deals with the removal of products from the premises since few kitchen workers also handle cash, as is the case with bartenders. Kitchen workers can, however, work with service personnel to defraud the operation (see Chapter 11). In addition, kitchen workers have access to valuable food and beverage products. The following product security tips are helpful when designing control systems to ensure the safety and security of food and beverage products:

Product Security Tips

1. Keep all storage areas locked and secure.
2. Issue food only with proper authorization and management approval.
3. Monitor the use of all carryovers.
4. Do not allow food to be prepared unless a guest check or written request precedes the preparation.
5. Maintain an active inventory management system.
6. Ensure that all food received is signed for by the appropriate receiving clerk.
7. Do not pay suppliers for food products without an appropriate and signed invoice.
8. Do not use "petty cash" to pay for food items unless a receipt and the product can be produced.
9. Conduct systematic physical inventories of all level A, B, and C products.
10. Do not allow employees to remove food from the premises without management's specific approval.

Determining Actual and Attainable Product Costs

When you have implemented proper control procedures, you can create accurate product cost data. As we have seen, it is important to know and control your overall cost of food sold and your food cost percentage. Truly effective management of the food and beverage production process, however, requires you to know more. For this reason, we now turn our attention to answering an important series of questions:

1. What are our actual product costs?
2. What should our product costs be?
3. How close are we to this attainable goal?

Determining Actual Product Cost

Knowledge of actual product cost begins with a standardized recipe cost for each menu item. Just as each menu item should have a standardized recipe, it should also have a **standardized recipe cost sheet.** The standardized recipe cost sheet is a record of the ingredient costs required to produce an item sold by your operation. This standardized cost sheet may take the form of a physical piece of paper or index card. Increasingly, however, effective managers are using computerized spreadsheet programs to handle this task. Standard spreadsheet programs are an excellent means of creating these records and keeping them current. Properly maintained, cost sheets provide you with up-to-date information that can help with pricing decisions in addition to assisting in comparing your actual costs with those you should incur.

Figure 5.14 shows the format you might use for recipes if you operate Steamer's, a small soup and sandwich carryout kiosk. The recipe, in this example, is for beef stew, which yields a cost per portion of $1.07. A standard recipe cost sheet can be produced in seconds today using a personal computer. This formerly tedious task has become so simplified there is just no reason for management not to have accurate, up-to-date costing sheets on all its recipes. To do any less would mean that we are selling items for a set price when we have no idea what we, ourselves, are paying for that item! The point to remember here is that it is easy today to know exactly what it should cost to produce a menu item if you begin the process with a standardized recipe.

FUN ON THE WEB!

Look up the following sites to view several companies that sell software designed for recipe costing and much more!

www.computrition.com Link to "Products," and click on any category you desire.

www.cbord.com First, link to "Products." Then try out "NetRecipe" and its online demo. Or, click on any of the other products offered.

www.foodsoftware.com Click on "Restaurant Computer Products Catalog," then scroll down to "Incredibly Simple Inventory" and click on it. Scroll down once again and click on "Screen Examples from Incredibly Simple Inventory" to see samples of screens in the program.

www.restaurantplus.com Scroll down and click on "Recipe Costing" to learn about the features and reports available with this software.

www.foodtrak.com Click on "Food-Trak for Windows," then click on "Product Information" or "Sample Reports" to see what this comprehensive food and beverage management software has to offer.

FIGURE **5.14** ● Standardized Recipe Cost Sheet

Unit Name: Steamer's
Menu Item: Beef Stew   Recipe Number: 146

Special Notes: _____   Recipe Yield: _____ 40

All ingredients weighed as edible   Portion Size: _____ 8 oz.

portion (EP) _____   Portion Cost: _____ $ 1.07

Ingredients   Ingredient Cost

Item	Amount	Unit Cost	Total Cost
Corn, Frozen	3 lb.	0.60 lb.	$ 1.80
Tomatoes	3 lb.	1.40 lb.	4.20
Potatoes	5 lb.	0.40 lb.	2.00
Beef Cubes	5 lb.	5.59 lb.	27.95
Carrots	2 lb.	0.36 lb.	0.72
Water	2 gal.	N/A	–
Salt	2 T	0.30 lb.	0.02
Pepper	2 t	12.00 lb.	0.12
Garlic	1 clove	0.80/clove	0.80
Tomato Juice	1 qt.	4.00 gal.	1.00
Onions	4 lb.	1.00 lb.	4.00
Total Cost			**42.61**

Total Recipe Cost: _____ $42.61   Recipe Type: Soups/Stews
Portion Cost: _____ $ 1.07   Date Costed: 4/1
Previous Portion Cost: _ $ 1.01   Previous Date Costed: 1/1

Some managers have difficulty in computing recipe costs because recipes often contain ingredient amounts that are used in a different quantity than they are purchased. For example, you may purchase soy sauce by the gallon, but your recipes may call for it to be added by the cup or tablespoon. When situations such as this arise, the ingredient conversion table presented in Figure 5.15 can be of great value in calculating recipe costs. Weights, measures, and sizes must be accurately computed if your recipe costs are to be precise.

FUN ON THE WEB!

Look up the following site to calculate a variety of recipe conversions!

www.chefdesk.com First, check out "Book of Yields" to learn about a book that would be useful in any kitchen. Next, click on "Free Online Foodservice Calculators," then click on "Conversion Calculator." This is a cool site that will help you cost out almost any recipe!

When costing standardized recipes, many foodservice managers prefer to use whole cent figures rather than fractions of a cent. In addition, many elect to omit seasoning costs completely. They prefer to add a predetermined standard cost to those standardized recipes that contain seasonings. This amount, a percentage of total recipe cost, is determined annually. Thus, if 3% represents the total product category of seasoning cost per year, then 3% would be added to the total ingredient cost to account for seasonings. Still others prefer to identify spices as high or low cost. In our example, salt is designated as a low-cost spice, and a $0.02 cost is assigned to its two tablespoons of product. Pepper is identified as a high-cost spice, and $0.12 has been added to the total recipe to account for its usage. Note that all ingredients are to be costed in their edible-portion, or EP, state. This is extremely important due to the need for accuracy in costing recipes. If EP costs are to be accurate, you must thoroughly understand the concept of product yield presented in Chapter 3, and the effect of that yield on costs. It is to this matter that you must turn your attention if you want to be sure that your standardized recipe cost data are accurate.

Yield Testing

In order to determine actual recipe costs, it may sometimes be necessary to conduct a **yield test** to determine actual EP ingredient costs. A yield test is a procedure used for computing your actual costs on a product that will experience weight or volume loss in preparation. In the beef stew example (Figure 5.14), you would need to compute the EP cost of the beef cubes used in its preparation. Since beef is a major portion of the total recipe cost,

FIGURE **5.15** ● Ingredient Conversion Table

Weight and Measure Equivalents

Item	Equivalent
60 drops	1 teaspoon
3 teaspoons	1 tablespoon
2 tablespoons	1 liquid ounce
4 tablespoons	$1/4$ cup
16 tablespoons	1 cup
2 cups	1 pint
2 pints	1 quart
4 quarts	1 gallon
4 pecks	1 bushel
16 ounces	1 pound

Select Spices*

Pepper: 4.20 tablespoons	1 ounce
Salt: 1.55 tablespoons	1 ounce

Common Can Sizes

Can Size	Quantity
No. 303	$1^3/4$ cups
No. 2	$2^1/2$ cups
No. $2^1/2$	$3^1/2$ cups
No. 5	$7^1/3$ cups
No. 10	13 cups

Conversion Formulas

To Convert	Multiply	By
Ounces to Grams	Ounces	28.35
Grams to Ounces	Grams	0.035
Liters to Quarts	Liters	0.950
Quarts to Liters	Quarts	1.057
Inches to Centimeters	Inches	2.54
Centimeters to Inches	Centimeters	0.39

*Spices have different conversions based on their individual weights.

you would want to make sure that you computed the cost of the beef cubes accurately. As-purchased (AP) meat prices do not include any losses you will incur due to trimming, cooking, or carving. These activities, if undertaken, will, of course, affect the EP cost of the meat products. The same is true for many vegetables, fruits, seafood, and other products.

To illustrate how a yield test results in the determination of actual product cost, assume that you purchased 10 pounds of beef short ribs from which you will cut the beef cubes for your stew recipe. You know that you will have losses because of bone and fat removal, but unlike some other products, such as roast beef, you will have no cooking or slicing loss. You can use a form, such as the one presented in Figure 5.16, to determine your EP meat yields and, thus, your cost per portion. In the case of the beef short ribs for beef stew, if you conducted a yield test you would find the data listed in Figure 5.16.

FIGURE **5.16** ● Butcher's Yield Test Results

Unit Name: <u>Steamer's</u>   Item: <u>Beef Cubes</u>   Date Tested: <u>1/1</u>

Specification: <u># 842</u>   Item Description: <u>Short Ribs</u>

AP Amount Tested: <u>10 lb.</u>

Price per Pound AP: <u>$3.60</u>

Loss Detail	Weight	Use % of Original
AP	10 lb. 0 oz.	100.0%
Fat Loss	1 lb. 6 oz.	13.8%
Bone Loss	2 lb. 3 oz.	21.9%
Cooking Loss	0	0%
Carving Loss	0	0%
Total Product Loss	**3 lb. 9 oz.**	**35.6%**

Net Product Yield: <u>64.4%</u>   EP Cost per Pound: <u>$5.59</u>

Yield Test Performed By: <u>L. D.</u>

In the preceding example, net product yield equals 64.4%. This can be determined by the following formula:

$$\frac{\text{Product Loss}}{\text{AP Weight}} = \text{Net Waste \%}$$

In this example, total product loss is 3 pounds and 9 ounces. If you convert all pounds to ounces for ease of computation, your product loss of 3 pounds and 9 ounces becomes 57 ounces (48 ounces + 9 ounces). Your as-purchased, or AP, weight of 10 pounds equals 10 × 16 ounces, or 160 ounces. Thus:

$$\frac{57 \text{ oz.}}{160 \text{ oz.}} = 35.6\% \text{ Net Waste}$$

To determine the product yield %, you simply subtract the net waste % from 1.00 (100%). In this example, the net product yield % is, therefore, determined to be

1.00 Total − 0.356 Net Waste = 0.644 Product Yield

Another way to determine net product yield % is to compute it directly using the following formula:

$$\frac{\text{EP Weight}}{\text{AP Weight}} = \text{Product Yield \%}$$

In this example, the EP weight is equal to the AP weight of 10 pounds less the product loss of 3 pounds and 9 ounces. Thus, the EP weight equals 6 pounds and 7 ounces (103 ounces), and the product yield % is computed as follows:

$$\frac{103 \text{ oz.}}{160 \text{ oz.}} = 64.4\%$$

To compute the actual EP cost, you must now simply divide the AP price per pound by the product yield % to determine EP cost.

In our example, with an AP price per pound of short ribs of $3.60 and a product yield of 0.644, the EP cost would be $5.59, which is computed using the EP cost formula:

$$\frac{\text{AP Price per Pound}}{\text{Product Yield \%}} = \text{EP Cost (per pound)}$$

or

$$\frac{\$3.60}{0.644} = \$5.59$$

You know, now, that your actual EP cost when buying short ribs of *this particular specification* is $5.59. You should conduct additional butcher yield tests if you are considering changing suppliers, beef short rib specifications, or the source of your beef ribs. In addition, you would want to conduct yield tests on all of your meat items at least twice per year.

Many items, including meats, fruits, vegetables, and the like, should be periodically yield tested. Some computer programs on the market today, including those mentioned previously in this chapter, have components that will conduct yield calculations and compute EP costs for you.

Determining Attainable Product Cost

If you are to draw reasonable conclusions regarding your facility's operational efficiency, you must be able to compare how well you are doing with how well you *should* be doing. This process, which is absolutely necessary, begins with determining **attainable product cost.** Attainable product cost is defined as that cost of goods sold figure that should be achievable given the product sales mix of a particular operation. Simply put, when you compare attainable product cost to actual product cost, you get a measure of operational efficiency. The formula for this operational efficiency ratio is as follows:

$$\frac{\text{Actual Product Cost}}{\text{Attainable Product Cost}} = \text{Operational Efficiency Ratio}$$

To illustrate, assume again that you own Steamer's, the small soup and sandwich carryout kiosk referred to in the previous example. You determine your attainable product cost for a week to be $850, and you actually achieve a product cost of $850 for that same week. Applying the operational efficiency ratio, your results would be evaluated as follows:

$$\frac{\$850 \text{ Actual Product Cost}}{\$850 \text{ Attainable Product Cost}} = 100\%$$

These results represent perfection in the relationship between attainable and actual operational results. More likely, however, if attainable product cost were $850, actual product cost might be higher, say $900. In this case, the formula would be computed as:

$$\frac{\$900 \text{ Actual Product Cost}}{\$850 \text{ Attainable Product Cost}} = 105.9\%$$

In this case, you would know that your actual product usage and, thus, cost is 5.9% higher than your attainable product cost goal.

Chapter 3 described the method used to determine actual product usage through the cost of goods sold formula. Attainable product cost is determined through the use of a form as illustrated in Figure 5.17.

As is evident, total product cost for this week, as determined by the standardized recipes, should have been $1,207.90. Sales were $4,590. You would know your attainable product cost percentage through the use of the following formula:

$$\frac{\text{Cost as per Standardized Recipes}}{\text{Total Sales}} = \text{Attainable Product Cost }\%$$

In our example, then,

$$\frac{\$1,207.90}{\$4,590.00} = 26.3\%$$

FIGURE **5.17** ● Attainable Product Cost

Unit Name: <u>Steamer's</u>

Date Prepared: <u>1/8</u>   Time Period: <u>1/1–1/7</u>
Prepared By: <u>J. M.</u>

Item	Number Sold	Attainable Portion Cost	Total Cost	Menu Price	Total Sales
Beef Stew	150	$1.07	$ 160.50	$1.90	$ 285.00
Corn Chowder	140	0.44	61.60	1.90	266.00
Ham and Bean Soup	160	0.82	131.20	1.90	304.00
Turkey Sandwich	130	1.02	132.60	5.90	767.00
Ham Sandwich	190	1.20	228.00	5.20	988.00
Roast Beef Sandwich	125	1.74	217.50	5.90	737.50
Coffee	175	0.20	35.00	1.85	323.75
Soda	525	0.46	241.50	1.75	918.75
Total			$1,207.90		$4,590.00

Note that this cost excludes any losses due to overcooking, overportioning, waste, theft, and the like. Therefore, the attainable food cost is rarely achieved. Consider, for example, the cost of a product like fresh brewed coffee. While you may be able to compute the cost of producing an 8-ounce cup of coffee, it is much more difficult to estimate the amount of product that must be thrown away on a regular basis to ensure guests are getting only freshly brewed coffee. In addition, every foodservice operation employs people, and people make errors at work. Some managers prefer to compute attainable cost data on specific items, for example, steaks, in a steakhouse restaurant. In this manner, data collection and analysis is simplified, but, at the same time, management can maintain close control over its most important items. In all cases, the use of the operational efficiency ratio can help management answer the question made famous by the former mayor of New York City, Ed Koch: "How'm I doing?"

The attainable food cost and, thus, the operation efficiency ratio is designed to address just that issue. In general, operational efficiency ratings in the range of 100 to 110% are attainable. Variance beyond that, however, can indicate serious control problems. Ratios that are too high, that is, ratios above 110%, could be an indication of excessive waste, ingredient theft, spoilage, or inaccurate recipe cost sheet computation. Operating efficiency ratings that are too low, that is, ratings in the 80 to 90% range, could be the result of miscalculation of the number of items sold, inaccurate ingredient costing, incorrect standardized cost sheets, or errors in valuing inventory. Many managers find that it is helpful to share the operational efficiency results with employees since they also are interested in the question: "How are *we* doing?"

Acceptable and Unacceptable Variance   It is important to realize that you will not treat all variances from expected results in the same manner. For example, a variance of one or two dollars from an expected result of several thousand dollars is small enough that it constitutes an acceptable level of variation. A variance of one or two dollars from an expected result of ten dollars might well be cause for concern and, thus, is likely unacceptable. Figure 5.18 displays the operational efficiency ratios, dollar variances, and percentage variances that might result if you were to compute individual efficiency ratios on a variety of individual products in a steakhouse. The concept that is important here is a simple one. Your attention, as a manager, should be directed toward those areas where the need is greatest. It simply makes little sense to devote the same amount of time addressing a 1% variance as it does a variance of 10%.

As can be seen, results such as those in Figure 5.18 call upon you to make decisions about the acceptability of the variances you may encounter. Efficiency ratings in this example range from 0.90 to 2.00. The $10.00 variance in actual steak cost is likely within an acceptable range. The $10.00 variance in coffee costs is likely unacceptable. In a similar manner, the 10% variance in the cost of Bolla Soave wine may well be worth investigating, while the 10% variation in horseradish and parsley costs may be too small to merit your immediate attention. While it is not

FIGURE **5.18** ● Acceptable and Unacceptable Variance

Item	Actual Cost	Attainable Cost	Efficiency Ratio	Dollar Variance	Percentage Variance
Steaks	$1,010	$1,000	1.01	$10	1%
Coffee	20	10	2.00	10	100
Bolla Soave	550	500	1.10	50	10
Horseradish	22	20	1.10	2	10
Parsley	45	50	0.90	5	10

possible to determine one range of variance acceptability that is appropriate for all food facilities, it is important for you to establish acceptability ranges for your own facility.

Reducing Overall Product Cost Percentage

Once management has determined what costs actually are and has compared them to what costs should be, we often find that Walt Kelly's Pogo character was correct when he said: "We have met the enemy, and they is us!"

Foodservice managers (and their bosses) seem to be on a never-ending quest to reduce food and beverage production costs. While you must remember to guard against inappropriate cost cutting, you will, on occasion, find yourself in a position where food and beverage production costs are deemed to be too high and, thus, must be reduced. When that is the case, effective managers turn to the solutions inherent in the product cost equation.

The food cost percentage equation is extremely interesting. In its simplest form, it can be represented as:

$$\frac{A}{B} = C$$

where:

A = **Cost of Goods Sold**
B = **Sales**
C = **Cost Percentage**

This formula can, however, become extremely complex. Its analysis occupies many a food organization staff meeting and can give the food-service operator many sleepless nights! Essentially, only six reduction strategies are available to influence this rather simple formula. A quick al-gebra lesson, however, prior to our discussion of these six approaches may be useful. In general, the rules of algebra say the following things about the $A/B = C$ formula:

1. If A is unchanged and B increases, C decreases.
2. If A is unchanged and B decreases, C increases.
3. If A increases at the same proportional rate B increases, C remains unchanged.
4. If A decreases and B is unchanged, C decreases.
5. If A increases and B is unchanged, C increases.

Put into foodservice management terms, these five algebraic state-ments can be translated as follows:

1. If costs can be kept constant but sales increase, the cost percentage goes down.
2. If costs remain constant but sales decline, the cost percentage increases.
3. If costs go up at the same rate sales go up, your cost of goods sold percentage will remain unchanged.
4. If costs can be reduced but sales remain constant, the cost percentage goes down.
5. If costs increase with no increase in sales, the cost percentage will go up.

Rarely do foodservice operators feel their product costs are too low. In general, foodservice managers work to control the six variables that impact product cost percentage and, thus, strive to reduce the overall value of C in the equation. A list of these six approaches to reducing overall product cost percentage and a summary of each are presented here to help you devise your own cost reduction strategies:

Reducing Overall Product Cost Percentage

1. Decrease portion size relative to price.
2. Vary recipe composition.
3. Adjust product quality.
4. Achieve a more favorable sales mix.
5. Ensure that all product purchased is sold.
6. Increase price relative to portion size.

To reduce your food costs, you will ultimately select an appropriate strategy from this relatively small number of alternatives. It is the judicious selection and mixing of these approaches that differentiate the successful operator from the unsuccessful one.

For instance, assume that you own and operate a nightclub. You compute your actual liquor cost percentage and determine that it is four percentage points higher than you have budgeted for. If you have approximately six cost-reducing options available to you, by the mathematics law of permutations, this yields ($6 \times 5 \times 4 \times 3 \times 2$), or 720, possible combinations of these differing cost reduction methods. No wonder, then, there is so much information written about reducing costs!

It is not the authors' contention that all product cost reduction methods are exhausted by these six points, but rather they are presented here as a means of systematically analyzing the various alternatives available. While, for illustration purposes, these approaches will be applied to reducing beverage cost %, *they apply equally* to the cost of food sold formula and, thus, to the reduction of food cost.

Decrease Portion Size Relative to Price

Too often, bar operators assume that their standard drink sizes must conform to some unwritten rule of uniformity. This is simply not the case. Most guests would prefer 1 ounce of liquor in a 3- or 4-ounce glass over 1½ ounces in a 6-ounce glass. The point here is that a smaller, high-quality, well-proportioned product is preferable to a drink that may include more liquor but is of such a large overall size that the guest feels his or her drink is "weak." Glass selection becomes very important here, and most glassware salespersons are more than willing to work with you in establishing optimal glass sizes for your specific operation.

The table in Figure 5.19 represents the effect on liquor cost percentage of varying the standard drink size served in an operation using $16.00

FIGURE **5.19** ● Impact of Drink Size on Liquor Cost Percentage at Constant Selling Price of $5.00 per Drink

Drink Size	Drinks per Liter	Cost per Liter	Cost per Drink (cents)	Sales per Liter	Liquor Cost % per Liter
2 oz.	16.5	$16.00	97.0	$ 82.50	19.4%
1³/₄ oz.	18.9	16.00	84.7	94.50	16.9
1¹/₂ oz.	22.0	16.00	72.7	110.00	14.5
1¹/₄ oz.	26.4	16.00	60.6	132.00	12.1
1 oz.	33.0	16.00	48.5	165.00	9.7

per liter as the standard cost of liquor and assuming 0.8-ounce evaporation per 33.8-ounce (1-liter, or 1,000-ml) bottle and a standard $5.00 selling price per drink, which is the amount used to compute sales value in each category.

Certainly, the matter of the perfect drink size is subjective. As such, you must determine the proper drink size for your establishment, taking into account such variables as location, price structure, competition, bar atmosphere, and clientele, to name just a few. While the decision about the proper alcohol content of a drink calls for the balancing of many factors, the effect on liquor cost percentage in varying this content is unmistakable.

Vary Recipe Composition

The proportion of alcohol to mixer has a profound effect on liquor cost percentage. This is especially true for those "specialty" drinks that many operators find so profitable. One option available is to replace high-cost items (fresh juices, coconut milk, etc.) with less expensive alternatives. Indeed, overall drink sizes can be increased by the additional use of such bar extenders as milk, juices, and soda. This often contributes to a feeling of satisfaction by the guest, while allowing the operator to increase profitability. A second way to vary the recipe composition of a drink and, thus, reduce beverage costs is simply to reduce the amount of alcohol served in each drink. For example, a 2-ounce portion of Kahlua in a Kahlua and cream may simply become 1¾ ounces instead, with no reduction in the amount of cream used in the drink's preparation. As with all cost reduction strategies, this one must be carefully considered before implementation.

Adjust Product Quality

This is definitely an area to be approached with caution. It is true, however, that one should strive to use the quality of product appropriate for its intended use. A *specific* coffee liqueur and cream, when called for, must, of course, include that name brand liqueur and cream! It may be wise, however, to use an alternative brand for the many specialty drinks (black Russian, brave bull, black magic, sombrero, etc.) that include coffee liqueur as a major or minor ingredient. In this example, a generic-type coffee liqueur might be used with totally satisfactory results. This is, of course, just one of many possibilities.

With appropriate care, you can determine the quality of ingredients necessary for your operation and then purchase that quality. This is a case where the *appropriate* ingredient, rather than the *highest cost* ingredient, is actually the best possible ingredient. Certainly, the same is true in the area of food products. For example, it simply makes little sense to buy fresh, perfectly shaped strawberries to make a baked strawberry pie, because you must first slice and then cook the fruit. A frozen, sliced strawberry that is less costly, but every bit as wholesome and tasty may be a perfectly acceptable alternative in this case.

Achieve a More Favorable Sales Mix

Typically, each beverage (and food) item you sell will carry a unique cost percentage. This is true because most operators set standard drink prices and ignore minor variances in the cost of differing types of liquor. Most operators, for example, set a particular price for each type of drink they sell. One and one-half ounce of all well liquors plus cola, for example, may sell for the same price. The various spirits ingredients that make up these drinks, however, do not all represent the same cost to the operator. Thus, there exist small differences in liquor cost percentages for these various drinks. The weighted sum total of these various percentages, due to the sales mix concept, yields the overall liquor cost percentage.

The selection of drinks, which you wish to market heavily, has a distinct effect on total profitability. Figure 5.20 illustrates the effect of a shift in consumer buying habits away from a high-cost item to a more profitable one. That is, it shows how the sales mix concept can be used to vary profitability.

While the difference in overall liquor cost percentage in this illustration is only 1.44% (17.92 − 16.48 = 1.44), it represents an increase in cost savings per drink of 7.2 cents (89.6 cents cost − 82.4 cents cost = 7.2 cents).

FIGURE **5.20** ● Impact of Sales Mix on Beverage Cost %

	Sales per Drink	Number Sold	Total Sales	Cost per Drink	Total Cost	Liquor Cost %
Rum/Cola	$5	60	$300	$1.04	$62.40	20.80%
Fruit Brandy/Cola	5	40	200	0.68	27.20	13.60
Combination 1 Total		**100**	**500**	**0.896**	**89.60**	**17.92**
Rum/Cola	5	40	200	1.04	41.60	20.80
Fruit Brandy/Cola	5	60	300	0.68	40.80	13.60
Combination 2 Total		**100**	**500**	**0.824**	**82.40**	**16.48**

In cost control, it's the little things that add up. If you were to be open 365 days a year, serve 100 drinks per day, and each drink costs 7.2 cents less than it would ordinarily, the net result is an extra profit of $2,628 (365 × 100 × 0.072 = $2,628). Effective merchandising of the right product has a positive effect on profitability while, at the same time, allowing the portion size, recipe composition, and product quality to remain constant.

Ensure That All Product Purchased Is Sold

These seven words have tremendous implications. They include all phases of purchasing, receiving, storage, inventory, issuing, and cash control. Perhaps the hospitality industry's greatest challenge in the area of cost control is ensuring that all products, once purchased, do indeed generate cash that makes it to the bank!

Increase Price Relative to Portion Size

This area must be approached with the greatest caution of all. There is no greater temptation in foodservice than to raise prices in an effort to conceal ineffectiveness at controlling costs. This temptation must be resisted. There are times, of course, when prices on selected items must be increased. This is especially true in inflationary times. Price increases should be considered, however, only when all necessary steps to control costs have been effectively implemented. Any price increases should reflect only increases in your costs, not your inefficiency.

On the other hand, many operators are afraid to be 25 or 50 cents higher per menu item than their competition. In some instances, keeping prices in line with competitors' is a good strategy. Frequently, however, decor, quality of product, and service may allow you to be slightly higher in price than your competition. Given the proper ambiance, most guests will not react negatively to small variances in prices because it is perceived value, not price alone, that drives a guest's purchase decision.

Managing the food and beverage production process effectively is indeed at the heart of all foodservice operations. The combination of equipment and product and employee and guest makes the foodservice industry one of the most fascinating professions in the world. If you find joy and a challenge in this process, you are well on your way to a successful foodservice management career. All of the preplanning, ordering, receiving, storing, and issuing systems in the world are for naught if the product cannot be produced well and delivered to the guest with a sense of style and hospitality. Cost control systems can never take the place of the sense of welcome you must impart to your guests. The latter must remain a priority; the former are additions to the personal attention you give your guests and not substitutions for it!

Managing the food and beverage production process is a complex task, and it must be accomplished with the utmost grace and skill. While it is important that your food and beverages are prepared correctly and at an appropriate cost to you, it is just as important to ensure that these products are *sold* for the proper price. It is to this task that we next turn our attention.

Key Terms and Concepts

The following are terms and concepts discussed in the chapter that are important for you as a manager. To help you review, please define the terms below.

Requisition	Free-pouring
Issued	Jigger
Ingredient room	Open bar
Empty for full system	Head size
Physical inventory	Hydrometer
Perpetual inventory	Spotter
Bin card	Standardized recipe cost sheet
Perpetual inventory card	Yield test
Category food cost %	Attainable product cost
Back of the house	

Test Your Skills

1. Loralei owns Loralei's Electra Club, a nightclub in a midsized coastal city. She has set a standard beverage cost of 27% for her club, and she wants to make sure that her beverage costs are in line with her standard. Loralei wants to estimate her beverage cost after the first 10 days of the month. Since she doesn't have time to take a physical inventory, she decides to use her issues to estimate her costs. Help Loralei complete her six-column beverage cost estimate. Based on the first 10 days of the month, is her beverage cost within acceptable limits?

Six-Column Beverage Cost Estimate

Unit Name: Loralei's Electra Club   Date: 1/1–1/10

	Issues		Sales		Beverage Cost Estimate	
Date	Today	To Date	Today	To Date	Today	To Date
1/1	$ 701.89		$2,232.56			
1/2	650.21		2,536.56			
1/3	857.96		2,764.23			
1/4	852.65		2,656.82			
1/5	1,223.35		6,123.54			
1/6	1,300.50		6,445.36			
1/7	785.56		2,545.87			
1/8	1,200.80		3,568.91			
1/9	655.85		2,258.75			
1/10	601.25		2,379.96			
Total						

2. Guests come from all over the county to sample the surf and turf special at Mike's Seaside Café. However, Mike is concerned about his food cost %. He thinks that his seafood costs may be causing the problem. Help him calculate his category food cost percentages and his product usage ratios (portion of total cost). Then list six suggestions for Mike to help him lower his food cost %.

Monthly Food Cost Category Percentage/Proportion

Unit Name: Mike's Seaside Café

Sales: $271,795

Category	Cost of Food Consumed	Food Cost %	Portion of Total Cost
Seafood	$38,500		
Meat	25,850		
Dairy	6,145		
Produce	12,500		
Other	4,315		
Total			

3. Dave would like to add a new menu item to his standard menu. Upper management has approved such an addition if his total product cost percentage does not exceed 31.5% of his allowable selling price. The selling price allowed is $9.75. Using the standardized recipe cost sheet below, can Dave add the new menu item?

Standardized Recipe Cost Sheet

Menu Item: **Dave's Pork Surprise**   Recipe Number: ____15____

Special Notes: _____   Recipe Yield: ____24____

____Boston Butt Net____   Portion Size: ____5 oz.____

____All ingredients weighed as EP____   Portion Cost: _____

_____

Ingredients		Ingredient Cost		
Item	Amount	Unit	Unit Cost	Unit	Total Cost
Boston Butt	10	lb.	$ 5.90	lb.	
Jones Spicy Sauce	4	oz.	8.00	lb.	
Onion	8	oz.	1.20	lb.	
Water	1/4	C	N/A	N/A	
Salt	2	T	0.40	lb.	
Pepper	1	t	12.00	lb.	
Garlic	1	clove	0.60	clove	
Pineapple Juice	1/2	C	3.78	gal.	
Total					

Total Recipe Cost: _____

Portion Cost: _____   Date Costed: ____4/13____

Previous Portion Cost: ___N/A___   Previous Date Costed: ___N/A___

Selling Price: ___$9.75_____

Food Cost Percentage (by portion): _____

Food Cost Percentage Goal: 31.5% _____

4. Elaine owns a fine dining restaurant in the midwest, and she has asked her manager, Gerry, to increase Sunday revenues. To achieve this, Gerry decides to start a buffet line for Sunday brunch at the restaurant, and he is trying to decide what carving meats to serve. He must first determine the EP costs and yields of the various kinds of meats. Help Gerry calculate the EP cost and yield of the inside round.

Butcher's Yield Test Results

Unit Name: Elaine's   Date Tested: May 20

Item: Inside Round
Specification: # 138
AP Amount Tested: 20 lb.
Price per Pound AP: $6.00

Loss Detail	lb.	oz.	Total Ounces	% of Original
AP Weight	20	0		
Fat Loss	3	6		
Bone Loss	2	4		
Cooking Loss	1	12		
Carving Loss	0	8		
Total Production Loss				
EP Weight				

Net Product Yield: _____
Yield Test Performed By: _____ G.W. _____
EP Cost: _____

5. Kathey operates a takeout cookie store in the mall. Business is good, and guests seem to enjoy the products. Her employees, mostly young teens, are a problem since they seem to like the products also. Kathey takes a physical inventory on a weekly basis. This week, her total cost of goods sold figure was $725.58. Kathey has determined that this week she will also compute her attainable food cost and her operational efficiency ratio. Help Kathey by completing the following information using the attainable food cost form. After completing the form, give Kathey five suggestions to keep her employees from eating all of her profits.

Attainable Food Cost

Unit Name: ___Kathey's___

Date Prepared: ___1/8___   Time Period: _1/1–1/7_
Prepared By: ___S. L.___

Item	Number Sold in Dozens	Cost per Dozen	Total Cost	Menu Price per Dozen	Total Sales
Chocolate Chip	85	$1.32		$3.40	
Macadamia	60	$1.61		$4.10	
Coconut Chip	70	$0.83		$2.95	
Fudge	141	$1.42		$3.80	
M&M	68	$1.39		$3.40	
Soft Drinks	295	$0.16		$0.85	
Coffee	160	$0.09		$0.75	
Attainable Product Cost					

Actual Product Cost: _____

Attainable Product Cost: _____

Operational Efficiency Ratio: _____

Attainable Food Cost %: _____

Chapter

6 MANAGING FOOD AND BEVERAGE PRICING

OVERVIEW   In this chapter, you will learn to identify and use the menu formats you will most often encounter as a hospitality manager. Knowledge of these menu formats will help you reduce costs through effective utilization of food and beverage products as well as better utilization of your staff. In addition, you will examine and analyze the factors that influence the prices you charge for the menu items you will sell. Finally, you will learn the procedures used to assign individual menu item prices based on cost and sales data you have collected. By fully understanding the hospitality pricing process, you can help ensure that your menu items will generate the sales revenue needed to meet your profit goals.

CHAPTER OUTLINE

Menu Formats
Factors Affecting Menu Pricing
Assigning Menu Prices
Special Pricing Situations
Key Terms and Concepts, and Test Your Skills

HIGHLIGHTS   At the conclusion of this chapter, you will be able to:

○ Choose and apply the best menu type to an operation you manage.
○ Identify the variables you must consider before establishing your menu prices.
○ Assign menu prices to menu items based on their cost, popularity and ultimate profitability.

Menu Formats

If you have determined that your purchasing, receiving, storing, issuing, and production controls are well in line, you have an excellent chance of reaching your profit goals. It is possible to find, however, that these areas are properly controlled yet food and beverage costs are not in line with your projections. When this is true, the problem may well lie in the fundamental areas of menu format, product pricing, or both. It makes good sense to analyze menu format first, as menu design decisions drive most pricing decisions.

Menus in foodservice establishments generally fall into one of the following three major categories:

1. Standard menu
2. Daily menu
3. Cycle menu

Each of these can be an asset to your effort to control food costs if they are used in the proper setting. The most commonly used menu is the standard menu.

Standard Menu

The **standard menu** is printed, recited by service staff, or otherwise communicated to the guest. The standard menu is fixed day after day. While you may periodically add or delete an item, the standard menu remains virtually constant. There are many operational advantages to a standard menu. First, the standard menu simplifies your ordering process. Since the menu remains constant each day, it is easy to know which products must be purchased to produce these specific menu items. Second, guests tend to have a good number of choices when selecting from a standard menu. This is true because virtually every item that can be produced by the kitchen is available for selection by each guest entering the operation.

A third advantage of the standard menu is that guest preference data are easily obtained since the total number of menu items that will be served stays constant and, thus, is generally smaller than in some alternative menu formats. As you learned in Chapter 3, menu item sales histories can be used to accurately compute percent selecting data and, thus, production schedules and purchasing requirements. In addition, standard menus often become marketing tools for your operation since guests soon become familiar with and return for their favorite menu items.

The standard menu is most typically found in the traditional restaurant or hotel segment of the hospitality industry. It tends to dominate those segments of the business where the *guest* selects the location of the dining experience, as contrasted with situations where a guest's choice is restricted. Examples of restricted-choice situations include a college dormitory cafeteria where students are required to dine in one location, a hospital where patients during their stay must choose their menu selections from that hospital only, or an elementary school cafeteria.

Despite its many advantages, the standard menu does have drawbacks from a control standpoint. First, standard menus are often not developed to utilize carryovers effectively. In fact, in many cases, items that are produced for a standard menu and remain unsold must be discarded, as the next day their quality will not be acceptable. An example would be a quick-service restaurant that produces too many hamburgers for lunch and does not sell all of them. Indeed, for some quick-service restaurants, a burger that is made but not sold within five minutes would be discarded. Contrast that cost control strategy with one that says that cooked burgers not sold within five minutes will be chopped and added to the house specialty chili, and it is easy to see how menu design and the items placed on the menu affect food cost control. A second disadvantage of the standard menu is its lack of ability to respond quickly to market changes and product cost changes. A restaurant that does not list green beans on the menu cannot take advantage of the seasonal harvest of green beans, a time when they can be purchased extremely inexpensively. Conversely, if management has decided that its two house vegetables will be broccoli and corn, even considerable price increases in these two items will have to be absorbed by the operation since these two menu items are listed on the permanent menu. An extreme example of this kind of problem was found in a quick-service seafood restaurant chain that found itself paying almost three times what it had the previous year for a seafood item that constituted approximately 80% of its menu sales. A foreign government had restricted fishing for this product off its shores, and the price skyrocketed. This chain was nearly devastated by this turn of events. Needless to say, management quickly moved to add chicken and different seafood products to the menu in order to dilute the effect of this incredible price increase. Whenever possible, you should monitor food prices with an eye to making seasonal adjustments. The standard menu makes this quite difficult, although some restaurant groups respond to this problem by changing their standard menu on a regular basis. That is, they develop a standard menu for the summer, for example, and another for the winter. In this manner, they can take advantage of seasonal cost savings, add some variety to their menus, but still maintain the core menu items for which they are known.

In summary, the standard menu presents you with both benefits and liabilities. A careful look at what you are serving and how those items affect your costs is in your best interest if you operate from a standard menu.

Daily Menu

In some restaurants, you might elect to operate without a standard or fixed menu and, instead, implement a **daily menu,** that is, a menu that changes every day. This concept is especially popular in some upscale restaurants where the chef's daily creations are viewed with great anticipation, and some awe, by the eager guest. The daily menu would seem to offer some advantages over the standard menu since management can respond very quickly to changes in the price of the raw materials needed to produce the menu items. In fact, that is one of the daily menu's great advantages. In addition, carryovers are less of a problem because any product unsold from the previous day has at least the potential of being incorporated, often as a new dish, into today's menu. Every silver lining has its cloud, however. For all its flexibility, the daily menu is recommended only for very special situations due to the tremendous control drawbacks associated with its implementation. First, guests' percent selecting data are difficult to come by since the items on any given day's menu may never have been served in that particular combination in that restaurant. Thus, the preparation of specific items in certain quantities is pure guesswork and a dangerous way of determining production schedules. Second, it may be difficult for you to plan to have the necessary ingredients on hand to prepare the daily menu if the menu is not known ahead of time. And how does one decide on Monday whether one should order tuna or sirloin steak for the menu on Thursday? Obviously, this situation requires that even the daily menu be planned far enough in advance to allow the purchasing agent to select and order the items necessary to produce the menu. Third, the daily menu may sometimes serve as a marketing tool, but can just as often serve as a disappointment to guests who had a wonderful menu item the last time they dined at this particular establishment and have now returned only to find that their favorite item is not being served. On the other hand, it is very unlikely that any guest will get bored with a routine at a daily menu restaurant, since the routine is, in fact, no routine at all.

Both the standard and the daily menus have advantages and disadvantages. The cycle menu is an effort by management to enjoy the best aspects of both of these approaches and minimize their respective disadvantages.

Cycle Menu

A **cycle menu** is a menu in effect for a specific time period. The length of the cycle refers to the length of time the menu is in effect. Thus, we refer to a 7-day cycle menu, 21-day cycle menu, 30-day cycle menu, or one of any other length of time. Typically, the cycle menu is repeated on a regular basis. Thus, for example, a particular cycle menu could consist of four

FIGURE **6.1** ● Sample Cycle Menu Rotation

Days	Cycle
1–7	A
8–14	B
15–21	C
22–28	D
29–35	A
36–42	B
43–49	C
50–56	D
57–63	A

7-day periods. If each of the four periods were labeled as A, B, C, and D, the cycle periods would rotate as illustrated in Figure 6.1.

Within each cycle, the menu items vary on a daily basis. For example, cycle menu A might consist of the following seven dinner items:

Day 1	Monday	Cheese Enchiladas
Day 2	Tuesday	Turkey and Dressing
Day 3	Wednesday	Corned Beef and Cabbage
Day 4	Thursday	Fried Chicken
Day 5	Friday	Chop Suey
Day 6	Saturday	Lasagna
Day 7	Sunday	Pot Roast

These menu items would be served again when cycle menu A repeated itself on days 29–35 as follows:

Day 29	Monday	Cheese Enchiladas
Day 30	Tuesday	Turkey and Dressing
Day 31	Wednesday	Corned Beef and Cabbage
Day 32	Thursday	Fried Chicken
Day 33	Friday	Chop Suey
Day 34	Saturday	Lasagna
Day 35	Sunday	Pot Roast

In the typical case, cycle menus B, C, and D would, of course, consist of different menu items. In this manner, no menu item would be repeated more frequently than desired by management.

Cycle menus make the most sense when your guests dine with you on a very regular basis, either through the choice of the individual, such as a college student or summer camper eating in a dining hall, or through the choice of an institution, such as a hospital or correctional facility feeding situation. In cases like this, menu variety is very important. The cycle menu provides a systematic method for incorporating that variety into the menu. At a glance, the foodservice manager can determine how often, for example, fried chicken will be served per week, month, or year, and how frequently bread dressing rather than saffron rice is served with baked chicken. In this respect, the cycle menu offers more to the guest than does the standard menu. With cycle menus, production personnel can be trained to produce a wider variety of foods than with the standard menu, thus improving their skills, but requiring fewer skills than might be needed with a daily menu concept.

Cycle menus have the advantage of being able to systematically incorporate today's carryovers into tomorrow's finished product. This is an important management advantage. Also, because of its cyclical nature, management should have a good idea of guest preferences and, thus, be able to schedule and control production to a greater degree than with the daily menu.

Purchasing, too, is simplified since the menu is known ahead of time and menu ingredients that will be appear on all the different cycles can be ordered with plenty of lead time. Inventory levels are easier to maintain as well because, as is the case with the standard menu, product usage is well known.

To illustrate the differences and the impact of operating under the three different menu systems, consider the case of Larry, Moe, and Curly Jo, three foodservice operators who wish to serve roast turkey and dressing for their dinner entrée on a Saturday night in April. Larry operates a restaurant with a standard menu. If he is to print a standard menu that allows him to serve turkey in April, he may be required to have it available in January and June also. If he is to utilize any carryover parts of the turkey, he must incorporate a second turkey item, which also must be made available every day. Larry is not sure all the trouble and cost is worth it! In addition, consider the expense involved in a national chain restaurant with thousands of outlets. Reprints of menus in this situation are very costly. If Larry is the CEO (chief executive officer) of an organization such as this, any decision to change the standard menu is indeed a major undertaking.

Moe operates a restaurant with a daily menu. For him, roast turkey and dressing on a Saturday in April is quite easy. His problem, however, is that he has no idea how much to produce since he has never before served this item at this time of the year in his restaurant. Also, few of the guests he has served in the past year are likely to know about his decision to serve the menu item. What if no one orders it?

Curly Jo operates on a cycle menu. She can indeed put roast turkey and dressing on the cycle. If it sells well, she will keep it on the cycle. If it does not, it will be removed from the next cycle. Curly Jo makes a note to herself that she should record how well it sells and leave a space in the cycle for the utilization of any carryover product that might exist within the next few days. The advantages of the cycle menu, in this situation, are apparent.

Menu Specials

Regardless of the menu type used, you can generally incorporate minor menu changes on a regular basis. This is accomplished through the offering of daily or weekly **menu specials,** that is, menu items that will appear on the menu as you desire and be removed when they are either consumed or discontinued. These daily or weekly specials are an effort to provide variety, take advantage of low-cost raw ingredients, utilize carryover products, or test-market potential new menu items. The menu special is a powerful cost control tool. Properly utilized, it helps shape the future menu by testing guest acceptance of new menu items while, at the same time, providing opportunities for you to respond to the challenges of using carryover or new food and beverage products you have in inventory.

Related Menu Issues

Some aspects of menu development apply to any of the previously mentioned menu types. Proper employee scheduling, for example, is an essential factor in controlling not only labor cost, but food cost as well. Certainly, the operation's menu must allow for the correct number of employees to be in place and to work at a pace that is productive and not wasteful of time or products. Failure to do so will result in increased costs. If your bar is improperly staffed, for example, so that drink preparation personnel are unduly rushed, product waste is sure to increase. In addition, proper menu planning of all types must include the assessment of production equipment utilization. No piece of equipment should be overloaded, even at peak time periods, or product quality, as well as guest service, may suffer.

Another important aspect of menu planning, and the one that we shall explore next, is the concept of price and value for each menu item served. Care must be taken to develop a positive **price/value relationship,** that is, to match menu items with a price that guests are willing to pay and for which they feel a good value is received. Too often, management sees increasing menu price as a way to make up for poor cost control systems. It is never wise, however, to ask guests to subsidize management inefficiency. In the end, this is simply a bankrupt guest strategy.

Strategic pricing is important and you must understand it well. While it is not the total solution to cost control problems, it does play a part because proper pricing strategies help assure that an improper price/value relationship is not the cause of any cost control problems.

Factors Affecting Menu Pricing

A great deal of important information has been written in the area of menu pricing and strategy. For the serious foodservice operator, menu pricing is a topic that deserves its own significant research and study. Pricing is related to cost control by virtue of the basic formula from Chapter 1:

Revenue − Expense = Profit

When foodservice operators find that profits are too low, they frequently question whether prices (revenues) are too low. It is important to remember, however, that revenue and price are not synonymous terms. **Revenue** means the amount spent by *all guests,* while **price** refers to the amount charged to *one guest.* Thus, total revenue is generated by the following formula:

Price × Number Sold = Total Revenue

From this formula, it can be seen that there are two components of total revenue. While price is one component, the other is the number of items sold and, thus, guests served. It is a truism that as price increases, the number of items sold will generally decrease. For this reason, price increases must be evaluated based on their impact on total revenue and not price alone. Assume, for example, that you own a quick-service restaurant chain. You are considering raising the price of small drinks from $1.00 to $1.25. Figure 6.2 illustrates the possible effects of this price increase on total revenue in a single unit. Note especially that, in at least one alternative result, increasing price has the effect of actually *decreasing* total revenue. Experienced foodservice managers know that increasing prices without giving added value can result in higher prices but, frequently, lower revenue because of reduced guest counts.

Perhaps no area of hospitality management is less understood than the area of pricing. This is not surprising when you consider the many fac-

FIGURE **6.2** ● Alternative Results of Price Increases

Old Price	New Price	Number Served	Total Revenue	Revenue Result
$1.00		200	$200.00	
	$1.25	250	$312.50	Increase
	$1.25	200	$250.00	Increase
	$1.25	160	$200.00	No Change
	$1.25	150	$187.50	Decrease

tors that play a part in the pricing decision. For some foodservice operators, inefficiency in cost control is passed on to the guest in terms of higher prices. In fact, sound pricing decisions should be based on establishing a positive price/value relationship in the mind of the guest. Most foodservice operators face similar product costs when selecting their goods on the open market. Whether the product is oranges or beer, wholesale prices vary little from supplier to supplier. In some cases, this variation is due to volume buying, while, in others, it is the result of the relationship established with the vendor. Regardless of their source, the fact remains that the variations are small relative to variations in menu pricing. This becomes easier to understand when you realize that selling price is a function of much more than product cost. It may be said that price is significantly affected by all of the following factors:

Factors Influencing Menu Price

1. Local competition
2. Service levels
3. Guest type
4. Product quality
5. Portion size
6. Ambiance
7. Meal period
8. Location
9. Sales mix

Local Competition

This factor is often too closely monitored by the typical foodservice operator. It may seem to some that the average guest is vitally concerned with price and nothing more. In reality, small variations in price generally make little difference to the average guest. If a group of young professionals goes out for pizza and beer after work, the major determinant will *not* be whether the selling price for the beer is $3.00 in one establishment or $3.25 in another. Your competition's selling price is somewhat important when establishing price, but it is a well-known fact in foodservice that someone can always sell a lesser quality product for a lesser price. The price a competitor charges for his or her product can be useful information in helping you arrive at your own selling price. It should *not*, however, be the only determining factor in your pricing decision. Successful foodservice operators spend their time focusing on building guest value in their *own* operation and not in attempting to mimic the efforts of the competition.

Service Levels

Guests expect to pay more for the same product when service levels are higher. The can of soda sold from a vending machine is generally less expensive than one served by a human being. In a like manner, many pizza chains charge a lower price, for example, for a large pizza that is picked up by the guest than for that same pizza when it is delivered to the guest's door. This is as it should be. The hospitality industry is, in fact, a service industry. As the personal level of service increases, prices may also increase. This personal service may range from the delivery of products, as in the pizza example, to simply increasing the number of servers in a dining room and, thus, reducing the number of guests each must serve. This is not to imply that menu price increases based on service levels are reserved exclusively to pay for the labor required to increase those service levels. Guests are willing to pay more for increased service levels, but this higher price should provide for extra profit as well. In the hospitality industry, those companies that have been able to survive and thrive over the years have done so because of their uncompromising commitment to high levels of guest service. This trend will continue.

Guest Type

Some guests are simply less price sensitive than others. All guests, however, want value for their money. The question of what represents value can vary, of course, due to the type of clientele. If you truly understand this principle, you can use it to benefit your operation. An example of this can clearly be seen in the pricing decisions of convenience stores across the United States. In these facilities, food products such as sandwiches, fruit, drinks, cookies, and the like are sold at relatively high prices. The guests these stores cater to, however, value speed and convenience above all else. For this convenience and a wider range of products than would be found at most quick-service restaurants, they are willing to pay a premium price. In a like manner, guests at an expensive steakhouse restaurant are less likely to respond negatively to small variations in drink prices than are guests at a corner tavern. A thorough analysis of whom their guests are and what they value most is critical to the success of foodservice operators.

Product Quality

In nearly every instance, the guest's quality perception of any specific product offered for sale in the foodservice business can range from very low to very high. This is not to say that the wholesomeness or safety of the product will vary. They should not. But the guest's perception of quality will be based on a variety of factors. As the product itself and those quality-influencing factors vary, so, too, does the guest's perception of quality. For example, when average foodservice guests think of a "hamburger," they actually think, not of one product, but of a range of products. A hamburger may be a rather small burger patty on a regular bun, wrapped in paper and served in a sack. If so, its price will be low and so perhaps may service levels and, thus, perceived quality. If, however, the guest's thoughts turn to an 8-ounce gourmet burger with avocado slices and alfalfa sprouts on a toasted whole-grain bun served in a white-tablecloth restaurant, the price will be much higher and so, probably, will service levels and perceived quality.

As an effective foodservice manager, you will choose from a variety of quality levels when developing product specifications and, consequently, planning menus and establishing prices. If you select the market's cheapest bourbon as your well brand, you will likely be able to charge less for drinks made from it than your competitor who selects a better brand. Your drink quality levels, however, may also be perceived by your guests as lower. To be successful, you should select the quality level that best represents your guests' anticipated desire as well as your goals, and then price your products accordingly.

Portion Size

Portion size plays a large role in determining menu pricing. It is a relatively misunderstood concept, yet it is probably the second most significant factor (next to sales mix) in overall pricing. The great chefs know that people "eat with their eyes first!" This relates to presenting food that is visually appealing. It also relates to portion size. A 4-ounce drink in a 5-ounce glass looks good. The same 4-ounce drink in a 6-ounce glass looks as if the operator is attempting to skimp at the guest's expense. A burger and fries may fill an 8-inch plate, but will be lost on an 11-inch plate. Portion size, then, is a function of both food quantity and how it is presented. It is no secret why successful cafeteria chains use smaller than average dishes to plate their food. For their guests, the image of price/value comes across loud and clear.

In some dining situations, particularly in an "all you care to eat" operation, the previously mentioned principle again holds true. The proper dish size is just as critical as the proper size scoop or ladle when serving the food. Of course, in a traditional table service operation, management controls (or should control!) portion size. Simply put, the larger the portion size, the higher your costs. One very good way to determine whether portion sizes are too large is simply to watch the dishwashing area and see what comes back from the dining room as uneaten. In this regard, the dishroom operator becomes an important player in the cost control team.

Many of today's consumers prefer lighter food with more choices in fruits and vegetables. The portion sizes of these items can be increased at a fairly low increase in cost. At the same time, average beverage sizes are increasing, as are the size of side items such as French fries. Again, these tend to be lower cost items. This can be good news for the foodservice operator if prices can be increased to adequately cover the larger portion sizes.

Every menu item should be analyzed with an eye toward determining if the quantity being served is the "proper" quantity. You would, of course, like to serve this proper amount, but no more than that. The effect of portion size on menu price is significant, and it will be your job to establish and maintain strict control over proper portion size.

Ambiance

If people ate only because they were hungry, few restaurants would be open today. People eat out for a variety of reasons, some of which have little to do with food. Fun, companionship, time limitations, adventure, and variety are just a few reasons diners cite for eating out rather than eating at home. For the foodservice operator who provides an attractive ambiance, menu prices can be increased. In fact, the operator in such a situation is selling much more than food and, thus, justly deserves this increased price. A caveat is in order, however, since some foodservice operations that counted on ambiance alone to carry their business started well but were not ultimately successful. Excellent product quality with outstanding service goes much further over the long run than do clever restaurant designs. Ambiance may draw guests to a location the first time. When this is true, prices may be somewhat higher if the quality of products also supports the price structure. It is always the price/value relationship, however, that will bring the guest back again and again.

Meal Period

In some cases, diners expect to pay more for an item served in the evening than that same item served at a lunch period. Sometimes this is the result of a smaller "luncheon" portion size, but in other cases the portion size, as well as service levels, may be the same in the evening as earlier in the day. You must exercise caution in this area. Guests should clearly understand *why* a menu item's price changes with the time of day. If this cannot be answered to the guest's satisfaction, it may not be wise to implement a time-sensitive pricing structure.

Location

Location can be a major factor in determining price. One need look no further than America's many themed amusement parks or sports arenas to see evidence of this. Foodservice operators in these places are able to charge premium prices because they have, in effect, a monopoly on food sold to the visitors. The only all-night diner on the interstate highway exit is in much the same situation. Contrast that with an operator who is one of 10 seafood restaurants on restaurant row. It used to be said of restaurants that success was due to three things: location, location, and location! This may have been true before so many operations opened in the United States. There is, of course, no discounting the value of a prime restaurant location, and location alone can influence price. It does not, however, guarantee success. Each foodservice operator must analyze his or her own operation. Location can be an asset or a liability. If it is an asset, menu prices may reflect that fact. If location is indeed a liability, menu prices may need to be lower to attract a sufficient clientele to ensure the operation's total revenue requirements.

Sales Mix

Of all the factors mentioned thus far, sales mix would most heavily influence the menu pricing decision, just as guest purchase decisions will influence total product costs. Recall that sales mix refers to the specific menu items selected by guests. Managers can respond to this situation by employing a concept called **price blending.** Price blending refers to the process of pricing products, with very different individual cost percentages, in groups with the intent of achieving a favorable overall cost situation. The ability to knowledgeably blend prices is a useful skill and one that is well worth mastering. As an example, assume that you are the operations vice president for a chain of upscale hamburger restaurants known as Texas Red's. Assume also that you hope to achieve an overall food cost of 40% in your units. For purposes of simplicity, assume that Fig-

FIGURE **6.3** ● Unblended Price Structure

Texas Red's Burgers			
Item	Item Cost	Desired Food Cost	Proposed Selling Price
Hamburger	$1.50	40%	$3.75
French Fries	0.32	40	0.80
Soft Drinks (12 oz.)	0.18	40	0.45
Total	2.00	40	5.00

ure 6.3 illustrates the three products you sell and their corresponding selling price if each is priced to achieve a 40% food cost.

In Chapter 3, you learned that the formula for computing food cost percentage is as follows:

$$\frac{\text{Cost of Food Sold}}{\text{Food Sales}} = \text{Food Cost \%}$$

This formula can be worded somewhat differently for a single menu item without changing its accuracy. Consider that:

$$\frac{\text{Cost of a Specific Food Item Sold}}{\text{Food Sales of That Item}} = \text{Food Cost \% of That Item}$$

It is important to understand that the food sales value in the preceding formula is a synonymous term to the selling price when evaluating the menu price of a single menu item. The principles of algebra allow you to rearrange the formula as follows:

> **Cost of a Specific Food Item Sold**
> **Food Cost % of That Item**
> **= Food Sales (Selling Price) of That Item**

Thus, in Figure 6.3, the hamburger's selling price is established as

$$\frac{\$ 1.50}{0.40} = \$3.75$$

Notice that in Figure 6.3 all products are priced to sell at a price that would result in a 40% food cost. Certainly, under this system, sales mix, that is, the individual menu selections of guests, would not affect overall food cost %. The sales mix resulting from this pricing strategy could, however, have very damaging results on your profitability. The reason is very simple. If you use the price structure indicated previously, your drink prices are too low. Most guests expect to pay far in excess of 45 cents for a soft drink at a quick-service restaurant. You run the risk, in this example, of attracting many guests who are interested in buying only soft drinks at your restaurants. Your French fries may also be priced too low. Your burger itself, however, may be priced too high relative to your competitors. However, if you use the price-blending concept, and if you assume that each guest coming into your restaurants will buy a burger, French fries, and a soft drink, you can create a different menu price structure and still achieve your overall cost objective as seen in Figure 6.4.

Note that, in this example, you would actually achieve a total food cost slightly lower than 40%. Your hamburger price is now less than $2.50 and in line with local competitors. Note also, however, that you have assumed each guest coming to Texas Red's will buy one of each item. In reality, of course, not all guests will select one of each item. Some guests will not elect fries, while others may stop in only for a soft drink. It is for this reason that guest selection data, discussed in Chapter 3, is so critical. These histories let you know exactly what your guests are buying when they visit your outlets. You can then apply percent selecting figures to your pricing strategy. To illustrate how this works, assume that you monitored a sample of 100 guests who came into one of your units and found the results presented in Figure 6.5.

As you can see from Figure 6.5, you can use the price-blending concept to achieve your overall cost objectives if you have a good understanding of how many people buy each menu item. In this example, you have achieved the 40% food cost you sought. It matters little if the burger

FIGURE **6.4** ● Blended Price Structure

Texas Red's Burgers			
Item	Item Cost	Proposed Food Cost %	Proposed Selling Price
Hamburger	$1.50	60.2%	$2.49
French Fries	0.32	21.5	1.49
Soft Drinks (12 oz.)	0.18	16.5	1.09
Total	2.00	39.4	5.07

FIGURE **6.5** ● Sample Sales Mix Data

Texas Red's Burgers

Total Sales: ____$449.25____   Guests Served: __100__

Total Food Cost: $180.20____   Food Cost %: __40.1%__

Item	Number Sold	Item Cost	Total Food Cost	Selling Price	Total Sales	Food Cost %
Hamburger	92	$1.50	$138.00	$2.49	$229.08	60.2%
French Fries	79	0.32	25.28	1.49	117.71	21.5
Soft Drink (12 oz.)	94	0.18	16.92	1.09	102.46	16.5
Total			180.20		449.25	40.1

has a 60.2% food cost *if* the burger is sold in conjunction with the sample number of soft drinks and fries. Obviously, there may be a danger if your guests begin to order nothing but hamburgers when they come to your establishment. Again, careful monitoring of guest preferences will allow you to make price adjustments, as needed, to keep your overall costs and prices in line. A word of caution regarding the manipulation of sales mix and price blending is, however, in order. Since price itself is one of the factors that impact percent selecting figures, a change in menu price may cause a change in item popularity. If, in an effort to reduce overall product cost percentage, you were to increase the price of soft drinks at Texas Red's, for example, you might find that a higher percentage of guests would elect *not* to purchase a soft drink. This could have the effect of actually increasing your overall product cost percentage since fewer guests would choose to buy the one item with an extremely low food cost percentage. The sales mix and the concept of price blending will have a major impact on your overall menu pricing philosophy and strategy.

FUN ON THE WEB!

Look up the following site to evaluate restaurants' pricing strategies based on reviewers' perceptions of service levels, guest type, product quality, ambiance, location, and much more!

www.zagat.com First, choose a city. Then click on your specific restaurant criteria or just click on "Most Popular." Then click on any restaurant for a review that includes a features list, reviewers' ratings, prices, and much more! Look at several restaurant reviews. Evaluate whether you think the menu prices and the features/review are a "good fit," in your opinion. Spend about 30 minutes viewing this site!

Assigning Menu Prices

The methods used to assign menu prices are as varied as foodservice managers themselves. In general, however, menu prices are most often assigned on the basis of one of the following two concepts:

1. Product cost percentage
2. Product contribution margin

Product Cost Percentage

This method of pricing is based on the idea that product cost should be a predetermined percentage of selling price. As was illustrated earlier in this chapter, if you have a menu item that costs $1.50 (EP) to produce, and your desired cost percentage equals 40%, the following formula can be used to determine what the item's menu price should be:

$$\frac{\underline{\text{Cost of a Specific Food Item Sold}}}{\text{Food Cost \% of That Item}} = \text{Food Sales (Selling Price) of That Item}$$

or

$$\frac{\$1.50}{0.40} = \$3.75$$

Thus, the recommended selling price, given a $1.50 product cost, is $3.75. If the item is sold for $3.75, then a 40% food cost should be achieved for that item. A check on this work can also be done using the food cost percentage formula:

$$\frac{\$1.50}{3.75} = 40\%$$

When management uses a predetermined food cost percentage to price menu items, it is stating its belief that product cost in relationship to selling price is of vital importance. Experienced foodservice managers know that a second method of arriving at appropriate selling prices based on predetermined food cost % goals can be employed. This method uses a cost factor or multiplier that can be assigned to each desired food cost percentage. This factor, when multiplied times the item's EP cost, will result in a selling price that yields the desired food cost percentage. Figure 6.6 details such a factor table.

In each case, the factor is arrived at by the following formula:

$$\frac{1.00}{\text{Desired Product Cost \%}} = \text{Pricing Factor}$$

Thus, if one were attempting to price a product and achieve a product cost of 40%, the computation would be

FIGURE **6.6** ● Pricing Factor Table

Desired Product Cost %	Factor
20	5.000
23	4.348
25	4.000
28	3.571
30	3.333
33$\frac{1}{3}$	3.000
35	2.857
38	2.632
40	2.500
43	2.326
45	2.222

$$\frac{1.00}{0.40} = 2.5$$

This pricing factor of 2.5 when multiplied by any product cost will yield a selling price that is based on a 40% product cost. The formula is as follows:

Pricing Factor × Product Cost = Menu Price

To return to our example, you could use the previous version of the formula to establish your selling price if you hope to achieve a 40% product cost and your item costs $1.50 to produce. The computation would be as follows:

$$2.5 \times 1.50 = \$3.75$$

As can be seen, these two methods of arriving at the proposed selling price yield the same results. One formula simply relies on division, while the other relies on multiplication. The decision about which formula to use is completely up to you. With either approach, the selling price will be determined with a goal of achieving a given product cost percentage for each item. Obviously, due to sales mix and the price-blending concept, the appropriate product cost percentage desired for any given item may vary according to your own view of the best selling price for each menu item.

Product Contribution Margin

Some foodservice managers prefer an approach to menu pricing that is focused not on product cost percentage, but rather on a menu item's contribution margin. **Contribution margin,** in this case, is defined as the amount that remains after the product cost of the menu item is subtracted from the item's selling price. Contribution margin, then, is the amount that "contributes" to paying for your labor and other expenses and providing a profit. Thus, if an item sells for $3.75 and the product cost for this item is $1.50, the contribution margin would be computed as follows:

$$\text{Selling Price} - \text{Product Cost} = \text{Contribution Margin}$$

or

$$\$3.75 - \$1.50 = \$2.25$$

When this approach is used, the formula for determining selling price is

$$\text{Product Cost} + \text{Contribution Margin Desired} = \text{Selling Price}$$

Establishing menu price, in this case, is a simple matter of combining product cost with a predetermined contribution margin. Management's role here is to determine the desired contribution margin for each menu item. When using this approach, you would likely establish different contribution margins for various menu items or groups of items. For example, in a cafeteria where items are priced separately, entrées might be priced with a contribution margin of $2.50 each, desserts with a contribution margin of $1.25, and drinks, perhaps, with a contribution margin of $0.75. Again, menu price would be established by combining desired contribution margin with actual product cost. Those managers who rely on the contribution margin approach to pricing do so in the belief that the average contribution margin per item is a more important consideration in pricing decisions than food cost percentage.

Product Cost Percentage or Product Contribution Margin?

Proponents exist for both of these approaches to menu pricing. Indeed, there are additional methods to menu pricing, beyond the scope of an introduction to pricing theory. Some large foodservice organizations have established highly complex computer-driven formulas for determining appropriate menu prices. For the average foodservice operator, however, product cost percentage, contribution margin, or a combination of both will suffice when attempting to arrive at appropriate pricing decisions.

While the debate over the "best" pricing method is likely to continue for some time, you should remember to view pricing not as an attempt to take advantage of the guest, but rather as an important process with an end goal of establishing a good price/value relationship in the mind of your guest.

Each foodservice manager may, of course, have his or her own method of pricing menu items. In all cases, however, pricing should be based on the total cost of goods sold. It is not appropriate for management to pass on to guests the cost of production errors or simple managerial inefficiencies. If management is not committed to controlling food and beverage as well as other expenses, and thus providing consumers with high-quality products at fair prices, the operation will suffer. Regardless of whether the pricing method used is based on food cost percentage or contribution margin, the selling price selected must provide for a predetermined operational profit. For this reason, it is important that the menu not be priced so low that no profit is possible or so high that you will not be able to sell a sufficient number of items to make a profit. In the final analysis, it is the market that will eventually determine what your sales will be on any given item.

Being sensitive to both required profit and your guests–their needs, wants, and desires–is very critical to a pricing philosophy. *Menu Pricing and Strategy* by Jack Miller and David Pavesic, provides an excellent treatment of the menu development, marketing strategies, price support systems, and pricing strategies necessary to effectively design and assign price to a menu. It is highly recommended as an addition to your management library.

Special Pricing Situations

Some pricing decisions faced by foodservice managers call for a unique approach. In many cases, pricing is used as a way to influence guests' purchasing decisions or to respond to particularly difficult pricing situations. The following are examples:

1. Coupons
2. Value pricing
3. Bundling
4. Salad bars and buffets
5. Bottled wine
6. Beverages at receptions and parties

Coupons

Coupons are a popular way to vary menu price. Essentially, there are two types of coupons in use in the hospitality industry. The first type generally allows the guest to get a free item when he or she buys another item. This has the effect of reducing by 50% the menu price of the couponed item. In the second type, some form of restriction is placed on the coupon. The restriction, for example, may be that the coupon can only be used at a certain time of day or that a specific reduction in price is given if the guest purchases a designated menu item. In either case, coupons have the effect of reducing sales revenue from each guest in the hope that the total number of guests increases to the point that total sales revenue increases. Coupons are a popular marketing tool but their use should be carefully evaluated in terms of effect on menu price, product cost percentage, and product contribution margin.

Value Pricing

Value pricing refers to the practice of reducing all or most prices on the menu in the belief that, as in couponing, total guest counts will increase to the point that total sales revenue also increases. A potential danger, of course, with value pricing is that if guest counts do not increase significantly, total sales revenue may, in fact, decline rather than increase.

Bundling

Bundling refers to the practice of selecting specific menu items and pricing them as a group, in such a manner that the single menu price of the group is lower than if the items comprising the group were purchased individually. The most common example is the combination meals offered by many quick-service hamburger restaurants. In many cases, these bundled meals consist of a sandwich, French fries, and a drink. These bundled meals, often promoted as "value priced" or "combo" meals, encourage each individual guest to buy one of each menu item rather than only one or two of them. The bundled meal generally is priced so competitively that a strong value perception is established in the guest's mind.

When bundling, as in couponing or value pricing, lower menu prices are accepted by management in the belief that this pricing strategy will increase total sales revenue and, thus, profit by increasing the number of guests served.

Salad Bars and Buffets

The difficulty in establishing a set price for either a salad bar or a buffet is, of course, that total portion cost can vary greatly from one guest to the next. A person weighing 100 pounds will, most likely, consume fewer products from a buffet or an all-you-can-eat line than a 300-pound person will. The general rule, however, is that each of these guests will pay the same price to go through the salad bar or buffet line. Short of charging guests for the amount they actually consume (a technique that has been tried by some operators with little success), a method of determining a single selling price must be established. This price must be based on a known, overall cost for the average diner who selects the all-you-can-eat option.

This price may be different, of course, if your average clients weigh 300 pounds rather than 100 pounds. The point is that the selling price must be established and monitored so that either guest could be accommodated at a price you find acceptable. This can be accomplished rather easily if record keeping is accurate and timely. The secret to keeping the selling price low in a salad bar or buffet situation is to apply the ABC inventory approach. That is, A items, which are expensive, should comprise no more than 20% of the total product available. B items, which are moderate in price, should comprise about 30% of the item offerings. And C items, which are inexpensive, should comprise 50% of the offerings. Using this approach, a menu listing of items can be prepared to ensure that only items that stay within these predetermined ranges are offered for sale.

Regardless of the buffet items to be sold, their usage must be accurately recorded. Consider the situation of Mei, the manager of Lotus Gardens, a Chinese restaurant where patrons pay one price, but may return as often as they like to a buffet table. Mei finds that a form such as that presented in Figure 6.7 is helpful in recording both product usage and guests served. Note that Mei uses the ABC method to determine her menu items. She does so because total food costs on a buffet line or salad bar are a function of both *how much* is eaten and *what* is eaten. She also notes the amount of product she puts on the buffet to begin the dinner meal period (Beginning Amount), any additions during the meal period (Additions), and the amount of usable product left at the conclusion of the meal period (Ending Amount). From this information, Mei can compute her total product usage and, thus, her total product cost.

FIGURE **6.7** ● Salad Bar or Buffet Product Usage

Unit Name: **Lotus Gardens**   Date: 1/1 (Dinner)

Item	Category	Beginning Amount	Additions	Ending Amount	Total Usage	Unit Cost	Total Cost
Sweet and Sour Pork	A	6 lb.	44 lb.	13 lb.	37 lb.	$4.40/lb.	$162.80
Bean Sprouts	B	3 lb.	17 lb.	2 lb.	18 lb.	1.60/lb.	28.80
Egg Rolls	B	40 each	85 each	17 each	108 each	0.56 each	60.48
Fried Rice	C	10 lb.	21.5 lb.	8.5 lb.	23 lb.	0.60/lb.	13.80
Steamed Rice	C	10 lb.	30 lb.	6.5 lb.	33.5 lb.	0.40/lb.	13.40
Wonton Soup	C	2 gal.	6 gal.	1.5 gal.	6.5 gal.	4.00/gal.	26.00
Total Product Cost							305.28

Total Product Cost: $305.28

Guests Served: 125   Cost per Guest: $2.44

Based on the data in Figure 6.7, Mei knows that her total product cost for dinner on January 1 was $305.28. She can then use the following formula to determine her buffet product cost per guest:

$$\frac{\text{Total Buffet Product Cost}}{\text{Guest Served}} = \text{Buffet Product Cost per Guest}$$

or

$$\frac{\$305.28}{125} = \$2.44$$

Thus, on her buffet, Mei had a portion cost per guest of $2.44. She can use this information to establish a menu price that she feels is appropriate. Assume, for example, that Mei uses the food cost percentage approach to establishing menu price and she has determined a 25% food cost to be her goal. Using the pricing factor table in Figure 6.6, Mei would use the following formula to establish her per-person buffet price:

$$\$2.44 \text{ (Per-Person Cost)} \times 4.00 \text{ (Pricing Factor)} = \$9.76$$

For marketing purposes, and to ensure her desired food cost percentage, Mei may well round her buffet selling price up, to say, $9.99 per person. The significant point to remember here is that the amount consumed by any individual guest is relatively unimportant. It is the consumption of the average, or typical, guest that is used to establish menu price.

It is to be expected that Mei's buffet product cost per guest will vary somewhat each day. This is not a cause for great concern. Minor variations in product cost per guest should be covered if selling price is properly established. By monitoring buffet costs on a regular basis, you can be assured that you can keep good control over both costs per guest and your most appropriate selling price.

Bottled Wine

Few areas of menu pricing create more controversy than that of pricing wines by the bottle. The reason for this may be the incredible variance in cost among different **vintages,** or years of production, as well as the quality of alternative wine offerings. If your foodservice operation will sell wine by the bottle, it is likely that you will have some wine products that appeal to value-oriented guests and other, higher priced wines that are preferred by higher spending guests. An additional element that affects wine pricing is the fact that many wines that are sold by the bottle in restaurants are also sold in retail grocery or liquor stores. Thus, guests have a good idea of what a similar bottle of wine would cost them if it were purchased in either of these locations. How you decide to price the bottled-wine offerings on your own menu will definitely affect your guest's perception of the price/value relationship offered by your operation.

Properly pricing wine by the bottle calls for skill and insight. Consider the case of Claudia, who owns and manages a fine-dining Italian restaurant. Using the product cost percentage method of pricing, Claudia attempts to achieve an overall wine product cost in her restaurant of 25%. Thus, when pricing her wines and using the pricing factor table in Figure 6.6, Claudia multiplies the cost of each bottled wine she sells by four to arrive at her desired selling price. Following are the four wines she sells and the costs and prices associated with each type:

Wine	Product Cost	Selling Price	Product Cost %
1	$ 4.00	$16.00	25%
2	6.00	24.00	25
3	15.00	60.00	25
4	20.00	80.00	25

Claudia decides that she would like to explore the contribution margin approach to wine pricing. She, therefore, computes the contribution margin (selling price − product cost = contribution margin) for each wine she sells and finds the following results:

Wine	Selling Price	Product Cost	Contribution Margin
1	$16.00	$ 4.00	$12.00
2	24.00	6.00	18.00
3	60.00	15.00	45.00
4	80.00	20.00	60.00

Her conclusion, after evaluating the contribution margin approach to pricing and what she believes to be her customers' perception of the price/value relationship she offers, is that she may be hurting sales of wines 3 and 4 by pricing these products too high, even though they are currently priced to achieve a 25% product cost as are wines 1 and 2. In the case of bottled wine, the contribution margin approach to price can often be used to your advantage. Guests appear to be quite price conscious when it comes to bottled wine. When operators seek to achieve profits guests feel are inappropriate, bottled-wine sales may decline. Following is an alternative pricing structure that Claudia has developed for use in her restaurant. She must, however, give this price structure a test run and monitor its affect on overall product sales and profitability if she is to determine whether this pricing strategy will be effective.

Wine	Product Cost	Selling Price	Contribution Margin	Product Cost %
1	$ 4.00	$19.00	$15.00	21.1%
2	6.00	22.00	16.00	27.3
3	15.00	33.00	18.00	45.5
4	20.00	39.00	19.00	51.3

Note that, while selling price has been increased in the case of wine 1, it has been reduced for wines 2, 3, and 4. Contribution margin still is higher for wine 4 than for wine 1. The difference is, however, not as dramatic as before. Product cost percentages have, of course, been altered due to the price changes Claudia is proposing. Note also that the **price spread,** defined as the range between the lowest and the highest priced menu item, has been drastically reduced. Where the price spread was previously $16.00 to $80.00, it is now $19.00 to $39.00. This reduction in price spread may assist Claudia in selling more, higher priced wine because her guests may be more comfortable with the price/value relationship perceived under this new pricing approach. It is important to remember, however, that Claudia must monitor sales and determine if her new strategy is successful. As a rule, it may be stated that pricing bottled wine only by the product percentage method is a strategy that may result in overall decreased bottled-wine sales. In this specific pricing situation, the best approach to establishing selling price calls for you to evaluate both your product cost percentage and your contribution margin.

Beverages at Receptions and Parties

Pricing beverages for open-bar receptions and special events can be very difficult, but the reason for this is very simple. Each consumer group can be expected to behave somewhat differently when attending an open-bar or hosted-bar function. Clearly, we would not expect the guests at a formal wedding reception to consume as many drinks during a one-hour reception as a group of fun-loving individuals celebrating a sports victory.

Establishing a price per person in these two cases may well result in quite different numbers. One way to solve this problem is to charge each guest for what he or she actually consumes. In reality, however, many party hosts want their guests to consume beverage products without having to pay for each drink. When this is the case, you are required to charge the host either for the amount of beverage consumed or on a per-person, per-hour basis. When charging on a per-person, per-hour basis, you must have a good idea of how much the average attendee will consume during the length of the party or reception so that an appropriate price can be established.

For example, assume that you are the food and beverage director at the Carlton, a luxury hotel. Ms. Swan, a potential food and beverage guest, approaches you with the idea of providing a one-hour champagne reception for 100 guests prior to an important dinner that she is considering booking at your facility. The guest would like all of the attendees to drink as much champagne during the reception as they care to. Ms. Swan's specific question is, "How much will I be charged for the reception if 100 guests attend?" Clearly, an answer of "I don't know" or "It depends on how much they drink" is inappropriate. It is, of course, your business to know the answer to such questions, and you *can* know. If you are aware from past events and records you have kept on such events of what the average consumption *for a group of this type* has been previously, you can establish an appropriate price. To do so, records for this purpose must be maintained. Figure 6.8 is an example of one such device that can be used. Note that average consumption of any product type can be recorded. In this example, assume that you had recently recorded the data from the Gulley Wedding, an event very similar to the one requested by Ms. Swan. In this case, a wedding reception, which also requested champagne, was sold to 97 guests. The product cost per guest for that event, based on your records in Figure 6.8, equaled $3.37.

Based on what you know about the drinking pattern of a similar group, you could use either the product cost percentage method or the contribution margin pricing method to establish your reception price. For purpose of illustration, assume that you used the product contribution margin approach to pricing alcoholic beverage receptions. Further, assume that the contribution margin desired per person served is $15.00.

FIGURE **6.8** ● Beverage Consumption Report

Event: <u>Gulley Wedding</u>   Date: <u>1/1</u>

Unit Name: **The Carlton Hotel**

Beverage Type	Beginning Amount	Additions	Ending Amount	Total Usage	Unit Cost	Total Cost
Liquor A						
B						
C						
D						
E						
F						
G						
Beer A						
B						
C						
D						
E						
Wine A						
B						
C						
D						
Other: Champagne: A. Sparkling	8 bottles	24	9	23	6.00/btl.	$138.00
B. Sparkling Pink	8 bottles	24	11	21	9.00/btl.	$189.00
Total Product Cost						327.00

Total Product Cost: <u>$327.00</u>

Guests Served: <u>   97   </u>   Cost per Guest: <u>$3.37</u>

Remarks: <u>Mild group; very orderly; no problems.</u>

The computation of selling price using the contribution margin formula would be as follows:

> **Product Cost + Desired Contribution Margin = Selling Price**
>
> *In this example:*
>
> $ 3.37 (Per-Person Product Cost)
> + $15.00 (Desired Contribution Margin)
> = $18.37 Selling Price Per Person

Armed with this historical information, as well as that from other similar events, you can be well prepared to answer Ms. Swan's question; "How much will I be charged for the reception if 100 guests attend?"

Establishing product costs and then assigning reasonable menu prices based on these costs is a major component of your job as a foodservice manager. You must be able to perform this task well. Increasingly, however, the cost of labor, rather than the cost of products, has occupied a significant portion of the typical foodservice manager's cost control efforts. In fact, in some foodservice facilities, the cost of labor exceeds that of the food and beverage products sold. Because this area of cost control is so important, we will now turn our attention to the unique set of skills and knowledge you must acquire to adequately manage and control your labor costs.

Key Terms and Concepts

The following are terms and concepts discussed in the chapter that are important for you as a manager. To help you review, please define the terms below.

Standard menu	Price blending
Daily menu	Contribution margin
Cycle menu	Value pricing
Menu specials	Bundling
Price/value relationship	Vintage
Revenue versus price	Price spread

Test Your Skills

1. Bill owns Bill's Burger Barn, and he is dissatisfied with his consistently high food cost percentage. In an effort to drop his food cost % *below*

35%, he has decided to incorporate price blending into his pricing strategy. He has developed three combo items, and he wants to find out if his food cost % has been lowered after the first week of sales. Help Bill calculate the food cost % for his combo items.

Price Blending

Bill's Burger Barn Combo

Item	Number Sold	Item Cost	Total Cost	Selling Price	Total Sales	Food Cost %
Hamburger	200	$1.50		$3.49		
French Fries (large)	185	0.40		1.60		
Soft Drink (16 oz.)	190	0.20		1.35		
Total						

Bill's Bacon Cheeseburger Combo

Item	Number Sold	Item Cost	Total Cost	Selling Price	Total Sales	Food Cost %
Bacon Cheeseburger	160	$1.65		$4.29		
Onion Rings	135	0.30		1.40		
Soft Drink (16 oz.)	155	0.20		1.35		
Total						

Bill's Chicken Sandwich Combo

Item	Number Sold	Item Cost	Total Cost	Selling Price	Total Sales	Food Cost %
Chicken Sandwich	75	$1.10		$3.15		
French Fries (large)	75	0.40		1.60		
Soft Drink (16 oz.)	75	0.20		1.35		
Total						

Should Bill continue with this pricing strategy?

2. Tonekwa has priced her menu items using the product cost percentage method in the past. She has asked her evening shift manager to price new menu items, and she believes that he will feel more comfortable using the factor method to price the new items. Help Tonekwa convert her desired product cost percentages to factors.

Pricing Factor Table

Desired Product Cost	Factor
18%	
21%	
22%	
24%	
26%	
31%	
32%	
36%	
37%	
41%	
42%	
44%	
46%	

3. Bess and David own two small diners in a midsized city in Oklahoma. Bess has primary responsibility for the diner in the suburbs, and David has primary responsibility for the diner in the inner city. The menu items and product costs are the same in both diners, but the market in the inner city demands lower menu prices than that in the suburbs. So, Bess has set her desired product cost percentage at 40%, and David's desired product cost percentage is 42% since he can't charge as much as Bess. Bess likes to use the product cost percentage method to price menu items, and David likes to use the factor method. Help both of them determine their selling prices.

Bess and David's Diner—Suburbs (Bess)

Desired Product Cost Percentage: __40%__

Product Cost Percentage Method

Item	Cost of Product	Desired Product Cost Percentage	Selling Price
Chicken Breast Dinner	$2.25		
Seafood Platter	3.45		
Steak Dinner	4.99		
Turkey Sandwich	1.25		
Pork Chop	2.45		
Hamburger	1.50		
Cheeseburger	1.75		
Fries	0.45		
Meat Loaf	1.25		
Small Drink	0.35		

Bess and David's Diner—Inner City (David)

Desired Product Cost Percentage: 42%

Factor Method

Item	Cost of Product	Factor	Selling Price
Chicken Breast Dinner	$2.25		
Seafood Platter	3.45		
Steak Dinner	4.99		
Turkey Sandwich	1.25		
Pork Chop	2.45		
Hamburger	1.50		
Cheeseburger	1.75		
Fries	0.45		
Meat Loaf	1.25		
Small Drink	0.35		

4. Frankie Marie owns Frankie's Cafeteria in a small southern town. She has decided to price her menu items using the contribution margin method. She has determined the following contribution margins for her food categories:

Contribution Margins

Salad	$1.20
Entrées	$4.25
Desserts	$1.50
Drinks	$1.10

Help her price her menu items.

Contribution Margin Approach

Item	Product Cost	Desired Contribution Margin	Selling Price
Salads			
Dinner Salad	$0.30		
Macaroni Salad	$0.55		
Potato Salad	$0.65		
Carrot and Raisin Salad	$0.40		
Bavarian Salad	$0.60		
Entrées			
Liver and Onions	$2.50		
Steak Patty	$2.75		
Meat Loaf	$2.85		
Chicken Fried Steak	$2.10		
Fried Catfish	$2.35		
Chicken Casserole	$2.25		
Turkey and Dressing	$2.55		
Desserts			
Chocolate Cream Pie	$0.75		
Coconut Cream Pie	$0.75		
Pecan Pie	$1.25		
Chocolate Cake	$0.60		
Pudding	$0.20		
Jello	$0.20		
Carrot Cake	$0.70		
Drinks			
Coffee	$0.15		
Tea	$0.15		
Soft Drink	$0.15		

5. Gabriel Hinojosa owns Gabriel's Tex-Mex Restaurant, an extremely popular, 250-seat establishment in a large California city. Gabriel has decided to offer a four-hour Sunday brunch buffet for his guests because he thinks he can achieve a guest count of 625 (2½ turns). Last Sunday, June 1, he offered the buffet for the first time, and he charged $12.00 per guest. However, he only served 400 people. He thinks that maybe he could attract more guests if he offered the buffet at a lower price. He collected information on last Sunday's buffet product usage, and he used the ABC method to put his menu items into categories. His desired food cost percentage is 40%. Help him complete the buffet product usage report.

   After completing this analysis, what should be Gabriel's selling price? If he uses this new selling price *and* he serves 625 guests next Sunday, June 8, will his total revenue increase? If so, how much?

6. This is a fun assignment! Go to your favorite restaurant and evaluate the menu prices based on the following:
   a. Local competition
   b. Service level
   c. Guest type
   d. Product quality
   e. Portion size
   f. Ambiance
   g. Meal period
   h. Location
   i. Sales mix

   Write a critique summarizing your opinion of the restaurant's pricing based on the factors you observed. Do you think that the prices adequately reflect your view of the criteria?

Buffet Product Usage (Sunday, June 1): Gabriel's Tex-Mex Restaurant

Item	Category	Unit	Beginning Amount	Additions	Ending Amount	Total Usage	Unit Cost	Total Cost
Steak Fajitas	A	lb.	20	60	6		$4.50	
Chicken Fajitas	A	lb.	15	70	10		4.00	
Carne Asada	A	lb.	10	50	4		4.25	
Cheese Enchiladas	B	lb.	2	80	15		2.00	
Beef Enchiladas	B	lb.	3	60	10		2.50	
Enchiladas Verde	B	lb.	1	70	8		2.00	
Chili Rellenos	B	lb.	10	45	5		2.75	
Tacos	C	each	0	150	20		0.30	
Bean Chalupas	C	each	0	175	5		0.25	
Tortilla Soup	C	gal.	2	10	4		0.30	
Spanish Rice	C	lb.	5	70	12		0.20	
Refried Beans	C	lb.	15	75	6		0.20	
Sopapillas	C	each	25	200	30		0.15	
Total Product Cost								

Guests Served: 400

Total Product Cost: _____

Cost per Guest: _____

Desired Food Cost %: 40

Total Sales: _____

Desired Selling Price: _____

Revenues, June 1: _____   Projected Revenues, June 8: _____   Difference: _____

Chapter

7 MANAGING THE COST OF LABOR

OVERVIEW   This chapter details the techniques used to control costs by establishing and monitoring labor cost standards. In this chapter, you will learn about the factors that affect labor productivity, as well as methods for improving labor productivity. The chapter will teach you how to schedule employees based on established labor standards, as well as how to compute the labor cost percentage and other measures of labor productivity.

CHAPTER OUTLINE

Labor Expense in the Hospitality Industry
Assessing Labor Productivity
Maintaining a Productive Workforce
Measuring Current Labor Productivity
Managing Payroll Costs
Reducing Labor-Related Costs
Key Terms and Concepts, and Test Your Skills

HIGHLIGHTS   At the conclusion of this chapter, you will be able to:

○ Identify the factors that affect employee productivity.
○ Develop appropriate labor standards and employee schedules for use in your foodservice operation.
○ Analyze and evaluate your actual labor utilization.

Labor Expense in the Hospitality Industry

Having the correct amount of food and beverage products in the operation to serve guests is important. Knowing how those products should be prepared is vital also. Consider, however, the case of Pauline. She manages the cafeteria of a large urban hospital. Generally speaking, the quality of food she provides is quite good. Both hospital staff and patients' visitors, who constitute the majority of her guests, have good things to say about the quality of her food. They complain often, however, about the slowness of her cafeteria line, the dirty tables during the busy lunch hour, and the frequent running out of items on both the beverage and the salad bars. Pauline often feels that she needs more employees. She knows, however, that her current staff is actually larger than it was a few years ago. Of course, business is better today also. Many more guests are served per day now than before Pauline was the manager. Her question is, "Do I have the right number of employees scheduled at the right times for the number of guests I anticipate today?" Unfortunately, Pauline is so busy "helping" her employees get through the meal periods that there seems to be little time for thinking and planning about the strategies and techniques she will have to apply if she is to solve her labor-related customer service problems. In years past, when labor was relatively inexpensive, Pauline might have responded to her need for more workers by simply hiring more employees. Today's foodservice manager, however, does not have that luxury. In the current tight and increasingly costly labor market, you will need to learn the supervisory skills to motivate your current staff, as well as the cost control skills required to effectively evaluate their efforts. When you do, you will be able to accomplish all necessary tasks and stay within your allotted labor budget.

At one time, labor-related expenses were much less important to the foodservice manager than they are today. In some foodservice establishments, the cost of labor exceeds the cost of food and beverage products. Today's competitive workforce would indicate that future foodservice managers may well find it even more difficult to recruit, train, and retain an effective cadre of employees. Therefore, the control of labor expenses takes on a greater level of importance than ever before. In some sectors of the foodservice industry, a reputation for long hours, poor pay, and undesirable working conditions has caused quality employees to look elsewhere for a more satisfactory job or career. It does not have to be that way, and it is up to you to help ensure that in your organization it is not. When labor costs are adequately controlled, management has the funds necessary to create both desirable working conditions and pay a wage necessary to attract the very best employees the labor pool has to offer. In every service industry, better employees mean better service and, ultimately, better profits.

Labor Expense Defined

Payroll is the term generally used to refer to the salaries and wages you will pay your employees. **Labor expense** includes salaries and wages, but it consists of other labor-related costs as well. In addition to salaries and wages, the following expenses are also related to employees and, thus, are considered labor expenses:

1. FICA (Social Security) taxes
2. Unemployment taxes
3. Workman's compensation
4. Group life insurance
5. Health insurance
6. Pension/retirement plan payments
7. Employee meals
8. Employee training expense
9. Employee transportation
10. Employee uniforms, housing, and other benefits
11. Vacation/sick leave
12. Employee incentives and bonuses

Not all foodservice units will incur all of the preceding costs. Some will have additional costs. You can be sure, however, that regardless of the facility you manage, you will incur some labor-related expenses in addition to payroll costs. The critical question you must answer is similar to the one posed by Pauline in the previous example. That is, "How much should I spend on payroll and labor expense to provide the quality of products and service that I feel is appropriate?" Before turning to that question, it is important that you fully understand the components of payroll and labor expense.

Payroll

Payroll refers to the gross pay received by an employee in exchange for his or her work. That is, if an employee earns $8.00 per hour and works 40 hours for his or her employer, the gross paycheck (the employee's paycheck before any mandatory or voluntary deductions) would be $320 ($8.00 per hour × 40 hours = $320). This amount is considered a payroll expense.

If the employee earns a salary, that salary amount is also a payroll expense. A **salaried employee** receives the same income per week or month regardless of the number of hours worked. Thus, if a salaried employee is paid $500 per week whether he or she works 40 hours in that week or more than 40 hours, we consider that $500 part of the payroll expense also. Payroll, then, is one part of labor expense.

Fixed Payroll Versus Variable Payroll When you manage a foodservice facility, you must make choices regarding the number and type of employees you will hire to help you serve your guests. Some employees are needed simply to open the doors for minimally anticipated business as, for example, a manager whose payroll includes one server, one cook, and the manager. In this case, the cost of providing payroll to these three individuals is called a **minimum-staff** payroll. Minimum staff is used to designate the least number of employees, or payroll dollars, required to operate a facility or department within the facility.

Suppose, however, that you anticipate much greater volume on a given day. The increased number of guests expected means that you must have more cooks, more servers, added cashiers, more dishroom personnel, and, perhaps, more supervisors to handle the additional workload. Clearly, these additional staff positions create a work group that is far larger than the minimum staff, but is of a size that you feel is needed to adequately service the anticipated number of guests. In this case, your staff size would far exceed that of the minimum staff.

Some managers confuse the minimum-staff concept with that of fixed payroll and variable payroll. **Fixed payroll** refers to the amount an operation pays in salaries. This amount is fixed in that it remains unchanged from one pay period to the next unless the individual receiving the pay separates employment from the organization. **Variable payroll** consists of those dollars paid to hourly employees. Thus, variable payroll is the amount that "varies" with changes in volume. Generally, as you anticipate increased volume levels in your facility, you will add additional hourly employees. When lower levels of volume are anticipated, the number of hourly employees scheduled will likely decrease. In a similar manner, if increased volume levels are anticipated to sustain themselves over a long period of time, you may determine that additional salaried employees are beneficial to your organization. The distinction between fixed and variable labor is an important one, since you may sometimes have little control over your fixed labor expense, while, at the same time, exerting nearly 100% control over variable labor expenses that are above your minimum-staff levels.

Labor Expense

Labor expense refers to the total of *all* costs associated with maintaining your foodservice workforce. As such, labor expense is always larger than payroll expense. Foodservice managers must keep in mind that total labor expense will always exceed that of payroll. As the cost of providing employee benefits increases or employment taxes go up, labor expense will increase, even if payroll expense remains constant.

Most foodservice operators have total control over their payroll expense. It is, therefore, often referred to as a "controllable" labor expense. Those labor expenses, on the other hand, over which an operator has little or no control are called "noncontrollable" labor expenses. These expenses include items such as federal- or state-mandated payroll taxes, insurance premiums, and retirement plan payments. In reality, however, you can exert some control even over these noncontrollable labor expenses as, for example, a foodservice manager who works very hard to ensure a well-trained workforce in a safe environment and achieves, thereby, a lower rate on accident and health insurance for his or her employees.

In this chapter, we shall deal primarily with payroll-related expenses. This is in keeping with the concept that these are the most controllable of our labor-related expenses, and the ones most managers will evaluate when they are called upon to control labor expenses.

In order to determine how much labor is needed to operate the business, a foodservice manager must be able to determine how much work each fixed and variable employee can perform. If too few employees are scheduled on any given day, poor service and lack of sales can result, as guests go elsewhere. If too many employees are scheduled, payroll and other labor expenses will be too high for the day, resulting in reduced profits. The solution is to know how many employees are required given the estimated number of guests anticipated on any given day. In order to determine this number of employees, you must have a clear idea of the **productivity** of each of your employees. Productivity, simply put, is the amount of work performed by an employee in a fixed period of time.

Assessing Labor Productivity

There are many ways to assess labor productivity. In general, productivity is measured in terms of the **productivity ratio** as follows:

$$\frac{\text{Output}}{\text{Input}} = \text{Productivity Ratio}$$

Take, for example, a restaurant in which four servers are employed to serve 60 guests. Using the productivity ratio formula, the *output* is guests served, the *input* is servers employed, as follows:

$$\frac{60 \text{ Guests}}{4 \text{ Servers}} = 15 \text{ Guests per Server}$$

This formula demonstrates that, for each server employed, 15 guests can be served. The productivity ratio is one server per 15 guests (1/15) or, stated another way, 15 guests to one server (15 to 1).

There are several ways of defining foodservice output and input; thus, there are several types of productivity ratios. Some of these will be presented later in this chapter. All of these productivity ratios are helpful in determining the answer to the question, "How much should I spend on labor?" The answer, however, is more complicated than it might seem at first glance. In the preceding example, you know that, on average, one server can serve 15 guests. But how many guests will a slow server serve? How about your best server? How much do we pay for our best server? Our poorest? Are you better off scheduling your best server if you anticipate 20 guests or should you schedule two of your slower servers? How can the slower server be developed into an above-average server? At what cost? These are the types of questions that must be answered daily if you are to effectively manage payroll costs. These costs can, however, be managed. Each foodservice operator must develop his or her method for managing payroll because each foodservice unit is different. Consider the differences between managing payroll costs at a small, quick-service food kiosk in a shopping mall and a large banquet kitchen in a convention hotel. While the actual application of the methods may vary, payroll costs can be controlled in any foodservice operation you may manage.

Maintaining a Productive Workforce

Before we discuss how to establish and use productivity ratios, however, it is important to examine the factors that make employees more productive and, thus, directly affect productivity. The following are 10 key employee-related factors that affect employee productivity:

---

10 Key Factors Affecting Employee Productivity

1. Employee selection
2. Training
3. Supervision
4. Scheduling
5. Breaks
6. Morale
7. Menu
8. Convenience versus scratch preparation
9. Equipment
10. Service level desired

Employee Selection

Choosing the right employee from the beginning is vitally important in developing a highly productive workforce. Good foodservice managers know that proper selection procedures go a long way toward establishing the kind of workforce that can be both efficient and effective. This involves matching the right employee with the right job. The process begins with the development of the job description.

Job Description   A **job description** is a listing of the tasks that must be accomplished by the employee hired to fill a particular position. For example, in the case of a room service delivery person in a large hotel, the tasks might be listed as indicated on the job description card labeled Figure 7.1.

A simple job description like the one in Figure 7.1 should be maintained for every position in the foodservice operation. From the job description, a job specification can be prepared.

Job Specification   A **job specification** is a listing of the personal characteristics needed to perform the tasks contained in a particular job description. Figure 7.2 shows the job specification card that would match the job description in Figure 7.1.

As can be seen, this position requires a specific set of personal characteristics and skills. When a room service delivery person is hired, the job specification requirements must be foremost in management's mind. If the job specs do not exist or are not followed, it is likely that employees may be hired who are simply not able to be highly productive. Each employee must bring either the skills necessary to do the job or the ability to acquire those skills. It is your role to develop and maintain both job descriptions and job specifications so that employees know what their jobs are, and you know the characteristics that your employees must have, or be trained in, to do their jobs well. When actually beginning to select employees for your vacancies, you will likely use one or more of the following selection aids:

1. Applications
2. Interviews
3. Preemployment testing
4. Background/reference checks

Applications   The employment application is a document completed by the candidate for employment. It will generally list the name, address, work experience, and related information of the candidate. It is important that each employment candidate for a given position be required to fill out an identical application, and that an application be on file for each candidate who is ultimately selected for the position.

Interviews   From the employment applications submitted, you will select some candidates for the interview process. It is important to realize that the types of questions that can be asked in the interview are highly restricted. This is because job interviews, if improperly performed, can subject an employer to legal liability. If a candidate is not hired based on his or her answer to–or refusal to answer–an inappropriate question, that candidate has the right to file a lawsuit. The Equal Employment Opportunity Commission suggests that an employer consider the following three

FIGURE **7.1** ● Job Description

Job Description

Unit Name: **Thunder Lodge Resort**   Position Title: **Room Service Delivery Person**

Primary Tasks:

1. Answer telephone to receive
   guest orders

2. Set up room service trays
   in steward area

3. Deliver trays to room, as requested

4. Remove tray covers upon delivery

5. Remove soiled trays from floors

6. Maintain guest check control

7. Balance room service cash drawer

8. Clean room service setup area
   at conclusion of shift

9. Other duties, as assigned by
   supervisor

10. _____

11. _____

12. _____

Special Comments: Hourly rate excludes tips. Uniform allowance is $35.00
per week
_____
_____

Salary Range: $8.00–$10.25/hour   Signature: Matt V.

FIGURE **7.2** ● Job Specification

Job Specification

Unit Name: **Thunder Lodge Resort**   Position Title: **Room Service Delivery Person**

Personal Characteristics Required:

1. Good telephone skills; clear, easily understood English

2. Ability to operate cash register

3. Bondable

4. Detail oriented

5. Pleasant personality

6. Discreet

Special Comments: Good grooming habits are especially important in this position as employee will be a primary guest contact person.

Job Specification Prepared By: Matt V.

---

questions in deciding whether to include a particular question on an employment application or in a job interview:

1. Does this question tend to screen out minorities or females?
2. Is the answer needed in order to judge this individual's competence for performance of the job?
3. Are there alternative, nondiscriminatory ways to judge the person's qualifications?

In all cases, questions asked both on the application and in the interview should focus on the applicant's job skills and nothing else.

Preemployment Testing Preemployment testing is a common way to help improve employee productivity. In the hospitality industry, preemployment testing will generally fall into one of the following categories:

1. Skills tests
2. Psychological tests
3. Drug screening tests

Skills tests can include activities such as typing tests for office employees, computer application tests for those involved in using word processing or spreadsheet tools, or food production tasks, as in the case of chefs. **Psychological testing** can include personality tests, tests designed to predict performance, or tests of mental ability.

Preemployment drug testing is used to determine if an applicant uses drugs. It is allowable in most states, and can be a very effective tool for reducing insurance rates and potential employee liability issues. It is permissible to ask an applicant if he or she uses drugs. It is also allowable to ask candidates if they are willing to submit to a voluntary drug test as a condition of employment. Of course, potential employees have a right to refuse to submit to a drug screening test, just as you have a right to insist that all prospective employees submit to such a test. The important point to remember is that, if you are using drug screening, it must be used on all employees and not just those you may suspect of drug use. To selectively, rather than uniformly, require drug screening could place you and your organization in legal jeopardy if you were subject to charges of discrimination.

A drug-free environment tends to attract better quality employment candidates, with the resulting impact of a higher quality workforce with greater productivity. Most hospitality companies find that drug testing as a preemployment screening device not only boosts employee productivity, but reduces job-related accidents as well.

Background/Reference Checks Increasingly, hospitality employers are utilizing background checks prior to hiring employees in selected positions. Common verification points include the following:

○ Name
○ Social security number
○ Address history
○ Dates of past employment and duties performed
○ Education/training
○ Criminal background

Background checks, like preemployment testing, can leave an employer subject to litigation if the information secured during a check is false or used in a way that violates employment law. In addition, if the information is improperly disclosed to third parties, it could violate the employee's right to privacy. Not conducting background checks on some positions can, however, subject the employer to potential litigation under the doctrine of **negligent hiring,** that is, a failure on the part of an employer to exercise reasonable care in the selection of employees. When background checks are performed, a candidate for employment should be required to sign a consent form authorizing you to conduct the background check.

In the past, employment references were a very popular tool for managers to use in the screening process. In today's litigious society, however, they are much more difficult to obtain. While many organizations still seek information from past employers about an employee's previous work performance, few sophisticated companies will divulge such information. To help minimize the risk of litigation related to reference checks, it is best to secure the applicant's permission in writing before contacting an ex-employer. Even with such authorization, however, many employers are reluctant to give out information about former employees. Verification of such application entries such as dates of employment and duties performed can be helpful to you in making decisions about the potential "fit" and, thus, productivity of a potential employee.

The advertising for, interviewing, and selection of the right employee for the right job is a specialized area of human resources, and you will often be able to rely on a human resources department in your organization for assistance when undertaking this important task. Selection of employees is, in the final analysis, critically important in creating a productive workforce in your facility.

Training

Perhaps no area under your control holds greater promise for increased employee productivity related to current employees than improvement through training. In fact, the human being is the only asset we can expand without spending money. In too many cases, however, training in the hospitality industry is poor or almost nonexistent. Highly productive employees are well-trained employees, and, frequently, employees with low productivity are poorly trained. Every position in a foodservice operation should have a specific, well-developed, and ongoing training program. Effective training will improve job satisfaction and instill in employees a sense of well-being and accomplishment. It will also reduce confusion, product waste, and loss of guests. In addition, supervisors find that a well-trained workforce is easier to manage than one in which the employees are poorly trained. An additional advantage of a well-trained workforce is that management will be more effective because of reduced stress, in terms of both work completion and interpersonal relationships.

Effective training begins with a good orientation program. The following list includes some of the concerns that most employees have when they start a new job. You should identify which items are relevant to your new employees, and take care to provide information in each area, in written or verbal form.

Orientation Program Information

1. Payday
2. Annual performance review
3. Probationary period
4. Dress code
5. Telephone call policy
6. Smoking policy
7. Uniform allowance
8. Disciplinary system
9. Educational assistance
10. Work schedule
11. Mandatory meetings
12. Tip policy
13. Transfers
14. Employee meal policy
15. Sexual harassment policy
16. Lockers/security
17. Jury duty
18. Leave of absence
19. Maternity leave
20. Alcohol/drug policy
21. Employee assistance programs
22. Tardy policy
23. Sick leave policy
24. Vacation policy
25. Holidays and holiday pay
26. Overtime pay
27. Insurance
28. Retirement programs
29. Safety/emergency procedures
30. Grievance procedures

Most employees truly want to do a good job for their employer. To achieve this, most employees look forward to and enjoy participating in training sessions. Managers who like to train tend to find themselves with motivated employees. Managers who, on the other hand, dislike or can find no time for training usually encounter less productive, less motivated individuals.

Training programs need not be elaborate. They must, however, be continual. Hospitality companies can train in many different areas. Some training seeks to influence attitudes and actions as, for example, when training to prevent work-related harassment is presented. In other cases, training may be undertaken to assist employees with stress or other psychologically related job aspects. In most cases, however, the training you will be responsible for as a unit manager is **task training.** Task training is the training undertaken to ensure an employee has the skills to meet productivity goals. The development of a training program for any task involves the following:

1. Determine how the task is to be done.
2. Plan the training session.
3. Present the training session.
4. Evaluate the session's effectiveness.
5. Retrain at the proper interval.

Determine How the Task Is to Be Done Often, jobs can be done in more ways than one. An employee making a salad may elect to clean carrots prior to washing the lettuce, with no effect on the total amount of time it takes to prepare the salad. In other areas, for example, in taking table service orders on a guest check, management may have very specific procedures that must be followed so that both cooks and cashiers can receive the guest's order and process it properly. When management has determined how a task should be completed, that method should be made part of the training program and should be strictly maintained unless a better method can be demonstrated. If this is not done, employees will find that "anything goes," and product consistency, along with service levels, will vary tremendously. Employees watch management very carefully. If management is not diligent in the enforcement of standard operating procedures, employees may perform tasks in a manner that is easiest for them. This may, of course, not be the manner that is best for your operation. This is not to underestimate the value of employee input in job design. They should certainly have input into the execution of a task, but once management has made the decision to follow a certain procedure, it must be communicated and enforced. This enforcement is best done through a positive approach. Managers should focus less on people who are "doing it wrong" than on those who are "doing it right." Positive reinforcement and praise, as well as rewarding employees for a job well done, are powerful management tools since most employees truly want to be recognized by management for that good job.

Plan the Training Session Like any other important management task, the training session must be planned. This includes asking and appropriately answering the following questions:

1. Who should be trained?
2. Who should do the training?
3. Where should the training occur?
4. When should the session occur?
5. What tools, materials, or supplies are needed to conduct the session?
6. What should the length of the session be?
7. How frequently should the sessions occur?
8. How and where will the attendance and completion records regarding each training session offered be kept?

Good training sessions are the result of a felt need by management to train personnel, matched with a management philosophy that training is important. Taking time to effectively plan the training session is a good way for you to let employees know that you take the training process seriously. Whether the training session is a video, a demonstration, or a lecture/presentation, time spent planning the session is time well spent.

Present the Training Session   Many managers feel that they have no time for training. But management is about teaching, encouraging, and coaching. You must find the time. Any manager who is interested in the long-term success of his or her operation and employees will set aside time each week to conduct a formal training session. Some managers maintain that all of the training in *their* unit must be of the **OJT** type (on-the-job training). They feel that structured training either takes too long or is inappropriate. In nearly all cases, this is incorrect and is a major cause of the rather low rate of productivity so prevalent in the hospitality industry.

The best training sessions are presented with enthusiasm and an attitude of encouragement. Make sure that training is presented not because employees "don't know," but rather because management wants them to "know more." Involve employees in the presentation of training exercises. Seek their input in the sessions. Ask questions that encourage discussion and always conclude the sessions on a positive note.

A brief, but effective, outline for each session could be as follows:

1. Tell the employees what you hope to teach them and why.
2. Present the session.
3. Reemphasize main points and discuss why they are important.
4. Ask for questions to ensure understanding.

Evaluate the Session's Effectiveness   There is a saying in education that "if the student hasn't learned, then the teacher hasn't taught." This concept, when applied to hospitality training, implies that presenting a training session is not enough. Training should cause behavior to change. Either employees improve or gain a new skill, knowledge, or information, or they have not learned. If you are to know which of these is the case, you must evaluate the training session. This can be as simple as observing employee behavior (to test skill acquisition) or as detailed as preparing written questions (to test knowledge retention).

Posttraining evaluation should also be directed at how the sessions were conducted. Were they too long? Planned well? Delivered with the appropriate attitude? The evaluation of training is as important as its delivery. Both the content of the session and the delivery itself should be evaluated. The bottom line, of course, is changed behavior. A workforce that is trained well is more productive. In fact, employees who are well trained are both more productive and more highly motivated.

Retrain at the Proper Interval   Few 35-year-old foodservice managers could walk into a room, sit down, and pass, with a good or better grade, the algebra final they took in high school some 18 or so years earlier. Why is that? The answer is not that they did not learn algebra. Clearly, they knew the answers at one time. Humans, however, do not learn and then remain stagnant. We learn, unlearn, and relearn on a regular basis. The telephone number we knew so well 10 years ago is now gone from memory. The friend or teacher's name we knew we would never forget, is forgotten. In the same way, employees who are well trained in an operation's policies and procedures need to be constantly reminded and updated if their skill level is to remain high. Declines in performance levels can come about through a change in the operational systems you have in place or changes in equipment used. When this is true, you must retrain your employees. Nearly every operating foodservice manager can remember an instance when the conversation went something like this:

SUPERVISOR:	*"Alex, I thought I told you to . . ."*
ALEX:	*"I did!"*
SUPERVISOR:	*"Yes, you did it, but you did it wrong. That's not how we do it here!"*
ALEX:	*"Oh yeah, I forgot! I'll get it right next time."*
SUPERVISOR:	*"Good! Make sure you do!"*

The point is that, without a regular retraining program, Alex will *not* get it right the next time. It matters little whether Alex never got the correct training, or whether he got it, but now has forgotten. Conversations like this are a sure sign that effective training sessions are not in place on a regular basis.

Training a workforce is one, if not the best, method of improving employee productivity. Effective training costs a small amount in time in the short run, but pays off extremely well in dollars in the long run. The managers who have risen to the top in the hospitality industry have some specific characteristics and traits. Chief among these is their desire to teach and encourage their employees and, thus, get the best results from each and every one of them.

Supervision

All employees require proper supervision. This is not to say that all employees desire to have someone tell them what to do. Proper supervision means assisting employees in improving productivity. In this sense, the supervisor is a helper and facilitator who provides assistance. Supervising should be a matter of assisting employees to do their best, not just identifying their shortcomings. It is said that employees think one of two things when they see their boss approaching:

1. Here comes help!
   or
2. Here comes trouble!

For those supervisors whose employees feel that the boss is an asset to their daily routine, productivity gains are remarkable. Supervisors who see their position as one of power and taskmaster only can rarely maintain the quality workforce necessary to compete in today's competitive market. It is important to remember that it is the employee who services the guest and not management. When supervision is geared toward helping, the guest benefits and, thus, the operation benefits. This is why it is so important for managers to be **on the floor,** in other words, in the dining area, during meal periods. The foodservice manager is, in the final analysis, the individual in the best position to see what must be done to satisfy the guest. This means being where the action is when meals are served. Greeting guests, solving bottleneck problems, maintaining food quality, and ensuring excellent service are all tasks of the foodservice manager during the service period. When employees see that management is committed to customer service and is there to assist employees in delivering that service, their productivity will improve. Again, most employees want to please both the guest and the boss. When both can be pleased at once, productivity rises. If employees feel that they can only satisfy the guest *or* the operation, difficulties will arise.

Consider, for example, the employee who has been instructed to serve one 2-ounce portion of tartar sauce with a particular fried fish dinner. When she does so, she finds that 80% of the guests request a second portion of the tartar sauce. If management does not respond to this consumer demand and adjust the portion size, the employee is faced with a difficult choice: "Do I satisfy management (serve one portion) or the guest (serve two portions)?" Clearly, situations such as this can, and do, occur, but they must be resolved by management. Good managers do this by involving themselves closely with the work of their employees.

This does not mean that the supervisor *does* the employees' work, but rather that employees know that they can go to management with their problems or, better yet, that they can say: "Here comes help" when they see the boss approaching.

Scheduling

Even with highly productive employees, poor employee scheduling by management can result in low productivity ratios. Consider the example in Figure 7.3, where management has determined a schedule for potwashers in a unit that is open for three meals a day.

In Schedule A, four employees are scheduled for 32 hours at a rate of $8.00 per hour. Payroll, in this case, would be $256 per day (32 hours/day × $8.00/hour = $256/day). Each shift, breakfast, lunch, and dinner, has two employees scheduled.

In Schedule B, three employees are scheduled for 24 hours. At the same rate of $8.00 per hour, payroll would be $192 per day (24 hours/day × $8.00/hour = $192/day). Wages, in this case, are reduced by $64 ($256 − $192 = $64), not to mention the savings that will be made due to reduced benefits, employee meal costs, and other labor-related expenses. Schedule A assumes that the amount of work to be done is identical at all times of the day. Schedule B covers both the lunch and the dinner shifts with two employees, but assumes that one potwasher is sufficient in the early-morning period as well as very late in the day.

When scheduling is done to meet projected demand, productivity ratios will increase. If production standards are to be established and monitored, management must do its job in ensuring that employees are scheduled only when needed to meet the sales or volume anticipated. Returning to our formula for computing the productivity ratio, assume that 600 pots are to be washed and that four rather than three potwashers are scheduled to work. Figure 7.4 shows the effect on the productivity ratio of different scheduling decisions.

Proper scheduling ensures that the correct number of employees is available to do the necessary amount of work. If too many employees are scheduled, productivity ratios will decline. If too few employees are scheduled, customer service levels may suffer or necessary tasks may not be completed on time or as well as they should be.

Since work in the foodservice operation tends to occur in peaks and valleys, in other words, people in the United States tend to eat in three major time periods, the foodservice manager is often faced with uneven demands regarding the number of employees needed. In a hotel restaurant, the slow period might be a weekend when most business travelers are at home rather than in the hotel. In an upscale restaurant, the slow period may be during the week with volume picking up on the weekends. In a college foodservice operation, the summers may be slow, but a beach resort may be extremely busy during that time. Demand can also vary from morning to evening. In some restaurants with a busy lunch, 5 cooks and 15 servers may be necessary. At 3:00 in the afternoon at the same restaurant, one cook and one server may find themselves with few guests to serve. Scheduling efficiency can often be improved through the use of the **split-shift,** a technique used to match individual employee work shifts with peaks and valleys of customer demand. In using a split shift, the manager would require an employee to work a busy period, for example, lunch, then be off in the afternoon, only to return for the busy dinner period. Employee scheduling in the hospitality industry is difficult. It is important, however, that it be done well. Productivity standards help the foodservice operator match workload to the number of employees required.

FIGURE **7.3** ● Two Alternative Schedules

Schedule A

	7:30 to 8:30	8:30 to 9:30	9:30 to 10:30	10:30 to 11:30	11:30 to 12:30	12:30 to 1:30	1:30 to 2:30	2:30 to 3:30	3:30 to 4:30	4:30 to 5:30	5:30 to 6:30	6:30 to 7:30	7:30 to 8:30	8:30 to 9:30	9:30 to 10:30	10:30 to 11:30
Employee 1		■	■	■	■	■	■	■								
Employee 2		■	■	■	■	■	■	■								
Employee 3									■	■	■	■	■	■	■	■
Employee 4									■	■	■	■	■	■	■	■

Total Hours = 32

Schedule B

	7:30 to 8:30	8:30 to 9:30	9:30 to 10:30	10:30 to 11:30	11:30 to 12:30	12:30 to 1:30	1:30 to 2:30	2:30 to 3:30	3:30 to 4:30	4:30 to 5:30	5:30 to 6:30	6:30 to 7:30	7:30 to 8:30	8:30 to 9:30	9:30 to 10:30	10:30 to 11:30
Employee 1	█	█	█	█	█	█	█	█								
Employee 2					█	█	█	█	█	█	█	█				
Employee 3									█	█	█	█	█	█	█	█

Total Hours = 24

293

FIGURE **7.4** ● Effect of Scheduling on Productivity Ratios

Number of Pots to Be Washed	Number of Potwashers Scheduled	Productivity Ratio
600	4	150 pots/washer
600	3	200 pots/washer

FUN ON THE WEB!

Look up the following sites to view companies that sell software designed for employee scheduling and much more!

www.alohapos.com Once into the home page, scroll down and click on "Back Office." Then, click on "Labor Scheduler" to learn about this software's features. Have some fun, and try the demo!

www.foodsoftware.com Click on "Restaurant Computer Products Catalog," then click on "Employee Scheduling and Human Resources." Next, click on "Schedule Maker" to see what this company has to offer to help you with scheduling.

www.symbioticsys.com Click on "Foodservice Boss," then click on "Products." Scroll down and click on "Schedule Maker" to see how you can use this product for scheduling employees.

Breaks

It is a fact that employees cannot work at top speed for eight hours at a time. Employees have both a physical and a mental need for breaks from their work. These breaks give them a chance to pause, collect their thoughts, converse with their fellow employees, and, in general, prepare for the next work session. As management, the foodservice supervisor must determine both the frequency and the length of designated breaks. In some cases, especially regarding the employment of students and minors, both federal and state law may mandate breaks for employees; as a manager, you will need to check these laws.

Employees need to know that management cares enough about them to establish a break schedule and then maintain it. Of course, employees must be prepared to alter their break schedule when the workload requires it. Short, frequent breaks have been shown to increase employee productivity and morale. Management should not view breaks as lost or wasted time; instead, they should be viewed as a necessary part of maintaining a highly productive workforce. The truth is that employees who are given frequent, short breaks will outproduce those who are not given any. It simply makes no sense, then, for management to behave as if they begrudge their staff the breaks that are so beneficial to the organization, as well as to the employee.

Morale

Employee morale is not often mentioned in a discussion about controlling foodservice costs. Yet, as experienced managers will attest, it is impossible to overestimate the value of a highly motivated employee or crew. While it is a truism that employees motivate themselves, it is also true that effective managers provide an environment that makes it easy for employees to want to be motivated. Management creates this environment. History is filled with examples of groups who have achieved goals that seemed impossible because they were highly motivated. Serving people is fun. It is exciting. If this fun and excitement can be instilled in each employee, work also becomes fun and exciting.

Volumes have been written about the manner in which managers can create a highly motivated workforce. It is the authors' opinion, however, that those work groups with high morale share a common trait. In general, these groups work for a manager or management team that has the following characteristics:

1. Management has created a vision.
2. The vision is constantly communicated to employees.
3. The vision is shared and embraced by both management and employees.

Creating a vision is nothing more than finding a "purpose" for the workforce. Any manager who communicates that the purpose for a potwasher is simply to clean pots cannot expect to have a fired-up, turned-on employee. Yet, potwashers can have high morale. They can be a critical part of management's overall purpose for the work crew. Consider, for purposes of illustration, some of the following techniques you could use to communicate a customer service vision to potwashers:

1. If your unit has been, as it should be, free from cases of foodborne illness, part of the credit goes to your potwashing staff. Recognize them for this achievement on a quarterly basis.
2. Conduct regular "potwashing station inspections." Score the area for cleanliness on a scale of 1 to 100. Present each potwasher with a certificate when the area score exceeds 90. If it does not exceed 90, increase training until it does!

3. Recognize your "best" potwasher at an annual employee recognition luncheon or dinner for:
   a. Best attendance
   b. Best productivity
   c. Cleanest work area
   d. Most improved
   e. Most thorough
   f. Most often in proper uniform
4. Include a potwasher on your safety committee. Publicly recognize all committee members on a regular basis.
5. Make it a point to go to the potwashing area on a daily basis to thank those employees for a job well done. Emphasize the importance of their efforts.
6. Encourage food production employees (your potwashers' customers) to take the time to thank the potwashers for their contribution to the food production process.

If the purpose or vision that management creates is only financial profit for the organization or owners, the vision will not likely be shared by employees, even if it is strongly communicated. If management's vision, however, includes the vital importance of each employee, each employee can share that vision. This vision might be to be the number one unit in sales volume, or the unit with the highest percentage sales increase, or the unit with the lowest food cost. Whatever management's vision for the unit, it must be communicated to the employees with a sense that they can share and benefit from its pursuit. A shared purpose between management and employee is important for the development and maintenance of high morale. It is just not enough for management to feel that employees should be "glad to have a job." This type of attitude by management results in high employee turnover and lost productivity.

Employee turnover *is* high in some sections of the hospitality industry. By some estimates, it exceeds 200% per year. You can measure your turnover by using the following formula:

$$\text{Employee Turnover Rate} = \frac{\text{Number of Employees Separated}}{\text{Number of Employees in Workforce}}$$

For example, assume that you have a total of 50 employees in your foodservice operation. In the past year, you replaced 35 employees. Your turnover rate is computed as follows:

$$\frac{35 \text{ Employees Separated}}{50 \text{ Employees in Workforce}} = 70\% \text{ Turnover Rate}$$

Separated is the term used to describe employees who have either quit, been terminated, or in some other manner have "separated" themselves from the operation. The number of employees in the workforce is computed by adding the number of employees at the beginning of the accounting period to the number of employees at the end of the accounting period, and dividing the sum by two. The number of employees in the workforce, then, refers to the average number of people employed by the operation during a given time period.

Some foodservice operators prefer to use the terms voluntary separation and involuntary separation. A **voluntary separation** is one in which the employee made the decision to leave the organization. This may have been due, for example, to retirement, a better opportunity in another organization, or relocation to another state. An **involuntary separation** is one in which management has caused the employee to separate from the organization. This may have been, for example, firing the employee because of poor attendance, violation of procedures or policy, or a reduction in workforce. Some managers want to know the amount of turnover that is voluntary as opposed to involuntary. For example, excessively high voluntary turnover rates may be a signal that wages and salaries are too low to keep your best employees. High involuntary turnover rates may mean that employee screening and selection techniques may need to be reviewed and improved.

If it is your preference, you can modify the turnover formula to create these two ratios:

Involuntary Employee Turnover Rate
$$= \frac{\text{Number of Employees Involuntarily Separated}}{\text{Number of Employees in Workforce}}$$

Voluntary Employee Turnover Rate
$$= \frac{\text{Number of Employees Voluntarily Separated}}{\text{Number of Employees in Workforce}}$$

Whether separation is involuntary or voluntary, turnover is expensive. Employee turnover costs you in terms that are both actual and hidden. Actual costs, such as those involved in advertising the vacancy, relocation costs, interviewing and training time, and record keeping, are easy to determine. The hidden costs of increased dishroom breakage due to a new warewasher, slower customer service and, thus, smaller stations in the dining room by a new server, or an increase in improperly prepared food by a new cook–all are expenses that can cost dearly an operation with high turnover rates. Good foodservice managers calculate and closely monitor their turnover rates. High turnover rates mean trouble.

Low rates mean that employees feel good about the operation they work for.

To counteract the turnover syndrome, management can decide to be smart. It can seek to give job satisfaction by providing a healthy environment and wholesome working conditions. It can create and train a strong and loyal workforce that will be willing and committed to work under many different conditions, some pleasant, some less so. If the understanding between management and the workforce is established over time, on good faith, the relationship will transcend and exceed the monetary value attached to the job and allow for the establishment of a committed, dependable, and permanent staff.

A belief that both managers and employees share a common vision, and a noble one at that, creates the kind of environment that yields high employee productivity and morale and reduced turnover rates, which will result in your staff providing excellent service to your guests.

Menu

A major factor in employee productivity is the foodservice operation's actual menu. The items that you elect to serve on your menu will have a profound effect on your employees' ability to produce the items quickly and efficiently.

In general, the more variety of items a kitchen is asked to produce, the less efficient that kitchen will be. Of course, if management does not provide the guest with enough choices, loss of sales may result. Clearly, neither too many nor too few menu choices should be offered. The question for management is, "How many are too many?" The answer depends on the operation, the skill level of employees, and the level of variety management feels is necessary to properly service the guests.

Menus that continue to grow and grow cost in other ways as well. The quick-service unit that elects to specialize in hamburgers can prepare them quickly and efficiently. The same restaurant that decides to add pizza, tacos, salads, and fried chicken may find that employees are not only less productive, but guests are confused as to what the operation really is. Again, the dilemma management faces is to serve the widest variety possible, but not so many things as to markedly reduce employee productivity.

While the number of items produced is important, so is the type of item. Obviously, a small diner with one deep-fat fryer will have production problems if the day's specials are fried fish, fried chicken, and a breaded fried vegetable platter! Menu items must be selected to complement the skill level of the employees and the equipment available to produce the menu item. Most foodservice operations change their menu fairly infrequently. Print costs are often high, and restaurateurs are reluctant to radically change their product offerings. Thus, it is extremely important that the menu items selected by management are items that can be prepared efficiently and well. If this is done, productivity rates will be high, as will guest satisfaction.

Convenience Versus Scratch Preparation

Few, if any, foodservice operators today make all of their menu items from scratch. Indeed, there is no real agreement among operators as to what "scratch cooking" is. Canned fruits, frozen seafood, and prebaked pastries are examples of foods that would not be available to many guests if it were not for the fact that they were processed to some degree before they were delivered to the foodservice operator's door. At one time, presliced white bread was considered a convenience item. Today, this is considered a staple. Some foods, like canned cheese sauce, can be modified by the operator to produce a unique item. This can be done by the addition of special ingredients according to the standardized recipe, with the intent of creating a product served only by *that* foodservice operation.

The decision of whether to "make" or "buy" involves two major factors. The first is, of course, product quality. In general, if an operation can make a product that is superior to the one it can buy from a supplier, it should produce that item. The second factor, product cost, is also a major issue for management. It is possible that management determines that a given menu item can be made in house and that it is a superior product. The cost of preparing that product, however, may be so great that it is simply not cost effective to do so. Fortunately, convenience products are becoming more quality driven and less expensive due to advances in technology and increased competition among the major food suppliers.

Consider the situation that would arise if you managed a quick-service Mexican restaurant. One of the items that you use is frijoles, or cooked pinto beans, which are seasoned and mashed. Assume that you use 50 EP pounds of beans like this per day. You can buy the beans in a can for 80 cents per pound. Your cost per pound with the canned product includes only the cost of the beans. In addition, you would incur the labor cost required to open the cans and the cost of cooking fuel to heat the beans.

If you were to consider making the frijoles from scratch, your food cost would go down to 36 cents per pound (the price of the dried pinto beans), a savings of over 50%. The complete story, however, can only be viewed when you consider the labor required to produce the frijoles. Figure 7.5 details the hypothetical costs involved in the decision that you must make, assuming a usage of 50 pounds of product per day and a labor cost of $8.00 per hour to both cook the beans and clean up the production process.

As you can see in this example, you would experience a reduction in your cost of food if you made the frijoles from scratch but an increase in the cost of labor, since your own employees must now complete the cooking process. In the case of frijoles, your decision may well be to purchase

FIGURE **7.5** ● Frijoles: 50 Pounds

Component	Cost of Convenience Product	Cost of Scratch Product
Beans	$40.00 ($0.80/lb.)	$18.00 ($0.36/lb.)
Seasoning	0	2.00
Labor	8.00 (1 hour)	32.00 (4 hours)
Fuel	1.40	4.40
Total Cost	49.40	56.40

the convenience item rather than make it from scratch because the overall cost would be less.

Management, often in consultation with kitchen production staff, must resolve make or buy decisions. It is important to note, however, that these decisions affect both food and labor costs. One cannot generally achieve food cost savings without expending additional labor dollars. Conversely, when a manager elects to buy rather than make an item from scratch, food costs tend to rise but labor costs should decline. In general, productivity in your operation will rise when you elect to buy, rather than make from scratch, any item that you cannot produce efficiently. This may be due to specialized skills required, as is the case with some purchased bakery items, or it could simply be a case of your supplier having the tools and equipment necessary to do a time-consuming task at a great savings to you, such as the case in buying a prechopped, frozen onion.

In many cases, convenience items will save you significant money by reducing your overall labor costs. Productivity of your staff will increase. It is important, however, that you not fall into the trap of electing to buy more convenience-type items, without reducing your labor expenditures. When that happens, you lose in terms of both high food costs and higher than required labor costs, thus causing your labor productivity ratios to decrease.

Equipment

In most cases, foodservice productivity ratios have not increased in recent years, as have those of other businesses. Much of this is due to the fact that ours is a labor-intensive, not machine-intensive, industry. In some cases, equipment improvements have made kitchen work much easier. Slicers, choppers, and mixers have replaced human labor with mechanical labor. However, robotics and automation are not yet a part of our industry in any major way. Nonetheless, it is critical for you to understand the importance of a properly equipped workplace to improve productivity. This can be as simple as understanding that a sharp knife cuts more quickly and better than a dull one, or as complex as deciding which Internet service will be used to provide communication links to the 1,000 stores in a quick-service restaurant chain. In either case, management must ask itself the fundamental question: "Am I providing my employees with the tools necessary to effectively do their job?" The key word in that question is "effectively." If the proper tools are provided, but they are at the wrong height, in the wrong location, or unavailable at the right time, the tools will not be used effectively. Similarly, if the proper tools are provided but employees are not adequately trained in their use, productivity will suffer. One need look no further than the 1980s and early 1990s, when large numbers of personal computers were purchased but not effectively used, to see evidence of mismanagement, poor training, and its impact on productivity. When tools are provided but instruction in their use is not, productivity gains will not occur.

Equipment should be properly maintained (see Chapter 8) and updated if employees are to be held accountable for productivity standards or gains. It is your obligation to provide your employees with the tools they need to do their jobs quickly and effectively.

Service Level Desired

It is a fact that the average quick-service employee can serve more guests in an hour than the best server can at an exclusive French-style restaurant. The reason for this is, of course, quite obvious. In the quick-service situation, speed, not total service rendered, is of the utmost importance. In the French-style restaurant, service is to be more elegant and the total service rendered of a much higher level. Thus, when you vary service levels, you also vary employee productivity ratios. In the past, foodservice managers focused very heavily on speed of service. While that is still important today, many operators are finding that guests expect and demand higher levels of service than ever before. If this trend continues, one could expect that foodservice productivity levels would tend to go down. In order to prevent this from happening, foodservice operators will need to become very creative in finding ways to improve employee productivity in other areas, say through training and improved morale, so that these "savings" can be used to provide the higher level of customer service demanded by today's sophisticated foodservice consumer.

Now that we have discussed some of the factors that impact employee productivity and what management can do to affect them, we return to the question of knowing "how many employees are needed" to effectively operate the foodservice unit. As previously stated, the key to answering that question lies in developing productivity standards for the foodservice unit. There are many measures of employee productivity. Next, you will learn about the most popular of these and identify their weaknesses and strengths. In the final analysis, the best productivity measure for any unit you manage is, of course, the one that makes the most sense for your unique operation.

FUN ON THE WEB!

Look up the following site to explore the U.S. Department of Labor Web site.

www.dol.gov Look up this site for government information regarding labor issues and laws in the United States. Click on "Quick Guide" for a table of contents. You will find information on things like minimum wage and overtime pay, family and medical leave, employment discrimination, and much more! Also, click on "Laws and Regs" to find the most recent and pertinent information on legal issues and employment.

Measuring Current Labor Productivity

There are a variety of ways to measure productivity in the hospitality industry. We shall examine five of them as follows:

1. Labor cost percentage
2. Sales per labor hour
3. Labor dollars per guest served
4. Guests served per labor dollar
5. Guests served per labor hour

Labor Cost Percentage

A very commonly used measure of employee productivity in the foodservice industry is the labor cost percentage. The labor cost percentage is computed as follows:

$$\frac{\text{Cost of Labor}}{\text{Total Sales}} = \text{Labor Cost \%}$$

It is important to realize that there are several ways to define cost of labor. You should select the one that makes the most sense for your own operation. Cost of labor, as previously mentioned, includes both payroll and total labor costs. To measure productivity, you may elect, for example, only to include payroll costs and not total labor costs. In a like manner, some managers elect to include the cost of management when computing their labor cost percentage, while others do not. Again, the most important point is that you should compute a labor cost percentage that makes sense for your operation. Remember, however, that when comparing your labor cost percentage with those of other similar units, it is important that you make sure both your unit and the one you are comparing use the same formula for your computations. If you do not, your comparisons will not accurately reflect true differences between the two units.

Controlling the labor cost percentage is extremely important in the foodservice industry since it is the most widely used measure of productivity and, thus, is often used to determine the effectiveness of management. If labor cost percentage increases, management may be held accountable and penalized. A labor cost percentage that increases too much may result in management turnover, even if, as in many cases, the management did not want to turn over!

Fortunately, labor cost percentages are fairly easy to compute and analyze. Consider the case of Roderick, a foodservice manager in charge of a table service restaurant in a year-round theme park. The unit is popular and has a $20 per guest check average. Roderick uses only payroll (wages and salaries) when determining his overall labor cost percentage. Other labor-related expenses are considered by Roderick's supervisor to be noncontrollables and beyond Roderick's immediate control. Roderick has computed his labor cost percentage for each of the last 4 weeks using the labor cost percentage formula. His supervisor has given Roderick a goal of 35% for the 4-week-period. Roderick feels that he has done well in meeting that goal. Figure 7.6 shows Roderick's 4-week performance.

Roderick's supervisor, Madeline, is concerned because she received many comments in week 4 regarding poor service levels in Roderick's unit. As she analyzes the numbers in Figure 7.6, she sees that Roderick exceeded his goal of a 35% labor cost in weeks 1 through 3, then reduced his labor cost to 27.9% in week 4. While the monthly overall average of 35% is within budget, she knows all is not well in this unit. Roderick elected to reduce his payroll in week 4, and yet it is clear from the negative guest comments that, at a 27.9% labor cost, service to guests suffers. That is, too few employees were on staff to provide the necessary guest attention. Unfortunately, one disadvantage of using overall labor cost percentage is that it can hide daily or weekly highs and lows. As in Roderick's case, labor costs were too high the first 3 weeks, too low the last week, but acceptable overall. Recall that the total labor cost of 35% indicates that, for each dollar of sales generated, 35 cents is to be paid to the employees who assisted in generating those sales.

FIGURE **7.6** ● Roderick's Labor Cost % Report

Week	Cost of Labor	Sales	Labor Cost %
1	$ 7,100	$18,400	38.6%
2	8,050	21,500	37.4
3	7,258	19,100	38.0
4	6,922	24,800	27.9
Total	29,330	83,800	35.0

Using the labor cost percentage formula and the data from Figure 7.6, we find the following:

$$\frac{\text{Cost of Labor}}{\text{Total Sales}} = \text{Labor Cost \%}$$

or

$$\frac{\$29,330}{\$83,800} = 35\%$$

Thus, management can use the 35% figure to measure employee productivity and, to some degree, management's skill. The labor cost percentage does, however, have some limitations as a measure of productivity. Notice, for example, what happens to this measure of productivity if all Roderick's employees are given a 5% raise in pay. If this were the case, Roderick's labor cost percentages for last month would have been as shown in Figure 7.7.

Note that labor now accounts for 36.8% of each dollar sales value. It is important to realize that Roderick's workforce did *not* become less productive because they got a 5% increase in pay. Labor cost percentage varies with changes in the price paid for labor. When the price paid for labor increases, labor cost percentage increases. When the price paid for labor decreases, labor cost percentage goes down. Because of this, labor cost percentage by itself is not a complete measure of workforce productivity.

FIGURE **7.7** ● Roderick's Revised Labor Cost % Report

(Includes 5% Raise)					
Week	Original Cost of Labor	5% Raise	Total Cost of Labor	Sales	Labor Cost %
1	$ 7,100	$ 355.00	$ 7,455.00	$18,400	40.5%
2	8,050	402.50	8,452.50	21,500	39.3
3	7,258	362.90	7,620.90	19,100	39.9
4	6,922	346.10	7,268.10	24,800	29.3
Total	29,330	1,466.50	30,796.50	83,800	36.8

To see another example of the limitations of labor cost percentage as a complete measure of productivity, consider the effect on labor cost percentage of increasing the selling prices of your products. Return to the data in Figure 7.6 and assume that Roderick's unit raised prices by 5% prior to the beginning of the month. Figure 7.8 shows how an increase of this size in selling price would affect the labor cost percentage.

As demonstrated, increases in selling price (assuming no decline in guest count or buying behavior) will result in decreases in the labor cost percentage. Alternatively, lowering the selling price without increasing total sales generally results in increased labor cost percentage. While labor cost percentage is easy to compute and widely used, it is difficult to use as a measure of productivity over time, since it depends on labor dollars spent and sales dollars received for its computation. Even in relatively noninflationary times, wages do increase and menu prices are adjusted upward. Both activities affect the labor cost percentage. In addition, institutional foodservice settings, which have no sales figures to report, find that it is not possible to measure labor productivity using labor cost percentage, since they generally count guests or meals served rather than sales dollars earned.

Sales per Labor Hour

It has been said that the most perishable commodity any foodservice operator buys is the labor hour. When not productively used, it disappears forever. It cannot be "carried over" to the next day like an unsold head of

FIGURE **7.8** ● Roderick's Revised Labor Cost % Report

(Includes 5% Increase in Selling Price)					
Week	Cost of Labor	Original Sales	5% Selling Price Increase	Total Sales	Labor Cost %
1	$ 7,100	$18,400	$ 920	$19,320	36.7%
2	8,050	21,500	1,075	22,575	35.7
3	7,258	19,100	955	20,055	36.2
4	6,922	24,800	1,240	26,040	26.6
Total	29,330	83,800	4,190	87,990	33.3

lettuce or a slice of turkey breast. Indeed, when one considers the product that a foodservice operator sells as the result of both food products and labor added to those products, the importance of effectively using each labor hour paid for is very clear. It is for this reason that some foodservice operators prefer to measure labor productivity in terms of the amount of sales generated for each labor hour used. The formula for computing this measure of labor productivity is as follows:

$$\frac{\text{Total Sales}}{\text{Labor Hours Used}} = \text{Sales per Labor Hour}$$

Labor hours used is simply the sum of all labor hours paid for by management in a given sales period. If Roderick had used this measure of productivity for his unit, he would, perhaps, have had data such as that presented in Figure 7.9.

Sales per labor hour ranged from a low of $19.50 in week 1 to a high of $28.66 in week 4. Those operators who compute sales per labor hour tend to do so because they feel it is a better measure of labor productivity than the labor cost percentage. Indeed, while sales per labor hour will vary with changes in menu selling price (as does the labor cost percentage), it will not vary based on changes in the price paid for labor. In other

FIGURE **7.9** ● Roderick's Sales per Labor Hour

Week	Sales	Labor Hours Used	Sales per Labor Hour
1	$18,400	943.5	$19.50
2	21,500	1,006.3	21.37
3	19,100	907.3	21.05
4	24,800	865.3	28.66
Total	83,800	3,722.4	22.51

words, increases and decreases in the price paid per hour will not affect this productivity measure. On the negative side, however, sales per labor hour neglects to consider the amount *paid* to employees per hour to generate the sales. A foodservice unit paying its employees an average of $8.00 per hour could, using this measure of productivity, have the same sales per labor hour as a similar unit paying $10.00 for each hour of labor used. Obviously, the manager paying $8.00 per hour has created a lower cost, yet equally productive workforce if the sales per labor hour used are the same in the two units. Sales per labor hour, however, may be useful in some situations. Consider, for example, the decision you would face as the food and beverage director of a private golf course/country club. One of the services you would like to offer your members is beverage service while golfers are on the course. The question you must answer is, "How many beverage carts should I place on the golf course at any given time of the day and week to adequately serve the club's members?" Too few beverage carts will result in thirsty, unserved members, while too many carts will cause the club to incur excessive labor costs. In this situation, you would want to monitor your beverage cart sales per labor hour and make determinations on the number of carts that you should use at various times to ensure cost-effective, quality service.

It is relatively easy to compute total sales per labor hour used, because both the numerator and the denominator of the formula are generated on a regular basis. However, depending on the record-keeping system employed, it may be more difficult to determine total labor hours used than total labor dollars spent. This is especially true when large numbers of employees are salaried rather than hourly employees. Remember that the efforts of managers and supervisors, too, should be considered when computing a facility's overall sales per labor hour used.

Labor Dollars per Guest Served

Had Roderick preferred, he might have measured his labor productivity in terms of the labor dollars per guest served. The formula for this measure is as follows:

$$\frac{\text{Cost of Labor}}{\text{Guests Served}} = \text{Labor Dollars per Guest Served}$$

Using Roderick's data, the labor dollars per guest served computation would be as shown in Figure 7.10.

In this example, the labor dollars expended per guest served for the 4-week period would be computed as follows:

$$\frac{\$29,330}{4,190} = \$7.00$$

Using this measure of productivity, it is fairly easy to see why Roderick experienced guest complaints during the fourth week of operation. Note that in the first 3 weeks, he "supplied" his guests with more than $7.00 of guest-related labor costs per guest served, but in the fourth week that amount fell to less than $6.00 per guest. As is the case with labor cost percentage,

FIGURE **7.10** ● Roderick's Labor Dollars per Guest Served

Week	Cost of Labor	Guests Served	Labor Dollars per Guest Served
1	$ 7,100	920	$7.72
2	8,050	1,075	7.49
3	7,258	955	7.60
4	6,922	1,240	5.58
Total	29,330	4,190	7.00

labor dollars per guest served is limited in that it varies based on the price paid for labor.

Guests Served per Labor Dollar

A variation on the formula of labor dollars per guest served is to reverse the numerator and denominator to create a new productivity measure called guests served per labor dollar. The formula for this measure of productivity is as follows:

$$\frac{\text{Guests Served}}{\text{Cost of Labor}} = \text{Guests Served per Labor Dollar}$$

Had Roderick so desired, his productivity data could have been as presented in Figure 7.11.

In this situation, Roderick served for the 4-week average a total of 0.143 guest for each labor dollar expended. It is important to note, however, that cost of labor in this case represents *all* the labor required to serve the guests. This includes cooks, servers, dishwashers, and Roderick himself. It is, therefore, not surprising that each dollar spent services less than one complete guest. As a measure of productivity, guests served per labor dollar expended has advantages. It is relatively easy to compute, and can be used by foodservice units, such as institutions, that do not routinely

FIGURE **7.11** ● Roderick's Guests Served per Labor Dollar

Week	Guests Served	Cost of Labor	Guests Served per Labor Dollar
1	920	$ 7,100	0.130
2	1,075	8,050	0.134
3	955	7,258	0.132
4	1,240	6,922	0.179
Total	4,190	29,330	0.143

record dollar sales figures. When the number of guests to be served stays fairly constant, it can be a good measure of productivity. In addition, this measure is relatively easy to compute because you are very likely to get records on total guests served on a daily basis, as well as total payroll amounts each time payroll is paid.

If the number of guests anticipated varies widely, this measure of productivity will vary widely also, despite management's conscientious efforts at forecasting. Of course, that is true of even the best measures of labor productivity.

Guests Served per Labor Hour

Guests served per labor hour is the last measure of productivity we shall discuss. Had Roderick elected to use this measure, he would compute it as follows:

$$\frac{\text{Guests Served}}{\text{Labor Hours Used}} = \text{Guests Served per Labor Hour}$$

As is evident, the formula of guests served per labor hour has neither sales figures nor labor expense figures in its computation. It is, thus, free either from variations due to changes in the price paid for labor or from fluctuations due solely to changes in menu selling prices. Guests served per labor hour is a true measure of productivity, not a measure of either cost and productivity or sales and productivity. Guests served per labor hour is powerful in its ability to measure productivity gains across time due to changes that are unrelated to selling price or wages. It is extremely useful in comparing similar units in areas with widely differing wage rates or selling prices and is, thus, popular with multilocation corporations comparing one operational unit to another. It is also useful in comparing dissimilar facilities with similar wages and selling prices since it helps identify areas of weakness in management scheduling, employee productivity, facility layout and design, or other factors that can affect productivity.

Had Roderick elected to evaluate his workforce productivity through the use of the guests served per labor hour formula, his data might have looked as shown in Figure 7.12.

As the data demonstrate, Roderick's guests served per labor hour figure ranges from a low of 0.975 guest per hour (week 1) to a high of 1.433 guests per hour (week 4). The average for the 4-week period is 1.126 guests served per labor hour (4,190 guests served/3,722.4 hours used = 1.126 guests per labor hour).

FIGURE **7.12** ● Roderick's Guests Served per Labor Hour

Week	Guests Served	Labor Hours Used	Guests Served per Labor Hour
1	920	943.5	0.975
2	1,075	1,006.3	1.068
3	955	907.3	1.053
4	1,240	865.3	1.433
Total	4,190	3,722.4	1.126

Those managers who use guests served per labor hour as a measure of productivity generally do so because they like the focus of emphasizing service levels and not just reducing costs. It may be more difficult and time consuming to compute this measure of productivity, however, because you must compute the number of labor hours used, as well as make decisions on how to define a guest. For example, in a café, a guest who orders a cup of coffee is indeed a guest but requires much less service than one who consumes a full meal. Unless you decide differently, however, the guests served per labor hour productivity measure treats these two guests in the same manner.

Since it is widely believed that work really does expand to meet (and exceed) the number of people available to do the job, measures of productivity must be available to guide management in making productivity assessments. Figure 7.13 summarizes the five productivity measures discussed in this text and lists some advantages and disadvantages associated with each.

Each formula for measuring labor productivity has limitations, advantages, and disadvantages. You may select one or more of the measures described previously or create your own measure. In most cases, it is recommended that you monitor the labor cost percentage and at least one other measure of productivity if you are serious about controlling labor-related expenses.

Six-Column Daily Productivity Report

Many operators, upon selecting a productivity measure, prefer to compute that measure on a daily, rather than on a weekly or monthly, basis. This

FIGURE **7.13** ● Productivity Measures Summary

Measurement	Advantages	Disadvantages
Labor Cost % = Cost of Labor ───── Total Sales	1. Easy to compute 2. Most widely used	1. Hides highs and lows 2. Varies with changes in price of labor 3. Varies with changes in menu selling price
Sales per Labor Hour = Total Sales ───── Labor Hours Used	1. Fairly easy to compute 2. Does not vary with changes in the price of labor	1. Ignores price per hour paid for labor 2. Varies with changes in menu selling price
Labor Dollars per Guests Served = Cost of Labor ───── Guests Served	1. Fairly easy to compute 2. Does not vary with changes in menu selling price 3. Can be used by non-revenue-generating units	1. Ignores average sales per guest and, thus, total sales 2. Varies with changes in the price of labor
Guests Served per Labor Dollar = Guests Served ───── Cost of Labor	1. Fairly easy to compute 2. Does not vary with changes in menu selling price 3. Can be used by non-revenue-generating units	1. Ignores average sales per guest and, thus, total sales 2. Varies with changes in the price of labor
Guests Served per Labor Hour = Guests Served ───── Labor Hours Used	1. Can be used by non-revenue-generating units 2. Does not change due to changes in price of labor or menu selling price 3. Emphasizes serving guests rather than reducing costs	1. Time consuming to produce 2. Ignores price paid for labor 3. Ignores average sales per guest and, thus, total sales

can easily be done by using a six-column form similar to the one introduced in Chapter 3.

A six-column form for Roderick's restaurant sales and labor cost in week 1 is presented in Figure 7.14. It uses as a productivity measure, the standard labor cost percentage formula, cost of labor/total sales = labor

---

FIGURE **7.14** ● Six-Column Labor Cost %

Unit Name: **Roderick's**   Date: 1/1–1/7

	Cost of Labor		Sales		Labor Cost %	
Weekday	Today	To Date	Today	To Date	Today	To Date
1	$ 800	$ 800	$2,000	$ 2,000	40.0%	40.0%
2	880	1,680	1,840	3,840	47.8	43.8
3	920	2,600	2,150	5,990	42.8	43.4
4	980	3,580	2,300	8,290	42.6	43.2
5	1,000	4,580	2,100	10,390	47.6	44.0
6	1,300	5,880	4,100	14,490	31.7	40.6
7	1,220	7,100	3,910	18,400	31.2	38.6
Total	7,100		18,400		38.6	

cost %. Amounts in the Today columns are divided to create the Labor Cost % Today column, just as the amounts in the To Date columns are divided to create the Labor Cost % To Date column.

Roderick's daily labor cost percentage during week 1 ranged from a low of 31.2% (day 7) to a high of 47.8% (day 2). The labor cost percentage for the week was 38.6%. Again, you can see the effect of averaging highs and lows when using measures of labor productivity. Any of the five measures of labor productivity can be calculated on a daily basis using a modification of the six-column form located in Appendix C of this book. Figure 7.15 details the method to be used to establish six-column forms for each of the five productivity measures presented in this chapter. When using the six-column report, it is important to remember that the To Date column value, on any given day, is always the sum of the values of all the preceding Today columns, including the current day.

Determining Costs by Labor Category

Many operators find that a single measure of their labor productivity is insufficient for their needs. Consider the case of Otis, the owner and operator of a restaurant called the Squirrel Flats Diner, near a logging camp that services both backpacking tourists and loggers taking a break from work. Otis's sales last month were $100,000. His labor costs were $30,000. Thus, his labor cost percentage was 30% ($30,000/$100,000 = 0.30). Otis, however, knows more about his labor cost percentage than the overall number alone tells him. Figure 7.16 demonstrates the method Otis uses to compute his overall labor cost percentage.

Note that Otis divides his labor expense into four distinct labor subcategories. Production includes all those individuals who are involved with the actual preparation of the food products Otis sells. Service includes the servers and cashiers involved in delivering the products to the guests and receiving payment for these products. Sanitation consists of individuals who are responsible for warewashing and after-hour cleanup of the establishment. Management includes the salaries of Otis's two supervisors.

By establishing four labor categories, Otis has a better idea of where his labor dollars are spent than if only one overall figure had been used. Just as it is often helpful to compute more than one food cost percentage, it is helpful to calculate more than one labor cost percentage. Notice that the sum of Otis's four labor cost percentage subcategories equals the amount of his total labor cost percentage:

$$12\% + 9\% + 3\% + 6\% = 30\%$$

You may establish any number of labor subcategories that make sense for your own unique operation. Of course, you can apply any mea-

FIGURE **7.15** ● Six-Column Labor Productivity Form

Measure of Productivity	Columns 1 & 2	Columns 3 & 4	Columns 5 & 6
Labor Cost % = $\frac{\text{Cost of Labor}}{\text{Total Sales}}$	Cost of Labor Today Cost of Labor to Date	Sales Today Sales to Date	Labor Cost % Today Labor Cost % to Date
Sales per Labor Hour = $\frac{\text{Total Sales}}{\text{Labor Hours Used}}$	Sales Today Sales to Date	Labor Hours Used Today Labor Hours Used to Date	Sales per Labor Hour Today Sales per Labor Hour to Date
Labor Dollars per Guest Served = $\frac{\text{Cost of Labor}}{\text{Guests Served}}$	Cost of Labor Today Cost of Labor to Date	Guests Served Today Guests Served to Date	Labor Dollars per Guest Served Today Labor Dollars per Guest Served to Date
Guests Served per Labor Dollar = $\frac{\text{Guests Served}}{\text{Cost of Labor}}$	Guests Served Today Guests Served to Date	Cost of Labor Today Cost of Labor to Date	Guests Served per Labor Dollar Today Guests Served per Labor Dollar to Date
Guests Served per Labor Hour = $\frac{\text{Guests Served}}{\text{Labor Hours Used}}$	Guests Served Today Guests Served to Date	Labor Hours Used Today Labor Hours Used to Date	Guests Served per Labor Hour Today Guests Served per Labor Hour to Date

FIGURE **7.16** ● Labor Cost % for Squirrel Flats Diner

Time Period: 1/1–1/31   Sales: $100,000

Labor Category	Cost of Labor	Labor Cost %
Production	$12,000	12%
Service	9,000	9
Sanitation	3,000	3
Management	6,000	6
Total	30,000	30

sure of labor productivity to these labor subcategories, just as you would the overall total. The important points for you to remember when determining labor productivity measures by subcategory are:

1. Be sure to include all the relevant data, whether dollars spent, hours used, sales generated, or guests served.
2. Use the same method to identify the numerator and denominator for each category.
3. Compute an overall total to ensure that the sum of the categories is consistent with the overall total.

Keep these points in mind as you examine Figure 7.17, which details Otis's second measure of labor productivity. He has selected guests served per labor dollar as a supplement to his computation of labor cost percentage. Otis feels that this second measure helps him determine his effectiveness with guests without losing sight of the total number of dollars he spends on payroll expense. The formula he uses for this computation is:

$$\frac{\text{Guests Served}}{\text{Cost of Labor}} = \text{Guests Served per Labor Dollar}$$

Each labor category in Figure 7.17 yields a different guests served per labor dollar figure. As could be expected, when labor dollars in a category are small, guests served per labor dollar in that category is relatively high.

FIGURE **7.17** ● Guests Served per Labor Dollar for Squirrel Flats Diner

Guests Served: 25,000   Time Period: 1/1–1/31

Labor Category	Cost of Labor	Guests Served per Labor Dollar
Production	$12,000	2.083
Service	9,000	2.778
Sanitation	3,000	8.333
Management	6,000	4.167
Total	30,000	0.833

This is clearly demonstrated in the Sanitation category of Figure 7.17. When labor dollars expended are high, as in the Total category, guests served per labor dollar is lower. Any measure of labor productivity presented in this chapter can be categorized in any logical manner that is of value to management. The purpose of computing numbers such as these is, of course, because of their value in developing staff schedules and estimating future payroll costs. Assume, for example, that one month Otis finds his labor cost percentage has exceeded his goal of 30%. By computing his guests served per labor dollar subcategory values, Otis could quickly see exactly where he had exceeded his goal and, thus, make adjustments. In addition, if Otis knows, for example, that next month he is projecting 30,000 guests, he can estimate his labor costs for each subcategory. By following the rules of algebra and adding the word "estimated," the guests served per labor dollar formula can be restated as follows:

$$\frac{\text{Number of Estimated Guests Served}}{\text{Guests Served per Labor Dollar}} = \text{Estimated Cost of Labor}$$

From the data in Figure 7.17 and using the Production subcategory as an example, Otis would estimate his production labor costs on a month where 30,000 guests were anticipated as follows:

$$\frac{30,000}{2.083} = \$14,402.30$$

Of course, Otis could, using the same estimated cost of labor formula, project labor costs for each of his subcategories, as well as his overall total. Using this information, Otis could prepare an employee schedule that uses that amount of payroll cost and no more.

Managing Payroll Costs

Essentially, the management of payroll costs is a four-step process, which includes the following factors:

> Step 1. Determine productivity standards.
> Step 2. Forecast sales volume.
> Step 3. Schedule employees using productivity standards and forecasted sales volume.
> Step 4. Analyze results.

Step 1. Determine Productivity Standards

The first step in controlling payroll costs is to determine productivity standards for your operation. A **productivity standard** is defined as management's view of what constitutes an appropriate productivity ratio in a given foodservice unit or units. Thus, a productivity standard might be, as in this case, a particular labor cost percentage, a specific number of guests served per labor dollar expended, or any other predetermined productivity ratio you want to utilize. In other words, you must find the answers to the questions of how long it should take an employee to do a job and how many employees it takes to do the complete job. It was previously stated that a productivity ratio measures the units of output, such as guests served or meals served, relative to the units of input, such as the number of employees or hours worked. Productivity standards represent what you should reasonably expect in the way of output per unit of labor input. Assume, for example, that a cafeteria manager knows that a well-trained, motivated cashier can total seven guest trays per minute during a busy lunch period. Actual payment for these meals will be made at another station at the conclusion of the meal. Seven trays (output) per one labor minute (input) would be the productivity standard for a cashier totaling trays in this operation.

A productivity standard is simply management's expectation of the productivity ratio of each employee. Establishing productivity standards for *every* employee is an essential management task and the first step in controlling payroll costs.

Thus far, we have discussed some methods of measuring current productivity ratios based on historical data. This tells you where you are in relation to productivity, but does not say where you should be. To illustrate this concept, assume that you have decided to buy and operate a franchise unit within a themed steakhouse chain. Currently, four units of the same chain exist in your immediate geographic area, which has been designated a district by the **franchiser,** the entity responsible for selling and maintaining control over the franchise name.

The area franchise representative who monitors labor productivity by using labor cost percentage has shared the following data with you as shown in Figure 7.18. The figures for units 1 to 4 represent labor cost percentages in those franchise steakhouse units in your district. The district average is the *unweighted* mean of those four units. Company average refers to the overall labor cost percentage in the steakhouse chain that you are joining. Industry average refers to the average labor cost percentage reported by theme-style steakhouses of the type similar to the one you will own and operate.

Using the data presented in Figure 7.18, you would begin to establish your own desired productivity measures and goals. Since your restaurant is not open, you face the problem of not having historical data from your own unit to help you. Of course, this is the case when opening new restaurants, but it is also true when converting the theme, decor, or menu of an existing restaurant. Using your own judgment and the information you do have available, you could choose to use as your goal the lowest labor cost

FIGURE **7.18** ● Labor Cost % Summary

Unit Description	Labor Cost %
Unit 1	34.1%
Unit 2	35.5
Unit 3	34.3
Unit 4	35.2
District Average	34.8
Company Average	34.0
Industry Average	35.5

percentage (unit 1); the highest (unit 2); the district, company, or industry average; or even some other number not included in this listing. Any of these numbers could become your target, or ideal labor cost percentage. In the final analysis, you must use whatever data you have available to establish an appropriate productivity standard for your operation. Productivity standards are typically based on the following types of information:

1. Unit history
2. Company average
3. Industry average
4. Management experience
5. Combination of some or all of the above

In this case, you might choose to begin with a 35% labor cost as one of your productivity standards. This figure is close to the district average (34.9%) and is likely an aggressive, but realistic goal for your first year. As mentioned previously, you would likely want to choose at least one more measure of productivity to help you monitor your labor efficiency. In the years to come, you would want to effectively manage the factors that affect productivity, carefully monitor your actual productivity using the productivity measures you select, then establish a goal that is both realistic and attainable.

Step 2. Forecast Sales Volume

Sales volume forecasting (discussed in Chapter 2), when combined with established productivity standards, allows you to determine the number of employees needed to effectively service those guests who will visit your facility. All foodservice units must forecast volume if they are to supply an adequate number of employees to service that volume. This forecasting may be done in terms of either sales dollars or number of guests to be served.

An important, but frequently misunderstood distinction must be made between forecasting sales volume and forecasting the number of employees needed to service that volume. The distinction is simply that, as a manager, you will view guests coming to your operation in "block" fashion, that is, in groups at a time. Employees, on the other hand, are added to your schedule one individual at a time and, thus, will significantly affect productivity measures. A brief example will make this clear. Ted owns a small shop that sells only specialty coffees. His service staff productivity standard is one server for each 30 guests. Thus, he would schedule his employees as shown in Figure 7.19.

When 30 or less guests are expected, Ted needs only one server on duty. In effect, each time a block of 30 guests is added, Ted must add another server. Thus, if Ted anticipates 40 guests one day and 50 the next, no change in staff is necessary. That is, an addition of 10 extra guests does not

FIGURE **7.19** ● Ted's Coffee Shop Staffing Guide

Number of Guests Anticipated	Number of Servers Needed
1–30	1
31–60	2
61–90	3
91–120	4

dictate the addition of another server. On the other hand, if Ted anticipates 60 guests one day and 70 the next, an additional staff person is required since Ted has introduced a new block of guests.

It really does not matter how much of the new block actually arrives, since Ted has staffed for all of it. He hopes, of course, that all or nearly all of the block will arrive, as this will keep his cost per person served lower. If only a small portion of the block comes, Ted's cost per person served will, of course, rise unless he takes some action to reduce his labor-related expense.

Step 3. Schedule Employees Using Productivity Standards and Forecasted Sales Volume

Forecasting sales volume is important to cost control because it begins to take management out of the past and present and allows it to project into the future and influence what will happen then. To illustrate how established productivity standards (Step 1) are combined with sales forecasts (Step 2) to develop employee schedules (Step 3), consider the scenario of Darla, the foodservice director at Langtree, a small women's college in a rural area. Darla operates both a dormitory feeding situation and an open snack bar/cafeteria. The dormitory, Geier Hall, houses 1,000 young women. The snack bar/cafeteria, called Lillie's, is open to the students, staff, and faculty of the school. Darla is committed to controlling her labor-related expense. As such, she has carefully monitored her past labor productivity ratios, those of other similar schools, and national averages. In addition, she has considered the facilities she operates, the skill level and morale of her workforce, and the impact of her aggressive training program on her future productivity. Considering all of these factors, Darla has determined that Lillie's snack bar/cafeteria should be able to operate at a labor cost of 30% of gross sales. In the dormitory, where guest counts, but no dollar sales figures are kept on a daily basis, she has decided that her labor productivity measure should be established in terms of guests served per labor hour. Her goal is a ratio of 30 to 1, that is, 30 guests served per labor hour. Darla may now establish her labor cost expense budget in terms of both dollars (Lillie's) and labor hours used (Geier Hall).

Let us examine in Figure 7.20 how Darla would establish her labor budget for Lillie's using her productivity standards, her sales forecast, and the labor cost percentage formula you have already learned. Remember that the labor cost percentage formula is defined as

$$\frac{\text{Cost of Labor}}{\text{Total Sales}} = \text{Labor Cost \%}$$

If you include the words "forecasted," "standard," and "budget" and follow the rules of algebra, the labor cost percentage formula can be restated as follows:

$$\text{Forecasted Total Sales} \times \text{Labor Cost \% Standard} = \text{Cost of Labor Budget}$$

FIGURE **7.20** ● Labor Budget for Lillie's Using Labor Cost %

Time Period	Forecasted Total Sales	Labor Cost % Standard	Cost of Labor Budget
Week 1	$ 6,550	30%	$1,965
Week 2	6,850	30	2,055
Week 3	6,000	30	1,800
Week 4	8,100	30	2,430
Total	27,500	30	8,250

Thus, budgeted cost of labor in the preceding formula becomes Darla's targeted labor expense budget. To determine, for example, her targeted labor expense budget in week 1, Darla would compute the amount as follows:

$$\$6,550 \times 30\% = \$1,965$$

Figure 7.21 illustrates how Darla would establish a budget for total number of labor hours used to service Geier Hall. Recall that, in this food facility, sales refers to the number of guests served rather than dollars and this is reflected in Darla's sales forecast. Remember that the guests served per labor hour formula is defined as

$$\frac{\text{Guests Served}}{\text{Labor Hours Used}} = \text{Guests Served per Labor Hour}$$

If you include the words "forecasted," "standard," and "budget" and follow the rules of algebra, the guests served per labor hour formula can be restated as follows:

$$\frac{\text{Forecasted Number of Guests Served}}{\text{Guests Served per Labor Hour Standard}} = \text{Labor Hour Budget}$$

FIGURE **7.21** ● Labor Budget for Geier Hall Using Guests Served per Labor Hour

Time Period	Forecasted Number of Guests Served	Guests Served per Labor Hour Standard	Labor Hour Budget
Week 1	20,000	30 guests/hour	666.7
Week 2	18,600	30 guests/hour	620.0
Week 3	18,100	30 guests/hour	603.3
Week 4	17,800	30 guests/hour	593.3
Total	74,500	30 guests/hour	2,483.3

Using week 1 in Figure 7.21 as an example, the computation would be

$$\frac{20,000}{30} = 666.7$$

Note that, in Figures 7.20 and 7.21, Darla could have varied her *weekly* productivity standard and still have produced a 4-week budget. In other words, on weeks when volume was high, she could have elected to reduce her desired labor cost % or increase the guests served per labor hour standard. This can be a logical course of action if the operator feels that increased volume can have the effect of reducing the cost percentage of fixed labor or can increase the number of guests served per labor hour that can be served by staff persons in specific positions such as cashiers, managers, and so on. Experience tells Darla, however, that, in her case, a standard labor productivity ratio that remains unchanged across the 4 weeks is her best option.

From the labor budgets she developed, Darla can now schedule her production people in terms of both dollars to be spent for labor (Lillie's) or labor hours to be used (Geier Hall). *She must be careful to schedule employees only when they are needed.* To do this, she must forecast her volume in time blocks smaller than one-day segments. Perhaps, in her case, volume should be predicted in three groups such as breakfast, lunch, and dinner in the dormitory, and in one- or two-hour blocks in her snack bar/cafeteria.

Now let us examine how Darla might schedule her dormitory staff during week 1 of her 4-week projection. Let us assume that Darla's weekly projection of sales volume for Geier Hall is as demonstrated in Figure 7.22.

On any given day, Darla can match her volume projections with budgeted hours or dollars. To see exactly how she would use this information to determine her employees' schedules, let us examine day 1, in Figure 7.22, a day when Darla projects 3,000 guests served and 100 labor hours needed. She knows that she should "spend" no more than 100 total hours for labor on that day. She also knows from recording her productivity ratio in the past (Figure 7.23) where she has spent her labor hours in prior time periods.

Thus, Darla should invest approximately 60 hours (100 hours available × 0.60 average usage) for production employees, 30 hours for service employees, and 10 hours of management time for Monday if she is to stay within her labor budget.

Presented in a different way, Darla knows that, to stay within her labor goals, each labor category will have its own unique guest served per labor hour ratio, as noted in Figure 7.24.

It is important to note that, while guests served per labor hour varies by labor category, the overall total yields 30 guests per labor hour used, which is her productivity standard. Darla's employee schedule for the *production area* on Monday might look as shown in Figure 7.25.

FIGURE **7.22** ● Weekly Labor Hour Budget for Geier Hall

Day	Forecasted Number of Guests Served	Guests Served per Labor Hour Standard	Labor Hour Budget
1	3,000	30 guests/hour	100.0
2	2,900	30 guests/hour	96.7
3	2,900	30 guests/hour	96.7
4	2,850	30 guests/hour	95.0
5	3,000	30 guests/hour	100.0
6	2,700	30 guests/hour	90.0
7	2,650	30 guests/hour	88.3
Total	20,000	30 guests/hour	666.7

Because employee schedules can only be done in terms of either hours scheduled or dollars spent, an employee schedule recap form similar to the one in Figure 7.25 can be an effective tool in any daily analysis of labor productivity. Since labor is purchased on a daily basis, labor costs should be monitored on a daily basis. The labor schedule should be mod-

FIGURE **7.23** ● Recap of Percentage of Total Usage by Category

Geier Hall	
Labor Category	% of Total
Production	60%
Service	30
Management	10
Total	100

FIGURE **7.24** ● Recap of Guests Served per Labor Hour

Geier Hall			
Labor Category	Forecasted Number of Guests Served	Labor Hour Standard	Budgeted Guests Served per Labor Hour
Production	3,000	60	50
Service	3,000	30	100
Management	3,000	10	300
Total	3,000	100	30

ified, as needed, during the day. This constant adjustment is a key to the quick-service industry's profitability because schedule modifications by good managers in this segment of the industry are done hourly, not daily! In other words, if customer demand is lower than expected, employees should be released from the schedule to reduce costs. If volume is higher than expected, additional employees should be available on an "as needed" basis.

Some foodservice managers practice an **on-call** system whereby employees who are off duty are assigned to on-call status. This means that these employees can be contacted by management on short notice to cover for other employees who are absent or to come to work if customer demand suddenly increases. State laws vary regarding the compensation that must be paid to these on-call employees; thus, managers who practice this method should clarify existing state laws and their own company policies regarding the practice before it is implemented.

Other managers practice a **call-in** system. In this arrangement, employees who are off duty are required to check in with management on a daily basis to see if the volume is such that they may be needed. This is a particularly good way to make rapid changes in staffing because of unforeseen increases in projected sales volume.

Overtime, which must be paid at a higher than average rate, should be held to a minimum and should require written management approval before it is authorized. In the case of Geier Hall, the Rate and Total Cost columns in Figure 7.25 are not computed since, in this unit, they are not part of our productivity measure (remember that guests served per labor

FIGURE **7.25** ● Employee Schedule

Unit Name: **Geier Hall**   Date: <u>Monday 1/1</u>

Labor Category: **Production**   Shift: <u>A.M. & P.M.</u>   Labor Budget: <u>60 hours</u>

Employee Name	Schedule	Hours Scheduled	Rate	Total Cost
Sally S.*	6:00 A.M.–2:30 P.M.	8	N/A	N/A
Tom T.*	6:30 A.M.–3:00 P.M.	8		
Steve J.*	8:00 A.M.–4:30 P.M.	8		
Lucy S.*	10:00 A.M.–6:30 P.M.	8		
Janice J.	7:00 A.M.–11:00 A.M.	4		
Susie T.	6:30 A.M.–10:30 A.M.	4		
Peggy H.	10:30 A.M.–1:30 P.M.	3		
Marian D.	2:00 P.M.–5:00 P.M.	3		
Larry M.*	11:00 A.M.–7:30 P.M.	8		
Jill D.*	1:00 P.M.–7:30 P.M.	6		
Total		60	N/A	N/A

*Includes 30-minute meal break.

hour relies on neither cost of labor nor sales revenue for its computation). They would, of course, be filled out when determining the cost of the schedule for Lillie's because, in that unit, it is labor dollars, not hours used, that is the integral part of the productivity standard. An employee schedule, reviewed on a daily basis, should be established for each unit, labor category, and individual. It is critical to match labor usage with projected volume.

Step 4. Analyze Results

Darla has done a good job of using established labor standards and volume projections in building her employee schedule. To complete the job of managing labor-related expense, she must now analyze her results. Figure 7.26 represents the budgeted and actual results of the operation of Lillie's for the first 4 weeks of the year.

To determine the percentage of budget, the following formula, introduced in Chapter 1, is used:

$$\frac{\text{Actual Amount}}{\text{Budgeted Amount}} = \%\ \text{of Budget}$$

Note that total sales were somewhat less than we budgeted (98%), while total labor cost dollars were somewhat higher than we budgeted (102%). Consequently, labor cost % was somewhat higher than we had anticipated, in other words, a 31% actual result compared to a 30% budget percentage. Notice also that, when we project sales perfectly (week 3) but overspend on labor, our actual labor cost % will be too high (33%). Conversely, when we spend exactly what we budget for labor costs (week 4) but sales volume does not reach our estimate, our labor cost percent will similarly be too high (32%).

FIGURE **7.26** ● Labor Recap for Lillie's Actual Versus Budgeted Labor Cost

Week	Budgeted	Actual	% of Budget	Budgeted	Actual	% of Budget	Budgeted	Actual
1	$ 6,550	$ 6,400	98%	$1,965	$1,867	95%	30%	29%
2	6,850	7,000	102	2,055	2,158	105	30	31
3	6,000	6,000	100	1,800	1,980	110	30	33
4	8,100	7,600	94	2,430	2,430	100	30	32
Total	27,500	27,000	98	8,250	8,435	102	30	31

It may seem that a 1 percent variation in overall labor cost percentage is insignificant. In fact, in this case it represents $185 ($8,435 actual − $8,250 budgeted = $185). However, if a foodservice company achieved sales of $30,000,000 per year, 1% would represent $300,000 per year in cost overrun! Small percentages can add up! What constitutes a significant budget variation can only be determined by management. Darla may well want to review standard scheduling techniques with her supervisors since she exceeded her budgeted labor cost in 2 of the 4 weeks shown. In Darla's case, $185 is a significant budget variation.

When referring to labor costs, some foodservice operators prefer to use the term **standard cost,** that is, the labor cost needed to meet established productivity standards, rather than "budgeted cost." If productivity standards are used to establish budgeted labor costs, then, of course, the two terms are synonymous. It is important, however, not to confuse the concept of standard labor cost with that of standard food cost. A simple example will help to explain the difference. Assume that a restaurant serves each of four guests a ham steak for dinner. If the restaurant had 10 such steaks in the refrigerator and 6 remain at the end of the meal period, the food standard of one per guest has been maintained. Assume also, however, that these four guests are the only customers of the night and that labor staffing was established based on five guests. In this case, the standard cost, or budget, was not met in terms of guests served or perhaps dollar sales, yet management is in control. To further make the point, if one ham steak were missing, our food standard would be off by 10% (1 steak/10 total). This would represent a serious loss of food product control. In our labor example, our forecast was off by 20% (1 guest short/5 total projected), yet the variation is not due to lack of management control. In the case of labor, we are still within reasonable budget, though we may vary greatly from the standard.

For this reason, the authors prefer the term **budgeted labor** rather than **standard labor.** Labor standards will always vary a bit unless guest counts can be predicted perfectly, which, of course, is rarely the case. We can, however, compare budgeted labor expense with actual results to determine if the reasons for the variation from budget are valid and acceptable to management. The complete process for establishing the labor schedule is summarized in the checklist contained in Figure 7.27.

Reducing Labor-Related Costs

If you find, through your analysis, that labor costs are too high, problem areas must be identified and corrective action must be taken. If the overall productivity of your work group cannot be improved, other action must be taken. The approaches you can take to reduce labor-related costs, however, are different for fixed-payroll costs than for variable costs. Figure 7.28 indicates actions that can be taken to reduce labor-related expense in

FIGURE **7.27** ● 10-Point Labor Schedule Checklist

1. Monitor historical operational data (or alternative data if historical data are not available).
2. Identify productivity standards.
3. Forecast sales volume.
4. Determine budgeted labor dollars or hours.
5. Divide monthly budget into weekly budgets.
6. Divide weekly budget into daily budgets.
7. Segment daily budget into meal period budgets.
8. Build schedule based on the budget.
9. Analyze service levels during schedule period.
10. Review and adjust productivity standards as needed.

each of these two categories. Notice that you can only increase productivity, improve the scheduling process, eliminate employees, or decrease variable expense through reducing wages paid. Fixed expense can be reduced (as a percentage of revenue) by increasing sales volume. In all cases, however, the foodservice operation gains when increases in productivity mean that wages can remain high and, in fact, increase.

FIGURE **7.28** ● Reducing Labor-Related Expense

Category	Actions
Fixed	1. Improve productivity.
	2. Increase sales volume.
	3. Combine jobs to eliminate fixed positions.
	4. Reduce wages paid to the fixed-payroll employees.
Variable	1. Improve productivity.
	2. Schedule appropriately to adjust to changes in sales volume.
	3. Combine jobs to eliminate variable positions.
	4. Reduce wages paid to the variable employees.

Employee Empowerment

One way of increasing employee productivity, and thus reducing labor-related expense, is through employee empowerment. This is simply a step by management to involve employees in the decision-making process as far as guests and the employees themselves are concerned.

The shortage of skilled labor, shrinking numbers of qualified applicants, and increased competition from other industries all force management in the hospitality industry to act and think creatively when attempting to secure a productive workforce. This has resulted in new approaches to evaluate the manner in which the industry has dealt with its operation and employees over time and the adoption of techniques that would lead to improved interpersonal relationships in the workplace.

Contrary to what custom has dictated in the past, the workforce today is not as amenable to "forced" labor as in years gone by. Today's employees realize that there is more to life than work. They expect more from life than a 50-hour week with little time left for family and friends and with responsibilities that do not profit them. Blind allegiance to an organization with the likelihood of being dismissed when management is in a squeeze is no longer the norm. Employees are seeking job satisfaction in addition to salaries or wages. Absolutely, salaries and wages must be acceptable and fair. It has, however, become critical that management show its human side, its compassionate side, and provide for its employees those amenities that make life gentler, smoother, and more gratifying. Employees have been making demands, and management, unable to offer more money, has found itself in a position where it has had to come up with incentives of a different sort. Many companies are receiving satisfying returns for providing incentives to their employees and creating an open and healthy atmosphere in their work environment.

In addition to creating a good working climate, providing competitive benefits, and establishing strong and equitable conditions, management has found that one productive way of increasing employee productivity, and thus reducing related expense, is through the use of employee **empowerment.** Empowerment refers simply to the fact that, whereas it was once customary for management to make all decisions regarding every facet of the operational aspects of its organization and presenting them to its employees as inescapable facts to be accomplished, employees are now being given the "power" to get involved. They are being empowered to make decisions concerning themselves and, most important, the guests—the bread and butter of the hospitality industry. Employees, generally, work closely with guests; they see and observe; they talk to guests; they hear and listen to complaints; they can appease guests, if needed; they can find remedies to rectify problem situations. Most guest-related problems in the hospitality industry could be easily solved if employees were given the power to make it "right" for the guest. Management has found, in many cases, that, through a solid and constant training program and by giving their employees a share in the decision-making process, they are nurturing a loyal and committed workforce, supportive of management and willing to go that extra mile. Employee empowerment, which has been discussed in the hospitality industry primarily in terms of its positive effect on employees and guests, can also be of great assistance in freeing management to concentrate on running the business while allowing employees to service the guest. It has been said that management gets the quality of workforce it deserves. That is, managers who care little about the welfare of their employees get employees who care little for the welfare of the organization. Those managers, on the other hand, who demonstrate real care and concern for their employees and do their best to meet their needs as well as those of the guest find employees who return that care and concern to the organization.

Key Terms and Concepts

The following are terms and concepts discussed in the chapter that are important for you as a manager. To help you review, please define the terms below.

Labor expense	Task training
Payroll	OJT
Salaried employee	On the floor
Minimum staff	Split shift
Fixed payroll	Separated
Variable payroll	Voluntary separation
Productivity	Involuntary separation
Productivity ratio	Productivity standard
Job description	Franchiser
Job specification	On-Call
Skills test	Call-in
Psychological testing	Standard cost
Preemployment drug testing	Budgeted labor vs. standard labor
Negligent hiring	Empowerment

Test Your Skills

1. Rosa is the manager of a fine-dining Italian restaurant in a large Midwest city. She has experienced high turnover with her hourly employees over the past several months because they say that she isn't paying competitive wages. More employees have threatened to leave if she doesn't give them a raise. She has determined that she can compete with local restaurants if she raises the hourly wage from $8.00 per hour to $8.50, a 6.25% increase. Rosa is concerned about what this will do to her labor cost percentage. Her current labor cost % is at 35%, and she

has determined that 38% is the highest she can go and still make a profit. Using last month's data, help Rosa calculate the effect of a 6.25% increase in wages. Can she give the employees what they want and still make a profit?

Week	Original Cost of Labor	6.25% Raise	Total Cost of Labor	Sales	Labor Cost %
1	$10,650			$27,600	
2	12,075			32,250	
3	10,887			28,650	
4	10,383			37,200	
Total					

2. Jennifer operates Joe Bob's Bar-B-Q Restaurant in a quaint southwestern city of the United States. She specializes in beef brisket and blackberry cobbler. Her operation is very popular. The following data are taken from her last month's operation. She would like to establish labor standards for the entire year based on last month's figures because she believes *that* month represents a good level of both customer service and profitability for her operation. Jennifer has an average guest check of $12 and an overall average payroll cost of $8 per hour.

a. Use Jennifer's last month's operating results to calculate the following productivity standards: labor cost percentage, sales per labor hour, labor dollars per guest served, guests served per labor dollar, and guests served per labor hour.

Operating Results for Joe Bob's

Week	Number of Guests Served	Labor Hours Used
1	7,000	4,000
2	7,800	4,120
3	7,500	4,110
4	8,000	4,450
Total	30,300	16,680

Calculate:

Average Guest Check	$12
Average Wage per Hour	$ 8
Total Sales	
Total Labor Cost	

Productivity Measurement	Productivity Standard
Labor Cost Percentage	
Sales per Labor Hour	
Labor Dollars per Guest Served	
Guests Served per Labor Dollar	
Guests Served per Labor Hour	

b. Jennifer has subdivided her employees into the following categories: meat production, bakery production, salad production, service, sanitation, and management. She wants to develop a sales per labor hour standard for each of her labor categories. She believes this will help her develop future labor budgets based on forecasted sales. Help Jennifer calculate this, based on her current usage of labor hours.

Labor Category	% of Labor Hours Used	Labor Hours	Sales per Labor Hour
Meat Production	25%		
Bakery Production	15%		
Salad Production	10%		
Service	20%		
Sanitation	20%		
Management	10%		
Total	100%		

c. Now that Jennifer has calculated her productivity standards, she would like to use them to develop a labor hours budget for each day next week. She has forecasted 8,000 guests, and she wants to use the guests served per labor hour standard that was calculated in part a. Use this information to develop a labor hours budget for Jennifer.

Day	Forecasted Number of Guests Served	Guests Served per Labor Hour Standard	Labor Hours Budget
1	900		
2	925		
3	975		
4	1,200		
5	1,400		
6	1,600		
7	1,000		
Total	8,000		

3. Mikel owns Mikel's Steak House, a popular dining establishment just outside of town on a busy state highway. Mikel uses labor cost % as his productivity measure, but he has been calculating it only once per month. Since his monthly costs have been higher than he expected, Mikel has decided that he needs a *daily* measure of his labor cost % in order to control his costs better.

   a. Calculate Mikel's daily labor cost % using the six-column daily productivity report, which follows.

   b. Mikel wants to keep his labor cost % at 37%. Given the results of his six-column daily productivity report for the first week of March, will he be able to achieve his labor cost % standard if he continues in the same manner for the remainder of the month? If not, what actions can he take to reduce both his fixed and his variable labor-related expense?

Six-Column Labor Cost Percentage

Unit Name: <u>Mikel's Steak House</u>   Date: <u>3/1–3/7</u>

Weekday	Cost of Labor		Sales		Labor Cost %	
	Today	To Date	Today	To Date	Today	To Date
1	$ 950		$2,520			
2	1,120		2,610			
3	1,040		2,720			
4	1,100		2,780			
5	1,600		3,530			
6	1,700		4,100			
7	1,300		3,910			
Total						

4. Jeffrey operates a high-volume, fine-dining restaurant called the Baroness. His labor productivity ratio of choice is guests served per labor hour. His standard for both servers and buspersons is as follows:

Servers = 10 guests per labor hour.
Buspersons = 25 guests per labor hour.

On a busy day, Jeffrey projects the following volume in terms of anticipated guests. His projections are made in one-hour blocks. Determine the number of labor hours Jeffrey should schedule for each job classification for each time period.

How often in the night should Jeffrey check his volume forecast in order to ensure that he achieves his labor productivity standards and, thus, is within budget at the end of the evening?

Volume/Staff Forecasting for Saturday

The Baroness

Time	Forecasted Number of Guests Served	Server Hours Needed	Busperson Hours Needed
11:00–12:00	85		
12:00–1:00	175		
1:00–2:00	95		
2:00–3:00	30		
3:00–4:00	25		
4:00–5:00	45		
5:00–6:00	90		
6:00–7:00	125		
7:00–8:00	185		
8:00–9:00	150		
9:00–10:00	90		
10:00–11:00	45		
Total	1,140		

5. Steve is in trouble. He has never been a particularly strong labor cost control person. He likes to think of himself more as a "people person." His boss, however, believes that Steve must get more serious about controlling labor costs or he will make Steve an unemployed people person! Steve estimates his weekly sales, then submits that figure to his boss, who then assigns Steve a labor budget for the week. Steve's operating results and budget figures for last month are presented below.

a. Compute Steve's % of budget figures for both sales and labor cost. Also, compute Steve's budget and actual labor cost percentages per week and for the five-week accounting period.

Operating Results

Steve's Airport Deli

For Weeks 1–5

Week	Sales Budget	Sales Actual	Sales % of Budget	Labor Cost Budget	Labor Cost Actual	Labor Cost % of Budget	Labor Cost % Budget	Labor Cost % Actual
1	$2,500	$2,250		$ 875	$ 900			
2	1,700	1,610		595	630			
3	4,080	3,650		1,224	1,300			
4	3,100	2,800		1,085	1,100			
5	2,600	2,400		910	980			
Total								

b. Do you feel that Steve has significant variations from budget? Why do you think Steve's boss assigned Steve a lower labor cost % goal during week 3? How do you feel about Steve's overall performance? What would you do if you were Steve's boss? If you were Steve?

Chapter

8 CONTROLLING OTHER EXPENSES

OVERVIEW This chapter explains the management of foodservice costs that are neither food, beverage, nor labor. These other expenses must also be controlled if cost control goals are to be achieved in the operation you manage. You will learn how to identify the costs you can control as well as those that are considered to be noncontrollable expenses. In addition, you will learn to express other expenses in terms of both other expense per guest served and other expense as a percentage of sales revenue.

CHAPTER OUTLINE

Managing Other Expenses
Fixed, Variable, and Mixed Other Expenses
Controllable and Noncontrollable Other Expenses
Monitoring Other Expenses
Reducing Other Expenses
Key Terms and Concepts, and Test Your Skills

HIGHLIGHTS At the conclusion of this chapter, you will be able to:

○ Assign other expenses in terms of being fixed, variable, or mixed.
○ Differentiate controllable from noncontrollable other expenses.
○ Compute other expense costs in terms of both cost per guest and percentage of sales.

Managing Other Expenses

Food, beverage, and payroll expenses represent the greatest cost areas you will encounter as a foodservice manager. There are, however, expenses

339

you will encounter that are neither food, beverage, nor labor. These **other expenses** can account for significant financial expenditures on the part of your foodservice unit. Controlling these costs can be just as important to the success of your operation as controlling food, beverage, and payroll expenses. Remember that the profit margins in many restaurants are very small. Thus, the control of all costs is critically important. Even in those situations that are traditionally considered nonprofit such as hospitals, nursing homes, and educational institutions, dollars that are wasted in the foodservice area are not available for use in other areas of the institution.

You must look for ways to control all of your expenses, but sometimes the environment in which you operate will act upon your facility to influence some of your costs in positive or negative ways. An excellent example of this is in the area of energy conservation and waste recycling. Energy costs are one of the other expenses we will examine in this chapter. In the past, serving water to each guest upon arrival in a restaurant was simply **SOP** (standard operating procedure) for many operations. The rising cost of energy has caused many foodservice operations to implement a policy of serving water on request rather than with each order. Guests have found this change quite acceptable, and the savings in the expenses related to warewashing costs, equipment usage, energy, cleaning supplies, as well as labor, are significant. In a similar vein, many operators today are finding that recycling fats and oils, cans, jars, and paper can be good not only for the environment, but also for their bottom line. Recycling these items not only reduces your cost of routine garbage and refuse disposal, but, in some communities, the recycled materials themselves have a cash value.

Source reduction, that is, working with food manufacturers and wholesalers to reduce product packaging waste, is just one example of hospitality industry managers and suppliers working to reduce costs. When product packaging and wrapping are held to a minimum, delivery and storage costs are reduced, thus reducing the price foodservice operators must pay to wholesalers. This impacts other expenses in that the quantity of trash generated by this packaging is reduced, which, in turn, reduces garbage pickup fees to the foodservice operator.

FUN ON THE WEB!

Look up the following sites for ideas on how to cut other expenses through energy conservation, source reduction, and recycling.

www.epa.gov/smallbiz Check out this U.S. Environmental Protection Agency site, the Energy Star Small Business Web site. Click on "Restaurants" to find articles, products, and ideas on how to cut energy costs for restaurants.

www.cygnus-group.com This is a great place to learn about source reduction, packaging, and waste reduction. Browse through this site for reports, articles, and links to other interesting sites.

www.dinegreen.com This site is a good resource for recycling and other environmentally friendly practices. Learn about the Green Restaurant Association and find out what they do!

Other expenses can constitute almost anything in the foodservice business. If your restaurant is a floating ship, periodically scraping the barnacles off the boat is an "other expense." If an operator is serving food to oil field workers in Alaska, heating fuel for the dining rooms and kitchen is an other expense, probably a very large one! If a company has been selected to serve food at the Olympics in a foreign country, airfares for its employees may be a significant other expense.

It is important to note that each foodservice operation will have its own unique list of required other expenses. It is not possible, therefore, to list all imaginable expenses that could be incurred by the foodservice operator. It is possible, nonetheless, to group them into categories that make them easier to manage and understand. Napkins, straws, paper cups, and plastic lids, for example, might all be listed under the heading *paper supplies,* while stir sticks, coasters, tiny plastic swords, small paper umbrellas, and the like used in a cocktail lounge might be grouped under the listing *bar supplies.* Groupings, if used, should make sense to the operator and should be specific enough to let the operator know what is in the category. While some operators prefer to make their own groups, the categories used in this text come from the *Uniform System of Accounts for Restaurants* (USAR) recommended for use by the National Restaurant Association. The categories may be identified either by name, such as paper supplies, or by number, such as category 7420. The *Uniform System of Accounts for Restaurants* lists categories both by name and by number. For the purpose of our discussion, titles alone will suffice.

The following list details many of the other expenses associated with these groupings:

1. Costs related to food and beverage operations
2. Costs related to labor
3. Costs related to facility maintenance
4. Occupancy costs

Again, it should be pointed out that you should recognize and monitor the other expense costs you incur in a way that is meaningful to you. Only then can you begin to truly manage and thus control these costs.

Costs Related to Food and Beverage Operations

Direct Operating Expenses

Uniforms
Laundry and dry cleaning

Linen rental
Linen
China and glassware
Silverware
Kitchen utensils
Auto and truck expense
Cleaning supplies
Paper supplies
Guest supplies
Bar supplies
Menus and wine lists
Contract cleaning
Exterminating
Flowers and decorations
Parking lot expenses
Licenses and permits
Banquet expenses
Other operating expenses

Music and Entertainment

Musicians
Professional entertainers
Mechanical music
Contracted wire services
Piano rental and tuning
Films, records, tapes, and sheet music
Programs
Royalties to ASCAP, BMI
Booking agents fees
Meals served to musicians

Marketing

Selling and promotion
   Sales representative service
   Travel expense on solicitation
   Direct mail
   Telephone used for advertising and promotion
   Complimentary food and beverage (including gratis meals to customers)
   Postage
   Advertising
   Newspapers
   Magazines and trade journals
   Circulars, brochures, postal cards, and other mailing pieces
   Outdoor signs
   Radio and television

Programs, directories, and guides
Preparation of copy, photographs, etc.
Public relations and publicity
Civic and community projects
Donations
Souvenirs, favors, treasure chest items
Fees and commissions
Advertising or promotional agency fees
Research
Travel in connection with research
Outside research agency
Product testing

Utility Services

Electric current
Electric bulbs
Water
Removal of waste
Other fuel

Administrative and General Expenses

Office stationery, printing, and supplies
Data processing costs
Postage
Telegrams and telephone
Dues and subscriptions
Traveling expenses
Insurance–general
Commissions on credit card charges
Provision for doubtful accounts
Cash over or (short)
Professional fees
Protective and bank pickup services
Bank charges
Miscellaneous

Costs Related to Labor

Employee Benefits

FICA
Federal unemployment tax
State unemployment tax

Workmen's compensation
Group insurance
State health insurance tax
Welfare plan payments
Pension plan payments
Accident and health insurance premiums
Hospitalization, Blue Cross, Blue Shield
Employee meals
Employee instruction and education expenses
Employee Christmas and other parties
Employee sports activities
Medical expenses
Credit union
Awards and prizes
Transportation and housing

Costs Related to Facility Maintenance

Repairs and Maintenance

Furniture and fixtures
Kitchen equipment
Office equipment
Refrigeration
Air conditioning
Plumbing and heating
Electrical and mechanical
Floors and carpets
Buildings
Parking lot
Gardening and grounds maintenance
Building alterations
Painting, plastering, and decorating
Maintenance contracts
Autos and trucks
Other equipment and supplies

Occupancy Costs

Rent

Rent–minimum or fixed
Percentage rent

Ground rental
Equipment rental
Real estate taxes
Personal property taxes
Other municipal taxes
Franchise tax
Capital stock tax
Partnership or corporation license fees
Insurance on building and contents

Interest

Notes payable
Long-term debt
Other

Depreciation

Buildings
Amortization of leasehold
Amortization of leasehold improvements
Furniture, fixtures, and equipment

While there are many ways in which to consider other expenses, two views of these costs are particularly useful for the foodservice manager. They are:

1. Fixed, variable, or mixed
2. Controllable or noncontrollable

A short discussion of these two concepts will help you to understand other expenses.

Fixed, Variable, and Mixed Other Expenses

As a foodservice manager, some of the costs you will incur will stay the same each month, while others may vary. For example, if you elect to lease a building to house a restaurant and cocktail lounge you want to operate, your lease payment may be such that you pay the same amount for each month of the lease. In other instances, the amount you pay for an expense

(Source: *Uniform System of Accounts for Restaurants* published by the National Restaurant Association http:/www.restaurant.org.)

will vary based on the success of your business. Expenses you incur for paper cocktail napkins used at the cocktail lounge in your restaurant, for example, will increase as the number of guests you serve increases and decrease as the number of guests you serve decreases. As an effective cost control manager, it is important to recognize the difference between costs that are fixed and those that vary with sales volume.

A **fixed expense** is one that remains constant despite increases or decreases in sales volume. A **variable expense** is one that generally increases as sales volume increases and decreases as sales volume decreases. A **mixed expense** is one that has properties of both a fixed and a variable expense. To illustrate all three of these expense types, consider Jo Ann's Hot Dogs Deluxe, a midsize, freestanding restaurant outside a shopping mall, where Jo Ann features upscale Chicago-style hot dogs.

Assume that Jo Ann's average sales volume is $136,000 per month. Assume also that rent for her building and parking spaces is fixed at $8,000 per month. Each month, Jo Ann computes her rent as a percentage of total sales, using the following standard cost percentage formula:

$$\frac{\text{Other Expense}}{\text{Total Sales}} = \text{Other Expense Cost \%}$$

In this case, the other expense category she is interested in looking at is rent; therefore, the formula becomes:

$$\frac{\text{Rent Expense}}{\text{Total Sales}} = \text{Rent Expense \%}$$

Jo Ann has computed her rent expense % for the last six months. The results are shown in Figure 8.1.

Note that Jo Ann's rent expense % ranges from a high of 6.67% (February) to a low of 4.88% (May), yet it is very clear that rent itself was a constant, or fixed, amount of $8,000 per month. Thus, rent, in this lease arrangement, is considered to be a fixed expense. It is important to note that, while the dollar amount of her rent expense is fixed, the rent % declines as volume increases. Thus, the rent payment, as a percentage of sales or cost per item sold, is not constant. This is true because, as sales volume increases, the number of guests contributing to rent expense also increases so it takes a smaller dollar and percentage amount of each guest's sales revenue to generate the $8,000 fixed amount Jo Ann needs to pay her rent.

FIGURE **8.1** ● Jo Ann's Fixed Rent

For Period: 1/1–6/30

Month	Rent Expense	Sales	Rent %
January	$8,000	$121,000	6.61%
February	8,000	120,000	6.67
March	8,000	125,000	6.40
April	8,000	130,000	6.15
May	8,000	164,000	4.88
June	8,000	156,000	5.13
6-Month Average	8,000	136,000	5.88

It makes little sense for Jo Ann to be concerned about the fact that her rent expense % varies by a great amount based on the time of the year. If Jo Ann is comfortable with the six-month average rent percentage (5.88%), she is in control of and managing her other expense category called rent. If Jo Ann feels that her rent expense % is too high, she has only two options. She must increase sales and thereby reduce her rent expense %, or she must negotiate a lower monthly rental with her landlord. When rent is a fixed expense, as in this case, the expense, as expressed by the percentage of sales, may vary. The expense itself, however, is not affected by sales volume.

Some restaurant lease arrangements are based on the sales revenue an operator achieves in the leased facility. Assume, for example, that Jo Ann has a lease arrangement of this type, requiring Jo Ann to pay 5% of her monthly sales revenue as rent. If that were the case, Jo Ann's monthly lease payments would be completely variable as displayed in Figure 8.2. Note that the dollar amount of Jo Ann's rent, in this case, varies a great deal. It ranges from a low of $6,000 (February) to a high of $8,200 (May). The percentage of her sales revenue that is devoted to rent, however, remains at 5 percent.

A third type of lease that is common in the hospitality industry illustrates the fact that some other expenses are mixed; that is, there is both a fixed and a variable component to this type of expense. Figure 8.3 demon-

FIGURE **8.2** ● Jo Ann's Variable Rent

For Period: 1/1–6/30

Month	Sales	Rent %	Rent Expense
January	$121,000	5.00%	$6,050
February	120,000	5.00	6,000
March	125,000	5.00	6,250
April	130,000	5.00	6,500
May	164,000	5.00	8,200
June	156,000	5.00	7,800
6-Month Average	136,000	5.00	6,800

strates such a lease type. In it, Jo Ann pays a flat lease amount of $5,000 per month plus 1% of total sales revenue.

In this arrangement, a major portion ($5,000) of Jo Ann's lease is fixed, while a smaller amount (1% of revenue) varies based on sales revenue. Mixed expenses of this type are common and include items such as energy costs, garbage pickup, some franchise fees, and other expenses where the operator must pay a base amount and then additional amounts as sales volume increases.

In summary, the total dollar amount of fixed expenses does not vary with sales volume, while the total dollar amount of variable expenses changes as volume changes. As a percentage of total sales, however, a fixed-expense % decreases as sales increase, and a variable-expense % does not change. A mixed expense has both fixed and variable components; therefore, as sales increase, the mixed-expense % decreases and total mixed expenses increase. Figure 8.4 shows how fixed, variable, and mixed expenses behave as sales volume increases.

A convenient way to remember the distinction between fixed, variable, and mixed expenses is to consider a napkin holder and napkins on a cafeteria line. The napkin holder is a fixed expense. One holder is sufficient whether you serve 10 guests at lunch or 100 guests. The napkins themselves, however, are a variable expense. As you serve more guests (if each guest takes one napkin), you will incur a greater paper napkin expense. The cost of the napkin holder *and* napkins, if considered together,

FIGURE **8.3** ● Jo Ann's Mixed Rent

For Period: 1/1–6/30

Month	Sales	Fixed Rent Expense	1% Variable Rent Expense	Total Rent Expense
January	$121,000	$5,000	$1,210	$6,210
February	120,000	5,000	1,200	6,200
March	125,000	5,000	1,250	6,250
April	130,000	5,000	1,300	6,300
May	164,000	5,000	1,640	6,640
June	156,000	5,000	1,560	6,560
6-Month Average	136,000	5,000	1,360	6,360

would be a mixed expense. For some very large restaurant chains, it makes sense to separate some mixed expenses into their fixed and variable components, while smaller operations may elect, as in the case of the napkin holder and napkins, to combine these expenses. The choice of how you account for other expenses may be made by the company you work

FIGURE **8.4** ● Fixed, Variable, and Mixed Expense Behaviors as Sales Volume Increases

Expense	As a Percentage of Sales	Total Dollars
Fixed Expense	Decreases	Remains the Same
Variable Expense	Remains the Same	Increases
Mixed Expense	Decreases	Increases

for, or you may be free to consider other expense costs in a manner you feel is best for your own operation.

Good managers know that it is not possible to categorize fixed, variable, or mixed costs in terms of being either "good" or "bad." Some expenses are, by their very nature, related to sales volume. Others are not. It is important to remember that the goal of management is not to reduce, but to increase variable expenses in direct relation to increases in sales volume. Expenses are required if you are to service your guests. In the example of the paper napkins, it is clear that management would prefer to use 100 napkins at lunch rather than 10. As long as the total cost of servicing guests is less than the amount spent, expanding the number of guests served will not only increase variable other expenses, but will increase profits as well. Thus, increasing variable costs is desirable if management increases them in a way that makes sense for both the operation and the satisfaction of the guest.

As we saw in the case of labor expense (Chapter 7), the concept of fixed, variable, and mixed expense is quite useful. Variations in expense percentage that relate *only* to whether an expense is fixed, variable, or mixed should not be of undue concern to management. It is only when a fixed expense is too high or a variable expense is out of control that management should act. This is called the concept of **management by exception.** That is, if the expense is within an acceptable variation range, there is no need for management to intervene. You must take corrective action only when operational results are outside the range of acceptability. This approach keeps you from overreacting to minor variations in expense, while monitoring all important activities.

Examples of other fixed foodservice expenses include the areas of advertising (outdoor sign rentals), utilities (restroom light bulbs), employee benefits (employee-of-the-month prize), repairs and maintenance (parking lot paving), and occupancy costs (interest due on long-term debt). Many foodservice operation other expenses, however, are related to sales volume, and, thus, management has some daily control over these items. This control is both critical and necessary.

Controllable and Noncontrollable Other Expenses

While it is useful, in some cases, to consider other expenses in terms of their being fixed, variable, or mixed, it is also useful to consider some expenses in terms of their being controllable or noncontrollable. Consider, for a moment, the case of Steve, the operator of a neighborhood tavern/sandwich shop. Most of Steve's sales revenue comes from the sale of beer, sandwiches, and his special pizza.

Steve is, of course, free to decide on a weekly or monthly basis the amount he will spend on advertising. Advertising expense, then, is under Steve's direct control and, thus, would be considered a controllable expense. Some of his other expenses, however, are not under his control. Taxes on product sales are a familiar form of a noncontrollable expense. The state in which Steve operates charges a tax on all alcoholic beverage sales. As the state in which he operates increases the liquor tax, Steve is forced to pay more. In this situation, the alcoholic beverage tax would be considered a noncontrollable expense. That is, an expense beyond Steve's immediate control.

As an additional example, assume, for a moment, that you own a quick-service unit that sells takeout chicken. Your store is part of a nationwide chain of such stores. Each month, your store is charged a $500 advertising and promotion fee by the regional headquarters' office. The $500 is used to purchase television advertising time for your company. This $500 charge, as long as you own the franchise, is a noncontrollable operating expense.

A **noncontrollable expense,** then, is one that the foodservice manager can neither increase nor decrease. A **controllable expense** is one in which decisions made by the foodservice manager can have the effect of either increasing or reducing the expense. Simply stated, management has some control over controllable expenses, but has little or no control over noncontrollable expenses. Other examples of noncontrollable expenses include some insurance premiums, property taxes, interest on debt, and depreciation. In every one of these cases, the foodservice operator will find that even the best control systems will not affect the specific expense. Thus, as a manager, you should focus your attention on controllable rather than noncontrollable expenses.

Monitoring Other Expenses

When managing other expenses, two control and monitoring alternatives are available to you. They are:

1. Other expense cost %
2. Other expense cost per guest

Each alternative can be used effectively in specific management situations; thus, it is important for you to master each approach.

As you learned earlier in this chapter, the other expense cost % is computed as follows:

$$\frac{\text{Other Expenses}}{\text{Total Sales}} = \text{Other Expense Cost \%}$$

Thus, for example, in a situation where a restaurant you own incurs advertising expense of $5,000 in a month, serves 10,000 guests, and achieves sales of $78,000 for that same month, you would compute your advertising expense percentage for that month as follows:

$$\frac{\$5,000}{\$78,000} = 6.4\%$$

The other expense cost per guest is computed as follows:

$$\frac{\text{Other Expense}}{\text{Number of Guests Served}} = \text{Other Expense Cost per Guest}$$

In this example and using the preceding formula, you would compute your advertising expense cost per guest as follows:

$$\frac{\$5,000}{10,000} = \$0.50$$

As we have seen, the computation required to establish the other expense percentage requires the other expense category to be divided by total sales. In many cases, this approach yields useful management information. In some cases, however, this computation alone may not provide adequate information; therefore, using the concept of other expense cost per guest can be very useful. To illustrate, consider the following example. Scott operates Chez Scot, an exclusive, fine-dining establishment in a suburban area of a major city. One of Scott's major other expenses is linen. He uses both tablecloths and napkins. Scott's partner, Joshua, believes that linen costs are a variable operating expense and should be monitored through the use of a linen cost % figure. In fact, says Scott's partner, Figure 8.5 indicates that the linen cost % has been declining over the past five months; therefore, current control systems must be working. As is evident in Figure 8.5, the linen cost % has indeed been declining over the past five months.

Scott, however, is convinced that there *are* control problems. He has monitored linen costs on a cost per guest basis. His information is presented in Figure 8.6, which validates Scott's fears. There is indeed a control problem in the linen area.

Figures 8.5 and 8.6 both show that a linen control problem does exist, yet Figure 8.6 shows it most clearly since it is plain that linen cost per guest has gone from $1.06 in January to its May high of $1.22.

Chez Scot is enjoying increased sales ($68,000 in January vs. $74,000 in May), but its guest count is declining (2,566 in January vs. 2,305 in

FIGURE **8.5** ● Chez Scot Linen Cost %

Month	Total Sales	Linen Cost	Cost %
January	$ 68,000	$ 2,720	4.00%
February	70,000	2,758	3.94
March	72,000	2,772	3.85
April	71,500	2,753	3.85
May	74,000	2,812	3.80
Total	355,500	13,815	3.89

May). The check average has obviously increased. This is a good sign, as it indicates that each guest is buying more food. The fact that fewer guests are being served should, however, result in a decrease in demand for linen and, thus, a decline in cost. In fact, on a per-person basis, linen costs are up. Scott is correct to be concerned about possible problems in the linen control area.

FIGURE **8.6** ● Chez Scot Linen Cost per Guest

Month	Linen Cost	Number of Guests Served	Cost per Guest
January	$ 2,720	2,566	$1.06
February	2,758	2,508	1.10
March	2,772	2,410	1.15
April	2,753	2,333	1.18
May	2,812	2,305	1.22
Total	13,815	12,122	1.14

Other expense cost per guest may also be useful in a situation where no sales figure is received by the foodservice manager. Consider a college dormitory feeding situation where paper products such as cups, napkins, straws, and lids are placed on the serving line to be used by the students eating their meals.

In this case, Juanita, the cafeteria manager, wonders whether students are taking more of these items than is normal. The problem is, of course, that she is not exactly sure what "normal" use is when it comes to supplying paper products to her students. Juanita belongs to a trade association that asks its members to supply annual cost figures to a central location where they are tabulated and sent back to the membership. Figure 8.7 shows the tabulations from five colleges in addition to those from Juanita's unit.

Juanita has computed her paper products cost per student for the year and has found it to be higher than at P. University and the University of T., but lower than O. University, C. State University, and A. State University. Juanita's costs appear to be in line in the paper goods area. If, however, Juanita hopes to reduce paper products cost per student even further, she could, perhaps, call or arrange a visit to either P. University or University of T. to observe their operations or purchasing techniques.

The other expense cost per guest formula is of value when management believes it can be helpful or when lack of a sales figure makes the computation of other expense cost % impossible. Figure 8.8 presents a six-column form that is useful in tracking both daily and cumulative cost per

FIGURE **8.7** ● Average Paper Product Cost

Institution	Cost of Paper Products	Number of Students	Paper Product Cost per Student
O University	$140,592	8,080	$17.40
C. State University	109,200	6,500	16.80
P. University	122,276	7,940	15.40
University of T.	184,755	11,300	16.35
A. State University	61,560	3,600	17.10
5-University Average	123,676.60	7,484	16.53
Juanita's Institution	77,220	4,680	16.50

FIGURE **8.8** ● Six-Column Cost of Paper Products

Juanita's Institution   Date: 4/1–4/8

Weekday	Other Expense Cost		Number of Guests Served		Cost per Guest	
	Today	To Date	Today	To Date	Today	To Date
Monday	$ 145.50	$ 145.50	823	823	$0.18	$0.18
Tuesday	200.10	345.60	751	1,574	0.27	0.22
Wednesday	417.08	762.68	902	2,476	0.46	0.31
Thursday	0	762.68	489	2,965	0	0.26
Friday	237.51	1,000.19	499	3,464	0.48	0.29
Saturday	105.99	1,106.18	375	3,839	0.28	0.29
Sunday	0	1,106.18	250	4,089	0	0.27
Monday	157.10	1,263.28	841	4,930	0.19	0.26
Total	1,263.28		4,930		0.26	

guest figures. It is maintained by inserting Other Expense Cost and Number of Guests Served in the first two sets of columns. The third set of columns, Cost per Guest, is obtained by using the other expense cost per guest formula.

Reducing Other Expenses

Since other expenses can be broken down into four distinct areas, it is useful to consider these four areas when developing strategies for reducing overall other expense costs. It is important to remember that each food-service manager faces his or her own unique set of other expenses. A restaurant on a beach in southern Florida may well experience the expense of hurricane insurance. A similar restaurant in Kansas would not. Each foodservice operation is unique. Those operators who are effective are constantly on the lookout for ways to reduce unnecessary additions to any other expense categories.

Reducing Costs Related to Food and Beverage Operations

In many respects, some of these other expenses should be treated like food and beverage expenses. For instance, in the case of cleaning supplies, linen, uniforms, and the like, products should be ordered, inventoried, and issued in the same manner used for food and beverage products. In general, fixed costs related to food and beverage operations can only be reduced when measuring them as a percentage of total sales. This is done, of course, by increasing the total sales figure. Reducing total variable cost expenses is generally not desirable, since, in fact, each additional sale will bring additional variable expense. In this case, while total variable expenses may increase, the positive impact of the additional sales on fixed costs will serve to reduce the overall other expense percentage.

To see how this is done, let's examine a shaved-ice kiosk called Igloo's located in the middle of a small parking lot. Figure 8.9 demonstrates the impact of volume increases on both total other expense and

FIGURE **8.9** ● Igloo's Fixed and Variable Other Expense

Sales	Fixed Expense	Variable Expense (10%)	Total Other Expense	Other Expense Cost %
$ 1,000	$150	$ 100	$ 250	25.00%
3,000	150	300	450	15.00
9,000	150	900	1,050	11.67
10,000	150	1,000	1,150	11.50
15,000	150	1,500	1,650	11.00

other expense cost %. We assume, in this example, that some of the other expenses related to food and beverage operations are fixed and others are variable. The variable portion of other expense, in this example, equals 10% of gross sales. Fixed expense equals $150.

While variable expense increases from $100 to $1,500, total other expense percentage drops from 25% of sales to 11% of sales. Thus, to reduce costs related to food and beverage operations, increases in sales are quite helpful! If all other expenses related to food and beverage operations were 100% variable, however, this strategy would not have the effect of reducing other expense cost %, since the dollar amount of other expenses would increase proportionately to volume increases, and total other expense cost % would be unchanged.

Reducing Costs Related to Labor

As you learned in Chapter 7, some labor-related expenses can be considered partially fixed and partially variable. To help reduce other expense costs related to labor, it is necessary for you to eliminate wasteful labor-related expense. Examples include the cost of advertising, hiring, and training new employees because of excessive employee turnover. It also means implementing cost-reducing hiring practices such as preemployment drug screening that may result in lower health insurance premiums for employees, if these benefits are provided. Proper employment practices also impact the worker's compensation and unemployment tax rates you may pay. Remember that, in many states, the rate you pay for these two insurance programs is determined, in part, by your history of work-related injuries and employment separations. Careful hiring and providing excellent training to reduce the costs associated with worker's compensation claims and unemployment compensation will save you money and reduce your other expense related to labor.

Conversely, those operators who attempt to reduce other expenses related to labor too much, by not providing adequate health care, pension, or sick leave benefits, will find that the best employees prefer to work elsewhere. This would leave the operator with a less productive workforce than would otherwise be possible. In many ways, employees will be your most valuable assets. Effective management is not magic. If your employees feel they are treated fairly, they will be motivated to do their best. If they do not, they will not. Reducing employee benefits while attempting to retain a well-qualified workforce is simply management at its worst!

Reducing Costs Related to Facility Maintenance

Any employee knows that keeping his or her tools clean and in good working order will make them last longer and perform better. The same is true for foodservice facilities. A properly designed and implemented preventative maintenance program can go a long way toward reducing equipment failure and, thus, decreasing equipment and facility-related costs. Proper care of mechanical equipment not only prolongs its life, but also actually reduces operational costs. As the price of energy needed to operate facilities continues to rise, you must implement a facility repair and maintenance program that seeks to discover and treat minor equipment and facility problems before they become major problems.

One way to help ensure that costs are as low as possible is to use a competitive-bid process before awarding contracts for services you require. For example, if you hire a carpet cleaning company to clean your dining room carpets monthly, it is a good idea to annually seek competitive bids from new carpet cleaners. This can help to reduce your costs by ensuring that the carpet cleaner you select has given you a price that is competitive with other service providers. In the area of maintenance contracts, for areas such as the kitchen or for mechanical equipment, elevators, or grounds, it is recommended that these contracts be bid at least once per year. This is especially true if the dollar value of the contract is large.

Air-conditioning, plumbing, heating, and refrigerated units should be inspected at least yearly, and kitchen equipment, such as dishwashers, slicers, and mixers, should be inspected at least monthly for purposes of preventative maintenance. A form such as the one in Figure 8.10 is useful in this process.

Some foodservice managers operate facilities that are large enough to employ their own facility maintenance staff. If this is the case, make sure these employees have copies of the operating and maintenance manuals of all equipment. These documents can prove invaluable in the reduction of equipment and facility-related operating costs.

Reducing Occupancy Costs

Occupancy costs refer to those expenses incurred by the foodservice unit that are related to the occupancy of and payment for the physical facility it occupies.

For the foodservice manager who is not the owner, the majority of occupancy costs will be noncontrollable. Rent, taxes, and interest on debt are real costs but are beyond the immediate control of the foodservice manager. However, if you own the facility you manage, occupancy costs are a primary determinant of both profit on sales and return on dollars invested. When occupancy costs are too high because of unfavorable rent or lease arrangements or due to excessive debt load, the foodservice operation's owner may face extreme difficulty in generating profit. Food, beverage, and labor costs can only be managed to a point; beyond that, efforts to reduce costs will result in decreased guest satisfaction. If occupancy costs are unrealistically high, no amount of effective cost control can help "save" the operation's profitability.

FIGURE **8.10** ● Equipment Inspection Report

Unit Name: **Your Restaurant**   Time Period: 1/1–1/31

Item Inspected	Inspection Date	Inspected By	Action Recommended
A. Refrigerator #6	1/1	D.H.	Replace gasket
B. Fryer	1/7	D.H.	Inspected, no maintenance needed
C. Ice Machine	1/9	D.H.	Drain, de-lime
D.			
E.			

Total other expenses in an operation can range from 5% to 20% or more of the gross sales. These expenses, while considered as minor expenses, can be extremely important to overall operational profitability. This is especially true in a situation where the number of guests you serve is fixed, or nearly so, and the prices you are allowed to charge for your products is fixed also. In a case such as this, your ability to control other expenses is vital to your success.

Key Terms and Concepts

The following are terms and concepts discussed in the chapter that are important for you as a manager. To help you review, please define the terms below.

Other expenses   Mixed expense
SOP   Management by exception
Source reduction   Noncontrollable expense
Fixed expense   Controllable expense
Variable expense   Occupancy costs

Test Your Skills

1. Susie operates a restaurant in the ski resort town of Asvail. She has decided to group her other expense categories in terms of either fixed expense or variable expense. Place an "X" in the Variable Expense column for those expenses that vary with sales volume. For expenses that do not vary with sales, place an "X" in the Fixed Expense column.

Other Expenses	Variable Expense	Fixed Expense
Linen rental		
Piano rental		
Ice		
Insurance		
Pension plan payments		
Snow shoveling fees (parking lot)		
Paper products		
Kitchen equipment rental (mixer)		
Long-term debt payment		
Real estate tax		

2. Tutti owns a fine-dining restaurant in a suburb of a major coastal city. Last year, her sales were not as high as she would have liked. To help increase her sales volume, Tutti decided to hire a sales consultant, Tina Boniner, to help bring in more customers. Tutti hired Tina on a trial basis for the first six months of the year. Tina was paid a fixed fee of $1,000 per month and a commission of 1% of sales. At the end of June, Tutti wants to evaluate whether she should hire Tina for the next six months. Calculate Tutti's sales consultant cost %.

Mixed Expense—Sales Consultant

For Period: 1/1–6/30

Month	Sales	Fixed Fee	1% Variable Expense	Total Expense	Cost %
January	$ 81,000				
February	80,000				
March	88,000				
April	92,000				
May	110,000				
June	108,000				
6-Month Average					

a. Tutti has decided that she cannot spend more than 2.2% of total sales for Tina's services. Based on the six-month average cost %, can Tutti afford to hire Tina for another six months?

b. Last year's average sales for the first six months was $80,000. Based on the sales data, did Tina do a good job at increasing sales? Should she be hired again?

3. John owns and operates the End Zone Steakhouse. He would like to turn the operation over to his son Zeke, a graduate of Spartacus High School. Zeke, however, has no foodservice background. Zeke would like to prove that he can effectively operate the restaurant and would be good at controlling costs. Operating cost categories for the restaurant, in terms of other expenses, are as follows. Place an "X" in the Controllable column for those operating expenses that Zeke could control. If he could not control the cost, place an "X" in the Noncontrollable column.

Other Expenses	Controllable	Noncontrollable
Real estate tax		
Menu printing		
Professional musicians		
Interest on long-term debt		
Charitable donations		
Cleaning supplies		
Flowers and decorations		
Water		
Licenses and permits		
Electricity		

4. Shanna operates a lounge in an extremely popular downtown convention hotel. The hotel regularly operates around the 80% occupancy mark, and its lounge, Luigi's, is very often filled to capacity. On weeks when business at the hotel is slower, Shanna attempts to build local sales by scheduling a variety of popular bands to play on the stage. She must select one band to play on Saturday night, six weeks from now, when the hotel is not busy. She has kept records of the costs and sales volume of the last four bands she has booked.

a. Compute both band expense % and cost per guest served. Based on the cost % of the bands, which one should Shanna select for booking?

b. Would your answer change if you knew Shanna charged a $5.00 cover charge to enter the lounge on the nights she has a band, and the cover charge is reported separately from the lounge sales? If so, which band would you choose?

Expense % and Cost per Guest Served—Bands

Unit Name: Luigi's Lounge

Date	Band	Band Expense	Lounge Sales	Cost %	Number of Guests Served	Cost per Guest Served
1/1	Tiny and the Boys	$1,400	$11,400		1,425	
2/1	Shakin' Bill and the Billfolds	1,900	12,250		1,980	
3/1	La Noise	2,000	12,000		2,005	
4/1	The Hoppers	2,000	10,250		2,100	

5. Marjorie runs a 200-seat, white-tablecloth restaurant in a wealthy neighborhood. Since her guests expect her tablecloths and napkins to be *really* white, she sends her linens to a local laundry service daily. The laundry service charges her by the piece. She wants to keep track of her laundry cost per guest to see if she can use the information to control her laundry costs better. Help her complete her six-column cost per guest report. She has budgeted $0.60 per guest on average. How is she doing at controlling her costs?

Six-Column Cost per Guest—Laundry Service

Unit Name: <u>Marjorie's</u>   Date: <u>5/1–5/7</u>

	Laundry Service Cost		Number of Served		Cost per Guest	
Weekday	Today	To Date	Today	To Date	Today	To Date
1	$225		400			
2	204		375			
3	200		350			
4	240		425			
5	275		450			
6	300		500			
7	230		420			
Total						

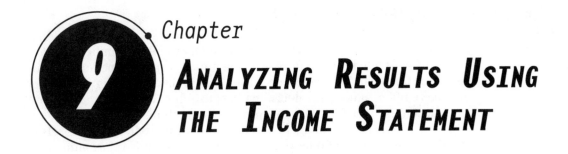

Chapter

9 ANALYZING RESULTS USING THE INCOME STATEMENT

OVERVIEW This chapter explains what you will do to analyze the cost effectiveness of your operation. You will learn to read and use the income statement, a financial document also known as the profit and loss (P&L) statement. Included are techniques to analyze your sales volume as well as expense levels, including food, beverage, labor, and other expenses. Finally, you will learn how to review the income statement to analyze your overall profitability.

CHAPTER OUTLINE

Introduction to Financial Analysis
Uniform System of Accounts
Income Statement (USAR)
Analysis of Sales/Volume
Analysis of Food Expense
Analysis of Beverage Expense
Analysis of Labor Expense
Analysis of Other Expenses
Analysis of Profits
Key Terms and Concepts, and Test Your Skills

HIGHLIGHTS At the conclusion of this chapter, you will be able to:

○ Prepare an income (profit and loss) statement.
○ Analyze sales and expenses using the P&L statement.
○ Evaluate your facility's profitability using the P&L statement.

Introduction to Financial Analysis

Far too many foodservice managers find that they collect numbers, fill out forms, or generate reams and reams of computer printout paper with little regard for what they should do with all these data. Some have said that managers often make poor decisions because they lack information, but when it comes to the financial analysis of an operation, the opposite is usually true. Foodservice managers more often than not will find themselves awash in numbers! It will be your job to sift through this information and select for analysis those numbers that can shed light on exactly what is happening in your operation. This information, in an appropriate form, is necessary not only to effectively operate your business, but to serve many interest groups that are directly or indirectly involved with the financial operation of your facility. Local, state, and federal financial records relating to taxes and employee wages will have to be submitted to the government on a regular basis. In addition, records showing the financial health of an operation may have to be submitted to new suppliers in order to establish credit worthiness. Also, if a foodservice operation has been established with both operating partners and investors, those owners and investors will certainly require accurate and timely updates that focus on the financial health of the business. Owners, stockholders, and investment bankers may all have an interest in the day-to-day efficiency and effectiveness of management. For each of these groups, and, of course, for the foodservice organization's own upper management, the accurate compilation and analysis of the operation's financial transactions is critical.

As a professional foodservice manager, you will be very interested in examining your cost of doing business. Documenting and analyzing sales, expenses, and profits is sometimes called **cost accounting,** but more appropriately is known as **managerial accounting** to reflect the importance managers place on this process. In this text, we will use the term managerial accounting when referring to documenting, analyzing, and managing sales, expenses, and profit data.

It is important for you to be keenly aware of the difference between simply recording and summarizing financial data and the process of analyzing that data. As an example, electronic cash registers or computer-based point of sales (POS) systems can be programmed to provide data about food and beverage sales per server. Management can track, per shift, the relative sales effort of each service employee. If this is done with the goal of either increasing the training of the less productive server or rewarding the most productive one, the cash register or POS system has, in fact, added information that is valuable and has assisted in the unit's operation. If, on the other hand, this information is dutifully recorded on a daily basis, filed away or sent to a regional office, and is then left to collect dust, the cash register or POS system has actually harmed the operation by taking management's time away from the more important task of running the business. It has converted the manager's role from that of cost analyst to one of a record keeper only, and a mindless record keeper at that. This type of situation must be avoided at all cost if you are to maximize your effectiveness by being in the production area or dining room during service periods and not by staying in the office catching up on your paperwork. Record keeping is essentially the summarizing and recording of data. Managerial accounting involves the summarizing, recording, and, most important, the analysis of that data.

You do not have to be a certified management accountant (CMA) or a certified public accountant (CPA) to analyze data related to foodservice revenue and expense. While this is not meant to discount the value of an accounting professional who assists the foodservice manager, it is important to establish that it is the professional foodservice manager, not an outside expert, who is most qualified to assess the effectiveness of the foodservice team in providing the service levels desired by management and in controlling production-related costs. The analysis of operating data, a traditional role of the accountant, must also be part of your role as manager. The process is not complex and, in fact, is one of the most fun and creative aspects of a foodservice manager's job.

A good foodservice manager is, in fact, a manager first and not an accountant. It is important, however, for you to be able to read and understand financial information and be able to converse intelligently and confidently with the many parties outside the operation who will read and use the information generated by accountants. This information will be crucial to the operation's overall health and success and can provide the needed data that will assist in sharpening the quality of your management decisions.

Uniform System of Accounts

Financial statements related to the operation of a foodservice facility are, of course, of interest to management, stockholders, owners, creditors, governmental agencies, and, often, the general public. To ensure that this financial information is presented in a way that is both useful and consistent, **uniform system of accounts** have been established for many areas of the hospitality industry. The National Restaurant Association, for example, has developed the *Uniform System of Accounts for Restaurants* (USAR). Uniform system of accounts also exist for hotels, clubs, nursing homes, schools, and hospitals. Each system seeks to provide a consistent and clear manner in which to record sales, expenses, and overall financial condition. Sales categories, expense classifications, and methods of computing relevant ratios are included in the uniform system of accounts. These uniform systems are typically available from the national associations involved with each hospitality segment.

It is important to note that the uniform system of accounts attempt to provide operator guidelines rather than mandated methodology. Small foodservice operations, for example, may use the *uniform system of accounts for restaurants* in a slightly different way than will large operations. In all cases, however, operators who use the uniform system of accounts "speak the same language," and it is truly useful that they do so. If each operator prepared financial statements in any manner he or she elected, it is unlikely that the many external audiences who must use them could properly interpret these statements. Thus, an effective manager will secure a copy of the appropriate uniform system of accounts for his or her operation and become familiar with its basic formats and principles.

FUN ON THE WEB!

Look up the following sites to review and obtain copies of the uniform system of accounts for restaurants, lodging facilities, and clubs.

www.restaurant.org Click on "Store," then click on "View Complete Product Listing." Next, click on "Business Planning and Financial Management," then "Uniform System of Accounts for Restaurants" to see a synopsis of the book and place an order.

www.ei-ahma.org Click on "Books." Scroll down to "Financial Management," and click on "Uniform System of Accounts for the Lodging Industry" to see a synopsis of the book and place an order.

www.clubnet.com Click on "Bookmart." Scroll down to "Successfully Manage Your Club's Financial Operations" and click on "Uniform System of Financial Reporting for Clubs" to see a synopsis of the book and place an order.

Income Statement (USAR)

The income statement, often referred to as the profit and loss (P&L) statement, is the key management tool for cost control. Essentially, the P&L statement seeks to show revenue and expense in a level of detail determined by management after review of the appropriate uniform system of accounts.

The word profit can mean many things; therefore, the profit and loss statement can be somewhat confusing if you are not familiar with it. Some operators use pretax profit on their P&L statements, while others do not. A tight definition of what is meant by profit must be established for each P&L statement if it is to be helpful. In all cases, however, a purpose of the profit and loss statement is to identify net income, or the profit generated after all appropriate expenses of the business have been paid.

Figure 9.1 details two years' profit and loss statements for Joshua's, Inc., a foodservice complex that includes a cocktail lounge, two dining areas, and banquet space. Joshua's fiscal year, that is, his accounting year, begins on October 1 and concludes on September 30 of the next year. This fiscal year coincides with the beginning of his busy season and, thus, gives him a logical starting point.

As can be seen in Figure 9.1, last year Joshua's generated $2,306,110 in total sales and achieved a net income of $101,772. This year, when the corporation generated total sales revenue of $2,541,206, Joshua achieved a net income of $114,923. The question Joshua must ask himself, of course, is, "How good is this performance?"

It is important to note that each operation's P&L statement will look slightly different. All of them, however, typically take a similar approach to reporting revenue and expense. Note that, while the detail is much greater, the layout of Joshua's P&L is similar in structure to the abbreviated P&L presented as Figure 1.3. Both statements list revenue first, then expense, and finally the difference between the revenue and expense figures. If this number is positive, it represents a profit. If expenses exceed revenue, a loss, represented by a negative number or a number in brackets, is shown. Operating at a loss is, for some unknown reason, often referred to as operating "in the red" or "shedding red ink." Regardless of the color of the ink, operating at a loss can cause an operator to shed a few tears!

To ensure that *your* operation does not produce a loss, you need to know some important components of the *Uniform System of Accounts for Restaurants*. The USAR can better be understood by dividing it into three sections: gross profit, operating expenses, and nonoperating expenses. Referring to Figure 9.1, the gross profit section consists of Sales through Total Gross Profit, the operating expenses section covers Operating Expenses through Operating Income, and the nonoperating expenses section includes Interest through Net Income. These three sections are arranged on the income statement *from most controllable to least controllable* by the foodservice manager. The **gross profit section** consists of food and beverage sales and costs that can and should be controlled by the manager on a daily basis. The majority of this book is devoted to controlling these items. The **operating expenses section** is also under the control of the manager but more so on a weekly or monthly basis (with the exception of wages, which you can control daily). Consider the Repairs and Maintenance category. Although repairs will be needed when equipment breaks down, maintenance is typically scheduled on a monthly basis. The manager can control, to some extent, how employees use the equipment, but he or she cannot control or predict the breakdown of equipment when it occurs. The third section of the USAR is the **nonoperating expenses section.** It is this section that is least controllable by the foodservice manager. Interest paid to creditors for short-term or long-term debt is due regardless of the ability of the manager to control operations. Furthermore, taxes are controlled by the government; to paraphrase Benjamin Franklin, the only sure things in life are death and taxes. So, the foodservice man-

FIGURE **9.1** ● Joshua's Income Statement (P&L)

Joshua's Inc.
Last Year Versus This Year

	Last Year	%	This Year	%
SALES:				
Food	$1,891,011	82.0%	$2,058,376	81.0%
Beverage	415,099	18.0	482,830	19.0
Total Sales	**2,306,110**	**100.0**	**2,541,206**	**100.0**
COST OF SALES:				
Food	712,587	37.7	767,443	37.3
Beverage	94,550	22.8	96,566	20.0
Total Cost of Sales	**807,137**	**35.0**	**864,009**	**34.0**
GROSS PROFIT:				
Food	1,178,424	62.3	1,290,933	62.7
Beverage	320,549	77.2	386,264	80.0
Total Gross Profit	**1,498,973**	**65.0**	**1,677,197**	**66.0**
OPERATING EXPENSES:				
Salaries and Wages	641,099	27.8	714,079	28.1
Employee Benefits	99,163	4.3	111,813	4.4
Direct Operating Expenses	122,224	5.3	132,143	5.2
Music and Entertainment	2,306	0.1	7,624	0.3
Marketing	43,816	1.9	63,530	2.5

FIGURE **9.1** ● Joshua's Income Statement (P&L) *(continued)*

Joshua's Inc.
Last Year Versus This Year

	Last Year	%	This Year	%
Utility Services	73,796	3.2	88,942	3.5
Repairs and Maintenance	34,592	1.5	35,577	1.4
Administrative and General	66,877	2.9	71,154	2.8
Occupancy	120,000	5.2	120,000	4.7
Depreciation	41,510	1.8	55,907	2.2
Total Operating Expenses	**1,245,383**	**54.0**	**1,400,769**	**55.1**
Operating Income	**253,590**	**11.0**	**276,428**	**10.9**
Interest	**86,750**	**3.8**	**84,889**	**3.3**
Income Before Income Taxes	**166,840**	**7.2**	**191,539**	**7.5**
Income Taxes	**65,068**	**2.8**	**76,616**	**3.0**
Net Income	**101,772**	**4.4**	**114,923**	**4.5**

Prepared By: M. Chaplin, CPA
Modified By: L. Dopson, Ed.D.

ager has little control over the amount of money "Uncle Sam" gets every year. Knowing the three sections of the income statement allows you to focus on those things that you have the most control over as a foodservice manager. This book helps you to focus on these controllable areas so that you can better manage your time and make the most out of your efforts to control costs.

Another facet of the uniform system of accounts that you should know is the supporting schedule. The income statement as shown in Figure 9.1 is an **aggregate statement.** This means that all details associated with the sales, costs, and profits of the foodservice establishment are *summarized* on the P&L statement. Although this summary gives the manager a one-shot look at the performance of the operation, the details are not included directly on the statement. These details can be found in **supporting schedules.** Each line item on the income statement should be accompanied by a schedule that outlines all of the information that you, as a manager, need to know to operate your business successfully. For example, the Food item under Cost of Sales could have an accompanying schedule that details costs incurred under the product categories of meat, seafood, poultry, produce, dairy, baked goods, and grocery (can, dry, and frozen) items. These categories could be broken down by costs and percentage of total food sales. The type of information and the level of detail that are included on the schedules are left up to you and what is appropriate for your operation. It is in the schedules that you collect the information you need to break down sales or costs and determine problem areas and potential opportunities for improving each item on the income statement.

Note also that each revenue and expense category in Figure 9.1 is represented in terms of both its whole dollar amount and its percentage of total sales. All ratios are calculated as a percentage of *total sales* except the following:

Food costs are divided by food sales.
Beverage costs are divided by beverage sales.
Food gross profit if divided by food sales.
Beverage gross profit is divided by beverage sales.

Food and beverage items use their respective food and beverage sales as the denominator so that these items can be evaluated separately from total sales. Since food costs and beverage costs are the most controllable items on the income statement, Joshua needs to separate these sales and costs out of the aggregate and evaluate these items more carefully. Notice also that Joshua's accountant presents this year's P&L statement along with last year's, as this can help Joshua make comparisons and analyze trends in his business.

The P&L statement, in conjunction with other financial documents, can provide useful data regarding rates of financial return based on various sales or profit measurements. The P&L statement alone, however, can yield important information that is critical to the development of your future management plans and budgets. The analysis of P&L statements is a fun and very creative process if basic procedures are well understood. In general, managers who seek to uncover all that their P&L will tell them undertake the following areas of analysis:

1. Sales/volume
2. Food expense
3. Beverage expense
4. Labor expense

5. Other expense
6. Profits

Using the data from Figure 9.1, each of these areas will be reviewed in turn.

Analysis of Sales/Volume

As discussed earlier in this text, foodservice operators can measure sales in terms of either dollars or number of guests served. In both cases, an increase in sales volume is usually to be desired. A sales increase or decrease must, however, be analyzed carefully if you are to truly understand the revenue direction of your business. Consider the sales portion of Joshua's P&L statement as detailed in Figure 9.2.

Based on the data from Figure 9.2, Joshua can compute his overall sales increase or decrease using the following steps:

1. Determine sales for this accounting period.
2. Calculate the following: this period's sales minus last period's sales.
3. Divide the difference in item 2 above by last period's sales to determine percentage variance.

For Joshua, the percentage variance is as indicated in Figure 9.3.
To illustrate the steps outlined using total sales as an example, we find:

1. $2,541,206
2. $2,541,206 − $2,306,110 = $235,096
3. $235,096/$2,306,110 = 10.2%

FIGURE **9.2** ● Joshua's P&L Sales Comparison

Sales	Last Year	% of Sales	This Year	% of Sales
Food Sales	$1,891,011	82.0%	$2,058,376	81.0%
Beverage Sales	415,099	18.0	482,830	19.0
Total Sales	2,306,110	100.0	$2,541,206	100.0

FIGURE **9.3** ● Joshua's P&L Sales Variance

Sales	Last Year	This Year	Variance	Variance %
Food Sales	$1,891,011	$2,058,376	$167,365	+ 8.9%
Beverage Sales	415,099	482,830	67,731	+16.3
Total Sales	2,306,110	2,541,206	235,096	+10.2

As can be seen, it appears that Joshua has achieved an overall increase in sales of 10.2%.

There are several ways Joshua could have experienced total sales volume increases in the current year. These are:

1. Serve the same number of guests at a higher check average.
2. Serve more guests at the same check average.
3. Serve more guests at a higher check average.

To determine which of these alternatives is indeed the case, Joshua must use a sales adjustment technique.

Assume, for a moment, that Joshua raised prices for food and beverage by 5% at the beginning of this fiscal year. If this was the case, and he wishes to determine fairly his sales increase, he must adjust for that 5% menu price increase. The procedure he would use to adjust sales variance for known menu price increases is as follows:

Step 1. Increase prior-period sales (last year) by amount of the price increase.
Step 2. Subtract the result in Step 1 from this period's sales.
Step 3. Divide the difference in Step 2 by the value of Step 1.

Thus, in our example, Joshua would follow the steps outlined previously to determine his real sales increase. In the case of total sales, the procedure would be as follows:

Step 1. $2,306,110 × 1.05 = $2,421,415.50
Step 2. $2,541,206 − $2,421,415.50 = $119,790.50
Step 3. $119,790.50/$2,421,415.50 = 4.95%

Figure 9.4 details the results that are achieved if this 5% adjustment

FIGURE **9.4** ● Joshua's P&L Sales Comparison with 5% Menu Price Increase

Sales	Last Year	Adjusted Sales (Last Year × 1.05)	This Year	Variance	Variance %
Food Sales	$1,891,011	$1,985,561.60	$2,058,376	$ 72,814.45	+ 3.67%
Beverage Sales	415,099	435,853.95	482,830	46,976.05	+10.78
Total Sales	2,306,110	2,421,415.50	2,541,206	119,790.50	+ 4.95

process is completed for all sales areas. Joshua's total sales figure would be up by 4.95% if he adjusted it for a 5% menu price increase.

There is still more, however, that the P&L can tell Joshua about his sales. If he has kept accurate guest count records, he can compute his sales per guest figure (see Chapter 2). With this information, he can determine whether his sales are up because he is serving more guests, or because he is serving the same number of guests but each one is spending more per visit, or because some of both has occurred. In fact, if each guest is spending quite a bit more per visit, Joshua may even have experienced a decrease in total guest count yet an increase in total sales. If this were the case, he would want to know about it since it is unrealistic to assume that revenue will continue to increase over the long run if the number of guests visiting his establishment is declining.

Other Factors Influencing Sales Analysis

In some foodservice establishments, other factors must be taken into consideration before sales revenue can be accurately analyzed. Consider the situation you would face if you owned a restaurant across the street from a professional basketball stadium. If you were to compare sales from this May to sales generated last May, the number of home games in May for this professional team would have to be determined before you could make valid conclusions about guest count increases or decreases. Also, if a foodservice facility is open only Monday through Friday, the number of operating days in two given accounting periods may be different for the facility. When this is the case, percentage increases or decreases in sales volume must be based on average daily sales, rather than the total sales figure. To illustrate this, consider a hot dog stand that operates in the city center Monday through Friday only. In October of this year, the stand was

Figure **9.5** ● Hot Dog! Sales Data

	Last Year	This Year	Variance	Variance %
Total Sales (October)	$17,710.00	$17,506.00	$−204	−1.2%
Number of Operating Days	22 days	21 days	1 day	
Average Daily Sales	$ 805.00	$ 833.62	$28.62	+3.6

open for 21 operating days. Last year, however, because of the number of weekend days in October, the stand operated for 22 days. Figure 9.5 details the comparison of sales for the stand, assuming no increase in menu selling price this year compared with last year.

While, at first glance, it appears that October sales this year are 1.2% lower than last year, in reality, average daily sales are up 3.6%! Are sales for October up or down? Clearly, the answer must be qualified in terms of monthly or daily sales. For this reason, effective foodservice managers must be careful to consider all of the relevant facts before making determinations about sales direction.

Every critical factor must be considered when evaluating sales revenue, including the number of operating meal periods or days; changes in menu prices, guest counts, and check averages; and special events. Only after carefully reviewing all details can you feel confident about generalizing statements concerning increases or decreases in revenue.

Analysis of Food Expense

In addition to sales analysis, the P&L statement, whether weekly, monthly, or annual, can provide information about other areas of operational interest. For the effective foodservice manager, the analysis of food expense is a matter of major concern. Figure 9.6 details the food expense portion of Joshua's P&L as outlined in the food expense schedule.

It is important to remember that the numerator of the food cost % equation is cost of food sold, while the denominator is total food sales, rather than total food and beverage sales. With total cost of food sold this year of $767,443 and total food sales of $2,058,376, the total food cost % is 37.3% ($767,443/$2,058,376 = 37.3%). A food cost percentage can be computed in a similar manner for each food subcategory. For instance, the cost

FIGURE **9.6** ● Joshua's P&L Food Expense Schedule

	Last Year	% of Food Sales	This Year	% of Food Sales
Food Sales	$1,891,011	100.0%	$2,058,376	100.0%
Cost of Food Sold				
Meats and Seafood	$ 297,488	15.7	$ 343,063	16.7%
Fruits and Vegetables	94,550	5.0	127,060	6.2
Dairy	55,347	2.9	40,660	2.0
Baked Goods	16,142	0.9	22,870	1.1
Other	249,060	13.2	233,790	11.4
Total Cost of Food Sold	712,587	37.7	767,443	37.3

percentage for the category Meats and Seafood for this year would be computed as follows:

Meats and Seafood Cost/Total Food Sales = Meats and Seafood Cost %

or

$343,063/$2,058,376 = 16.7%

At first glance, it appears that Joshua has done well for the year and that his total cost of goods sold expense has declined 0.4%, from 37.7% overall last year to 37.3% this year. This is true. Closer inspection, however, indicates that, while the categories Dairy and Other showed declines, Meats and Seafood, Fruits and Vegetables, and Baked Goods showed increases.

FIGURE **9.7** ● Joshua's P&L Variation in Food Expense by Category

Category	Last Year %	This Year %	Variance
Meats and Seafood	15.7%	16.7%	+1.0%
Fruits and Vegetables	5.0	6.2	+1.2
Dairy	2.9	2.0	−0.9
Baked Goods	0.9	1.1	+0.2
Other	13.2	11.4	−1.8
Total Cost of Food Sold	**37.7**	**37.3**	**−0.4**

Figure 9.7 shows the actual differences in food cost percentage for each of Joshua's food categories. While it is true that Joshua's overall food cost percentage is down by 0.4 percentage points, the variation among categories is quite marked. It is clear that it is to his benefit to subcategorize food products so that he can watch for fluctuations within and among groups, rather than merely monitor his overall increase or decrease in food costs. Without such a breakdown of categories, he will not know exactly where to look if costs get too high.

It would also be helpful for Joshua to determine how appropriate the inventory levels are for each of his product subgroups so that he can adjust the inventory sizes accordingly. To do this, Joshua must be able to compute his food inventory turnover.

Food Inventory Turnover

Inventory turnover refers to the number of times the total value of inventory has been purchased and replaced in an accounting period. Each time the cycle is completed once, we are said to have "turned" the inventory. For example, if you normally keep $100 worth of oranges on hand at any given time and your monthly usage of oranges is $500, you would have replaced your orange inventory five times in the month. The formula used to compute inventory turnover is as follows:

$$\frac{\text{Cost of Food Consumed}}{\text{Average Inventory Value}} = \text{Food Inventory Turnover}$$

Note that it is cost of food consumed rather than cost of food sold that is used as the numerator in this ratio. This is because all food inventory should be tracked so that you can better determine what is sold, wasted, spoiled, pilfered, or given to employees as employee meals.

Stated another way, inventory turnover is a measure of how many times the inventory value is purchased and sold to guests. In the foodservice industry, we are, of course, interested in high inventory turnover as it relates to increased sales. It simply makes sense that if a 5% profit is made on the sale of an inventory item, we would like to sell (turn) that item as many times per year as possible. If the item were sold from inventory only once a year, one 5% profit would result. If the item turned 10 times, a 5% profit on each of the 10 sales would result. However, you have to be sure that a high inventory turnover is caused by increased sales and not by increased food waste, food spoilage, or employee theft.

To compute his inventory turnover for each of his food categories, Joshua must first establish his average inventory value for each category. The average inventory value is computed by adding the beginning inventory for this year to the ending inventory for this year and dividing by 2 using the following formula:

$$\frac{\text{Beginning Inventory Value} + \text{Ending Inventory Value}}{2}$$
$$= \text{Average Inventory Value}$$

From his inventory records, Joshua creates the data recorded in Figure 9.8.

To illustrate the computation of average inventory value, note that Joshua's Meats and Seafood beginning inventory for this year was $16,520, while his ending inventory for that category was $14,574. His average inventory value for that category is $15,547 [($16,520 + $14,574)/2 = $15,547]. All other categories and the total average inventory value are computed in the same manner.

Now that Joshua has determined the average inventory values for his food categories, he can compute the inventory turnovers for each of these. As you recall from Figure 3.22, cost of food consumed is identical to cost of food sold when no reduction is made in cost as a result of employee meals. That is the case at Joshua's facility because he charges employees full price for menu items that he sells to them as employee meals. Therefore, employee meals are included in regular food cost because a normal food sales price is charged for these meals. Figure 9.9 shows the result of his computation using the food inventory turnover formula for this year.

To illustrate, Joshua's Meats and Seafood inventory turnover is 22.1 ($343,063/$15,547 = 22.1). That is, Joshua purchased, sold, and replaced his meat and seafood inventory, on average, 22 times this year, which was

FIGURE **9.8** ● Joshua's P&L Average Inventory Values

Inventory Category	This Year Beginning Inventory	This Year Ending Inventory	Average Inventory Value
Meats and Seafood	$16,520	$14,574	$15,547
Fruits and Vegetables	1,314	846	1,080
Dairy	594	310	452
Baked Goods	123	109	116
Other	8,106	9,196	8,651
Total	26,657	25,035	25,846

nearly twice per month. Note that all other food categories and the total inventory turnover are computed in the same manner. Note also that in categories such as fruits and vegetables, dairy, and baked goods the turnovers are very high, reflecting the perishability of these items. Joshua's overall inventory turnover is 29.7. If Joshua's *target* inventory

FIGURE **9.9** ● Joshua's P&L Food Inventory Turnover

Inventory Category	Cost of Food Consumed	Average Inventory	Inventory Turnover
Meats and Seafood	$343,063	$15,547	22.1
Fruits and Vegetables	127,060	1,080	117.6
Dairy	40,660	452	90.0
Baked Goods	22,870	116	197.2
Other	233,790	8,651	27.0
Total	767,443	25,846	29.7

turnover for the year was 26 times, then he should investigate why his actual inventory turnover is higher. It could be because of his increase in sales, which is a good sign of his restaurant's performance. Or it could be due to wastage, pilferage, and spoilage. He should use inventory turnover, in this case, to help him determine how he can more effectively control his costs in the future.

Analysis of Beverage Expense

Joshua's P&L (Figure 9.1) indicates beverage sales for this year of $482,830. With total sales of $2,541,206, beverages represent 19% of Joshua's total sales ($482,830/$2,541,206 = 19%). Also from Figure 9.1, beverage costs for this year are $96,566; thus, Joshua's beverage cost percentage, which is computed as cost of beverages divided by *beverage* sales, is 20% ($96,566/$482,830 = 20%). To completely analyze this expense category, Joshua would compute his beverage cost percentage, compare that to his planned expense, and compute a beverage inventory turnover rate, just as he did for his food products. It is important to remember that Joshua would compute his beverage inventory turnover using the following formula:

$$\frac{\text{Cost of Beverages Consumed}}{\text{Average Beverage Inventory Value}} = \text{Beverage Inventory Turnover}$$

If an operation carries a large number of rare and expensive wines, it will find that its beverage inventory turnover rate is relatively low. Conversely, those beverage operations that sell their products primarily by the glass are likely to experience inventory turnover rates that are quite high. The important concept here is to compute the turnover rates at least once per year (or more often if needed) to gauge whether inventory sizes should be increased or decreased. High beverage inventory turnovers accompanied by frequent product outages may indicate inventory levels that are too low, while low turnover rates and many slow-moving inventory items may indicate the need to reduce beverage inventory levels.

Figure 9.1 shows that last year's beverage cost percentage was 22.8% ($94,550/$415,099 = 22.8%). A first glance would indicate that beverage costs have been reduced, not in total dollars spent since sales were higher this year than last year, but in percentage terms. In other words, a beverage cost % of 22.8% last year versus 20% this year indicates a 2.8% overall reduction.

Assume, for a moment, however, that Joshua raised drink prices by 10% this year over last year. Assume also that Joshua pays, on average, 5% more for beverages this year compared with last year. Is his beverage operation more efficient this year than last year, less efficient, or the same? To determine the answer to this question in the beverage or any other expense category, Joshua must make adjustments to both his sales and his cost figures. Similar to the method for adjusting sales, the method for adjusting expense categories for known cost increases is as follows:

Step 1. Increase prior-period expense by amount of cost increase.
Step 2. Determine appropriate sales data, remembering to adjust prior-period sales, if applicable.
Step 3. Divide costs determined in Step 1 by sales determined in Step 2.

Thus, in our example, Joshua's beverage expense last year, adjusted for this year's costs, would be $94,550 × 1.05 = $99,277.50. His beverage sales from last year, adjusted for this year's menu prices, would be $415,099 × 1.10 = $456,608.90. His last year's beverage cost percentage, adjusted for increases in *this year's* costs and selling prices, would be computed as follows:

$$\frac{\$99,277.50}{\$456,608.90} = 21.7\%$$

In this case, Joshua's real cost of beverage sold has, in fact, declined this year, although not by as much as he had originally thought. That is, a 21.7% adjusted cost for last year versus a 20% cost for this year equals a reduction of 1.7%, not 2.8% as originally determined.

All food and beverage expense categories must be adjusted in terms of both costs and selling price if effective comparisons are to be made over time. When older foodservice managers remember back to the time when they purchased hamburger for $0.59 per pound, it is important to recall that the ¼-pound hamburger they made from it may have sold for $0.59 also! The 25% resulting product cost percentage is no different from today's operator paying $3.00 a pound for ground beef and selling the resulting ¼-pound burger for $3.00. Notice that it would not be possible to compare efficiency in food and beverage usage from one time period to the next unless you are making that comparison in equal terms. As product costs increase or decrease and as menu prices change, so, too, will food and beverage expense percentages change. As an effective manager, you must determine if variations in product percentage costs are caused by real changes in your operation or by differences in the price you pay for your products as well as your selling price for those products.

Analysis of Labor Expense

From Figure 9.1, it is interesting to note that, while the total dollars Joshua spent on labor increased greatly from last year to this year, his labor cost percentage increased only slightly. This was true in the Salaries and Wages category as well as the Employee Benefits category. Recall that, whenever your labor costs are not 100% variable costs, increasing sales volume will help you decrease your labor cost percentage, although the total dollars you spend on labor will increase. The reason for this is simple. When total dollar sales volume increases, fixed labor cost percentages will decline. In other words, the dollars paid for fixed labor will consume a smaller percentage of your total revenue. Thus, as long as any portion of total labor cost is fixed, increasing volume will have the effect of reducing labor cost percentage. Variable labor costs, of course, will increase along with sales volume increases, but the percentage of revenue they consume should stay constant.

When you combine a declining percentage (fixed labor cost) with a constant one (variable labor cost), you should achieve a reduced overall percentage, although your total labor dollars expended can be higher. Serving additional guests may cost additional labor dollars. That, in itself, is not a bad thing. In most foodservice situations, you will want to serve more guests. If labor expenses are controlled properly, you will find that an increase in the number of guests and sales will result in an appropriate increase in the labor costs required to service those guests. You must be careful, however, to always ensure that increased costs are appropriate to increases in sales volume.

Remember, too, that declining costs of labor are not always a sign that all is well in a foodservice unit. Declining costs of labor may be the result of significant reductions in the number of guests served. If, for example, a foodservice facility produces poor-quality products and gives poor service, guest counts can be expected to decline, as would the cost of labor required to service those guests who do remain. Labor dollars expended by management would decline, but it would be an indication of improper, rather than effective, management. An effective foodservice manager seeks to achieve declines in operational expense because of operational efficiencies, not reduced sales.

Figure 9.10 details the labor cost portion of Joshua's P&L. Note that all the labor-related percentages he computes are based on his total sales, that is, the combination of his food and beverage sales. This is different from computing expense percentages such as food and beverage because food cost percentage is determined using food sales as the denominator and beverage cost percentage computations use beverage sales as a de-

FIGURE **9.10** ● Joshua's P&L Labor Cost

Labor Cost	Last Year	% of Total Sales	This Year	% of Total Sales
Salaries and Wages	$641,099	27.8%	$714,079	28.1%
Employee Benefits	99,163	4.3	111,813	4.4
Total Labor Cost	740,262	32.1	825,892	32.5

nominator. Thus, Joshua's salaries and wages expense % for this year is computed as follows:

$$\frac{\text{Salaries and Wages Expense}}{\text{Total Sales}} = \text{Salaries and Wages Expense \%}$$

$$or$$

$$\frac{\$714,079}{\$2,541,206} = 28.1\%$$

A brief examination of the labor portion of Joshua's P&L would indicate an increase in both dollars spent for labor and labor cost percentage. Just as adjustments must be made for changes in food and beverage expenses before valid expense comparisons can be made, so, too, must adjustments be made for changes, if any, in the price an operator pays for labor. In Joshua's case, assume that all employees were given a **COLA** (cost of living adjustment), or raise, of 5% at the beginning of this year. This, coupled with an assumed 10% menu price increase, would indeed have the effect of changing overall the labor cost %, even if his labor productivity did not change.

From Figure 9.10, Joshua can see that his actual labor cost % increased from 32.1% last year to 32.5% this year, an increase of 0.4%. To adjust for the changes in the cost of labor and his selling prices, if these indeed occurred, Joshua uses the techniques previously detailed in this chapter. Thus, based on the assumption of a 5% increase in the cost of labor and a 10% increase in selling price, he adjusts both sales and cost of labor using the same steps as those employed for adjusting food or beverage cost percentage and computes a new labor cost for last year as follows:

Step 1. Determine sales adjustment:

$$\$2,306,110 \times 1.10 = \$2,536,721$$

Step 2. Determine total labor cost adjustment:

$$\$740,262 \times 1.05 = \$777,275.10$$

Step 3. Compute adjusted labor cost percentage:

$$\frac{\$777,275.10}{\$2,536,721} = 30.6\%$$

As can be seen, *last year* Joshua's P&L would have indicated a 30.6% labor cost percentage if he had operated under *this year's* increased costs and selling prices. This is certainly an area that Joshua would want to investigate. The reason is simple. If he were exactly as efficient this year as he was last year, and if he assumes a 10% menu price increase and a 5% labor cost increase, Joshua's cost of labor for this year should have been computed as follows:

> **This Year's Sales × Last Year's Adjusted Labor Cost %**
> **= This Year's Projected Labor Cost**
>
> *or*
>
> $$\$2,541,206 \times 0.306 = \$777,609.04$$

Put in another way, Joshua would have expected to spend 30.6% of sales for labor this year, given his 5% payroll increase and 10% menu price increase. In actuality, Joshua's labor cost was $48,282.96 higher ($825,892 actual this year − $777,609.04 projected = $48,282.96). A variation this large should obviously be of concern to Joshua and should be examined closely.

Increases in payroll taxes, benefit programs, and employee turnover can all affect labor cost percentage. Although, for our example, we assumed that employee benefits (including payroll taxes, insurance, etc.) increased at the same 5% rate as did salaries and wages, these are, of course, different expenses and may increase at rates higher or lower than salary and wage payments to employees. Indeed, one of the fastest increasing labor-related costs for foodservice managers today is cost of medical insurance benefit programs. These programs are needed to attract the best employees to the hospitality industry, but they can be expensive.

Controlling and evaluating labor cost is an important part of your job as a hospitality manager. In fact, many managers feel it is more important to control labor costs than product costs because, for many of them, labor and labor-related costs comprise a larger portion of their operating budgets than do food and beverage products.

Analysis of Other Expense

The analysis of other expenses should be performed each time the P&L is produced. Figure 9.11 details other expenses from Joshua's P&L statement.

Joshua's other expenses consist of both operating expenses (excluding salaries and wages and employee benefits) and nonoperating items, and he must review these carefully. In Joshua's operation, these costs have increased from last year's levels. Note that his Repairs and Maintenance category is also higher this year than it was last year. This is one area in which he both expects and approves a cost increase. It is logical to assume that kitchen repairs will increase as a kitchen ages. In that sense, a kitchen is much like a car. Even with a good preventative maintenance program, Joshua does not expect an annual decline in kitchen repair expense. In fact, he would be somewhat surprised and concerned should this category be smaller this year than in the previous year because his sales were higher and probably caused more wear and tear on his kitchen equipment. In the same way, his contributions to his state and national association political action funds, charged to Administrative and General expense, were up significantly. This is due to Joshua's belief that he, as part of the hospitality industry, needs to make his voice heard to his local and national political leaders. Joshua is a strong believer in taking a leadership role in his association on the local, state, and national levels. Indeed, one of his goals is to someday serve on the board of his national association! He knows that membership in that organization gives him a voice straight to the nation's law- and policymakers.

An analysis of other expenses proves difficult for Joshua since he is not sure how he compares with others in his area or with operations of a similar nature. For comparison purposes, he is, however, able to use industry trade publications to get national averages on other expense categories. One helpful source Joshua can use is an annual publication, *The Restaurant Industry Operations Report*, published by the National Restaurant Association and prepared by Deloitte & Touche (can be ordered through www.restaurant.org). For other operations (unlike Joshua's) that are a part of a corporate chain, unit managers can receive comparison data from district and regional managers who can chart performance against those of other operators in the city, region, state, and nation.

FIGURE **9.11** ● Joshua's P&L Other Expenses

Other Expenses	Last Year	% of Total Sales	This Year	% of Total Sales
Operating Expenses (excluding salaries and wages and employee benefits)				
Direct Operating Expense	$122,224	5.3%	$132,143	5.2%
Music and Entertainment	2,306	0.1	7,624	0.3
Marketing	43,816	1.9	63,530	2.5
Utility Services	73,796	3.2	88,942	3.5
Repairs and Maintenance	34,592	1.5	35,577	1.4
Administrative and General	66,877	2.9	71,154	2.8
Occupancy	120,000	5.2	120,000	4.7
Depreciation	41,510	1.8	55,907	2.2
Nonoperating Expenses				
Interest	$86,750	3.8%	$ 84,889	3.3%
Income Taxes	65,068	2.8	76,616	3.0

Analysis of Profits

As can be seen in Figure 9.1, profits for Joshua's, Inc., refer to the net income figure at the bottom of the income statement. Joshua's net income for this year was $114,923, or 4.5% of total sales, and his total sales for this year were $2,541,206. His profit percentage using the profit margin formula is as follows:

$$\frac{\text{Net Income}}{\text{Total Sales}} = \text{Profit Margin}$$

or

$$\frac{\$114,923}{\$2,541,206} = 4.5\%$$

Profit margin is also known as **return on sales (ROS).** For the food-service manager, perhaps no figure is more important than the ROS. This percentage is the most telling indicator of a manager's overall effectiveness at generating revenues and controlling costs in line with forecasted results. While it is not possible to state what a "good" return on sales figure should be for all restaurants, industry averages, depending on the specific segment, range from 1% to over 20%. Some operators prefer to use operating income (see Figure 9.1) as the numerator for profit margin instead of net income. This is because interest and income taxes are considered nonoperating expenses and, thus, not truly reflective of a manager's ability to generate a profit.

Joshua's results this year represent an improvement over last year's figure of $101,772, or 4.4% of total sales. Thus, he has shown improvement both in the dollar size of his net income and in the size of the net income as related to total sales. He realizes, however, that increased sales, rather than great improvements in operational efficiency, could have caused this progress, because his sales volume this year was greater than his sales volume last year. To analyze his profitability appropriately, he must determine how much of this increase was due to increased menu prices as opposed to increased guest count or check average. Joshua's improvement in net income for the year can be measured by the following formula:

$$\frac{\text{Net Income This Period} - \text{Net Income Last Period}}{\text{Net Income Last Period}}$$
$$= \text{Profit Variance \%}$$

or

$$\frac{\$114,923 - \$101,772}{\$101,772} = +12.9\%$$

How much of this improvement is due to improved operational methods versus increased sales will depend, of course, on how much Joshua actually did increase his sales relative to increases in his costs. Monitoring selling price, guest count, sales per guest, operating days, special events, and actual operating costs is necessary for accurate profit comparisons. Without knowledge of each of these areas, the effective analysis of profits becomes a risky proposition.

Key Terms and Concepts

The following are terms and concepts discussed in the chapter that are important for you as a manager. To help you review, please define the terms below.

Cost accounting
Managerial accounting
Uniform system of accounts
Gross profit section (of the USAR)
Operating expenses section
   (of the USAR)
Nonoperating expenses section
   (of the USAR)

Aggregate statement
Supporting schedules
Inventory turnover
COLA
Return on sales (ROS)

Test Your Skills

1. Lucir manages a German restaurant in a large western city. The owner wants to know how well Lucir did this year at generating sales, controlling costs, and providing a profit. The owner promised Lucir that he would give her a raise if she increased return on sales (profit margin) by at least 1%. Complete Lucir's P&L. Should she receive a raise?

Lucir's P&L

SALES:				
Food	$2,647,415		$2,675,889	
Beverage	498,119		965,660	
Total Sales				
COST OF SALES:				
Food	855,104		1,074,420	
Beverage	104,005		115,879	
Total Cost of Sales				
GROSS PROFIT:				
Food	1,792,311		1,601,469	
Beverage	394,114		849,781	
Total Gross Profit				
OPERATING EXPENSES:				
Salaries and Wages	769,319		785,487	
Employee Benefits	118,996		122,994	
Direct Operating Expenses	146,669		145,357	
Music and Entertainment	2,767		8,386	
Marketing	52,579		69,883	
Utility Services	88,555		97,836	
Repairs and Maintenance	41,510		39,135	
Administrative and General	80,252		78,269	
Occupancy	144,000		132,000	
Depreciation	49,812		61,498	
Total Operating Expenses				
Operating Income				
Interest	104,100		93,378	
Income Before Income Taxes				
Income Taxes	235,146		343,150	
Net Income				

2. Faye manages Faye's Tea Room in a small suburban town. She sells gourmet food and a variety of teas. This year, Faye increased her selling prices by 5%, and she increased her wages by 10%. Faye's condensed P&L follows. Help her calculate her variance and variance % from last year to this year. Use her adjusted sales and labor cost to provide a more accurate picture of her performance this year.

Faye's Condensed P&L

	Last Year	Adjusted Sales and Labor (for last year)	This Year	Variance	Variance %
Sales	$1,865,000		$2,315,000		
Cost of Food	615,450		717,650		
Cost of Labor	540,850		671,350		
Other Expenses	428,950		486,150		
Total Expenses					
Profit					

3. a. Rudolfo owns Rudolfo's Italian Restaurante in the Little Italy section of New York City. He wants to compare last year's costs to this year's costs on his food expense schedule to see how he performed in each food category. Help Rudolfo complete his schedule.

Rudolfo's Food Expense Schedule

	Last Year	% of Food Sales	This Year	% of Food Sales
Food Sales	$2,836,517		$3,087,564	
Cost of Food Sold				
Meats and Seafood	$ 386,734		$ 445,982	
Fruits and Vegetables	122,915		165,178	
Dairy	71,951		52,858	
Baked Goods	20,985		29,731	
Other	323,778		303,927	
Total Cost of Food Sold				

3. b. In addition to calculating the food cost % for each of his food categories, Rudolfo wishes to calculate his inventory turnover for the year. Rudolfo's inventory turnover target for this year was 32 times. Did he meet his target? If not, what may have caused this? (Assume that cost of food sold, part a, and cost of food consumed, part b, are the same for Rudolfo's.)

Rudolfo's Food Inventory Turnover

Inventory Category	This Year Beginning Inventory	This Year Ending Inventory	Average Inventory Value	Cost of Food Consumed	Inventory Turnover
Meats and Seafood	$21,476	$17,489		$445,982	
Fruits and Vegetables	1,708	1,015		165,178	
Dairy	772	372		52,858	
Baked Goods	160	131		29,731	
Other	10,538	11,035		303,927	
Total					

Chapter
10 PLANNING FOR PROFIT

OVERVIEW   This chapter shows you how to analyze your menu so you can identify which individual menu items make the most contribution to your profits. In addition, you will learn how to determine the sales dollars and volume you must achieve to break even and to generate a profit in your operation. Finally, the chapter will show you how to establish an operating budget and present techniques you will use to monitor your effectiveness in staying within that budget.

CHAPTER OUTLINE

      Financial Analysis and Profit Planning
      Menu Analysis
      Cost/Volume/Profit Analysis
      The Budget
      Developing the Budget
      Monitoring the Budget
      Key Terms and Concepts, and Test Your Skills

HIGHLIGHTS   At the conclusion of this chapter, you will be able to:

  ○ Analyze a menu for profitability.
  ○ Prepare a cost/volume/profit analysis.
  ○ Establish a budget and monitor performance to the budget.

Financial Analysis and Profit Planning

In addition to analyzing the P&L statement, you should also undertake a thorough study of three areas that will assist you in planning for profit.

393

These three areas of analysis, to which we now turn our attention, are menu analysis, cost/volume/profit (CVP) analysis, and budgeting.

Whereas menu analysis concerns itself with the profitability of each menu item you sell, CVP analysis deals with the sales dollars and volume required by your foodservice unit to avoid an operating loss and to make a profit. The process of budgeting allows you to plan your next year's operating results by projecting sales, expenses, and profits to develop the budgeted P&L statement.

Many foodservice operators practice the activity of "hoping for profit" instead of "planning for profit." Although hoping is an admirable pursuit when playing the lottery, it does little good when managing a foodservice operation. Therefore, planning is the key to ensuring that owners achieve the profit goals that will keep them in business.

Menu Analysis

A large number of methods have been proposed as being the best way to analyze the profitability of a menu and its pricing structure. The one you choose to use, however, should simply seek to answer the question, "How does the sale of this menu item contribute to the overall success of my operation?" It is unfortunate, in many ways, that the discussion of menu analysis typically leads one to elaborate mathematical formulas and computations. This is, of course, just one component of the analysis of a menu. It is not, however, nor should it ever be, the only component. Consider the case of Danny, who operates a successful family restaurant called Twins in a rural location. The restaurant has been in his family for three generations. One item on the menu is mustard greens with scrambled eggs. It does not sell often, but both mustard greens and eggs are ingredients in other, more popular items. Why does Danny keep the item in a prominent spot on the menu? The answer is simple and has little to do with finance. The menu item was Danny's grandfather's favorite. As a thank you to his grandfather, who started the business and inspired Danny to become service and guest oriented, the menu item survives every menu reprint. Menu analysis, then, is about more than just numbers. It involves marketing, sociology, psychology, and emotions. Remember that guests respond not to weighty financial analyses, but rather to menu copy, the description of the menu item, the placement of items on the menu, their price, and their current popularity. While the financial analysis of a menu is indeed done "by the numbers," you must realize that it is just one part, albeit an important part, of the total menu analysis picture.

For the serious foodservice manager, the analysis of a menu deserves special study. Many components of the menu such as pricing, layout, design, and copy play an important role in the overall success of a foodservice operation. The foodservice manager who does not seek to understand how a menu truly works is akin to the manager who does not seek to understand the essential components of making a good cup of coffee!

If you investigate the menu analysis methods that have been widely used, you will find that each seeks to perform the analysis using one or more of the following operational variables with which you are familiar:

1. Food cost percentage
2. Popularity
3. Contribution margin
4. Selling price
5. Variable expenses
6. Fixed expenses

Three of the most popular systems of menu analysis, shown in Figure 10.1, will be discussed here because they represent the three major philosophical approaches to menu analysis.

The **matrix analysis** referenced in Figure 10.1 provides a method for comparisons between menu items. A matrix allows menu items to be placed into categories based on whether they are above or below menu item averages such as food cost %, popularity, and contribution margin.

FIGURE **10.1** ● Three Methods of Menu Analysis

Method	Variables Considered	Analysis Method	Goal
1. Food cost %	a. Food cost % b. Popularity	Matrix	Minimize overall food cost %
2. Contribution margin	a. Contribution margin b. Popularity	Matrix	Maximize contribution margin
3. Goal value analysis	a. Contribution margin % b. Popularity c. Selling price d. Variable cost % e. Food cost %	Algebraic equation	Achieve predetermined profit % goals

Each approach to menu analysis has its proponents and detractors, but an understanding of each will help you as you attempt to develop your own philosophy of menu analysis.

Food Cost Percentage

Menu analysis that focuses on food cost percentage is the oldest and most traditional method used. When analyzing a menu using the food cost percentage method, you are seeking menu items that have the effect of minimizing your overall food cost percentage. The rationale for this is that a lowered food cost percentage leaves more of the sales dollar to be spent for other operational expenses. A criticism of the food cost percentage approach is that items that have a higher food cost percentage may be removed from the menu in favor of items that have a lower food cost percentage but also contribute fewer dollars to overall profit.

To illustrate the use of the food cost percentage menu analysis method, consider the case of Maureen, who operates a steak and seafood restaurant near the beach in a busy resort town. Maureen sells seven items in the entrée section of her menu. The items and information related to their cost, selling price, and popularity are presented in Figure 10.2.

To determine her average selling price, Maureen divides total sales by the total number of items sold. In this case, the computation is $11,583/700 = $16.55. To determine her total food cost percentage, she divides total cost by total sales. The computation is $4,002.77/$11,583 = 35%. The columns titled Item Contribution Margin and Total Contribution Margin are not used in the food cost percentage approach to menu analysis and, thus, will be discussed later in this chapter.

To analyze her menu using the food cost percentage method, Maureen must segregate her items based on the following two variables:

1. Food cost percentage
2. Popularity (number sold)

Since her overall food cost is 35%, she determines that any individual menu item with a food cost percentage above 35% will be considered *high* in food cost percentage, while any menu item with a food cost below 35% will be considered *low*. In a similar vein, with a total of 700 entrées served in this accounting period and seven possible menu choices, each menu item would sell 700/7, or 100 times, if all were equally popular. Given that fact, Maureen determines that any item sold more than 100 times during this week's accounting period would be considered high in popularity, while any item selling less than 100 times would be considered low in

FIGURE **10.2** ● Maureen's Menu Analysis Worksheet

Date: 1/1–1/7

Menu Item	Number Sold	Selling Price	Total Sales	Item Cost	Total Cost	Item Contribution Margin	Total Contribution Margin	Food Cost %
Strip Steak	73	$17.95	$ 1,310.35	$ 8.08	$ 589.84	$ 9.87	720.51	45%
Coconut Shrimp	121	16.95	2,050.95	5.09	615.89	11.86	1,435.06	30
Grilled Tuna	105	17.95	1,884.75	7.18	753.90	10.77	1,130.85	40
Chicken Breast	140	13.95	1,953.00	3.07	429.80	10.88	1,523.20	22
Lobster Stir-Fry	51	21.95	1,119.45	11.19	570.69	10.76	548.76	51
Scallops/Pasta	85	14.95	1,270.75	3.59	305.15	11.36	965.60	24
Beef Medallions	125	15.95	1,993.75	5.90	737.50	10.05	1,256.25	37
Total	700		11,583.00		4,002.77		7,580.23	
Weighted Average	100	16.55	1,654.71	5.72	571.82	10.83	1,082.89	35

popularity. Having made these determinations, Maureen can produce a matrix labeled as follows:

	Low Popularity (Below 100 Sales)	High Popularity (Above 100 Sales)
High Food Cost % (Above 35%)	1	2
Low Food Cost % (Below 35%)	3	4

The squares can be further defined as follows:

Square	Characteristics
1	High Food Cost %, Low Popularity
2	High Food Cost %, High Popularity
3	Low Food Cost %, Low Popularity
4	Low Food Cost %, High Popularity

Based on the number sold and food cost percentage data in Figure 10.2, Maureen can classify her menu items in the following manner:

Square	Characteristics	Menu Item
1	High Food Cost %, Low Popularity	Strip Steak, Lobster Stir-Fry
2	High Food Cost %, High Popularity	Grilled Tuna, Beef Medallions
3	Low Food Cost %, Low Popularity	Scallops/Pasta
4	Low Food Cost %, High Popularity	Coconut Shrimp, Chicken Breast

Note that each menu item finds itself in one, and only one, square. Using the food cost percentage method of menu analysis, Maureen would like as many menu items as possible to fall within square 4. These items have the characteristics of being low in food cost percentage but high in guest acceptance. Thus, both coconut shrimp and chicken breast have below-average food cost percentages and above-average popularity. When developing a menu that seeks to minimize food cost percentage, items in the fourth square are highly desirable. These, of course, are kept on the menu. They should be well promoted and have high menu visibility. Promote them to your best guests and take care not to develop and attempt to sell a menu item that is similar enough in nature that it could detract from the sales of these items.

The characteristics of the menu items that fall into each of the four matrix squares are unique and, thus, should be managed differently. Because of this, each of the menu items that fall in the individual squares requires a special marketing strategy, depending on their square location. These strategies can be summarized as shown in Figure 10.3.

It can be quite effective to use the food cost percentage method of menu evaluation. It is fast, logical, and time tested. Remember that if you achieve too high a food cost percentage, you run the risk that not enough percentage points will remain to generate a profit on your sales. Again, however, you should be cautioned against promoting low-cost items with low selling prices at the expense of higher food percentage items that contribute greater gross profits. For example, most foodservice operators would say it is better to achieve a 20% food cost than a 40% food cost. Consider, however, that a chicken dish that sells for $5.00 and cost you just $1.00 to make yields a 20% food cost ($1.00/$5.00 = 20%). In this case, there are $4.00 ($5.00 − $1.00 = $4.00) remaining to pay for the labor and other expenses of serving this guest. Compare that to the same guest buying steak for $10.00 that cost you $4.00 to make. Your food cost percentage would be 40% ($4.00/$10.00 = 40%). In this case, however, there are $6.00 ($10.00 − $4.00 = $6.00) remaining to pay for the labor and other expenses of serving this guest. For this reason, some operators prefer to analyze their menus using the contribution margin matrix.

Contribution Margin

When analyzing a menu using the contribution margin approach, the operator seeks to produce a menu that maximizes the overall contribution margin. Recall from Chapter 6 that **contribution margin per menu item** is defined as the amount that remains after the product cost of the menu item is subtracted from the item's selling price. Contribution margin is the amount that you will have available to pay for your labor and other expenses and to keep for your profit. Thus, from Figure 10.2, if an item on Maureen's menu such as strip steak sells for $17.95 and the prod-

FIGURE **10.3** ● Analysis of Food Cost Matrix Results

Square	Characteristics	Problem	Marketing Strategy
1	High food cost %, low popularity	Marginal due to both high product cost and lack of sales	a. Remove from the menu. b. Consider current food trends to determine if the item itself is unpopular or if its method of preparation is. c. Survey guests to determine current wants regarding this item. d. If this is a high-contribution-margin item, consider reducing price and/or portion size.
2	High food cost %, high popularity	Marginal due to high product cost	a. Increase price. b. Reduce prominence on the menu. c. Reduce portion size. d. "Bundle" the sale of this item with one that has a lower cost and, thus, provides better overall food cost %.
3	Low food cost %, low popularity	Marginal due to lack of sales	a. Relocate on the menu for greater visibility. b. Take off the regular menu and run as specials. c. Reduce menu price. d. Eliminate other unpopular menu items in order to increase demand for this one.
4	Low food cost %, high popularity	None	a. Promote well. b. Increase visibility on the menu.

uct cost for the item is $8.08, the contribution margin per menu item would be computed as follows:

Selling Price − Product Cost
= Contribution Margin per Menu Item

or

$17.95 − $8.08 = $9.87

When contribution margin is the driving factor in analyzing a menu, the two variables used for the analysis are contribution margin and item popularity. To illustrate the use of the contribution margin approach to menu analysis, the data in Figure 10.2 are again used. In this case, Maureen must again separate her items based on high or low popularity. This, of course, results in the same figures as those obtained when using the food cost percentage method; thus, any item that sells 700/7, or 100 times, or more is considered to be a high-popularity item, while any menu choice selling less than 100 times would be considered low in popularity. To employ the contribution margin approach to menu analysis, Maureen computes her average item contribution margin. When computing average contribution margin for the entire menu, two steps are required. First, to determine the total contribution margin for the menu, the following formula is used:

Total Sales − Total Product Costs = Total Contribution Margin

or

$11,583.00 − $4,002.77 = $7,580.23

Because 700 total menu items were sold, you can determine the average contribution margin per item, using the following formula:

$$\frac{\text{Total Contribution Margin}}{\text{Number of Items Sold}}$$
= Average Contribution Margin per Item

or

$$\frac{\$7,580.23}{700} = \$10.83$$

To develop the contribution margin matrix, you proceed along much the same lines as with the food cost percentage matrix. In this case, average item popularity is 100 and average item contribution margin is $10.83. The matrix is developed as follows:

High Contribution Margin (Above $10.83)	1	2
Low Contributin Margin (Below $10.83)	3	4
	Low Popularity (Below 100 Sales)	**High Popularity (Above 100 Sales)**

The squares can further be defined as follows:

Square	Characteristics
1	High Contribution Margin, Low Popularity
2	High Contribution Margin, High Popularity
3	Low Contribution Margin, Low Popularity
4	Low Contribution Margin, High Popularity

Maureen now classifies her menu items according to the contribution margin matrix in the following manner:

Square	Characteristics	Menu Item
1	High Contribution Margin, Low Popularity	Scallops/Pasta
2	High Contribution Margin, High Popularity	Coconut Shrimp, Chicken Breast
3	Low Contribution Margin, Low Popularity	Strip Steak, Lobster Stir-Fry
4	Low Contribution Margin, High Popularity	Grilled Tuna, Beef Medallions

Again, each menu item finds itself in one, and only one, matrix square. Using the contribution margin method of menu analysis, Maureen would like as many of her menu items as possible to fall within square 2, that is, high contribution margin and high popularity. From this analysis, Maureen knows that both coconut shrimp and chicken breast yield a higher than average contribution margin. In addition, these items sell very well. Just as Maureen would seek to give high menu visibility to items with low food cost percentage and high popularity when using the food cost percentage method of menu analysis, she would seek to give that same visibility to items with high contribution margin and high popularity when using the contribution margin approach.

Each of the menu items that fall in the other squares require a special marketing strategy, depending on their square location. These strategies can be summarized as shown in Figure 10.4.

A frequent criticism of the contribution margin approach to menu analysis is that it tends to favor high-priced menu items over low-priced ones, since higher priced menu items, in general, tend to have the highest contribution margins. Over the long term, this can result in sales techniques and menu placement decisions that tend to put in the guest's mind a higher check average than the operation may warrant or desire.

FIGURE **10.4** ● Analysis of Contribution Margin Matrix Results

Square	Characteristics	Problem	Marketing Strategy
1	High contribution margin, low popularity	Marginal due to lack of sales	a. Relocate on menu for greater visibility. b. Consider reducing selling price.
2	High contribution margin, high popularity	None	a. Promote well. b. Increase prominence on the menu.
3	Low contribution margin, low popularity	Marginal due to both low contribution margin and lack of sales	a. Remove from menu. b. Consider offering as a special occasionally, but at a higher menu price.
4	Low contribution margin, high popularity	Marginal due to low contribution margin	a. Increase price. b. Reduce prominence on the menu. c. Consider reducing portion size.

The selection of either food cost percentage or contribution margin as a menu analysis technique is really an attempt by the foodservice operator to answer the following questions:

1. Are my menu items priced correctly?
2. Are the individual menu items selling well enough to warrant keeping them on the menu?
3. Is the overall profit margin on my menu items satisfactory?

In reality, however, with the matrix method neither the food cost nor the contribution margin approach is tremendously effective in analyzing menus. This is the case because the axes on the matrix are determined by the mean (average) of food cost percentage, contribution margin, or sales level (popularity). When this is done, some items will always fall into the less desirable categories. This is so because high food cost percentage, for instance, really means food cost percentage *above* the mean or average. Obviously, then, some items must fall below the mean regardless of their contribution to operational profitability. Eliminating the poorest items only shifts other items into undesirable categories. To illustrate this drawback to matrix analysis, consider the following example. Assume that Homer, one of Maureen's competitors, sells only four items, as follows:

Homer's #1 Menu

Item	Number Sold
Beef	70
Chicken	60
Pork	15
Seafood	55
Total	200
Average Sold	50 (200/4)

Homer may elect to remove the pork item, since its sales range is below the average of 50 items sold. If Homer adds turkey to the menu and removes the pork, he could get the following results:

Homer's #2 Menu

Item	Number Sold
Beef	65
Chicken	55
Turkey	50
Seafood	30
Total	200
Average Sold	50 (200/4)

As can be seen, the turkey item drew sales away from the beef, chicken, and seafood dishes and did not increase the total number of menu items sold. In this case, it is now the seafood item that falls below the menu average. Should it be removed because its sales are below average? Clearly, this might not be wise. Removing the seafood item might serve only to draw sales *from* the remaining items *to* the seafood replacement item. Obviously, the same type of result can occur when you use a matrix to analyze food cost percentage or contribution margin. As someone once stated, half of us are always below average in anything. Thus, the matrix approach *forces* some items to be below average. How, then, can an operator answer questions related to price, sales volume, and overall profit margin? One answer is to avoid the overly simplistic and ineffective matrix analysis and employ a more effective method of menu analysis called goal value analysis.

Goal Value Analysis

Goal value analysis was introduced by Dr. David Hayes and Dr. Lynn Huffman in an article titled "Menu Pricing: A Better Approach," published by the respected hospitality journal *The Cornell Quarterly,* in 1985. Ten years later, at the height of what was known as the "value pricing" (i.e., extremely low pricing strategies used to drive significant increases in guest counts) debate, goal value analysis proved its effectiveness in a second article based on its methodology, which was published in the *Cornell Quarterly.*

Essentially, goal value analysis uses the power of an algebraic formula to replace less sophisticated menu average techniques. Before the widespread introduction of spreadsheet programs, some managers found the computations required to use goal value analysis challenging. Today, however, such computations are easily made. The advantages of goal value analysis are many, including ease of use, accuracy, and the ability to simultaneously consider more variables than is possible with two-dimensional matrix analysis. Mastering its power can truly help you design menus that are effective, popular, and, most important, profitable.

Goal value analysis evaluates each menu item's food cost percentage, contribution margin, and popularity and, unlike the two previous analysis methods introduced, includes the analysis of the menu item's nonfood variable costs as well as its selling price. Returning to the data in Figure 10.2, we see that Maureen has an overall food cost % of 35%. In addition, she served 700 guests at an entrée check average of $16.55. If we knew about Maureen's overall fixed and variable costs, we would know more about the profitability of each of Maureen's menu items. One difficulty, of course, resides in the assignment of nonfood variable costs to individual menu items. The issue is complex. It is very likely true, for example, that different items on Maureen's menu require differing amounts of labor to prepare. For instance, the strip steak on her menu is purchased precut and vacuum-sealed. Its preparation simply requires opening the steak package, seasoning the steak, and placing it on a broiler. The lobster stir-fry, on the other hand, is a complex dish that requires cooking and shelling the lobster, cleaning and trimming the vegetables, then preparing the item when ordered by quickly cooking the lobster, vegetables, and a sauce in a wok. Thus, the *variable* labor cost of preparing the two dishes is very different. It is assumed that Maureen responds to these differing costs by charging more for a more labor-intensive dish and less for one that is less labor intensive. Other dishes require essentially the same amount of labor to prepare; thus, their variable labor costs figure less significantly in the establishment of price. Because that is true, for analysis purposes, most operators find it convenient to assign variable costs to individual menu items based on menu price. For example, if labor and other variable costs are 30% of total sales, all menu items may be assigned that same variable cost percentage of their selling price.

For the purpose of her goal value analysis, Maureen determines her total variable costs. These are all the costs that vary with her sales volume, excluding the cost of the food itself. She computes those variable costs from her P&L statement and finds that they account for 30% of her total sales. Using this information, Maureen assigns a variable cost of 30% of selling price to each menu item.

Having compiled the information in Figure 10.2, Maureen can use the algebraic goal value formula to create a specific goal value for her entire menu, then use the same formula to compute the goal value of each individual menu item. Menu items that achieve goal values higher than that of the overall menu goal value will contribute greater than average profit percentages. As the goal value for an item increases, so, too, does its profitability percentage. The overall menu goal value can be used as a "target" in this way, assuming that Maureen's average food cost %, average number of items sold per menu item, average selling price (check average), and average variable cost % all meet the overall profitability goals of her restaurant. The goal value formula is as follows:

$$A \times B \times C \times D = \text{Goal Value}$$

where

A = 1.00 − Food Cost %
B = Item Popularity
C = Selling Price
D = 1.00 − (Variable Cost % + Food Cost %)

Note that A in the preceding formula is really the contribution margin percentage of a menu item and that D is the amount available to fund fixed costs and provide for a profit after all variable costs are covered.

Maureen uses this formula to compute the goal value of her *total menu* and finds that:

$$A \times B \times C \times D = \text{Goal Value}$$

$$(1.00 - 0.35) \times 100 \times \$16.55 \times [1.00 - (0.30 + 0.35)] = \text{Goal Value}$$

or

$$0.65 \times 100 \times \$16.55 \times 0.35 = 376.5$$

According to this formula, any menu item whose goal value equals or exceeds 376.5 will achieve profitability that equals or exceeds that of Maureen's overall menu. The computed goal value carries no unit designation; that is, it is neither a percentage nor a dollar figure because it is really a numerical target or score. Figure 10.5 details the goal value data Maureen needs to complete a goal value analysis on each of her seven menu items.

Figure 10.6 details the results of Maureen's goal value analysis. Note that she has calculated the goal values of her menu items and ranked

FIGURE **10.5** ● Maureen's Goal Value Analysis Data

Item	Food Cost % (in decimal form)	Number Sold	Selling Price	Variable Cost % (in decimal form)
Strip Steak	0.45	73	$17.95	0.30
Coconut Shrimp	0.30	121	16.95	0.30
Grilled Tuna	0.40	105	17.95	0.30
Chicken Breast	0.22	140	13.95	0.30
Lobster Stir-Fry	0.51	51	21.95	0.30
Scallops/Pasta	0.24	85	14.95	0.30
Beef Medallions	0.37	125	15.95	0.30

FIGURE **10.6** ● Goal Value Analysis Results

Rank	Menu Item	A	B	C	D	Goal Value
1	Chicken Breast	(1 − 0.22)	140	$13.95	1 − (0.30 + 0.22)	731.2
2	Coconut Shrimp	(1 − 0.30)	121	16.95	1 − (0.30 + 0.30)	574.3
3	Scallops/Pasta	(1 − 0.24)	85	14.95	1 − (0.30 + 0.24)	444.3
4	Beef Medallions	(1 − 0.37)	125	15.95	1 − (0.30 + 0.37)	414.5
	Overall Menu (Goal Value)	(1 − 0.35)	100	$16.55	1 − (0.30 + 0.35)	376.5
5	Grilled Tuna	(1 − 0.40)	105	17.95	1 − (0.30 + 0.40)	339.3
6	Strip Steak	(1 − 0.45)	73	17.95	1 − (0.30 + 0.45)	180.2
7	Lobster Stir-Fry	(1 − 0.51)	51	21.95	1 − (0.30 + 0.51)	104.2

them in order of highest to lowest goal value. She has also inserted her overall menu goal value in the appropriate rank order.

Note that the grilled tuna falls slightly below the profitability of the entire menu, while the strip steak and lobster stir-fry fall substantially below the overall goal value score. Should these two items be replaced? The answer, most likely, is no *if* Maureen is satisfied with her current target food cost percentage, profit margin, check average, and guest count. Every menu will have items that are more or less profitable than others. In fact, some operators develop items called **loss leaders.** A loss leader is a menu item that is priced very low, sometimes even below total costs, for the purpose of drawing large numbers of guests to the operation. If, for example, Maureen has the only operation in town that serves outstanding lobster stir-fry, that item may, in fact, contribute to the overall success of the operation by drawing people who will buy it, while their fellow diners may order items that are more profitable.

The accuracy of goal value analysis is well documented. Used properly, it is a convenient way for management to make shorthand decisions regarding required profitability, sales volume, and pricing. Because all of the values needed for the goal value formula are readily available, management need not concern itself with puzzling through endless decisions about item replacement.

Items that do not achieve the targeted goal value tend to be deficient in one or more of the key areas of food cost percentage, popularity, selling price, or variable cost percentage. In theory, all menu items have the potential of reaching the goal value, although management may determine that some menu items can indeed best serve the operation as loss leader–type items. For example, examine the goal value analysis results for the item, strip steak:

$$A \quad \times B \times C \quad \times D \qquad = \text{Goal Value}$$

$$\text{Strip Steak } (1 - 0.45) \times 73 \times \$17.95 \times [1 - (0.30 + 0.45)] = \text{Goal Value}$$

$$0.55 \quad \times 73 \times \$17.95 \times 0.25 \qquad = 180.2$$

This item did not meet the goal value target. Why? There can be several answers. One is that the menu item has a food cost %, 45%, that is too high. This can be addressed by reducing portion size or changing the item's recipe since both of these actions have the effect of reducing the food cost % and, thus, increasing the A value. A second approach to improving the goal value score of the strip steak is to work on improving the B value, that is, the number of times the item is sold. This may be done through merchandising or, since it is one of the more expensive items on the menu, incentives to waitstaff for upselling this item. Variable C, menu price, while certainly in line with the rest of the menu, can also be adjusted upward; however, you must remember that adjustments upward in C may well result in declines in the number of items sold (B value)! Increases in the menu price will also have the effect of *decreasing* the food cost % of the menu item. This is because item food cost % = food cost of the item/menu price. Obviously, the changes you undertake as a result of menu analysis are varied and can be complex. As you gain experience in knowing the tastes and behavior of your guests, however, your skill in menu-related decision making will quickly improve.

Goal value analysis can be modified if you prefer, and this modification can increase the accuracy of the goal value model. In the area of variable costs, a menu item might be assigned a low, medium, or high variable cost. If overall variable costs equal 30%, for example, management may choose to assign a variable cost of 25% to those items with very low labor costs attached to them, 30% to others with average labor costs, and 35% to others with even higher costs. This adjustment affects only the D variable of the goal value formula and can be accommodated quite easily.

Goal value analysis will also allow you to make better decisions more quickly. This is especially true if you know a bit of algebra and realize that anytime you determine a desired goal value *and* when any three of the four variables contained in the formula are known, you can solve for the fourth unknown variable by using goal value as the numerator and placing the known variables in the denominator. Figure 10.7 shows you how to solve for each unknown variable in the goal value formula.

To illustrate how the information in Figure 10.7 can be used, let's return to the information in Figure 10.6 and assume that, in Maureen's case, she feels the 12-ounce strip steak she is offering may be too large for her typical guest and that is why its popularity (B value) is low. Thus, Maureen elects to take three actions:

1. She reduces the portion size of the item from 12 ounces to 9 ounces, resulting in a reduction in her food cost from $8.08 to $6.10.
2. Because she knows her guests will likely be hesitant to pay the same price for a smaller steak, she also *reduces* the selling price of this item by $1.00 to $16.95. She feels that this will keep the strip steak from losing any popularity resulting from the reduction in portion size. Her new food cost percentage for this item is 36% ($6.10/$16.95 = 36%).
3. Since the labor required to prepare this menu item is so low, she assigns a below-average 25% variable cost to its D value.

Maureen now knows three of the goal value variables for this item and can solve for the fourth. Maureen knows her A value (1.00 − 0.36), her C value ($16.95), and her D value [1.00 − (0.25 + 0.36)]. The question she would ask is this, "Given this newly structured menu item, how many must be sold to make the item achieve the targeted goal value?" The answer requires solving the goal value equation for B, the number sold.

FIGURE **10.7** ● Solving for Goal Value Unknowns

Known Variables	Unknown Variables	Method to Find Unknown
A, B, C, D	**Goal Value (GV)**	$A \times B \times C \times D$
B, C, D, GV	A	$\frac{GV}{B \times C \times D}$
A, C, D, GV	B	$\frac{GV}{A \times C \times D}$
A, B, D, GV	C	$\frac{GV}{A \times B \times D}$
A, B, C, GV	D	$\frac{GV}{A \times B \times C}$

From Figure 10.7, recall that, if B is the unknown variable, it can be computed by using the following formula:

$$\frac{\text{Goal Value}}{A \times C \times D} = B$$

In this case:

$$\frac{376.5}{(1.00 - 0.36) \times \$16.95 \times [1.00 - (0.25 + 0.36)]} = B$$

Thus:

$$89 = B$$

According to the formula, 89 servings of strip steak would have to be sold to achieve Maureen's target goal value. Again, goal value analysis is a very useful estimation tool for management. You can use it to establish a desired food cost percentage, target popularity figure, selling price, or variable cost percentage.

Goal value analysis is also powerful because it is not, as is matrix analysis, dependent on past performance to establish profitability but can be used by management to establish future menu targets. To explain, assume, for a moment, that Maureen wishes to achieve a greater profit margin and a $17.00 entrée average selling price for next year. She plans to achieve this through a reduction in her overall food cost to 33% and her other variable costs to 29%. Her overall menu goal value formula for next year, assuming no reduction or increase in guest count, would be as follows:

$$A \qquad \times B \ \times C \quad \times D \qquad\qquad = \text{Goal Value}$$

$$(1.00 - 0.33) \times 100 \times \$17.00 \times [1.00 - (0.29 + 0.33)] = \text{Goal Value}$$

or

$$0.67 \qquad \times 100 \times \$17.00 \times 0.38 \qquad\qquad = 432.8$$

Thus, each item on next year's menu should be evaluated with the new goal value in mind. It is important to remember, however, that Maureen's actual profitability will be heavily influenced by sales mix. Thus, all pricing, portion size, and menu placement decisions become critical. Note that Maureen can examine each of her menu items and determine whether she wishes to change any of the item's characteristics in order to meet her goals. It is at this point that she must remember that she is a foodservice operator and not merely an accountant. A purely quantitative approach to menu analysis is neither practical nor desirable. Menu analysis and pricing decisions are always a matter of experience, skill, and educated predicting because it is difficult to know in advance how changing any one menu item may affect the sales mix of the remaining items.

Cost/Volume/Profit Analysis

Each foodservice operator knows that some accounting periods are more profitable than others. Often, this is because sales volume is higher or costs are lower during certain periods. The ski resort that experiences tremendous sales during the ski season but has a greatly reduced volume or may even close during the summer season is a good example. Profitability, then, can be viewed as existing on a scale similar to the following:

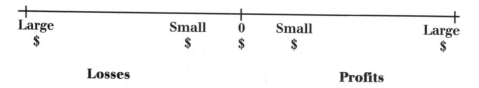

The midpoint on the scale, indicated by the zero, is called the break-even point. At the **break-even point,** operational expenses are exactly equal to sales revenue. Stated in another way, when sales volume in your operation equals the sum of your total variable and fixed costs, your break-even point has been reached. Most operators would like to know their break-even point on a daily, weekly, or monthly basis. In effect, by determining the break-even point, the operator is answering the question, "How much sales volume must I generate before I begin to make a profit?"

Beyond the break-even point, you will want to answer another question, "How much sales dollars and volume must I generate to make a *desired* profit level?" To answer this question, you must conduct a **cost/volume/profit (CVP) analysis.** A CVP analysis helps predict the sales dollars and *volume* required to achieve desired *profit* (or break even) based on your known *costs.*

The answer to these questions may be found either by constructing a CVP graph or by arithmetical calculation. While there are advantages to both methods, the arithmetical calculation is typically the most accurate.

FIGURE **10.8** ● Contribution Margin Income Statement

Jennifer's			
Total Sales	$125,000	Sales per Guest	$12.50
Variable Costs	50,000	Guests Served	10,000
Contribution Margin	75,000		
Fixed Costs	60,000		
Before-Tax Profit	15,000		
Taxes (40%)	6,000		
After-Tax Profit	9,000		

CVP calculations can be done either on the dollar sales volume required to break even or achieve the desired profit, or on the basis of the number of guests (covers) required.

Consider the case of Jennifer, who operates an Asian restaurant in a suburban northwestern city. Based on her income statement and sales records of last month, Jennifer has converted her P&L statement to a **contribution margin income statement** in Figure 10.8. A contribution margin income statement simply shows P&L items in terms of sales, variable costs, contribution margin, fixed costs, and profit.

As discussed in Chapter 8, foodservice expenses can generally be classified as either fixed or variable. Of course, some expenses have both a fixed and a variable component and, thus, are, in reality, mixed. For the purpose of engaging in a CVP analysis, however, it is necessary for the operator to assign costs to either a fixed or a variable category, as Jennifer has done. In addition, the **contribution margin for her overall operation** is defined as the dollar amount that *contributes* to covering fixed costs and providing for a profit. Contribution margin is calculated for Jennifer's as follows:

> **Total Sales − Variable Costs = Contribution Margin**
>
> *or*
>
> **$125,000 − $50,000 = $75,000**

Jennifer can also view her contribution margin income statement in terms of per-unit (guest) and percentage sales, variable costs, and contribution margin as shown in Figure 10.9.

Notice the dark box in Figure 10.9 that includes per unit (guest) and percentage calculations for sales per guest (selling price, SP), variable costs (VC), and contribution margin (CM). Note also that fixed costs are not calculated as per unit or as a percentage of sales. This is because fixed costs do not vary with sales volume increases.

FIGURE **10.9** ● Contribution Margin Income Statement with per Unit and Percentage Calculations

Jennifer's			
Total Sales	$125,000		
Variable Costs	50,000		
Contribution Margin	75,000		
Fixed Costs	60,000		
Before-tax Profit	15,000		
Taxes (40%)	6,000		
After-tax Profit	9,000		

	Per Unit (Guest)	Percentage
SP	$12.50	100%
VC	5.00	40
CM	7.50	60
Guests served		10,000

To calculate these numbers, the following steps apply:

Step 1. Divide total sales, variable costs, and contribution margin by the number of guests served (units) to get per-unit (guest) values.

$$SP/unit = \$125,000/10,000 \text{ units} = \$12.50$$

$$VC/unit = \$50,000/10,000 \text{ units} = \$5.00$$

$$CM/unit = \$75,000/10,000 \text{ units} = \$7.50$$

$$SP/unit - VC/unit = CM/unit$$

$$\$12.50 - \$5.00 = \$7.50$$

Step 2. Divide VC/unit by SP/unit, and CM/unit by SP/unit to get percentage values.

$$SP\% = 100\%$$

$$VC\% = \$5.00/\$12.50 = 40\%$$

$$CM\% = \$7.50/\$12.50 = 60\%$$

$$SP\% - VC\% = CM\%$$

$$100\% - 40\% = 60\%$$

Once Jennifer's P&L statement has been converted to a contribution margin income statement and per-unit values and percentages have been calculated, she can proceed to determine her operational break-even point and sales required to achieve her desired profit. She wants to do this based both on dollar sales and on the number of units (guests) required to do so.

To determine the dollar sales required to break even, Jennifer uses the following formula:

$$\frac{\text{Fixed Costs}}{\text{Contribution Margin \%}} = \text{Break-Even Point in Sales}$$

or

$$\frac{\$60,000}{0.60} = \$100,000$$

Thus, Jennifer must generate $100,000 in sales per month *before* she begins to make a profit. At a sales volume of less than $100,000, she would be operating at a loss. In terms of the number of guests that must be served in order to break even, Jennifer uses the following formula:

$$\frac{\text{Fixed Costs}}{\text{Contribution Margin per Unit (Guest)}}$$
$$= \text{Break-Even Point in Guests Served}$$

or

$$\frac{\$60,000}{\$7.50} = 8,000 \text{ Guests (Covers)}$$

Now, assume that Jennifer has decided that next month she will plan for $12,000 in after-tax profits. To determine sales dollars and covers to achieve her after-tax profit goal, Jennifer uses the following formula:

$$\frac{\text{Fixed Costs} + \text{Before-Tax Profit}}{\text{Contribution Margin \%}}$$
$$= \text{Sales Dollars to Achieve Desired After-Tax Profit}$$

Jennifer knows that her after-tax-profit goal is $12,000, but the preceding formula calls for *before-tax profit*. To convert her after-tax profit to before-tax profit, Jennifer must compute the following:

$$\frac{\text{After-Tax Profit}}{1 - \text{Tax Rate}} = \text{Before-Tax Profit}$$

or

$$\frac{\$12,000}{1 - 0.40} = \$20,000$$

Now that Jennifer knows her before-tax profit of $20,000, she can calculate her sales dollars to achieve her desired after-tax profit as follows:

$$\frac{\text{Fixed Costs + Before-Tax Profit}}{\text{Contribution Margin \%}}$$
$$= \text{Sales Dollars to Achieve Desired After-Tax Profit}$$

or

$$\frac{\$60,000 + \$20,000}{0.60} = \$133,333.33$$

Thus, Jennifer must generate $133,333.33 in sales per month to achieve her desired after-tax profit of $12,000. In terms of calculating the number of guests that must be served in order to make her profit, Jennifer uses the following formula:

$$\frac{\text{Fixed Costs + Before-Tax Profit}}{\text{Contribution Margin per Unit (Guest)}}$$
$$= \text{Guests to Be Served to Achieve Desired After-Tax Profit}$$

or

$$\frac{\$60,000 + \$20,000}{\$7.50}$$
$$= 10,666.67 \text{ Guests (Covers), Round up to 10,667 Guests}$$

When calculating sales and covers to achieve break-even and desired after-tax profits, you can easily remember which formulas to use if you know the following:

1. Contribution margin % is used to calculate sales *dollars*.
2. Contribution margin per *unit* is used to calculate sales volume in *units* (guests).

Once you fully understand the CVP analysis concepts, you can predict any sales level for break-even or after-tax profits based on your selling price, fixed costs, variable costs, and contribution margin. You can also make changes in your selling prices and costs to improve your ability to break even and achieve desired profit levels. This is where menu pricing and cost controls concepts covered in this text come into play. As you make changes in your control areas, you will be able to manage your operation efficiently so that losses can be prevented and planned profits can be achieved.

Minimum Sales Point

Every foodservice operator should know his or her break-even point. The concept of minimum sales point is related to this area. **Minimum sales point (MSP)** is the dollar sales volume required to justify staying open for a given period of time. The information necessary to compute MSP is as follows:

1. Food cost %
2. Minimum payroll cost for the time period
3. Variable cost %

Fixed costs are eliminated from the calculation because, even if the volume of sales equals zero, fixed costs still exist and must be paid. Consider the situation of Richard, who is trying to determine whether he should close his steakhouse at 10:00 P.M. or 11:00 P.M. Richard wishes to compute the sales volume necessary to justify staying open the additional hour. He can make this calculation because he knows that his food cost equals 40%, his minimum labor cost to stay open for the extra hour equals $150, and his variable costs (taken from his P&L statement) equal 30%. In calculating MSP, his food cost % + variable cost % is called his **minimum operating cost.** Richard applies the MSP formula as follows:

$$\frac{\text{Minimum Labor Cost}}{1 - \text{Minimum Operating Cost}} = \text{MSP}$$

or

$$\frac{\text{Minimum Labor Cost}}{1 - (\text{Food Cost \%} + \text{Variable Cost \%})} = \text{MSP}$$

In this case, the computation would be as follows:

$$\frac{\$150}{1 - (0.40 + 0.30)} = \text{MSP}$$

or

$$\frac{\$150}{1 - 0.70} = \text{MSP}$$

or

$$\frac{\$150}{0.30}$$

thus

$$\$500 = \text{MSP}$$

If Richard can achieve a sales volume of $500 in the 10:00 P.M. to 11:00 P.M. time period, he should stay open. If this level of sales is not feasible, he should consider closing the operation at 10:00 P.M. Richard can use MSP to determine the hours his operation is most profitable. Of course, some operators may not have the authority to close the operation, even when remaining open is not particularly profitable. Corporate policy, contractual hours, promotion of a new unit, competition, and other factors must all be taken into account before the decision is made to modify operational hours.

The Budget

In most managerial settings, you will also be concerned with preparing and maintaining a **budget** for your foodservice operation. This budget, or financial plan, will detail the operational direction of your unit and your expected financial results. The techniques used in managerial accounting will show you how close your actual performance was when compared to your budget, while providing you with the information you need to make changes to your operational procedures or budget. This will ensure that your operation achieves the goals of your financial plan. It is important to note that the budget should not be a static document. It should be modified and fine-tuned as managerial accounting presents data about sales and costs that affect the direction of the overall operation.

For example, if you own a dance club featuring Latin music, and you find that a major competitor in your city has closed its doors, you may quite logically determine that you want to revise upward your estimate of the number of guests who will come to your club. This would, of course, affect your projected sales revenue, your costs, and your profitability. Not to do so might allow you to meet and exceed your original sales goals but would ignore a significant event that very likely will affect your financial plan for the club.

In a similar vein, if you are the manager of a delicatessen specializing in salads, sliced meats, and related items, and you find through your purchase orders that the price you pay for corned beef has tripled since last month, you must adjust your budget or you will find that you have no chance of staying within your food cost guidelines. Again, the point is that the foodservice budget should be closely monitored through the use of managerial accounting, which includes the thoughtful analysis of the data this type of accounting provides.

Just as the P&L tells you about your past performance, the budget is developed to help you achieve your future goals. In effect, the budget tells you what must be done if predetermined profit and cost objectives are to be met. In this respect, you are attempting to modify the profit formula, as presented in Chapter 1. With a well-thought-out and attainable budget, your profit formula would read as follows:

$$\text{Budgeted Revenue} - \text{Budgeted Expense} = \text{Budgeted Profit}$$

To prepare the budget and stay within it assures you predetermined profit levels. Without such a plan, management is left to guess about items such as expenditures and acceptable sales levels. The effective foodservice operator builds his or her budget, monitors it closely, modifies it when necessary, and achieves the desired results. Yet, many operators do not develop a budget. Some say that the process is too time consuming. Others feel that a budget, especially one shared with the entire organization, is too revealing. Budgeting can also cause conflicts. This is true, for example, when dollars budgeted for new equipment must be used for either a new kitchen stove or a new beer-tapping system. Obviously, the kitchen manager and the beverage manager may hold different points of view on where these funds can best be spent!

Despite the fact that some operators avoid budgets, they are extremely important. The rationale for having and using a budget can be summarized as follows:

1. It is the best means of analyzing alternative courses of action and allows management to examine these alternatives prior to adopting a particular one.
2. It forces management to examine the facts regarding what is necessary to achieve desired profit levels.
3. It provides a standard for comparison essential for good controls.
4. It allows management to anticipate and prepare for future business conditions.
5. It helps management to periodically carry out a self-evaluation of the organization and its progress toward its financial objectives.
6. It provides a communication channel whereby the organization's objectives are passed along to its various departments.
7. It encourages department managers who have participated in the preparation of the budget to establish their own operating objectives and evaluation techniques and tools.
8. It provides management with reasonable estimates of future expense levels and serves as an instrument for setting proper prices.

Budgeting is best done by the entire management team, for it is only through participation in the process that the whole organization will feel compelled to support the budget's implementation. Foodservice budgets can be considered as one of three main types:

1. Long-range budget
2. Annual budget
3. Achievement budget

Long-Range Budget

The **long-range budget** is typically prepared for a period of three to five years. While its detail is not great, it does provide a long-term view about where the operation should be going. It is also particularly useful in those cases where additional operational units may increase sales volume and accompanying expense. Assume, for example, that you are preparing a budget for a corporation you own. Your corporation has entered into an agreement with an international franchise company to open 45 cinnamon bun kiosks in malls across the United States and Canada. You will open a new store approximately every month for the next four years. To properly plan for your revenue and expense in the coming four-year period, a long-range budget for your company will be much needed.

Annual Budget

The annual, or yearly, budget is the type most operators think of when the word budget is used. As it states, the **annual budget** is for a one-year period or, in some cases, one season. This would be true, for example, in the case of a religious summer camp that is open and serving meals only while school is out of session and campers are attending, or a ski resort that opens in late fall but closes when the snow melts.

It is important to remember that an annual budget need not follow a calendar year. In fact, the best time period for an annual budget is the one that makes sense for your own operation. A college foodservice director, for example, would want a budget that covers the time period of a school year, that is, from the fall of one year through the spring of the next. For a restaurant whose owners have a fiscal year different from a calendar year, the annual budget may coincide with either the fiscal year or the calendar, as the owners prefer.

It is also important to remember that an annual budget need not consist of 12, one-month periods. While many operators prefer one-month budgets, some prefer budgets consisting of 13, 28-day periods, while others use quarterly (three-month) or even weekly budgets to plan for revenues and costs throughout the budget year.

Achievement Budget

The **achievement budget** is always of a shorter range, perhaps a month or a week. It provides current operating information and, thus, assists in making current operational decisions. A weekly achievement budget might, for example, be used to predict the number of gallons of milk needed for this time period or the number of servers to be scheduled on Tuesday night.

Developing the Budget

Some managers think it is very difficult to establish a budget, and, thus, they simply do not take the time to do so. Creating a budget is not that complex. You can learn to do it and do it well. To establish any type of budget, you need to have the following information available:

1. Prior-period operating results
2. Assumptions of next-period operations
3. Goals
4. Monitoring policies

To examine how prior-period operating results, assumptions of next-period operations, and goals drive the budgeting process, we will consider the case of Levi, who is preparing the annual foodservice budget for his 100-bed extended-care facility.

Prior-Period Operating Results

Levi's facility serves patient meals to an average occupancy of 80%, and he serves approximately 300 additional meals per day to staff and visitors. His department is allotted a flat dollar amount by the facility's administration for each meal he serves. His operating results for last year are detailed in Figure 10.10.

Patient and additional meals served were determined by actual count. Revenue and expense figures were taken from Levi's P&L statements by the year's end. It is important to note that Levi must have this information if he is to do any meaningful profit planning. Foodservice unit managers who do not have access to their operating results are at a tremendous managerial disadvantage. Levi has his operational summaries and the data that produced them. Because he knows how he has

FIGURE **10.10** ● Levi's Last Year Operating Results

Patient Meals Served: <u>29,200</u>   Revenue per Meal: <u>$3.46</u>

Additional Meals Served: <u>109,528</u>

Total Meals Served: <u>138,728</u>

	Amount	Percentage
Total Department Revenue	$480,000	100%
Cost of Food	192,000	40%
Cost of Labor	153,600	32%
Other Expenses	<u>86,400</u>	<u>18%</u>
Total Expenses	432,000	90%
Profit	48,000	10%

operated in the past, he is now ready to proceed to the assumptions section of the planning process.

Assumptions of Next-Period Operations

If Levi is to prepare a budget with enough strength to serve as a guide and enough flexibility to adapt to a changing environment, he must factor in the assumptions he and others feel will affect the operation. While each management team will arrive at its own conclusions given the circumstances of the operation, in this example, Levi makes the following assumptions regarding next year:

1. Food costs will increase by 3%.
2. Labor costs will increase by 5%.
3. Other expenses will rise by 10% due to a significant increase in utility costs.
4. Revenue received for all meals served will be increased by no more than 1%.
5. Patient occupancy of 80% of facility capacity will remain unchanged.

Levi would be able to establish these assumptions through discussions with his suppliers and union leaders, his own records, and, most important, his sense of the operation itself. In the commercial sector, when arriving at assumptions, operators must also consider new or diminished competition, changes in traffic patterns, and national food trends. At the highest level of foodservice management, assumptions regarding the acquisition of new units or the introduction of new products will certainly affect the budget process. As an operator, Levi predicts items 1, 2, and 3 by himself, while his supervisor has given him input about items 4 and 5. Given these assumptions, Levi can establish operating goals for next year.

Establishing Operating Goals

Given the assumptions he has made, Levi can now determine actual operating goals for the coming year. He will establish them for each of the following areas:

1. Meals served
2. Revenue
3. Food costs
4. Labor costs
5. Other expenses
6. Profit

Meals Served   Given the assumption of no increase in patient occupancy, and in light of his results from last year, Levi budgets to prepare and serve 29,200 patient meals. He feels, however, that he can increase his visitor and staff meals somewhat by being more customer service driven and by offering a wider selection of items on the facility's cycle menu. He decides, therefore, to raise his goal for additional meals from the 109,528 served last year to 115,000 for the coming year. Thus, his budgeted total meals to be served will equal 144,200 meals (29,200 + 115,000 = 144,200).

Revenue   Levi knows that his total revenue is to increase by only 1%. His revenue per meal will thus be $3.46 × 1.01 = $3.49. With 144,200 meals to be served, Levi will receive $503,258 (144,200 × $3.49 = $503,258) if he meets his meals-served budget.

Food Costs   Since Levi is planning to serve more meals, he expects to spend more on food. In addition, he assumes that this food will cost, on average, 3% more than last year. To determine a food budget, Levi computes the estimated food cost for 144,200 meals as follows:

1. Last year's food cost per meal = last year's cost of food/total meals served = $192,000/138,728 = $1.38
2. Last year's food cost per meal + 3% estimated increase in food cost = $1.38 × 1.03 = $1.42 per meal
3. $1.42 × 144,200 meals to be served this year = $204,764 estimated cost of food this year

Labor Costs Since Levi is planning to serve more meals, he expects to spend more on labor cost. In addition, he assumes that this labor will cost, on average, 5% more than last year. To determine a labor budget, Levi computes the estimated labor cost for 144,200 meals to be served as follows:

1. **Last year's labor cost per meal = last year's cost of labor/total meals served = $153,600/138,728 = $1.11 per meal**
2. **Last year's labor cost per meal + 5% estimated increase in labor cost = $1.11 × 1.05 = $1.17 per meal**
3. **$1.17 × 144,200 meals to be served this year = $168,714 estimated cost of labor this year**

Other Expenses Since Levi assumes a 10% increase in other expenses, they are budgeted as last year's amount plus an increase of 10%. Thus, $86,400 × 1.10 = $95,040.

Based on his assumptions about next year, Figure 10.11 details Levi's budget summary for the coming 12 months.

Profit Note that the increased costs Levi will be forced to bear, when coupled with his minimal revenue increase, caused his profit to fall from $48,000 for last year to a projected $34,740 for the coming year. If this is not acceptable, Levi must either increase his revenue beyond his assumption or look to his operation to reduce costs.

Levi has now developed concrete guidelines for his operation. Since his supervisor approves his budget as submitted, Levi is now ready to implement and monitor this new budget.

Monitoring the Budget

An operational plan has little value if management does not use it. In general, the budget should be monitored in each of the following three areas:

1. Revenue
2. Expense
3. Profit

Revenue Analysis

If revenue should fall below projected levels, the impact on profit can be substantial. Simply put, if revenues fall far short of projections, it will be difficult for you to meet your profit goals. If revenue consistently exceeds your projections, the overall budget must be modified or the expenses as-

FIGURE **10.11** ● Levi's Budget for Next Year

Patient Meals Budgeted: 29,200   Budgeted Revenue per Meal: $3.49

Additional Meals Budgeted: 115,000

Total Meals Budgeted: 144,200

	Amount	**Percentage**
Total Budgeted Revenue	$503,258	100.0%
Budgeted Expenses		
Cost of Food	204,764	40.7%
Cost of Labor	168,714	33.5%
Other Expense	95,040	18.9%
Total Expense	468,518	93.1%
Profit	34,740	6.9%

sociated with these increased sales will soon exceed budgeted amounts. Effective managers compare their actual revenue to that which they have projected on a regular basis.

It is clear that increases in operational revenue should dictate proportional increases in variable expense budgets, although fixed expenses, of course, need not be adjusted for these increases. For those foodservice operations with more than one meal period, monitoring budgeted sales volume may mean monitoring each meal period. Consider the case of Rosa, the night (P.M.) manager of a college cafeteria. She feels that she is busier than ever, but her boss, Lois, maintains that there can be no increase in Rosa's labor budget since the overall cafeteria sales volume is exactly in line with budgeted projections. Figure 10.12 shows the complete story of the sales volume situation at the college cafeteria after the first six months of the fiscal year. Note that the year is half (or 50%) completed at the time of this analysis.

Based on the sales volume she generates, Rosa *should* have an increase in her labor budget for the P.M. meal period. The amount of busi-

FIGURE **10.12** ● College Cafeteria Revenue Budget Summary

Time Period: <u>First 6 Months</u>

Meal Period	Budget	Actual	% of Budget
A.M.	$480,500	$166,698	35%
P.M.	350,250	248,677	71
Total	830,750	415,375	50

ness she is generating in the evenings is substantially higher than budgeted. Note that she is one-half way through her budget year, but has already generated 71% of the annual revenue forecasted by the budget. This, however, does not mean that the labor budget for the entire cafeteria should be increased. In fact, the labor budget for the A.M. shift should likely be reduced, as those dollars are more appropriately needed in the evening meal period.

Some foodservice operators relate revenue to the number of seats they have available in their operation. Since the size of a foodservice facility affects both total investment and operating costs, this can be a useful number. The formula for the computation of sales per seat is as follows:

$$\frac{\text{Total Sales}}{\text{Available Seats}} = \text{Sales per Seat}$$

To illustrate this, assume that, if Rosa's cafeteria has 120 seats, her P.M. sales per seat thus far this year would be as follows:

$$\frac{\$248,677}{120} = \$2,072.31$$

The A.M. sales per seat, given the same number of seats, would be computed as follows:

$$\frac{\$166,698}{120} = \$1,389.15$$

As can be seen, Rosa's sales per seat are much higher than that of her A.M. counterpart. Of course, part of that may be due to the fact that evening menu items in the cafeteria may sell for more, on average, than do breakfast items.

When sales volume is lower than originally projected, management must seek ways to increase revenue. As stated earlier, one of management's main tasks is to generate guests, while the employee's main task is to service these guests to the best of his or her ability. There are a variety of methods used for increasing sales volume, including the use of coupons, increased advertising, price discounting, and specials. For the serious foodservice manager, a thorough study of the modern techniques of foodservice marketing is mandatory if you are to be ready to meet all the challenges you may face.

Expense Analysis

Effective foodservice managers are careful to monitor operational expense because costs that are too high or too low may be cause for concern. Just as it is not possible to estimate future sales volume perfectly, it is also not possible to estimate future expense perfectly, since some expenses will vary as sales volume increases or decreases. To know that an operation spent $800 for fruits and vegetables in a given week becomes meaningful only if we know what the sales volume for that week was. In the same vein, knowing that $500 was spent for labor during a given lunch period can be analyzed only in terms of the amount of sales achieved in that same period. To help them make an expense assessment quickly, some operators elect to utilize the **yardstick method** of calculating expense standards so determinations can be made as to whether variations in expenses are due to changes in sales volume or other reasons such as waste or theft.

To illustrate the yardstick method, consider the case of Marion, who operates a college cafeteria during nine months of the year in a small southeastern city. Marion has developed both revenue and expense budgets. His problem, however, is that variations in revenue cause variations in expense. This is true in terms of food products, labor, and other expenses. As a truly effective manager, he wishes to know whether changes in his actual expenses are due to inefficiencies in his operation or to normal sales variation. To begin his analysis, Marion establishes a purchase standard for food products using a seven-step model.

Developing Yardstick Standards for Food

Step 1. Divide total inventory into management-designated subgroups, for example, meats, produce, dairy, and groceries.

Step 2. Establish dollar value of subgroup purchases for prior accounting period.

Step 3. Establish sales volume for the prior accounting period.

Step 4. Determine percentage of purchasing dollar spent for each food category.

Step 5. Determine percentage of revenue dollar spent for each food category.

Step 6. Develop weekly sales volume and associated expense projection. Compute % cost to sales for each food grouping and sales estimate.

Step 7. Compare weekly revenue and expense to projection. Correct if necessary.

To develop his yardstick standards for food, Marion collects data from last year as shown in Figure 10.13.

Assuming that Marion has created a revenue estimate of $52,000 per month for this year and that he was satisfied with both last year's food cost percentage and profits, he can now follow the steps outlined previously to establish his yardstick standards for food. Marion estimates a weekly sales volume of $52,000/4, or $13,000, for this year.

FIGURE **10.13** ● Marion's College Cafeteria Food Data

	Last School Year (9 Months)
Total Sales: $450,000	Average Sales per Month: $50,000

Purchases	
Meats	$ 66,600
Fish/Poultry	36,500
Produce	26,500
Dairy	20,000
Groceries	18,300
Total	167,900

Marion's Yardstick Standards for Food

Step 1.   Meat
             Fish/Poultry
             Produce
             Dairy
             Groceries

Step 2.   Meat $ 66,600
             Fish/Poultry   36,500
             Produce   26,500
             Dairy   20,000
             Grocery   18,300

             Total   167,900

Step 3. $450,000 total revenue in prior period (9 months)

Step 4.   Meat $ 66,600/167,900 =   39.7%
             Fish/Poultry   36,500/167,900 =   21.7
             Produce   26,500/167,900 =   15.8
             Dairy   20,000/167,900 =   11.9
             Groceries   18,300/167,900 =   10.9

             Total   167,900   100.0

Step 5.   Meat $ 66,600/450,000 =   14.8%
             Fish/Poultry   36,500/450,000 =   8.1
             Produce   26,500/450,000 =   5.9
             Dairy   20,000/450,000 =   4.4
             Groceries   18,300/450,000 =   4.1

             Total   167,900   37.3%

Step 6.

Category	% Cost to Total Cost	% Cost to Total Sales	Weekly Sales Estimate				
			$11,000	$12,000	$13,000	$14,000	$15,000
Meat	39.7%	14.8%	$1,628	$1,776	$1,924	$2,072	$2,220
Fish/Poultry	21.7	8.1	891	972	1,053	1,134	1,215
Produce	15.8	5.9	649	708	767	826	885
Dairy	11.9	4.4	484	528	572	616	660
Groceries	10.9	4.1	451	492	533	574	615
Total	100.0	37.3	4,103	4,476	4,849	5,222	5,595

Note that, to compute the data for Step 6, you must multiply % cost to total sales by the weekly sales estimate. When using the sales estimate of $13,000 for a week, for example, the meat budget would be computed as follows:

$$0.148 \times \$13,000 = \$1,924$$

Fish/poultry would be computed as follows:

$$0.081 \times \$13,000 = \$1,053$$

Step 7. Analysis

Marion can now compare his budgeted expense with actual performance over several volume levels. In a week in which sales volume equals $14,000, for example, Marion would expect that total meat invoices for that period, according to his yardstick measure, would equal approximately $2,072 ($14,000 × 14.8% = $2,072). Of course, this assumes that Marion has not changed the level of his meat inventory. If his invoices, or in the case of an issues and requisition system, his issues, exceed $2,072, he would know exactly where to direct his attention. Using the yardstick system, Marion can easily monitor any expense over any number of differing volume levels. The yardstick method of purchase estimation is especially helpful for those operations that experience great variation in sales volume. A hotel that has a slow season and a busy season, for instance, will find that the use of this method is quite helpful in estimating the money needed for inventory acquisition.

Developing Yardstick Standards for Labor Just as Marion used the yardstick method to estimate food expense at varying sales volume levels, he can also used it to estimate labor cost expenditures at those various levels. To develop a labor yardstick, he follows these steps:

Step 1. Divide total labor cost into management-designated subgroups, for example, cooks, warewashers, and bartenders.
Step 2. Establish dollar value spent for each subgroup during the prior accounting period.
Step 3. Establish sales volume for the prior accounting period.
Step 4. Determine percentage of labor dollar spent for each subgroup.
Step 5. Determine percentage of revenue dollar spent for each labor category.
Step 6. Develop weekly sales volume and associated expense projection. Compute % cost to sales for each labor category and sales estimate.
Step 7. Compare weekly revenue and expense to projection. Correct if necessary.

Marion collected labor-related data from last year's operation as shown in Figure 10.14.

FIGURE **10.14** ● Marion's College Cafeteria Labor Data

		Last School Year (9 Months)
Total Sales: $450,000		Average Sales per Month: $50,000

Labor Costs
Management	$ 40,000
Food Production	65,000
Service	12,000
Sanitation	18,000
Total	135,000

It is important to note that Marion can develop a labor yardstick based on guests served, labor hours worked, or, as is his preference, labor cost percentage. To develop the labor standard based on labor cost percentage, Marion follows the seven-step process outlined below.

Marion's Yardstick Standards for Labor

Step 1. Management
Food Production
Service
Sanitation

Step 2.
Management	$ 40,000
Food Production	65,000
Service	12,000
Sanitation	18,000
Total	135,000

Step 3. $450,000 total revenue in prior period (9 months)

Step 4.
Management	$ 40,000/135,000 =	29.6%
Food Production	65,000/135,000 =	48.2
Service	12,000/135,000 =	8.9
Sanitation	18,000/135,000 =	13.3
Total	135,000	100.0%

Step 5.
Management	$ 40,000/450,000 =	8.9%
Food Production	65,000/450,000 =	14.4
Service	12,000/450,000 =	2.7
Sanitation	18,000/450,000 =	4.0
Total	135,000	30.0%

Step 6.

Category	% Cost to Total Cost	% Cost to Total Sales	Weekly Sales Estimate				
			$11,000	$12,000	$13,000	$14,000	$15,000
Management	29.6%	8.9%	$ 979	$1,068	$1,157	$1,246	$1,335
Food Production	48.2	14.4	1,584	1,728	1,872	2,016	2,160
Service	8.9	2.7	297	324	351	378	450
Sanitation	13.3	4.0	440	480	520	560	600
Total	100.0	30.0	3,300	3,600	3,900	4,200	4,500

Note that, to compute the data for Step 6, Marion must multiply % cost to total sales by his weekly sales estimate. Using the sales estimate of $13,000, for example, the management portion of the budget would be computed as follows:

$$0.089 \times \$13,000 = \$1,157$$

The food production cost expense estimate, based on the same weekly sales, would be computed as follows:

$$0.144 \times \$13,000 = \$1,872$$

Step 7. Analysis

It is now easy for Marion to identify exactly where his labor variations, if any, are to be found.

The yardstick method may, of course, be used for any operational expense, be it food, labor, or one of the many other expenses you will incur. In all cases, however, you must monitor your actual expenditures as they relate to budgeted expenditures, while keeping changes in sales volume in mind.

Profit Analysis

As business conditions change, changes in the budget are to be expected. This is because budgets are based on a specific set of assumptions, and, as these assumptions change, so, too, does the budget that follows from the assumptions. Assume, for example, that you budgeted $1,000 in January for snow removal from the parking lot attached to the restaurant you own in New York State. If unusually severe weather causes you to spend $2,000 for snow removal in January instead, the assumption (normal levels of snowfall) was incorrect and the budget will be incorrect as well.

Budgeted profit must be realized if the operation is to provide adequate returns for owner and investor risk. Consider the case of James, the operator of a foodservice establishment with excellent sales but below-budgeted profits. James budgeted a 5% profit on $2,000,000 of sales; thus, $100,000 profit ($2,000,000 × 0.05 = $100,000) was anticipated. In reality, at year's end, James achieved only $50,000 profit, or 2.5% of sales ($50,000/$2,000,000 = 2.5%). If the operation's owners feel that $50,000 is an adequate return for their risk, James' services may be retained. If they do not, he may lose his position, *even though* the operation is profitable. Remember that your goal is not merely to generate a profit, but rather to generate budgeted profit. You will be rewarded when you meet this goal. The primary goal of management is to generate the profits necessary for the successful continuation of the business. Budgeting for these profits is a fundamental step in the process. Analyzing the success of achieving budget forecasts is of tremendous managerial concern. If profit goals are to be met, safeguarding your operational revenue is critical. It is to that task that we now turn our attention. The proper collection and accounting for guest payment of services is one of the final steps in a successful food and beverage cost control system.

FUN ON THE WEB!

Look up the following sites to review and obtain copies of books related to accounting and cost control.

www.amazon.com
www.borders.com
www.barnesandnoble.com

Search these sites using key words such as food and beverage, cost control, hospitality accounting, and menu engineering to find resources to add to your book collection.

Key Terms and Concepts

The following are terms and concepts discussed in the chapter that are important for you as a manager. To help you review, please define the terms below.

Matrix analysis
Contribution margin per menu
   item
Goal value analysis
Loss leaders
Break-even point
Cost/volume/profit (CVP) analysis
Contribution margin income
   statement

Contribution margin for
   overall operation
Minimum sales point (MSP)
Minimum operating cost
Budget
Long-range budget
Annual budget
Achievement budget
Yardstick method

Test Your Skills

1. Boniso operates Boniso's Mexican Restaurant in an urban city in the South. He has worked hard at setting up cost control systems, and he is generally happy with his *overall* results. However, he is not sure if all of his menu items are providing profitability for his restaurant. He decides to use food cost matrix and contribution margin matrix analyses to study each of his menu items.

a. Complete his menu analysis worksheet.

Menu Analysis Worksheet

Menu Item	Number Sold	Selling Price	Total Sales	Item Cost	Total Cost	Item Contribution Margin	Total Contribution Margin	Food Cost %
Fajita Plate	147	$12.95	1903.65	$4.92	723.24	8.03	1180.41	38
Enchilada Dinner	200	9.95	1990	3.48	696	6.47	1294	35
Menudo	82	6.95	569.90	1.74	142.68	5.21	427.22	25
Mexican Salad	117	7.95	930.15	2.39	279.63	5.56	650.52	30
Chalupa Dinner	125	8.95	1118.75	2.51	313.75	6.44	805	28
Burrito Dinner	168	9.95	1671.60	3.25	546	6.70	1125.60	33
Taco Dinner	225	5.95	1338.75	1.55	348.75	4.40	990	26
Total	1064	62.65	8522.8	19.84	3329.8	42.81	6472.75	215
Weighted Average								

b. Using the results of Boniso's menu analysis worksheet (in part a), place each menu item in its appropriate square in the following matrices.

Food Cost Matrix

High Food Cost %
(Above _____ %)

Low Food Cost %
(Below _____ %)

Low Popularity (Below ___ Sales)	High Popularity (Above ___ Sales)

Contribution Margin Matrix

High Contribution Margin
(Above $ _____)

Low Contributin Margin
(Below $ _____)

Low Popularity (Below ___ Sales)	High Popularity (Above ___ Sales)

2. Garikai is a manager at Boniso's Mexican Restaurant (from previous exercise), and he believes that goal value analysis, rather than Boniso's matrix analysis, is a better way to study the profitability of his menu items.

   a. Using the following goal value analysis data, help Garikai analyze the restaurant's menu items.

Goal Value Analysis Data

Item	Food Cost % (in decimal form)	Number Sold	Selling Price	Variable Cost % (in decimal form)
Fajita Plate	0.38	147	$12.95	0.28
Enchilada Dinner	0.35	200	9.95	0.28
Menudo	0.25	82	6.95	0.28
Mexican Salad	0.30	117	7.95	0.28
Chalupa Dinner	0.28	125	8.95	0.28
Burrito Dinner	0.33	168	9.95	0.28
Taco Dinner	0.26	225	5.95	0.28
Overall Menu (Goal Value)	0.32	152	8.95	0.28

After computing the following goal values, sort (in descending rank order) by goal value. Be sure to include the *overall menu* in the appropriate rank order.

Goal Value Analysis Results

Item	Food Cost % (in decimal form)	Number Sold	Selling Price	Variable Cost % (in decimal form)	Goal Value

b. After analyzing his menu items, Garikai believes he can improve the chalupa dinner by lowering the selling price to $7.95. He believes that this lower price will increase the number of chalupa dinners sold to 150. If he makes these changes, will the chalupa dinner meet or exceed the overall menu goal value? Should Garikai make these changes?

Results of Changes Made to Chalupa Dinner

Item	Food Cost % (in decimal form)	Number Sold	Selling Price	Variable Cost % (in decimal form)	Goal Value
Chalupa Dinner					

3. Eunice manages a Thai restaurant in a primarily Asian section of a major West Coast city. She is interested in determining dollar sales and number of guests needed to break even and to generate her desired

profits. Her check average (selling price) is $16.00, her variable cost per unit (guest) is $5.60, and her fixed costs are $170,000.

a. Complete the following grid and determine her before-tax profit.

	Per Unit (Guest)	Percentage
SP		
VC		
CM		

Fixed Costs $170,000
Desired after-tax profit $ 24,000
Tax rate   40%
Before-tax profit   _____

b. Using the information from part a, calculate the following:

Break-even point in   _____
  sales dollars
Break-even point in   _____   Rounded up = _____
  guests served
Sales dollars to achieve   _____
  desired after-tax profit
Guests served to achieve   _____   Rounded up = _____
  desired after-tax profit

c. Based on her calculations, Eunice doesn't think that she can attract as many guests as she needs to achieve her desired after-tax profit. Therefore, she has decided to make some changes to improve her situation. Due to these changes, she has been able to reduce her selling price by $1.00, decrease her variable cost % by 5%, and lower her fixed costs by $5,000. After these changes, what are Eunice's sales dollars and guests served to

	Per Unit (Guest)	Percentage
SP		
VC		
CM		

achieve her after-tax profit? Complete the following grid and calculations.

Fixed costs _____

Sales dollars to achieve desired after-tax profit _____

Guests served to achieve desired
after-tax profit _____ **Rounded up =** _____

4. Sinqobile runs a restaurant in an East Coast city that specializes in African-American cuisine. She has compiled her sales and cost data from last year, and she wants to develop a budget for this year. She has projected the following increases for this year:

Projected Increases

Meals served	3%
Selling price per meal	2%
Cost of food	5%
Cost of labor	10%
Other expenses	2%

	Last Year	Budget
Meals Served	122,000	
Selling Price per Meal	$12.50	

	Last Year $	Last Year %	Budget $	Budget %
Revenue	$1,525,000			
Cost of Food	583,680			
Cost of Labor	491,520			
Other Expenses	245,760			
Total Expenses	1,320,960			
Profit	204,040			

Using this information, help Sinqobile complete her budget.

5. Sitabiso manages an executive dining room in an office building of a major food manufacturing company. Her sales, on average, run be-

tween $17,000 and $21,000 per week. She has decided to use yardstick standards for labor to predict labor costs for varying sales levels. With these data, she can determine if variations in her expenses are due to changes in sales volume or other reasons such as waste or theft. She has compiled information from last year to help her predict her weekly labor costs. Using this information, help Sitabiso complete her yardstick standards for labor.

Yardstick Standards for Labor

Total Sales: $900,000   Average Sales per Month: $75,000
Labor Costs:
Management $ 84,000
Food Production   143,000
Service   27,600
Sanitation   34,200
      Total   288,800

Category	% Cost to Total Cost	% Cost to Total Sales	Weekly Sales Estimate				
			$17,000	$18,000	$19,000	$20,000	$21,000
Management							
Food Production							
Service							
Sanitation							
Total							

Chapter

MAINTAINING AND IMPROVING THE REVENUE CONTROL SYSTEM

OVERVIEW In this chapter, you will learn the principles of revenue control. This includes protecting your sales revenue from external and internal threats of theft. Also, you will find out how to establish an effective revenue security system that includes an extensive series of checks and balances and helps you protect your revenue from the time it is collected from your guests to the time it is deposited in your bank.

CHAPTER OUTLINE

Revenue Security
External Threats to Revenue Security
Internal Threats to Revenue Security
Developing the Revenue Security System
Key Terms and Concepts, and Test Your Skills

HIGHLIGHTS At the conclusion of this chapter, you will be able to:

○ Identify internal and external threats to revenue dollars.
○ Create effective countermeasures to combat internal and external theft.
○ Establish and monitor a complete and effective revenue security system.

Revenue Security

All the cost control systems you can develop will be of little use if you are unable to collect the revenue generated by your restaurant and then deposit that revenue into your bank account. Errors in revenue collection can come from simple employee mistakes or, in some cases, outright theft by either guests or employees. An important part of your job is to devise revenue security systems that protect your funds, whether that revenue is in the form of cash, checks, credit or debit card receipts, coupons, meal cards, or any other method of guest payment.

In its simplest form, revenue control and security is a matter of matching products sold with funds received. Thus, an effective revenue security system ensures that the following formula reflects what really happens in your foodservice operation:

$$\textbf{Product Issues = Guest Charges}$$
$$\textbf{= Sales Receipts = Sales Deposits}$$

Product issues, guest charges, sales receipts, and sales deposits will each be explained in detail later in this chapter. The potential for guest or employee theft or fraud exists in all of these areas, and it is important for you to remain alert to irregularities.

To illustrate the problem that can exist, assume that you own a chain of 10 coffee/dessert shops. You call your units The Pie Parlor. You sell pies of many varieties, all for the same price of $2 per slice or $15 for a whole pie. A whole pie consists of eight slices. In addition, you sell coffee for $2 per cup. Assume that Figure 11.1 details your sales record on a Monday for unit 6, which is one of your 10 stores.

If you have in place an effective system of controlling your revenue, you should have total receipts (revenue) of $1,400 for January 1 at this unit. If, in fact, at the conclusion of the day you have only $1,300 in actual revenue, a security problem exists, not perhaps in the control of products but rather in the control of receipts. If you were short $100 in revenue per day for each of your 10 units, and you were open 360 days per year, your revenue loss for the year would be a staggering $360,000 ($100 × 10 × 360 = $360,000)!

There are several reasons why you might be short in revenue. A discussion of the potential problems you could be facing will be helpful as we proceed to develop revenue security systems designed to address these issues. Revenue security problems can exist in either of the following areas:

1. External threats to revenue security
2. Internal threats to revenue security

FIGURE **11.1** ● Sales Record

Unit Name: **The Pie Parlor #6**   Date: 1/1

Item	Number Sold	Selling Price	Total Sales
Apple Pie			
Slices	60	$ 2.00	$ 120.00
Whole	11	15.00	165.00
Pumpkin Pie			
Slices	40	2.00	80.00
Whole	14	15.00	210.00
Cherry Pie			
Slices	75	2.00	150.00
Whole	5	15.00	75.00
Peach Pie			
Slices	25	2.00	50.00
Whole	10	15.00	150.00
Coffee	200	2.00	400.00
Total			**$1,400.00**

External Threats to Revenue Security

Your facility could, of course, have lost sales revenue because some guests simply try to defraud foodservice operators. This activity can take a variety of forms, and a very common one is for a guest to **walk,** or **skip,** the bill or guest check. A guest is said to have walked, or skipped, a check when he or she has consumed a product but has left the foodservice operation without paying the bill. This type of theft is obviously not present in, for example, a quick-service operation where payment is received at the time the food is given to the guest. In cases where a guest is in a busy dining room, however, it is quite possible for one or more members of a dining party to slip outside while the server is busy with other guests. In any case, the loss of revenue to your business can be substantial if you do not take the necessary steps to reduce this type of theft. The fact is, in a busy restaurant it can sometimes be relatively easy for a guest or an entire party to leave without settling their bill unless everyone on your staff is extremely vigilant. To help reduce this type of guest theft, implementation of the steps in Figure 11.2 is suggested.

It is, of course, also possible that a guest truly forgets to pay his or her bill and leaves the establishment without paying. However, if many of your guests walked their bills on your day of $1,400 sales in our Pie Parlor example, you would, of course, find that while the products had indeed been consumed, the money in your cash register would not equal the sales value of the pie and coffee served.

A second form of guest theft that you must guard against is that of fraudulent payment. This includes passing counterfeit money, bad checks, or, most commonly, the use of invalid credit or debit cards. In our society, fewer and fewer consumers carry large amounts of cash, and many facilities are reluctant to accept personal checks. Thus, most foodservice operations accept a variety of credit and debit cards. A **credit card,** as the name implies, obligates users to pay their credit card companies for the goods and services they themselves charge on the card. A **debit card** is different in that, when it is used, the funds to cover the purchase are automatically transferred from the user's bank account to the entity issuing the debit card.

Since both credit card and debit card transactions are billed and collected by a third party, the foodservice operator pays a percentage of each card's sale back to the credit or debit card company. If, for example, the card sale is $10.00 and an operator is charged 4% for accepting the card, the card company would receive $10.00 × 0.04, or $0.40, from the restaurant for the use of the card.

The number of stolen and fraudulent credit cards in use today is very high. It is, therefore, important for the foodservice operator to check the validity of the credit card before accepting it for payment. The federal government has passed a law prohibiting the fraudulent use of credit cards. Individuals who fraudulently use credit cards in interstate commerce to obtain goods or services of $1,000 or more in any given year could be subject to fines of up to $10,000 and prison terms of up to 10 years.

Fortunately, credit card security has come a long way since the early introduction of these cards. Today, credit cards are issued with three-dimensional designs, magnetic strips, encoded numbers, and other features that reduce the chance of guest fraud. In addition, today's electronic credit card verification systems are fast, accurate, and designed to reduce the chances of loss by your business. A verification service should be used, even if the number of times credit cards are used as payment by guests is relatively small. These services charge a fee, but they guarantee that the business will receive its money for a legitimate credit card charge, even if cardholders do not pay the bank that issues them their monthly statements.

FIGURE **11.2** ● Steps to Reduce Guest Walks, or Skips

1. If the custom of your restaurant is that guests order and con-
    sume their food prior to your receiving payment, instruct
    servers to present the bill for the food promptly when the
    guests have finished.

2. If your facility has a cashier in a central location in the
    dining area, have that cashier available and visible at all
    times.

3. If your facility operates in such a manner that each server
    collects for his or her own guest's charges, instruct the
    servers to return to the table promptly after presenting the
    guest's bill to secure a form of payment.

4. Train employees to be observant of exit doors near restrooms
    or other areas of the facility that may provide an unscrupu-
    lous guest the opportunity to exit the dining area without
    being easily seen.

5. If an employee sees a guest leave without paying the bill,
    management should be notified immediately.

6. Upon approaching a guest who has left without paying the bill,
    the manager should ask if the guest has inadvertently "forgot-
    ten" to pay. In most cases, the guest will then pay the bill.

7. Should a guest still refuse to pay or flee the scene, the man-
    ager should note the following on an incident report:

    a. Number of guests involved
    b. Amount of the bill
    c. Physical description of the guest(s)
    d. Vehicle description if the guests flee in a car, as well as
       the license plate number if possible
    e. Time and date of the incident
    f. Name of the server(s) who actually served the guest

8. If the guest is successful in fleeing the scene, the police
    should notified. In no case should your staff members or man-
    agers be instructed to attempt to physically detain the guest.
    The liability that could be involved should an employee be
    hurt in such an attempt is far greater than the value of a
    skipped food and beverage bill.

To collect your money from an entity that administers credit or debit cards, your staff will be required to follow the specific procedures of that card company. Because that is true, if you agree to accept credit and debit cards for payment, you should become very familiar with the procedures required by each card issuer and follow them carefully. To enhance your chances of collecting your money from these companies and reducing the risk of fraudulent card use, insist that your staff follow the steps in Figure 11.3.

FIGURE **11.3** ● Credit and Debit Card Verification

1. Confirm that the name on the card is the same as that of the individual presenting the card for payment. Drivers' licenses or other acceptable forms of identification can be used.

2. Examine the card for any obvious signs of alteration.

3. Confirm that the card is indeed valid, that is, that the card has not expired or is not yet in effect.

4. Compare the signature on the back of the card with the one produced by the guest paying with the card.

5. The employee processing the charge should initial the credit card receipt.

6. Carbon paper, if used, should be destroyed.

7. Credit card charges that have not yet been processed should be kept in a secure place to limit the possibility that they could be stolen.

8. Do not issue cash in exchange for credit card charges.

9. Do not write in tip amounts for the guest. These should be supplied by the guest only unless the "tip" is, in truth, a mandatory service charge and that fact has been communicated in advance to the guest.

10. Tally credit card charges on a daily basis, making sure to check that the above procedures have been followed. If they have not, corrective action should immediately be taken to ensure compliance.

FUN ON THE WEB!

Look up the following sites to see examples of credit card companies that you can use to provide payment services for your operation.

www.totalmerchant-ca.com Click on "Retail/Restaurant" to find merchant account rates and fees.

www.novusnet.com Click on "Discover Business Services," then click on "Become a Merchant" to find out the benefits of being a Discover Card merchant.

www.americanexpress.com Click on "Merchants," then choose your industry or business category (e.g., restaurants) to find out how to become an American Express merchant and what services American Express offers.

www.visa.com Click on "For Businesses," then click on "Visa Merchant Resource Center" to learn about the benefits and services that Visa offers to restaurants.

While many operations no longer accept personal checks, those that do find that they, too, must use a verification service before accepting these instruments for payment. These services do not actually certify that there are sufficient funds in the bank to complete the transaction, but rather they notify the foodservice operator if that particular checking account or individual has had difficulty in the past in covering checks written on that account. If you agree to accept checks, you will experience some loss. That is, despite your best efforts, some checks accepted will not be collectable. Costs experienced from this type of loss like all other costs must be reflected in your menu prices. It is imperative, however, that guest theft of this type be kept to an absolute minimum.

In addition to skipping a bill and fraudulent payment attempts, the last method of guest theft you must be aware of is that used by the **quick-change artist.** A quick-change artist is a guest who, having practiced the routine many times, attempts to confuse the cashier; in his or her confusion, the cashier gives the guest too much change. For example, a guest who should have received $5 in change may use a confusing routine to secure $15. To prevent this from happening, you must train your cashiers well and instruct them to notify management immediately if there is any suspicion of attempted fraud to your operation through quick-change routines by a guest.

Internal Threats to Revenue Security

While most foodservice employees are honest, some are not. In addition to protecting your revenue from unscrupulous guests, you must protect it from those few employees who attempt to steal the revenue your facility has earned from sales. Since cash is the most readily usable asset in a foodservice operation, it is a major target for dishonest employees. In general, theft from service personnel is not a matter of removing large sums of cash at one time, since this is too easy for management to detect. Rather, service personnel can use a variety of techniques to cheat an operation a small amount at a time.

One of the most common server theft techniques involves the omission of recording the guest's order. If, in our Pie Parlor example, a guest ordered both pie and coffee, but the pie sale is not recorded either by hand or by machine, you will find that a piece of pie was missing, but no record of sale was ever made. In this situation, the server might have chosen to charge the guest and keep the revenue from the piece of pie, or might have attempted to build favor with the guest by not charging for the product at all. Theft of this type is especially prevalent in bars. As an old foodservice story goes: "A guest walks into a bar that sells drinks for $5, has four drinks, and places $20 on the counter as he leaves. The bartender then turns to the manager and says, 'Hey, that guy didn't pay for his drinks . . . but he left a great tip!' " The manager, of course, is not amused. The point, however, is that all sales must be recorded if management is to develop a system that matches products sold to revenue received. Complete revenue control is a matter of developing the checks and balances necessary to ensure that the value of products sold and the amount of revenue received do indeed equal each other.

To understand how server theft could occur, it is important to know your options in recording sales. In the least effective option, no record is made of the sale at all. Guests are simply told how much they owe by the server. Obviously, this approach is ineffective. Servers can misrepresent the amount they charged guests, and no historical record of sales is available to help you make decisions in the future. A second, and improved approach, is to require a written **guest check** recording each sale. A guest check is simply a written record of what was purchased by the guest and how much the guest was charged for the item(s). The use of guest checks is standard in the industry, but dishonest employees can abuse them. If, for example, one of your guest's at the Pie Parlor orders peach pie and coffee, and the service person collects the revenue for these products, in some operations the same guest check could be used one hour later for another guest who orders peach pie and coffee. The server could then keep the money from the second sale, and, at the end of the day, your operation would find itself short on revenue relative to product used. To prevent fraud of this type, you must have a system of guest check controls in place so that each check can be used one time only and is subsequently put under the safekeeping of management. It should not be possible, for example, for a server to submit a guest check that had previously been used, while keeping a blank one. Hard-copy guest checks should be recorded by number and then safely stored or destroyed, as management policy dictates.

It is important to note that most guests do not know or care if the guest check presented to them is actually theirs or belongs to someone else. In fact, in many cases, if the guest check is accurate in terms of total charges and items ordered, guests would have no way of knowing if they are paying their own bill or someone else's.

Another method of service personnel fraud also involves the use of guest checks. In this case, the server gives the proper guest check to the guest, collects payment, and destroys the guest check but keeps the money. In this case, you would find that the money in your cash register indeed equaled the sum of the guest checks you have, but, of course, the actual amount of product you served is not equal to that indicated on the guest checks. For this reason, many operators implement a **precheck/postcheck system** for guest checks. In a precheck/postcheck system, the server records the order (prechecks) on a guest check, when it is given to him or her by the guest. Kitchen and bar personnel are, in this system, prohibited from issuing any products to the server without a prechecked guest check. When the guest is ready to pay his or her bill, the cashier recalls the prechecked total, and the guest pays that bill. In this case, products ordered by the guest and issued by the kitchen or bar should match the items and money collected by the cashier. Today, precheck/postcheck systems are sold as a component of nearly all point of sales (POS) systems.

There are a variety of components available to you as you seek to design a good guest check control system. These can include the use of management-issued guest checks, multicopy guest checks (carbonless paper), and guest checks generated by computerized POS systems. In all cases, however, the goal is the same, which is to reduce server theft through the proper recording and collecting of all product sales.

In a foodservice operation, guests frequently place an order and then change their minds and order something else. When this happens, so, too, does the opportunity for fraud. Service personnel may charge the guest for a higher priced item while serving a lower priced one, and then keep the difference in selling price. Similarly, the operation can be defrauded if a higher priced item is sold, but the guest is charged for a lower priced menu selection. To prevent this kind of abuse, manual guest checks should be filled out in pen, never pencil, and any changes should be made by drawing a line through the original item and writing the new item below it. In computerized systems, changes in the product ordered or served should be clearly indicated. In no case should service personnel be provided with guest checks that can be erased. Many types of guest checks manufactured today are done so on nonerasable paper. This is an excellent control device.

Not all service personnel are dishonest, of course, and sometimes honest mistakes can be made. This usually occurs when service personnel are required to total their guest checks by hand. Simple errors in addition and subtraction can cost an operation dearly in lost revenue. For this reason, it is critical that service personnel do not total guest checks without the use of a POS system, cash register, adding machine, or calculator. Guests also prefer to see that the guest check is totaled by machine. It strengthens their belief that the total they have been charged does indeed match the items they have consumed, and that no errors in arithmetic have been made. For this reason, many operators use a computerized system to record product sales, tally guest check totals, and compare money collected with money that should have been collected. It is important to remember, however, that even such sophisticated systems hold the potential for employee fraud. Consider, for example, the precheck/postcheck POS system that requires a server to enter his or her password before allowing that server to precheck items. In this case, an unscrupulous server who discovers another server's password could use that password to defraud the operation, then blame the fraud on the unsuspecting server. Regardless of the weaknesses that can exist in them, today's POS systems, properly used and managed, are a tremendous asset in helping to reduce server theft.

Cashier Theft

In some operations, servers act as their own cashiers; in others, the server function and cashier function fall to different individuals. Regardless of the system in place, if a cashier is responsible for the collection of money, several areas of potential fraud can exist. The cashier may collect payment from a guest but proceed to destroy the guest check that recorded the sale. Another method of cashier theft involves failing to ring up the sale indicated by the guest check while pocketing the money. Management must have systems in place to identify missing checks that cannot be accounted for and to match guest check totals with those of cash register sales.

In addition to theft of your own business financial assets, the hospitality industry affords some employees the opportunity to defraud guests as well. Some techniques include:

1. Charging guests for items not purchased, then keeping the overcharge.
2. Changing the totals on credit card charges after the guest has left or imprinting additional credit card charges and pocketing the cash difference.
3. Misadding legitimate charges to create a higher than appropriate total, with the intent of keeping the overcharge.
4. Purposely shortchanging guests when giving back change, with the intent of keeping the extra change.
5. Charging higher than authorized prices for products or services, recording the proper price, then keeping the overcharge.

In all but the most outdated cash register systems, the totals of guest checks rung on the machine during a predetermined period are mechanically tallied, so management can compare the sales recorded by the cash register with the money actually contained in the cash register. For example, a cashier working a shift from 7:00 A.M. to 3:00 P.M. might have recorded $1,000 in sales during that time period. If that were, in fact, the case, and if no errors in handling change occurred, the cash register should contain $1,000. If it contains less than $1,000, it is said to be **short;** if it contains more than $1,000, it is said to be **over.** Cashiers rarely steal large sums directly from the cash drawer because such theft is easily detected, but management must make it a policy that any cash shortages or overages will be investigated. Some managers believe that cash shortages, not overages, need to be monitored. This is not the case. Consistent cash shortages may be an indication of employee theft or carelessness and should, of course, be investigated. Cash overages, too, may be the result of sophisticated theft by the cashier. In this case, the victim may be either the operation or the guest.

If the cash register has a void key, a dishonest cashier could enter a sales amount, collect for it, and then void, or erase, the sale after the guest has departed. In this way, total sales would equal the amount of the cash drawer. If the cashier then destroys the guest check involved with this sale, the remaining guest checks, cash register total sales figure, and cash drawer would all balance. To prevent this, management should insist that all cash register voids be performed by a supervisor or at least be authorized by management on an individual basis. In addition, because cash registers record the number and often the time at which voids are performed, these, too, should be monitored by management.

Another method of cashier theft involves the manipulation of complimentary meals or meal coupons. Assume, for example, that, at your Pie Parlor, you have produced and distributed a large number of guest coupons good for a free piece of pie. If the cashier has access to these coupons, it is possible to collect the money from a guest without a coupon and then add the coupon to the cash drawer while simultaneously removing sales revenue equal to the value of the coupon. A variation on this theme is for the cashier to declare a check to be complimentary after the guest has paid the bill. In cases like this, the cashier would again remove sales revenue from the cash register in an amount equal to the "comped" check. This kind of fraud can be prevented by denying cashiers access to unredeemed cash value coupons and by requiring special authorization from management to "comp" guest checks.

While the previous scenarios do not list all possible methods of revenue loss, it should be clear that you must have a complete revenue security system if you are to ensure that all product sold generates sales revenue that finds its way into your bank account. It is to this matter, the development of an effective revenue control system, that we now turn our attention. It is important to remember that even good revenue control systems present the opportunity for theft if management is not vigilant or if two or more employees conspire to defraud the operation. It may not be possible to prevent all types of theft, but a good revenue control system should help you determine if, in fact, a theft has occurred. It is then up to you to investigate and take appropriate action, from disciplining employees to contacting the police for assistance.

Bonding

Employees of a foodservice establishment may be bonded as a method of insuring against employee theft. **Bonding** is simply a matter of purchasing an insurance policy against the possibility that an employee will steal. If an employee has been bonded and an operation can determine that he or she was indeed involved in the theft of a specific amount of money, the operation will be reimbursed for the loss by the bonding company. While bonding will not completely eliminate theft, it is relatively inexpensive and well worth the cost to require that all employees who handle cash or other forms of operational revenue be bonded. It is also an excellent pre-employment check to verify an employee's track record in prior jobs.

Developing the Revenue Security System

An effective revenue security system will help you accomplish the following important tasks:

1. Verification of product issues
2. Verification of guest charges
3. Verification of sales receipts
4. Verification of sales deposits

You must consider each of these four areas when developing a total revenue security system. Obviously, each foodservice operation will have a different manner of both selling products and accounting for revenue. It is useful, however, to view the revenue control system for any unit in terms of these four key points and how they relate to each other. In an ideal world, a product would be sold, its sale recorded, its selling price collected, and the funds deposited in the foodservice operation's bank account, all in a single step. Rapid advances in the area of computers and "smart" cards are making this a reality for more foodservice operators each day. The following example from the grocery industry helps illustrate just how this works.

A grocery store customer uses his or her bank-issued debit card when buying a frozen entrée dinner. The cashier, in this instance, uses a scanner to read the bar code printed on the frozen entrée dinner. The following actions then take place:

1. The amount the shopper owes the store is recorded in the POS system and the sale itself is assigned a tracking number (verification of product issued/sold).

2. The sale amount is displayed for the guest who is asked to confirm its correctness; if it is correct, a receipt is printed for the shopper (verification of guest check accuracy).

3. The store POS system records the amount of the sale as well as the form of payment used by this shopper (verification of sales receipts).

4. The shopper's debit card number is attached to this specific sales tracking number and a transfer of funds takes place from the shopper's account to that of the grocery store (verification of deposit).

Of course, not all foodservice operations have the technological sophistication to duplicate the system described in our grocery store example. Foodservice operators should, however, adapt the technology they currently have available to the development of good revenue control systems. This can be done without the use of computers, although few, if any, serious control system specialists today would recommend that a control system be built without a solid reliance on the speed and accuracy of a computer. It is important to note, however, that you must design the control system *first* and then decide which aspects of the system are best computerized. Remember that computers do not *bring* controls to an operation. They can, however, assist you in making your control systems work faster and with less human effort.

In all cases, the foodservice manager should have a thorough understanding of how the revenue security system works and, thus, what is required to maintain it. To illustrate the four-step process of revenue security, consider the situation of Faris, who operates a Lebanese restaurant in New York City. Faris considers his restaurant to be a family-oriented establishment. It has a small cocktail area and 100 guest seats in the dining room. Total revenue at Faris' exceeds $1 million per year. When he started the restaurant, he did not give a tremendous amount of thought to the design of his revenue control system because he was in the restaurant at all times. Due to his success, however, he spends more and more of his time developing a second restaurant and, thus, needs both the security of an adequate revenue security system and the ability to review it quickly to evaluate the sales levels of his original store. Thus, Faris has begun to develop a revenue security system, concentrating on the following formula:

Product Issues = Guest Charges = Sales Receipts = Sales Deposits

He knows that sophisticated computer systems are on the market because he regularly attends restaurant trade shows. However, he does not wish to overspend on a revenue security system in terms of either equipment or time. He wants to make sure that he does not find himself spending hours of labor or thousands of dollars buying a control system that does not achieve the goals he has set for his operation. Faris knows that the first goal he must achieve is that of verifying his product sales.

Step 1. Verification of Product Issues

The key to verification of product issues in the revenue security system is to follow one basic rule: *No product shall be issued from the kitchen or bar unless a permanent record of issue is made.* In its simplest terms, this means that the kitchen should not fill any server request for food unless that request has been documented in this step of the control system. In many restaurants, the server request for food or beverages will take the form of a multicopy, written guest check, designed specifically for the purpose of revenue control. When this is the case, the top copy of this multicopy form would generally be sent to the kitchen or bar. The guest check, in this case, becomes the documented request for the food or beverage product. In other cases, the order information could be sent to the production area by way of a computer. When this is the case, the order information is viewed by the production staff on a computer terminal, or, in other cases, the computer system prints a hard copy of the order for the production staff. In this case, the software within the computer keeps the permanent record of the request. In every case, however, there should be a permanent documented order that authorizes the kitchen to prepare food or the bar to prepare a drink. In a quick-service restaurant also, no food should be given to the guest unless that sale has been recorded. If a foodservice operation elects to supply its employees with meals during work shifts, these meals, too, should be recorded in the system.

In the bar, this principle of verifying all product sales is even more important. Bartenders should be instructed never to issue a drink unless that drink has first been recorded on a guest check or in the POS system. This should be the procedure, even if the bartender is working alone.

This rule regarding product issuing is important for two reasons. In the first place, requiring a permanent documented order ensures that there is a record of each product sale. Second, this record of product sales can be used to verify both proper inventory usage and product sales totals. Faris enforces this basic rule by requiring that no menu item be served from his kitchen or the bar without a written record of the sale. To do so, Faris implements a precheck/postcheck system. As stated earlier, a precheck/postcheck system is used to match product issues with sales receipts. The precheck portion of the system, however, also fills the requirement that no menu item be issued from kitchen or bar without first documenting its sale.

If his verification of product sales system is working correctly, Faris will find that the following formula should hold true:

Documented Product Requests = Product Issues

Documentation of product sales can be done with or without a precheck/postcheck system. Regardless of the approach you select, however, good revenue control demands that no product be issued without a written guest check or its documented equivalent.

Step 2. Verification of Guest Charges

When the production staff is required to distribute products only in response to a documented request, it is critical that those documented requests result in charges to the guest. It makes little sense to enforce a verification of product issues step without also requiring the service staff to ensure that guest charges match these requests. This concept can be summarized as follows: *Product issues must equal guest charges.* There are a variety of ways this can be achieved. To illustrate this point, consider the case of Faris who could use a manual guest check system of verifying guest charges or use a completely computerized POS system.

If Faris uses manually completed guest checks as a primary control device, the effort is to ensure that product issues equal guest check totals. If they do, all issued products will result in appropriate charges to the guest. Figure 11.4 is a sample of a guest check in use at Faris'. Note that the check is numbered on both the top and the bottom, or guest receipt portion.

If guest checks are used as a control device, it is important to remember that the numbers on the checks are of no operational value if the checks are not tightly controlled. Each guest check must be accounted for, and employees must know that they will be held responsible for each check they are issued. This is because an unscrupulous employee could present a guest check for payment to a guest, then destroy the check and keep the money. For this reason, "lost" guest checks should always be accounted for. To keep track of the checks issued to service personnel, you can use a guest check control form. Figure 11.5 is an example of such a form used at Faris'.

Note that this form recognizes that some guest checks can be lost or destroyed. When using the guest check system of verifying guest charges, you must be aware of these incidents when they occur and must investigate when it is determined that a check is missing. Each lost or destroyed check should be "approved" by management. That is, management should know why and how each missing check came to be missing!

As important as it is, manually controlling guest checks can be time consuming and arduous. A POS system simplifies this task and saves time by creating a unique transaction number (guest check) for each server request. That is, a documented request for products generates, within the

FIGURE **11.4**● Sample Guest Check

		Faris'		Phone #: 123-4567	
Date	**Table**	**Server**	**Guests**	**Check Number** 123456	
Items Ordered					**Price**
Subtotal					
Tax					
Gratuity					
Total					

Guest Receipt

Date	**Table**	**Server**	**Guests**	**Check Number** 123456	**Total**

FIGURE **11.5** ● Sample Guest Check Control Form

Faris'

Date: 1/1   Shift: Lunch

**Check Numbers
Issued**   **Check Numbers
Returned**

From	To	Issued To	From	To	Checks Used	Checks Accounted For	Number Missing
00001	00100	Beth	00055	00100	45	44	1
00101	00200	Sally	00130	00200	70	70	0
00201	00300	Gerry	00264	00300	36	36	0

Unaccounted Checks:

Check Number	Issued To	Explanation	Manager's Initials
00035	Beth	Torn by accident	D.K.H.

POS system, a guest check that is matched to that request. Guest checks cannot be "lost" on purpose, because the POS keeps a record of each transaction, as well as records attempts by employees to request a product, receive it from the kitchen or bar, and then "void" (subtract) the charge from the guest's bill.

When properly implemented, this second step of the revenue control system will result in the following formula:

Product Issues = Guest Charges

Regardless of whether Faris chooses to implement a manual guest check control system or purchase a POS system that includes this component, he now has two major revenue control components in place. The first one is that no product can be issued from the kitchen or bar unless the order is documented on a guest check; the second one is that all guest charges must match product issues.

With these two systems in place, Faris can deal with many problems. If, for example, a guest has "walked" his or her check, the kitchen would have a duplicate of the order. This allows management to know which products were sold to this guest, which server sold them, and perhaps additional information, such as the time of the sale, the number of guests in the party, and, of course, the sales value of the products. The precheck system Faris has in place is also useful in ensuring that service personnel do not attempt to write one item on the guest check but charge the guest a higher or lower price. A periodic audit of checks by management is necessary to help detect such fraud.

Furthermore, Faris has a strict policy regarding the documented prechecked record of employee meals. This has the added advantage of giving him a monthly total of the value of employee meals. Recall that he needs this figure to compute his cost of food sold. Faris is now ready for the next major component in a revenue security system, that is, the actual collection of guest payment.

Step 3. Verification of Sales Receipts

Sales receipts, as defined in this step, refer to actual revenue received by the cashier or other designated personnel, in payment for products served. In Faris' case, this means all sales revenue from his restaurant and lounge. If his revenue security system is working properly, he knows that the following formula should be in effect:

Guest Charges = Sales Receipts

Verifying sales receipts is more than a simple matter of counting cash at the end of a shift. In fact, cash handling, while it is an important part of the total sales receipt reconciliation, is only one part of the total sales receipt verification system. To illustrate this, consider Figure 11.6, the form Faris uses to verify his total sales receipts. He wishes to ensure that the amount of cash, checks, and bank card charges in his cash register matches the dollar amount of his guest checks. If this is so, he has accounted for all of his sales receipts, given that he has controlled for both product issues and guest charges.

As you can see, the form in Figure 11.6 registers both guest charges (from the guest checks) and the money Faris has collected. Depending on the type of operation, guest check totals may be done by machine only. This is the case in a cafeteria, where food purchases may be totaled and paid for at the same time. In such instances, the POS system or cash register itself provides the guest check total. In Faris' case, physical guest checks are used along with this essential principle: *Both the cashier and a supervisor must verify sales receipts.* Figure 11.6 indicates that the sales receipt verification is made by both the cashier and the supervisor. While this will not prevent possible collusion by this pair, it is extremely important that sales receipt verification be a two-person process.

Note that the function of Figure 11.6 is to require Faris' staff to reconcile guest check totals with actual revenue (sales receipts). Overages or shortages are entered and, if they exceed predetermined allowable limits, are investigated by management. Service charges, the second entry on the form, are special charges assessed to guests. Faris assesses a service charge of 15% on all parties larger than eight persons. Observe also that guest check revenue consists of all sales, service charges, and taxes. This is the total amount of revenue the operation should have received on this date. Sales receipts refer to all forms of revenue, such as cash, checks (if accepted), and bank cards. In addition, note that Faris must subtract the value of his starting cash bank and any tip-outs or gratuities due to service personnel. These gratuities are typically added to bank card vouchers by the guest, but paid out to the service personnel by management either in cash or on their paychecks as such income is taxable to the server.

Note also that Figure 11.6 has a space to indicate cash overages and shortages (variance). It will be up to you, as the manager, to determine the level of variance you are comfortable with as far as this reconciliation is concerned. Some foodservice operators allow no variance whatsoever. Others routinely ignore minor variances. The level of variance that is tolerated is greatly affected by the method of guest payment collection that is in place. In general, there are four basic payment arrangements in use in the typical foodservice operation. They are as follows:

1. Guest pays cashier.
2. Guest pays service personnel, who pay cashier.
3. Guest pays service personnel, who have already paid cashier.
4. Guest is direct billed.

FIGURE **11.6** ● Sales Receipt Report

Faris'

Date: 1/1
Shift: Dinner

Performed By:
Cashier: Tammi F.
Supervisor: Faris L.

Revenue per Guest Check

Guest check totals	$7,500.00	
Service charges	450.00	
Tax	618.00	
Total guest check revenue		$8,568.00

Receipts
Charge cards

VISA	893.00	
MasterCard	495.00	
Discover	1,200.00	
American Express	975.00	
Total charge cards receipts	3,563.00	

Cash

Twenties and larger	$4,840.00	
Tens	1,480.00	
Fives	240.00	
Ones	196.00	
Change	68.20	
Total cash	6,824.20	

Less: Bank	500.00	
Tip-outs	1,320.00	

Net cash receipts	5,004.20	
Net total receipts		8,567.20
Variance check revenue to net receipts		$ (0.80)

Guest Pays Cashier   In this situation, a common one in the hospitality industry, losses can occur primarily due to guest walks. Obviously, this collection system works best in quick-service and cafeteria settings where a guest does not actually receive his or her food or beverage until the bill has been paid. It works less well in a busy table service restaurant where a cashier may simply be too preoccupied to notice whether each individual who has consumed a product has indeed paid the bill before leaving. Only a few guests are dishonest, but these few will account for some walked checks in this collection system. In addition, under this system, cashiers could collect funds, destroy a guest check, and claim a guest has walked with his or her bill.

Guest Pays Service Personnel, Who Pay Cashier   In this situation, the server simply presents the bill to the guest and then accepts payment, which is taken to the cashier for processing. Under this system, the guest's change is returned by the service personnel along with the receipt, if appropriate. An advantage of this system is that it is more difficult for guests to walk their checks, since it is easier for servers to watch their own tables than it is for a cashier to observe an entire dining room. A second advantage is that the guest is not required to stand in line to pay his or her bill during a busy period. A disadvantage of the system is that guests may have to wait longer than desired to settle their bill if service personnel do not notice when they are finished with their meal. This can be the case especially when the operation is very busy.

From a control perspective, it is good practice to separate into at least two parts the processes of requesting food or beverage products and delivering them, and totaling the guest check and collecting payment. While this will not completely prevent collusion on the part of the service personnel and cashier, it does make it more difficult to defraud the operation.

Guest Pays Service Personnel, Who Have Already Paid Cashier   This method of payment, also known as working with individual cash drawers or cash banks, is popular in some restaurants and many beverage operations. In this scenario, each server begins his or her shift with a predetermined cash bank, which either is his or her own or is issued by management. As the kitchen or bar fills guest orders, the service personnel *purchase* these products from the kitchen or bar and use their own bank to fund the purchase. The server will then collect final payment from the guest. In this manner, each server is responsible for the total of his or her bank only, since all food and beverages were purchased at the time they were issued.

In some beverage operations, a record is made of each drink issued to an individual server. Funds equal to the sales value of those drinks are then collected from the server at the conclusion of his or her shift rather than having the bartender and server settle their cash accounts after each drink is issued because, in a very busy operation, this would require much time and effort. Using this system, where the guest pays the service personnel who have already "paid" the cashier, management has less concern regarding the cash overages or shortages of each server's bank, since all products are paid for at the time they are issued (or collected at the end of the shift). It is important to note, however, that this collection system is not under direct management control. Service personnel can defraud guests, and guest checks can be walked without management's knowledge. In addition, employees may resent this system as it makes them personally responsible for guest walks, instead of the operation itself sharing some of the risk.

Guest Is Direct Billed In some situations, guests are not billed immediately upon finishing their meal, beverages, or reception. This is often the case in hotel food and beverage operations as well as those restaurants with banquet facilities. When this is the case, creditworthy guests are invoiced for the value of the products they have consumed. When this form of billing is employed, it is important that the invoice accurately reflect all guest charges. Consider, for example, the case of Faris, who agrees to provide a wedding banquet. The guest who arranged the event guarantees a count of 90 guests, but on the evening of the dinner, 100 guests actually attend. The guest should be billed for 100 if all were served, and payment by the guest should reflect that. In this manner, the principles of revenue control are still in place; that is, guest charges should equal revenue collected. Figure 11.7 is an example of a banquet event order/invoice (guest check) for Faris' that is used in such a case.

Accounts receivable is the term used to refer to guest charges that have been billed to the guest but not yet collected. Too high an accounts receivable amount is not good, as the foodservice operation will have paid for the products consumed by the guest and the labor to serve the products but has not yet collected from the guests for these. In addition, collecting money after a guest has left your operation can be more difficult as time passes. For these reasons, you must be diligent in collecting accounts receivable.

Special Revenue Collection Situations In some cases, variations on the four payment systems can be in place. For example, consider the drink ticket, or coupon, often sold in hotel reception areas for use at cocktail receptions. These coupons should be treated as if they were cash, for, in fact, they are its equivalent. Thus, those individuals who are selling the coupons should not be the same ones as those dispensing the beverages. In addition, the collected drink coupons should equal the number of drinks served. While the form required to verify this will vary, based on each operation's drink price policy, such an instrument should be in use.

A second special pricing situation is the reduced-price coupon. Coupons are popular in the hospitality industry and can take a variety of forms such as 50 % off a specific purchase, "buy-one-get-one-free" pro-

FIGURE **11.7** ● Banquet Event Order/Invoice

Faris'   Date: 1/1

Banquet Event Order/Invoice

Day of Event: _____ Date of Event: _____

Time of Event: _____ to _____ Time Ready By: _____

Type of Event: _____ Location: _____

Expected Count: _____ Guaranteed Count: _____ Final Count: _____

Organization Hosting Event: _____

Organization Contact Person: _____

Organization Address: _____

Organization Telephone: _____ Fax: _____ E-Mail: _____

Price: _____ Tax: _____ Service Charge: _____ %

Deposit Amount: _____ Deposit Received: _____

Total Amount Due: _____ Payment Due Date: _____

Menu	**Setup (Style of Room, A/V)**
	Linen
Wines/Liquors	**Decor/Flowers**

Signature of Guest: _____ Date: _____

Signature of Manager: _____ Date: _____

motions, or a program whereby a guest who buys a predetermined number of meals gets the next one free. In all of these cases, the coupon should be treated as its cash equivalent because, from a revenue control perspective, these coupons are like cash.

With his guest charges reconciled to sales receipts, Faris now moves to Step 4 of the revenue security process.

Step 4. Verification of Sales Deposits

It is recommended that only management make the actual bank deposit of daily sales revenue. The deposit slip may be completed by a cashier or other clerical assistant, but management alone should bear the responsibility for monitoring the actual deposit of sales. This concept can be summarized as follows: *Management must personally verify all bank deposits.* This involves the actual verification of the contents of the deposit and the process of matching bank deposits with actual sales. These two numbers obviously should match. That is, if you deposit Thursday's sales on Friday, the Friday deposit should match the sales amount of Thursday. If it does not, you have experienced some loss of revenue that has occurred after your cashier has reconciled sales receipts to guest charges. **Embezzlement** is the term used to describe theft of a type where the money, although legally possessed by the embezzler, is diverted to the embezzler by his or her fraudulent action. Embezzlement is a crime that often goes undetected for long periods of time because the embezzler is usually a trusted employee. Falsification of bank deposits is a common method of embezzlement. To prevent this activity, you should take the following steps to protect your deposits:

1. Make bank deposits daily if possible.
2. Ensure that the individual making the daily deposit is bonded.
3. Establish written policies for completing bank reconciliations (comparison of monthly bank statements vs. daily deposits).
4. Review and approve bank statement reconciliations each month.
5. Employ an outside auditor to examine the accuracy of deposits on an annual basis.

If verification of sales deposits is done correctly and no embezzlement is occurring, the following formula should hold true:

$$\text{Sales Receipts} = \text{Sales Deposits}$$

If he follows these steps, Faris will have now completed his revenue security system. Its four key principles are as follows:

1. No product shall be issued from the kitchen or bar unless a permanent record of issue is made.
2. Product issues must equal guest charges.
3. Both the cashier and a supervisor must verify sales receipts.
4. Management must personally verify all bank deposits.

It is possible to develop and maintain a completely manual revenue control system. That is, each of the four major components of the revenue control system described in this chapter can be instituted without the aid of a computer or even a cash register. In today's world, however, such an approach is both wasteful of time and suspect in accuracy. The simple fact is that the amount of information you need to effectively operate your business grows constantly. Guest dining choices, vendor pricing, inventory levels, payroll statistics, and revenue control are simply a few of the issues involving the huge amount of data collection and manipulation your business demands. Fortunately, technologies exist to easily and quickly assemble the data you need to make good management decisions. It is dangerous for a foodservice manager to expect that a computer system will "bring" control to an operation. That happens rarely! A computer may, however, take good control systems that have been designed by management and add to them in terms of speed, accuracy, or additional information.

If you hope to improve your revenue security or any other cost control system in the operation, a computerized system will be of immense value. If, however, your operation has no controls and you are not committed to the control process, the computer will simply become a high-tech adding machine, used primarily to sum up guest checks and nothing more. Properly selected and understood, however, technology-enhanced systems can be a powerful ally in the cost control/revenue security system. It is to that use of technology and its successful integration that we now turn our attention in the next and final chapter of this text.

Key Terms and Concepts

The following are terms and concepts discussed in the chapter that are important for you as a manager. To help you review, please define the terms below.

Walk or skip (the bill)
Credit card
Debit card
Quick-change artist
Guest check
Precheck/postcheck system

Short
Over
Bonding
Accounts receivable
Embezzlement

Test Your Skills

1. Trisha Sangus manages a large hotel. Recently, her hotel controller identified a problem in one of the hotel dining rooms. Essentially, one of the evening cashiers was voiding product sales after they had been rung up on the cash register, then removing an equal amount of money from the cash drawer so that the drawer balanced at the end of the shift. What procedures would you recommend to Trisha to prevent a further occurrence of this type incident? Assume that a precheck/postcheck guest check system is in place.

2. Counterfeit money is a problem for all U.S. businesses, including those in the hospitality industry. The U.S. Department of Treasury has developed educational aids to assist managers who must train those who handle cash. To do so, they have compiled information that is critical in the detection of imitation currency and coins.

   FUN ON THE WEB!

   Go to this U.S. Secret Service site to learn about how to detect counterfeit money.

   www.treas.gov/usss Click on "Know Your Money," then click on "How to Detect Counterfeit Money" to see what discrepancies to look for on counterfeit bills.

   Prepare a training session appropriate for cashiers who may routinely be responsible for the detection of counterfeit money. Include a memo to your cashiers detailing what they should do if they suspect a bill is counterfeit.

3. Mary Margaret and Blue are the owners/operators of an extremely upscale bakery goods boutique, and they are interested in a complete asset control system that includes protection of both products and revenue. Identify two control devices/procedures that they could implement to help them control revenue security in the following areas, and explain your reason for choosing each.
   a. Product issues
   b. Guest charges
   c. Sales receipts
   d. Sales deposits

4. Each of the following payment methods allows for potential employee and/or guest theft. Assume that Debbie operates a semiprivate country club where club members and the general public may purchase products in a variety of settings. Specify at least two potential methods of

theft for each of the following, as well as a description of the specific procedures Debbie should implement to prevent such theft.

a. Guest pays cashier.
b. Guest pays service personnel, who pay cashier.
c. Guest pays service personnel, who have already paid cashier.
d. Guest is direct billed.

Chapter

USING TECHNOLOGY TO ENHANCE CONTROL SYSTEMS

OVERVIEW   In this chapter, you will learn how to evaluate current and changing technology and its potential impact on your cost control system. Technological advances occur rapidly and it is important that you understand their advantages and limitations as well. Because computer hardware, software, and communications systems are continuously evolving, it is critical that you realize both what is available currently and, just as important, how to monitor and evaluate advances in those technologies currently under development.

CHAPTER OUTLINE

Role of Technology in Cost Control Systems
Applications Programs for Cost Control
Purchasing Technology Products
Monitoring Advances in Cost Control Technology
Key Terms and Concepts, and Test Your Skills

HIGHLIGHTS   At the conclusion of this chapter, you will be able to:

○ Identify areas where technology can be used to improve the cost control system.
○ Evaluate cost control technology enhancements based on their ability to better existing control programs.
○ Monitor technological developments within the cost control area.

Role of Technology in Cost Control Systems

There is no question that the future of foodservice revenue and expense management will be heavily influenced by the ever-expanding capabilities of technologically advanced cost control–related systems. While it is not expected that you will become an expert in the area of developing technological applications for cost control systems, technology advances certainly will continue to influence how you and your competitors will operate your businesses. Having successfully mastered the material in this text, you *are* an expert at cost control systems. You can also become an expert at evaluating the appropriateness of purchasing and integrating advanced technological systems to assist you in your own cost control efforts.

According to the U.S. Bureau of the Census, total foodservice sales have risen approximately 4 to 7 percent each year during the 1990s, with an average increase of 6 to 7 percent from 2000 through the present. Business in the hospitality industry is good and getting even better. Increased growth in the foodservice industry has occurred at the same time significant advances have occurred in the following three cost control–related technology areas:

1. Software
2. Hardware
3. Communications systems

In most cases, operators seeking to use technology to enhance their cost control systems are interested in one or more of the following goals:

1. New information
2. More accurate information collection
3. More convenient collection of information
4. Better communication of information
5. Improved analysis of information

Consider the case of Csilla Pomeroy. After a successful career operating restaurants for others, Csilla has launched her own business as a restaurant consultant. Her new business is doing well. The owners of the End Zone, a large, successful urban steakhouse restaurant, have recently hired Csilla as a consultant. She has been asked to evaluate the cost control systems in place and make recommendations for systems improvements. Using one specific example, assume, for a moment, that Csilla determines beverage cost controls in the establishment are insufficient in the areas of product cost control, labor cost control, and revenue security. Assessing the five goals identified previously, Csilla can evaluate the effectiveness of the current cost control systems and communicate to the owners exactly why and where improvements should be undertaken.

While rapid advances in technology have made computer-related systems more versatile and flexible, there are disadvantages as well as advantages in using them. Unfortunately, they can sometimes become so complicated that they generate great quantities of data, much of which is ignored by management. It is important to remember that technological improvements can encompass everything from advancement in a simple electronic cash register to property-specific, networked training delivered via the Internet in a multilanguage format. Regardless of the system improvement you consider integrating, when you evaluate its appropriateness for your operation, you should analyze the proposed purchase with an eye toward answering the following questions:

1. What information am I currently collecting?
2. What information would be valuable to collect/disseminate if time permitted?
3. What specific management actions could be undertaken if the information in question 2 were known?
4. What savings are likely to result from these management actions?
5. If savings do not immediately result from the improved system, how will its purchase add to the profitability of the operation?

All managers collect information, either formally or informally. The problem is knowing what information is worth collecting and, most important, what to do with that information. That is, how will you use the information collected to make better decisions? If this question cannot be answered specifically, the information will likely be of little use.

Once you know what information is desirable to you and, just as important, with whom you must communicate that information, you can evaluate the appropriateness of purchasing enhanced software, hardware, and communications systems for your own operation.

Applications Programs for Cost Control

Perhaps no area of foodservice management has undergone more change in the last 10 years than that of applying improvements in technology to the task of controlling costs. Indeed, it is rare today to find any foodservice operation that does not incorporate some level of technology into its cost control efforts. A discussion of applying technology to cost control can be complex because the application of the technology itself can be complex. For purposes of cost control analysis, however, it is helpful to view technological applications as those involved with one of three areas:

1. Software
2. Hardware
3. Communication devices

It should be stated at the outset that this three-way division of technology, while very useful, is certainly an artificial one. Returning to the example of Csilla, the consultant hired to improve the cost control systems of the End Zone steakhouse, assume that she sent an e-mail documenting her findings to the owners of the restaurant. This rapid form of communication relies on the actual e-mail program (software) contained on Csilla's laptop computer (hardware), both of which combine to send the message via a telephone modem (communication device) to create a unique method of allowing her to inform the owners of her findings.

For purposes of this chapter, however, it will be useful to evaluate technology in the areas of software, hardware, and communication devices, despite the fact that these technologies indeed can overlap and in nearly all cases are interdependent on one another.

Software

It is the software that you will most often first think about when considering technological upgrades to your cost control system. **Software** consists of the actual computer programs that generate the cost-related information you will use in your job. In our hypothetical case of Csilla, the restaurant consultant, it is these software programs that will provide her and the restaurant's owners with the information they need to make good decisions about controlling and analyzing the costs at the End Zone steakhouse.

Many companies offer their own versions of software developed exclusively for the hospitality industry. Alternatively, you can purchase generic software such as Microsoft's Excel program (used in this text) and customize it to create some of your own control programs. Regardless of the source, it is important to remember that you should select and maintain only those programs you will find useful. There are usually real dollar costs associated with accumulating data. These costs can occur in staff time, training, equipment, materials, and management time. To gather data with no intention of using that data simply wastes your time and the money you invest in the program. Of course, since many cost control software programs are sold in a bundled form, that is, they include multiple pieces of applications, you may find that selecting software requires you to choose a program that gives you all the features you want but may also include some features you find less useful.

For example, assume that you are interested in carefully monitoring your *overtime* labor costs. You check the market and find that the best, most cost effective labor-related software package on the market has been designed to:

1. Compute check average per server.
2. Monitor tip allocation and tip credit information.
3. Track employee and management overtime.
4. Compute total wages for employees working at multiple pay rates in the same payroll-reporting period.

5. Maintain payroll check and total wages paid history by employee and department.
6. Monitor employee vacation, sick leave, and "comp" time records.

Note that the program offers six unique functions, including item 3, the one of interest to you. If this program is competitively priced and operates effectively, you might elect to purchase it, despite the fact that it may contain one or more features that, while they could be important to some managers, do not reflect your specific areas of concern.

If you visit a hospitality trade show at the state or national level, you will likely encounter a large number of vendors, each touting the virtues of their own software approach to cost control as well as other managerial tasks. While many of these software producers are quite good, the focus of this chapter is on "what" the programs can do, rather than who produces them.

One convenient way to assess the software programs on the market today is to match them with the cost control topics presented in this text. Csilla, the consultant to the End Zone steakhouse, could find it very helpful to follow this text's outline as she investigates the current software offerings available to the restaurant's owners.

Managing Revenue and Expense–Chapter 1 In Chapter 1 of this text, we introduced the concept of profit and the P&L (income) statement, which was further examined in Chapter 9. There are a variety of software programs on the market that develop this statement for you. You simply fill in the revenue and expense portions of the program, and a P&L is produced. Variations include programs that compare your results to budgeted figures or forecasts, to prior-month performance, or to prior-year performance. In addition, P&L's can be produced for any time period, including months, quarters, or years. Most income statement programs will have a budgeting feature and the ability to maintain historical sales and cost records.

Managing your overall operation will require you to communicate with employees, guests, and vendors. Thus, the software you will need includes office products for word processing, spreadsheet building, faxes, and e-mail. If Csilla were advising the owners of the End Zone steakhouse, she would certainly want them to select a P&L program and an office management program as part of their computerized cost efforts.

A second issue, and one that must be kept foremost in mind, is that of information accessibility. An executive chef, for example, would certainly need to have information on food cost available to him or her. At the same time, it may not be wise to allow servers access to payroll information that, while it certainly affects costs, should only be shared with those who need to know. Thus, as you examine the following technology-assisted cost control options available to you, keep in mind that not all information should be accessible to all parties, and that security of your cost information can be just as critical as accuracy.

Determining Sales Forecasts–Chapter 2 The importance of accurate sales histories for forecasting sales was presented in Chapter 2. Cost-related software in this area can be a tremendous asset and includes programs that can:

1. Track sales by guest count.
2. Track sales by date.
3. Monitor cash vs. credit sales.
4. Maintain products sold histories.
5. Maintain check average data.
6. Compare actual sales to prior-period sales.
7. Maintain rolling sales averages.
8. Forecast future sales in increments:
   a. Monthly
   b. Weekly
   c. Daily
   d. By meal period
   e. Hourly
   f. Portions of an hour (i.e., 15 min., 30 min., etc.)
9. Maintain actual sales to forecast sales histories.
10. Maintain reservations systems:
    a. Automate advanced bookings up to two years in advance.
    b. Track no-shows and cancellations.
    c. Build a guest database for mailings and e-mailings.
    d. Track guest birthdays, favorite tables, food preferences, etc.

For those operations that rely on reservations to control bookings, software of this type is available to instantly identify repeat guests, giving the operator a display screen that can include such information as frequency of visit, purchase preferences, and total dollars spent in the operation. In addition, reservations software makes it possible for operators to reward repeat guests by developing their own "frequent dining" programs, similar to the airlines' frequent-flyer programs. In addition, reservations-related programs like these can store information on reservation demand, predict optimal reservation patterns, identify frequent no-show guests, and even allow guests to make their own reservations via on-line Internet connections.

Depending on the level of information required by the owners of the End Zone steakhouse, Csilla would, of course, want her software recommendations to include one or more of the features mentioned previously so the management of the End Zone could accurately predict future sales levels.

Managing the Cost of Food—Chapter 3 In Chapter 3, the focus was on managing food-related costs by controlling the areas of purchasing, receiving, storage, and issuing. In addition, computing food costs through the use of the food cost percentage and average cost per guest was introduced. Software programs that can assist in this area include those related to the following items.

Recipes

1. Maintain standardized recipes.
2. Cost standardized recipes.
3. Allow for computer-assisted recipe quantity conversion.
4. Maintain and supply dietary information by portion.
5. Create ingredient lists for purchase or issue from storeroom.
6. Suggest alternative cooking methods.
7. Supply color picture of finished product.
8. Create purchase orders based on production forecasts.
9. Create suggested selling price based on cost.

Menus

1. Create and print physical menus.
2. Create cycle menus based on management-supplied parameters.
3. Produce production schedules based on selected menus.
4. Produce equipment usage plans based on selected menus.
5. Produce purchase orders based on selected menus.
6. Create and cost catering/special-event menus.
7. Forecast revenue and expense based on selected menu and forecasted sales.

Purchasing

1. Create vendor bid sheets based on forecasted ingredient needs.
2. Compare bids and make purchase recommendations based on best cost/best value.
3. Maintain vendor price histories.
4. Maintain vendor invoice database.
5. Establish minimum and maximum par values by ingredient.
6. Create purchase orders and auto-order based on established par levels with automatic electronic order confirmation.
7. Interface (if desirable) with other systems to create aggregate purchase orders (in multiunit settings).
8. Create purchase recap by item.
9. Create purchase recap by vendor.
10. Maintain a "red-flag" system for product purchasing variances that exceed forecasted usage.
11. Utilize purchase orders to predict actual profitability.
12. Purchase directly from vendor using vendor-supplied software.

Receiving

1. Prepare daily receiving report.
2. Compare product received (receiving records) with purchase orders (POs) in areas of:
   a. Weight
   b. Quantity
   c. Quality
   d. Price
3. Maintain outage and shortage records by vendor.
4. Verify vendor price extensions.
5. Maintain receiving histories.

Storage/Inventory

1. Maintain product inventory values by food category (i.e., produce, meat, dairy, etc.).
2. Create shopping lists through production of daily inventory and comparison with production schedules.
3. Report par stock levels.
4. Report daily storeroom issues.
5. Report daily product usage.
6. Maintain perpetual inventory.
7. Compute LIFO or FIFO inventory values.
8. Maintain inventory products database by vendor, storeroom location, product type, alpha order, etc.
9. Report below-par inventory levels.
10. Report daily cost of goods sold.
11. Report product usage variances based on actual sales.
12. Interface with handheld bar code readers for accurate inventory count and price extension.
13. Compute inventory loss rates.

Cost of Goods Sold

1. Compare forecasted to actual cost of goods sold.
2. Maintain employee meal records.
3. Compare actual cost of goods sold to ideal food cost.
4. Compute cost of goods sold by menu category (i.e., salad, entrée, dessert, etc.).
5. Compare current cost of goods sold with:
   a. Same unit historical data
   b. Same unit budgeted cost data
   c. Multiunit operation averages (for multiunit operations)
   d. Industry- or management-generated standards

Perhaps it is in the area of managing food products, from their purchase to usage, that you can most effectively utilize the technological tools available today. Remember that the amount of information that can be generated in this case is vast, and you should elect to gather and maintain only information that is of real value to you.

Managing the Cost of Beverages–Chapter 4 Chapter 4 introduced cost control concepts related to beverages. For those operations that sell a significant amount of alcoholic beverage products, there are a variety of programs designed to discourage theft and track product sales. In fact, the software and hardware available in the beverage area is generally more sophisticated than that found in most food-related areas. Programs available include those that can help you:

1. Monitor product sales.
2. Monitor product usage.
3. Calculate actual and targeted pour percentages.
4. Adjust product costs for happy hours and specials, as well as product transfers to and from the kitchen.
5. Maintain product inventory.
6. Establish par stock quantities and values.
7. Generate purchase orders.
8. Schedule employees based on forecasted sales levels.
9. Create and print wine and specials menus.
10. Maintain sales histories.

It is important to realize that some bar-related software is dependent on specific and sometimes expensive automated pour systems. This must be considered when selecting these programs. In the End Zone steakhouse example, Csilla would undoubtedly recommend that the owners select programs that could assist them in controlling bar-related costs.

Managing the Food and Beverage Production Process–Chapter 5 In the past, restaurants were slow to install working computer terminals in kitchen areas where production staff could easily use them. Increasingly, however, these installations are being made. Chapter 5 introduced the control concepts needed in the production area. These control efforts are often shared between management and the production staff. Programs available include those that can help both you and your production staff members:

1. Perform nutrition-related analysis of menu items, including:
    a. Recipe nutrient analysis
    b. Diet analysis
    c. FDA (Food and Drug Administration) food labels
    d. Diabetic exchange
    e. Weight management components
2. Develop production schedules based on forecasted sales:
    a. Weekly
    b. Daily
    c. By meal period
3. Create product requisition (issues) lists based on forecasted sales.

4. Compute actual versus ideal costs based on product issues.
5. Estimate and compute daily food cost.
6. Maintain physical or perpetual inventory; compute inventory turnover rates.
7. Maintain product usage record by:
   a. Vendor
   b. Product
   c. Food category
   d. Menu item
8. Compare portions served to portions produced to monitor overportioning.
9. Suggest usage for carryover products.
10. Conduct "make versus buy" calculations to optimize employee productivity and minimize costs.

Managing Food and Beverage Pricing–Chapter 6 Chapter 6 introduced the menu formats most often encountered by hospitality managers, the factors affecting menu prices, and the procedures used to assign individual menu item prices based on cost and sales data. The mathematical computations required to evaluate the effectiveness of individual menu items and to establish their prices can be complex, and there is a wide range of software available that can help you:

1. Develop menus and cost recipes.
2. Design and print menu "specials" for meal periods or happy hours.
3. Compute and analyze item contribution margin.
4. Compute and analyze item and overall food cost percentage.
5. Price banquet menus and bars based on known product costs.
6. Evaluate profitability of individual menu items.
7. Estimate future item demand based on past purchase patterns.
8. Assign individual menu item prices based on management-supplied parameters.

Menu analysis and pricing software is often packaged as part of a larger program. Its importance, however, is great. It is an area that will likely see rapid development in the future as software makers seek additional ways to improve their products.

Managing the Cost of Labor–Chapter 7 Increasingly, the cost of labor exceeds that of food products for many foodservice managers. Chapter 7 detailed procedures for controlling these labor costs. If the End Zone steakhouse were like most restaurants, Csilla would find this an extremely important area as she seeks to help the restaurant's owners. In fact, her reputation as a consultant able to consistently assist her clients is likely to be made, in large part, on her ability to help her clients control labor costs. Current software programs that can help control labor costs include those that:

1. Maintain employment records such as:
   a. Required employment documents (i.e., applications, I-9's, W-2's, etc.)
   b. Tax data
   c. Pay rates
   d. Department/cost center affiliation
   e. Benefits eligibility
   f. Training records
2. Conduct and record the results of on-line or computer-based training programs.
3. Compute voluntary and involuntary employee turnover rates by department.
4. Track employee lost days due to injury/accident.
5. Maintain employee availability records (requested days off, vacation, etc.).
6. Develop employee schedules and interface employee schedules with time clock systems.
7. Monitor overtime costs.
8. Maintain job descriptions and specifications.
9. Develop and maintain daily, weekly, and monthly productivity reports, including:
   a. Labor cost percentage
   b. Sales per labor hour
   c. Labor dollars per guest served
   d. Guests served per labor dollar
   e. Guests served per labor hour
   f. Optimal labor costs based on actual sales achieved
10. Interface employee scheduling component with forecasted sales volume software.

As the annual increase in the cost of labor continues to exceed that of food, you will find it ever more important to control the costs of labor. Monitoring your ability to do so will also become increasingly important. There is no doubt Csilla will want to carefully explain the advantages of the labor cost control software available to the owners of the End Zone so they fully understand its benefits as well as its limitations.

Controlling Other Expenses–Chapter 8 Those expenses that are neither food nor labor related were introduced in Chapter 8. Software that can be purchased to assist in this area include applications that relate to:

1. Monitoring utilities cost
2. Managing equipment maintenance records
3. Tracking marketing costs/benefits
4. Analysis of communications costs
5. Insurance-related cost analysis
6. Analysis of all other expense costs on a per-guest basis

7. Analysis of all other expense costs on a "cost per dollar sale" basis
8. Tax management

The unique needs of an individual restaurant will heavily influence which other expense–related software packages would be helpful. At the minimum, Csilla is likely to recommend that the owners of the End Zone computerize their records related to taxes at all levels to ensure accuracy, safekeeping, and timeliness.

Analyzing Results Using the Income Statement–Chapter 9 Chapter 9 introduced the concept of analysis as it relates to sales, expenses, and profits. In this area, software is quite advanced and the choices available to you will be many. The best of the programs on the market will:

1. Analyze operating trends (sales and costs) over management-established time periods.
2. Analyze food and beverage costs.
3. Analyze labor costs.
4. Analyze other expenses.
5. Analyze profits.
6. Compare operating results of multiple profit centers within one location or across several locations.
7. Interface with the point of sales (POS) system.
8. "Red flag" areas of potential management concern.
9. Suggest revisions to future budget periods based on current operating results.

The End Zone steakhouse will, without doubt, need an analysis package to help it evaluate the results of owners', managers', and staff efforts. A particularly important aspect of this package will be its ability to interface (connect) easily to other cost control packages and POS systems used in the facility.

Planning for Profit–Chapter 10 Chapter 10 introduced the concepts of conducting individual menu item analysis and identifying a break-even point for your operation. When this break-even point is known, an effective operational budget can be produced. While menu analysis software is often packaged as part of a larger program and is somewhat limited, the software required to do an overall break-even analysis is readily available, as well as that required for budgeting. Thus, software in this area is available to help you:

1. Evaluate item profitability based on:
   a. Food cost percentage
   b. Popularity
   c. Contribution margin
   d. Selling price

2. Conduct menu matrix analysis.
3. Perform break-even analysis.
4. Budget revenue.
5. Budget expense.
6. Budget profit levels.
7. Assemble budgets based on days, weeks, months, years, etc.
8. Conduct performance to budget analysis.
9. Maintain performance to budget histories.
10. Blend budgets from multiple profit centers.
11. Perform budgeted cash flow analysis.

It is not wise to attempt to operate an effective foodservice unit without a properly developed budget. In the case of the End Zone steakhouse, Csilla would certainly recommend a software package that includes this component.

Maintaining and Improving the Revenue Control System–Chapter 11
In Chapter 11, the principles of revenue control were introduced. In years past, the manual counting of money and balancing of cash drawers was time consuming and, in many cases, tedious. With the advent of credit card sales and debit cards, the process has become easier, but its importance has not diminished. Protecting sales revenue from external and internal threats of theft requires diligence and attention to detail. Software on the market that can help in this area includes that which will:

1. Maintain daily cash balances from all sources.
2. Reconcile inventory reductions with product issues from kitchen.
3. Reconcile product issues from kitchen with guest check totals.
4. Reconcile guest check totals with revenue totals.
5. Create over and short computations by server, shift, and day.
6. Balance daily bank deposits with daily sales revenue.
7. Maintain database of returned checks.
8. Interface with POS.
9. Interface with budget/income statement software.

It is important to note that interfacing (connecting) the various software programs you select is very helpful. For example, a program that forecasts sales revenue, which also supplies that data to the software program you are using to schedule labor hours needed, will be more effective and helpful to you than one that does not connect to the scheduling feature. In a similar manner, a software program that compares sales recorded on the POS with daily bank deposits is preferable to one that does not connect these two independent but correlated functions.
When her work is complete, Csilla will have recommended that the owners of the End Zone select only those software programs they feel are important and useful. Again, it is important to remember that any mathematical process can be computerized; however, it is the wise manager that

implements only those software systems that will be carefully monitored and utilized.

FUN ON THE WEB!

Although you have already browsed these sites in previous chapters of the text, review them again to find evidence of the software applications outlined in this chapter. Also, try out the demos, where available.

www.micros.com
www.squirrelsystems.com
www.datatrakpos.com
www.computrition.com
www.cbord.com
www.foodsoftware.com
www.restaurantplus.com
www.foodtrak.com
www.alohapos.com
www.symbioticsys.com

Hardware

Hardware, for purposes of this discussion, consists of point of sales systems terminals, personal computers (PCs), time clocks, inventory/bar code reading equipment, and other devices required to manage the cost control software you will purchase. In some cases, your selection of software will partially or completely determine the hardware required to operate the software. If, for example, you elect to buy a software program built around a touch screen order entry system for servers, the required hardware (touch screens) will, of course, need to be purchased. The primary function of the hardware you select is to allow easy entering, storage, and retrieval of the information you have deemed important through your selection of your software.

If, however, you do have options as to the hardware to be purchased, you will find that the speed, capacity, and features of these machines change incredibly quickly over time. Even so, a brief review of the major hardware components can be helpful.

Microprocessor The **microprocessor** powers the central processing unit (CPU), which is the heart of your computer hardware system. A faster, more powerful microprocessor will give you better performance, but increased power and speed typically come at an increased price. A CPU's performance depends on the processor's design and its speed, which is measured in millions of cycles per second, or MHz. A good rule of thumb is to buy no more power than you actually need to run, at an appropriate speed, the software programs you have selected.

Random Access Memory **Random access memory** (RAM) is required to operate your software programs. The more memory you have, the faster and more reliably your computer will work. In this case, it is a good idea to buy more memory than you currently need, as newer software programs require increasing amounts of memory for optimum operation.

Hard Drive Your **hard drive** provides permanent storage for your software programs and data files such as reports, financial records, and so forth. Its capacity is measured in gigabytes, or billions of bytes. A gigabyte is enough to store 1,000 average-sized novels or 16 hours of compressed digital music. When you evaluate the required size of your hard drive before buying, make sure you have adequate capacity for both current applications and anticipated additions.

Multimedia Most computers come with **multimedia,** three-dimensional (3-D) video circuitry and a compact disc (CD) or digital video disc (DVD) drive. The 3-D capability is valuable for training applications, and the CD or DVD components are necessary for installing software.

Modem/Internet Connection It is highly recommended that any advanced technology system you purchase have, as one component, a dependable **modem** that provides you with the ability to connect to the Internet. This technology is advancing the most rapidly of all. The Internet holds the potential for tremendous cost reduction by allowing users to share information, software programs, and access far greater amounts of information than previously possible. The implications for improving cost control systems are clear and significant.

Monitor The **monitor** is one of the most important parts of your system because it's the component you and your employees will spend hours staring at. It's a good idea to shop carefully and check out as many alternatives as you can. As a rule, buy the largest screens that fit your application. Although some low-end personal computers come with 15-inch monitors, you'll be far more comfortable with a 17-inch or larger screen. When they were first introduced in the 1980s, touch screen monitors were not very reliable. Currently, however, these monitors, which combine viewing screen with input device, are quite satisfactory.

Printers The **printer(s)** you select will serve two purposes. One is to create for your guests a record of their charges. The second is for your own usage. You will utilize your system's printer for report documents, internal and external communications, and, increasingly, to create your own in-house marketing materials. Essentially, you will likely choose from a laser printer, ink jet printer, or digital printer/copier. Laser printers are more expensive, faster, and use less ink per page printed. Ink jet printers are less expensive, slower in most cases, and use more ink per page printed. Digital printer/copiers combine the speed and flexibility of digital printing with the convenience of a copy machine. In all cases, the printers you select should operate at a speed and cost that you find acceptable and, as with all critical equipment, should be able to be serviced quickly and affordably.

Handheld Devices Increasingly, computer hardware manufacturers are reducing the physical size of their products. In the foodservice industry, this is very helpful because so many of your cost control efforts will take place in the dining room, storage areas, kitchen, and receiving dock; thus, portability is important. Clearly, it would not be cost effective to have complete hardware-intensive cost control systems in place in each of these several areas. Wireless **handheld devices,** such as computers, pagers, printers, bar code readers, and other devices, will continue to play ever-increasing roles in the development of cost systems.

When cost control systems first began to advance beyond manual cash registers, time clocks, and adding machines, the data required for use in the control systems were often stored in an on-site PC. As multiunit operators began to see the value of linking these independent PCs into interconnected networks, the data stored began to require vast amounts of disk space, as well as large amounts of memory to operate the software portions of the cost control systems. Today, more and more companies are reducing hardware as well as software costs by relying on the Internet to provide the storage and transferability of the software they require. This trend should continue as operators and vendors look more to the Internet and less to on-site systems to provide the best approach to cost control.

Communication Devices

Perhaps it is in the area of communication devices that the greatest progression is taking place in the technological advancement of current cost control systems. Consider that communication devices have, as their main function, the transfer of information from one person or entity to another, and you can see their importance. **Communication devices** often used by foodservice managers include items such as cellular telephones, fax machines, e-mail, pagers, and the Internet. Just as the telegraph and later the telephone revolutionized the world by making it easier for two individuals to rapidly share information, the following communication devices have done the same for foodservice managers wishing to communicate with their own corporate offices, suppliers, employees, and others.

Cellular Telephones **Cellular telephones** allow mobile voice transmittal that is not tied to traditional telephone line locations. In addition to verbal communication, other advanced uses of the cellular telephone include paging, e-mail, and Internet accessibility.

Fax Machines   While the heaviest use of these machines involves purchase orders and credit information, **fax machines** are commonly used to supply guests with backup copies of their guest checks, as well as communicating between foodservice units in multiunit companies.

E-Mail   Faster than the traditional U.S. mail service and easier to send than a fax, **e-mail** has replaced the U.S. mail as the preferred method of rapidly exchanging, sharing, and revising internal documents for most foodservice companies. However, it has, as yet, been underutilized as a consumer marketing device. Expect this to change as more and more consumers look to their e-mail rather than traditional mail or newspapers for such restaurant-related communication as daily, weekly, or monthly specials, special coupons or promotions, job announcements, and a variety of other areas of communication.

Pagers   Originally used in restaurants primarily as a means of informing guests that their tables were ready, **pagers** are now used to communicate between the kitchen and dining room, as well as between staff and guests.

Internet   While the **Internet** is not merely a communication device in the traditional sense (because its use combines software, hardware, *and* communication), it does allow for the most rapid storage, retrieval, and transfer of information available today. Its uses, from the delivery of training to the execution of online purchasing, continue to grow. In fact, its future applications are likely to be among the most significant technological advancements to cost control in the first decade of the 21st century. As one example, coupon production and distribution is becoming ever more expensive. Some large operators have found that computer technology can help them reduce these costs. By developing a home page on the World Wide Web, operators can instruct those who view the site to simply "Print This Page" and then bring it to the restaurant to receive the special discount or promotion being advertised. In addition, Web page viewers who complete a guest profile survey can instantly qualify for a discount when they arrive at the restaurant. The possibilities are endless, and they are being rapidly developed.

Purchasing Technology Products

While your cost control efforts can be greatly enhanced by well-designed and integrated software, hardware, and communication products, there are limitations to the role technology can reasonably be expected to play in your operation. It is important to remember that computers can only be programmed to imitate processes that are already understood. This is not to imply that computers should be used only for those tasks that management currently performs. Indeed, a creative foodservice manager should be able to use technology to perform useful tasks that were never before attempted because they were too complex or time consuming. It is true, however, that a computer will not do the thinking required to initiate the new process. That task is up to you. Technology alone will not bring controls to an operation, but an effective, technologically advanced system can free you from spending excessive time on routine data collection and analysis tasks so you can focus on the more important responsibility of providing outstanding service to your guests.

Any proposed improvement in technology should be considered in light of its ability to:

1. Enhance guest satisfaction.
2. Increase revenue.
3. Reduce costs through improved decision making.
4. Increase employee or management productivity.
5. Improve communications.
6. Provide a competitive advantage.

An overreliance on technology or a misapplication of its features can result in frustration, and wasted time and money. To avoid such a situation, carefully consider the following essential elements before selecting and purchasing any technological enhancement to your existing cost control efforts.

Cost

It can be difficult to cost-justify any investment in technology. Consider an item as simple as the telephone. When telephones first appeared, it may have been difficult to show, by dollars and cents, that the telephone was an important technological advancement for a restaurant. Today, of course, no restaurant could be without a voice-activated communication device.

Cost legitimately does, however, play an important role in the decision of how much technology your facility can afford. When it is possible to demonstrate that the technological advancement will pay for itself (such as in reduced labor or product cost) relatively quickly, the decision can be an easy one. Often, however, it is complex to identify actual savings. Your technology vendors can be helpful in this area, but remember that their ultimate goal is to sell their products. Remember also that technology is a tool to be used by you and your staff. If the cost of the tool exceeds its value to your operation, its purchase is questionable.

Complexity

Some technology systems are so advanced that their implementation and routine operation requires very high levels of skills. A recipe conversion software package, for example, may require knowledge of both computer entry and basic cooking skills. If your staff is not sophisticated enough to use the technology you purchase, difficulties can arise. These may be reduced or eliminated through the implementation of thorough training programs. Again, your technology vendor should be more than willing to help you secure such programs at little or no cost to you.

System Warranty/Maintenance

Because technology items are machines, they need routine maintenance and can break down. When they do, it will be critical that you receive quality repair service in a timely manner and at a fair price. Typically, your technology purchase will include a warranty. Read this warranty carefully. Items of particular importance to you will be:

1. A listing of precisely which items are covered under the terms of the warranty
2. The length of the warranty
3. The hourly rate charged for repair service for non-warranty-covered items
4. Expected response time of the service/repair technicians

Item 4 is of particular importance. Many standard warranties specify 24-hour response time to service problems. Imagine, however, that your POS system goes down on a busy Friday evening. You certainly want it repaired sooner than 24 hours! Ask your technology vendor for the price of upgrading your service response time to no more than four hours. It may well be worth the extra cost.

Upgradability

While it is certainly difficult to know what new technological developments may occur in the future, it is true that advancements that are compatible with your current system will likely prove to be less expensive than those that require completely new software, hardware, or communication devices. Because this is so, many operators prefer to work with larger, more established technology vendors as these organizations generally will ensure that advancements in their products are compatible with the products they already have marketed. Smaller and newer technology companies may offer some features that are desirable, but their systems may be subject to complete obsolescence if newer technology makes the old systems incompatible with newer ones offered by alternative vendors.

Reliability

Where reliability is concerned, two areas are of importance. These are the reliability of the product or service and the reliability of the vendor. To help ensure that you select a product or service that is reliable, insist that your potential vendor share with you a list of current customers who can be contacted for information about the reliability of the products they have purchased. Unfortunately, at this time, there are no rating systems in place for hospitality-related technology items. Perhaps there should be. Until that time, the experience of others, as well as your own knowledge, will be important factors in assessing the reliability of the new technology products and services you select.

Vendor reliability is also very important. There is no more consequential consideration when electing to integrate a new technology than the quality of the vendor supplying that technology. While a variety of factors can influence vendor reliability, the following are worthy of close examination.

Location   Generally, the closer the location of the vendor to your operational unit(s), the more successful you will be in establishing a solid relationship with him or her. Long-distance contact can work, but only if the vendor is highly motivated and has field representatives who can quickly come onto your site if needed.

Experience   While even Microsoft was once a start-up company, in general it is best to deal with technology suppliers who have an established record of accomplishment. If you do select a company that is very new, perhaps due to a significant technological development, realize that the failure rate of technology start-ups, like restaurants, can be very high regardless of the product's quality.

Quality of Service Staff   If a problem develops, it will be the quality of the service/repair department, not the vendor's sales department, that will be of most importance to you. Before selecting a technology vendor, insist that you meet with the service person(s) responsible for your account. Ask the questions needed to ensure that the service provider understands your business well enough to help you work through any integration problems you may encounter.

Response Time   Response time is critical when your system is down. Regardless of the warranty in place, service response time, rather than who is to pay for that service, can be of critical importance. Be cautious if the service person provided by your vendor works as an independent contractor or for a company not directly related to the one from which you are buying. Subcontracted service can be acceptable, but is often a sign that you may have difficulty acquiring a prompt response to potential problems. The best technology companies provide their own service representatives and in a timely fashion.

Reputation   Perhaps the most important factor in selecting a technology vendor is the same one your guests use when evaluating your foodservice operation. The reputation of your vendor is as critical to you as the reputation of your own facility and, in fact, will be tied together in the eyes of your guests. Honesty, integrity, and a willingness to stand behind their promises are characteristics that you should seek in all vendors, but especially those involved in technology integration.

As is also true in purchasing foodservice equipment, reliability in your technology products can make the difference between a successful integration and an unsuccessful one. Be sure that you purchase a reliable system from a reliable vendor who provides reliable service!

Monitoring Advances in Cost Control Technology

It is simply not possible to immediately know about every software, hardware, or communication advance that could directly affect your business. You can, however, stay abreast of the commercial application of these advances. And it is important that you do. Your choices for continuing education in this area are varied and depend on your own preferences, but most foodservice managers can choose from one or more of the following methods:

1.   Trade shows/professional associations
2.   Publications
3.   Current vendors
4.   Competitive vendors
5.   Technology-related classes
6.   Your own organization

Trade Shows/Professional Associations

As a hospitality professional, you will likely elect to join one or more **professional trade associations.** These associations typically serve the certification, educational, social, and legislative goals of its members. Typically, such associations hold annual gatherings, and, in conjunction with these meetings, they invite exhibitors who sell products and services of interest to interact with their members at trade shows. These trade shows bring together a variety of vendors, all of whom are interested in exhibiting their latest product offerings. Trade shows are an extremely efficient way to see the product offerings of a large number of vendors in a very short time.

Many trade associations also have both state and local chapters, some of which will host their own trade shows. Some of the largest of these associations, as well as their Internet locations, are as follows.

FUN ON THE WEB!

Visit these association sites to find out when and where they will be holding their next trade shows.

Association	Web Address
National Restaurant Association	www.restaurant.org
American Hotel and Motel Association	www.ahma.com
American Dietetic Association	www.eatright.com
Dietary Managers Association	www.dmaonline.org
American Culinary Federation	www.acfchefs.org
Club Managers Association of America	www.cmaa.org
American School Foodservice Association	www.asfsa.org
National Association of Catering Executives	www.ienace.org
Hospitality Financial and Technology Professionals	www.iaha.org
International Hotel and Restaurant Association	www.ih-ra.com

On a local level, chambers of commerce and professional service organizations often hold meetings and schedule speakers who can update you on the newest business applications of technology. Membership in these organizations is generally well worth its modest cost.

Publications

The publications listed in Figure 12.1 are examples of those that can be of significant help in monitoring changes in technology that affect cost control. Regularly reading about the hospitality industry will not only make you a better manager, but will also keep you abreast of the latest technological trends. In many cases, technology and its application have become such a large part of the editorial interest of these publications that a special technology editor is employed to monitor technological changes that could be of interest to the publication's readers.

Some of these publications are distributed free to qualified members of the hospitality industry, while others are not. Be sure to ask if you qualify for a free subscription when you contact the publication.

Current Vendors

Your current supplier of software, hardware, or communications systems should be a valuable source of no cost information. All of these vendors

FIGURE **12.1** ● Selected Hospitality Publications List

Publication	Subscription Information
Cooking for Profit	(414) 923-3700
Cornell Quarterly	(607) 255-3025
Nation's Restaurant News	(212) 756-5000
Restaurant Business	(212) 592-6500
Restaurant Hospitality	(216) 696-7000
Restaurants & Institutions	(847) 635-8800
Restaurants USA	(202) 331-5900

will make improvements in their products as competitive pressures and the desire to grow drive their development efforts. An added advantage of working with your current technology suppliers is the fact that the new systems they develop are highly likely to be compatible with those systems you already have and maintain. This can reduce staff training time and the errors that sometimes come with new system implementation. In addition, your current vendors may be more competitive on pricing their new offerings because, in most cases, they very much would like to retain your business.

Competitive Vendors

While your current vendors can certainly help you know about their own efforts, competition in the area of cost control–related products and services is robust and getting stronger. Whether your interest is software, hardware, or communications, identifying your current vendor's strongest and best competitors is a good way to monitor advances in technology. At a minimum, annual visits, either in person or by telephone, can help you quickly identify improvements in procedures and features that your own vendor may have overlooked or dismissed. Don't hesitate to contact small vendors you may see advertised in publications or exhibiting at trade shows. Often, these start-up companies offer the most innovative and cutting-edge programs available. Conversely, their small size may limit their ability to adequately service your account. In any case, they can be a source of tremendous information and are well worth monitoring.

Technology-Related Classes

Many community colleges and private training organizations offer instruction on the application of technology to your business. For example, successfully completing an advanced course in word processing techniques may allow you to design and print your own "daily special" menu. Similarly, a course in the applications of database programs (those programs designed to manipulate and store information such as street addresses, e-mail addresses, and telephone numbers) may allow you to efficiently develop your own direct-marketing programs.

If, in your community, there is a four-year hospitality management program offered by a college or university, you will likely find that it is an excellent source of information regarding the latest technological advances in all areas of the hospitality industry, including cost control.

Finally, your current technology vendor may be a source of free or reduced-cost instruction. Be sure to contact the companies that currently provide your software, hardware, and communications services to see if they do, in fact, offer free or low-cost classes on effectively using their current products or instruction on newer products they are offering.

Your Own Organization

For those managers employed by a national chain or large company, the parent organization can be an excellent source of information about changing management tools. Often, a large company will produce newsletters, conduct in-service training, or hold regularly scheduled conventions that can be a source of information on changing technology. All of these resources should be monitored and utilized if they are available. Sometimes, a simple discussion with your area or regional supervisor regarding the technological changes affecting your company can be of tremendous value. These professionals are in a position to see the best of what is happening both within your own company and with your competitors.

As a wise professional, you know that it is only by staying aware of changes in technology and being committed to implementing the best and most cost effective of these that your business and your career will continue to flourish. Advances in technological capabilities will continue to change society and the hospitality industry as well. When those advances help you to better manage your business, you, your employees, and, most important, your guests are all beneficiaries. Good luck.

Key Terms and Concepts

The following are terms and concepts discussed in the chapter that are important for you as a manager. To help you review, please define the terms below.

Software   Handheld device
Hardware   Communication device

Microprocessor	Cellular telephone
RAM memory	Fax machine
Hard drive	E-mail
Multimedia	Pager
Modem	Internet
Monitor	Professional trade association
Printer	

Test Your Skills

1. One of the most significant changes in the hospitality industry in the past two decades has been the introduction of the drive-through window in the quick-service segment. Analyze that development in terms of its dependence on technology-related software, hardware, and communication devices. Which of these do you think has had the most influence on the development of the drive-through? Defend your answer.

2. Increasingly, employers are using advances in technology such as monitors and surveillance cameras to both observe and reduce employee theft and to help ensure the safety and security of their assets. Placement of these devices in food and beverage storage, production, and, in some cases, service areas has become commonplace. Assume that you are employed by such a company. How would you respond to a guest who protested to you that he or she resented being videotaped while they dining? Draft a letter to that guest explaining your company's reason(s) for employing such a cost control method.

3. Review the following news release. It was taken from the hospitality law-related Web site, www.hospitalitylawyer.com. Such an incidence could, of course, take place in the hospitality industry.

Dow Chemical Fires Workers

Published: Lansing, MI

In a case that holds great interest for the hospitality industry, Dow Chemical Company has fired 50 workers and disciplined 200 others after its investigation showed these individuals had e-mailed offensive material from company computers. The material mailed was, in some cases, pornographic, and said a company representative, "This sort of activity creates a harassment environment that we can't tolerate."

While the company does not regularly monitor e-mail content, it certainly has the right to do so. Employees who simply opened e-mails they received, then deleted the material were not disciplined said company officials. Only those employees who distributed pornography and violent images got in trouble. The message here is clear. Work computers are for work. Employees should be reminded that employ-ers can routinely limit the speech and images that may be displayed on these machines. The best practice, of course, is to include your pri-vacy policy as part of your employee manual [for a sample privacy policy, see "Management Tools" on the hospitalitylawyer.com home page].

Draft a model policy that spells out your position on this sometimes-controversial issue for a multiunit company that routinely uses com-puters as a communication device.

4. Advances in technology are often associated with improvements in pro-duction-related cost control issues such as food and beverage prepara-tion, purchasing, storage, and inventory. Technological advances, how-ever, also influence human resource management. Identify three ways in which advances in technology have had a major influence on cost control in the area of human resource management. Also, identify three ways you believe technology advancements will influence both job seekers and employers in the future.

5. It is apparent that advances in software, hardware, and communication devices will continue to have an impact on foodservice managers and their operations. As you analyze the technology industry, which of these three areas do you believe will change the most in the next five years? What new uses for technologies do you foresee?

Appendix A

Spreadsheet Formulas

This appendix is designed to give you the formulas that you will need to complete the Test Your Skills exercises at the end of each chapter. The authors make the assumption that you have a basic understanding of how to use spreadsheets. These formulas will be used throughout the textbook. The authors have intentionally chosen the simplest formulas that have the widest use. More experienced spreadsheet users may want to use more advanced functions or macros.

When you are using the Excel spreadsheets to complete the Test Your Skills exercises, you may sometimes need to enter the raw data presented in the textbook. To complete the exercises, you will have to enter formulas in the spreadsheets to perform mathematical calculations just as you would when analyzing data as a manager in a foodservice operation.

Basics of Creating Spreadsheets

Assume that you are the manager of a fine-dining restaurant, and you want to see how many guests your waitstaff, Anne, Debra, and George served on Monday and Tuesday nights. To quickly add up the daily totals, you decide to set up the following spreadsheet:

	A	B	C	D	E
		Anne	Debra	George	Total Guests
1					
2	Monday	25	16	23	
3	Tuesday	18	24	21	
4					
5					

To calculate the total guests served for Monday and Tuesday, you must do the following:

1. Place the cursor in cell E2.
2. Type: **=sum(**
3. Highlight the cells that you wish to add (B2 through D2).
4. Excel will automatically add the cells to your formula so that it now looks like this: **=sum(B2:D2**
5. Complete the formula by closing the right parenthesis: **=sum(B2:D2)**
6. Hit "Enter."
7. The number 64 should appear in cell E2.
8. To copy the same formula for cell E3, use the Auto Fill function. Simply click on the cell, E2, and then position your mouse directly over the bottom right-hand corner of the cell. The cursor will change to look like a plus sign (see the following spreadsheet). Click on the plus and drag down to cell E3. This will copy the formula from E2 to E3. It will automatically change the cells you are adding to B3 and D3. The answer you should have in E3 should be 63. You can use the Auto Fill function to copy numbers or formulas horizontally or vertically.

	A	B	C	D	E
1		Anne	Debra	George	Total Guests
2	Monday	25	16	23	=sum(B2:D2)
3	Tuesday	18	24	21	=sum(B3:D3)
4					
5					

Formulas Needed for Test Your Skills Exercises

Formula	Example	Explanation
=cell	=B1	Copies a number from another cell of the worksheet.
=$column$row	=B1	"Anchors" a cell in a series of formulas. When using the same cell in a variety of formulas in a spreadsheet, place the "$" in front of the column reference and the row reference to indicate that each formula is using the same cell in the calculation. This is especially helpful when dragging the formula to copy it over a series of cells.

Formula	Example	Explanation
=sum(cell:cell)	=sum(B1:B5)	Adds numbers in a range of cells.
=sum(cell,cell)	=sum(B1,B5)	Adds two numbers in cells that are not adjacent to each other.
In the following formulas, the word "cell" may be replaced by an actual number, e.g., =(cell+25)		
=(cell+cell)	=(B1+B2)	Adds two numbers.
=(cell-cell)	=(B1-B2)	Subtracts one number from another.
=(cell*cell)	=(B1*B2)	Multiplies two numbers.
=(cell/cell)	=(B1/B2)	Divides one number into another.
=(cell/cell)*100	=(B1/B2)*100	Divides one number into another and multiplies the answer by 100 (changes answer to percentage).
=min(cell:cell)	=min(B1:B5)	Chooses minimum value out of cell range. (Good to use when doing price comparisons.)
=roundup(cell,0)	=roundup(B1,0)	Rounds fractions up to whole numbers. The "0" denotes that the number of decimal places will be 0. (Good to use when inventory indicates that you need 2½ cases and you can only buy in full cases; this function will round the cases up to 3.)
=roundup(cell,2)	=roundup(B1,2)	Rounds fractions up to two decimal places. The "2" denotes that the number of decimal places will be 2. (Good to use for money: When one cell is being used in a formula of a second cell, this will guarantee that no rounding errors will occur in the second cell.)

Note that, for percentages, you don't necessarily have to type "*100" in the formula. You could, instead, so the following:

1. Highlight the cell.
2. Go to the menu at the top of the page and click on "Format."
3. Under "Format," click on "Cells."
4. Under "Cells," click on "Number."
5. Under "Number," click on "Percentage."
6. You will also find a box in "Number" that will allow you to choose the number of decimal places.

How to Create a Pie Chart

Although this looks like a *long* list of things to do to create a pie chart, it should really only take you approximately two minutes to do (once you get the hang of it). So please give it a try.

Following is an example of a P&L statement set up in Excel. Your task is to illustrate expenses and profit as a percentage of revenues in a pie chart.

	A	B	C	D
1			%	
2	Revenue	$250,000	100.0	
3	F&B Expense	130,000	52.0	
4	Labor Expense	70,000	28.0	
5	Other Expense	40,000	16.0	
6	Total Expenses	240,000	96.0	
7	Profit	10,000	4.0	

1. Highlight "F&B Expense," "Labor Expense," and "Other Expense" in Column A and highlight their respective dollar amounts in Column B (all at the same time). Then hold down the "Ctrl" key on your keyboard and highlight "Profit" and its respective dollar amount. This will allow you to skip the "Total Expenses" row.

2. Go to the menu at the top of the screen and click on "Insert," then click on "Chart." A Chart Wizard will appear on your screen.

3. In the Chart Wizard, you have two choices: "Standard Types" and "Custom Types." Usually, the Chart Wizard will open up automatically to "Standard Types," which is the one you want to use.

4. Click on "Pie" and click on the "Chart Sub-type" (pictured at the right) that you want to use. Then click on "Next" at the bottom of the page.

5. In the next screen, you have two choices: "Data Range" and "Series." "Data Range" is the one you want to use.

6. If you have already highlighted your columns in the spreadsheet as instructed in Step 1, you will not have to type in anything on this screen. Just click on "Next" at the bottom of the page.

7. In the next screen, you have three choices: "Titles," "Legend," and "Data Labels." Click on "Titles" first.

8. Under "Titles," you will see a space labeled "Chart Title." Type in the title that you want for your chart in that space (or do nothing if you do not want a title).

9. Now, click on "Legend." This option is available for you if you want the legend to show. If you want a legend, make sure the "Show Legend" box is checked and then click on a "Placement" for the legend (where you want it to appear on the chart). If you do not want a legend and it has a check mark next to it, click on the check mark to remove it.

10. Now, click on "Data Labels." You will see a list of options for labeling the pieces of the pie. The authors of this text like to use "Show Label and Percent." If you click on this, you will see that both the data labels (words) and percentages appear next to the corresponding piece of the pie. This also makes a legend redundant; so, if you are using this option, you will not want to click on "Show Legend" in the "Legend" section (see Step 9). Click on "Next" at the bottom of the page.

11. In the next screen, you have two choices: Place chart "as new sheet" and "as object in." This is referring to where you want the pie chart to appear, either in a new Excel spreadsheet or in an existing spreadsheet in your workbook. In most cases, you will click on "as object in." Next to "as object in" is a scroll down list. Choose the sheet in which you want the object to appear. The current sheet you are working in is the default sheet.

12. Click on "Finish" at the bottom of the page, and you should see your finished chart!

13. To move the pie chart to a specific location on the spreadsheet, click on any white space within the chart, hold down the mouse button, and drag the chart to the desired location.

14. To resize the pie chart, click on any of the eight dots on the border of the chart. The side middle dots make the chart larger or smaller

horizontally, and the top and bottom middle dots make the chart larger or smaller vertically. The dots in the corners of the chart will resize the entire chart (larger or smaller) within the same proportions.

15. The Chart Wizard defaults percentages to zero decimal places (e.g., 12%). If you want percentages to have one or more decimal places (e.g., 12.3% or 12.34%), double-click on one of the percentages shown in your pie chart. A window will pop up that is labeled "Format Data Labels." Click on the "Number" tab at the top of the window (this is the default). Then click on "Percentage" (this is the default). You will see "Set Decimal Places" on the right and a box next to it. Type in the number of decimal places you want and then click "OK" at the bottom of the window. This will set all of the percentages in your chart to the same number of decimal places.

16. Sit back and admire your work!

How to Sort a Table

Following is an example of *Goal Value Analysis* set up in Excel. Your task is to sort the menu items by Goal Value from highest to lowest.

Rank	Menu Item	A	B	C	D	Goal Value
	Overall menu (Goal Value)	(1-.35)	100	$16.55	1-(.30+.35)	376.5
	Lobster Stir-Fry	(1-.51)	51	21.95	1-(.30+.51)	104.2
	Chicken Breast	(1-.22)	140	$13.95	1-(.30+.22)	731.2
	Beef medallions	(1-.37)	125	15.95	1-(.30+.37)	414.5
	Coconut Shrimp	(1-.30)	121	16.95	1-(.30+.30)	574.3
	Grilled Tuna	(1-.40)	105	17.95	1-(.30+.40)	339.3
	Scallops/Pasta	(1-.24)	85	14.95	1-(.30+.24)	444.3
	Strip Steak	(1-.45)	73	17.95	1-(.30+.45)	180.2

1. Highlight the table to be sorted including the header row.
2. Go to the menu at the top of the screen and click on "Data," then click on "Sort."
3. A "Sort" window will appear on your screen. At the bottom of the "Sort" window you will see "My list has." Click on "Header row" to indicate that your table has a header row.
4. At the top of the "Sort" window, you will see "Sort by." Use the drop down menu to choose the appropriate column. In this example, you will choose the "Goal Value" column.
5. To the right of the drop down menu, you need to choose "Ascending" or "Descending." For this example, choose "Descending" because you want the menu items to be sorted from highest to lowest. Click "OK" at the bottom of the window to sort the table.
6. After your table is sorted, type in the appropriate ranking numbers in the "Rank" column.

Your table should now appear as follows:

Rank	Menu Item	A	B	C	D	Goal Value
1	Chicken Breast	(1-.22)	140	$13.95	1-(.30+.22)	731.2
2	Coconut Shrimp	(1-.30)	121	16.95	1-(.30+.30)	574.3
3	Scallops/Pasta	(1-.24)	85	14.95	1-(.30+.24)	444.3
4	Beef medallions	(1-.37)	125	15.95	1-(.30+.37)	414.5
5	*Overall menu (Goal Value)*	*(1-.35)*	*100*	*$16.55*	*1-(.30+.35)*	*376.5*
6	Grilled Tuna	(1-.40)	105	17.95	1-(.30+.40)	339.3
7	Strip Steak	(1-.45)	73	17.95	1-(.30+.45)	180.2
8	Lobster Stir-Fry	(1-.51)	51	21.95	1-(.30+.51)	104.2

Appendix B

Frequently Used Formulas for Managing Operations

Chapter 1—Managing Revenue and Expense

Revenue − Expense = Profit

Revenue − Desired Profit = Ideal Expense

$$\frac{Part}{Whole} = Percent$$

$$\frac{Expense}{Revenue} = Expense \%$$

$$\frac{Profit}{Revenue} = Profit \%$$

$$\frac{Desired\ profit}{Revenue} = Desired\ Profit \%$$

Revenue − (Food and Beverage Cost + Labor Cost + Other Expense) = Profit

$$\frac{Food\ and\ Beverage\ Cost}{Revenue} = Food\ and\ Beverage\ Cost \%$$

$$\frac{Labor\ Cost}{Revenue} = Labor\ Cost \%$$

$$\frac{Other\ Expense}{Revenue} = Other\ Expense \%$$

$$\frac{\text{Total Expense}}{\text{Revenue}} = \text{Total Expense \%}$$

$$\frac{\text{Profit}}{\text{Revenue}} = \text{Profit \%}$$

$$\frac{\text{Actual}}{\text{Budget}} = \text{\% of Budget}$$

Chapter 2–Determining Sales Forecasts

$$\frac{\text{Total Sales}}{\text{Number of Guests Served}} = \text{Average Sales per Guest}$$

Sales This Year − Sales Last Year = Variance

$$\frac{\text{Sales This Year} - \text{Sales Last Year}}{\text{Sales Last Year}} = \text{Percentage Variance}$$

$$\frac{\text{Variance}}{\text{Sales Last Year}} = \text{Percentage Variance}$$

(Sales This Year/Sales Last Year) − 1 = Percentage Variance

Sales Last Year + (Sales Last Year × % Increase Estimate)
   = Revenue Forecast

Sales Last Year × (1 + % Increase Estimate) = Revenue Forecast

Guest Count Last Year + (Guest Count Last Year × % Increase Estimate)
   = Guest Count Forecast

Guests Last Year × (1 + % Increase Estimate) = Guest Count Forecast

Last Year's Average Sales per Guest
   + Estimated Increase in Sales per Guest = Sales per Guest Forecast

$$\frac{\text{Revenue Forecast}}{\text{Guest Count Forecast}} = \text{Average Sales per Guest Forecast}$$

Chapter 3–Managing the Cost of Food

$$\frac{\text{Total Number of a Specific Menu Item Sold}}{\text{Total Number of All Menu Items Sold}} = \text{Popularity Index}$$

Number of Guests Expected × Item Popularity Index
= Predicted Number of That Item to Be Sold

$$\frac{\text{Yield Desired}}{\text{Current Yield}} = \text{Conversion Factor}$$

$$\frac{\text{Ingredient Weight}}{\text{Total Recipe Weight}} = \% \text{ of Total}$$

Ingredient % of Total × Total Amount Required = New Recipe Amount

Desired Servings × Ounces per Portion = Ounces Required

$$\frac{\text{Product Loss}}{\text{AP Weight}} = \text{Waste } \%$$

1 − Waste % = Yield %

$$\frac{\text{EP Required}}{\text{Yield } \%} = \text{AP Required}$$

AP Required × Yield % = EP Required

Par Value − On Hand + Special Order = Order Amount

Unit Price × Number of Units = Extended Price

Item Amount × Item Value = Item Inventory Value

```
  Beginning Inventory
+ Purchases
  Goods Available for Sale
− Ending Inventory
  Cost of Food Consumed
− Employee Meals
  Cost of Food Sold
```

```
  Beginning Inventory
+ Purchases
  Goods Available for Sale
− Ending Inventory
− Value of Transfers Out
+ Value of Transfers In
  Cost of Food Sold
```

$$\frac{\text{Cost of Food Sold}}{\text{Food Sales}} = \text{Food Cost \%}$$

$$\frac{\text{Purchases Today}}{\text{Sales Today}} = \text{Cost \% Today (six-column food cost \% estimate)}$$

$$\frac{\text{Purchases to Date}}{\text{Sales to Date}} = \text{Cost \% to Date (six-column food cost \% estimate)}$$

Chapter 4—Managing the Cost of Beverages

$$\frac{\text{Cost of Beverage Sold}}{\text{Beverage Sales}} = \text{Beverage Cost \%}$$

Beginning Inventory
+Purchases
Goods Available for Sale
−Ending Inventory
−Transfers from Bar
+Transfers to Bar
Cost of Beverages Sold

$$\frac{\text{Item Dollar Sales}}{\text{Total Beverage Sales}} = \text{Item \% of Total Beverage Sales}$$

Chapter 5—Managing the Food and Beverage Production Process

Prior-Day Carryover + Today's Production
   = Today's Sales Forecast ± Margin of Error

$$\frac{\text{Issues Today}}{\text{Sales Today}} = \text{Beverage Cost Estimate Today}$$

$$\frac{\text{Issues to Date}}{\text{Sales to Date}} = \text{Beverage Cost Estimate to Date}$$

$$\frac{\text{Issues to Date} - \text{Inventory Adjustment}}{\text{Sales to Date}} = \text{Cost of Beverage Sold}$$

$$\frac{\text{Cost in Product Category}}{\text{Total Cost in All Categories}} = \text{Proportion of Total Product Cost}$$

$$\frac{\text{Product Loss}}{\text{AP Weight}} = \text{Net Waste \%}$$

$$1 - \text{Net Waste} = \text{Product Yield}$$

$$\frac{\text{EP Weight}}{\text{AP Weight}} = \text{Product Yield \%}$$

$$\frac{\text{AP Price per Pound}}{\text{Product Yield \%}} = \text{EP Cost (per pound)}$$

$$\frac{\text{Actual Product Cost}}{\text{Attainable Product Cost}} = \text{Operational Efficiency Ratio}$$

$$\frac{\text{Cost as per Standardized Recipes}}{\text{Total Sales}} = \text{Attainable Food Cost \%}$$

Chapter 6—Managing Food and Beverage Pricing

$$\text{Revenue} - \text{Expense} = \text{Profit}$$

$$\text{Price} \times \text{Number Sold} = \text{Total Revenues}$$

$$\frac{\text{Cost of Food Sold}}{\text{Food Sales}} = \text{Food Cost \%}$$

$$\frac{\text{Cost of a Specific Food Item Sold}}{\text{Food Sales of That Item}} = \text{Food Cost \% of That Item}$$

$$\frac{\text{Cost of a Specific Food Item Sold}}{\text{Food Cost \% of That Item}} = \text{Food Sales (Selling Price) of That Item}$$

$$\frac{1}{\text{Desired Product Cost \%}} = \text{Pricing Factor}$$

$$\text{Pricing Factor} \times \text{Product Cost} = \text{Menu Price}$$

$$\text{Selling Price} - \text{Product Cost} = \text{Contribution Margin}$$

$$\text{Product Cost} + \text{Contribution Margin Desired} = \text{Selling Price}$$

$$\frac{\text{Total Buffet Product Cost}}{\text{Guests Served}} = \text{Buffet Product Cost per Guest}$$

Chapter 7—Managing the Cost of Labor

$$\frac{\text{Output}}{\text{Input}} = \text{Productivity Ratio}$$

$$\frac{\text{Number of Employees Separated}}{\text{Number of Employees in Workforce}} = \text{Employee Turnover Rate}$$

$$\frac{\text{Number of Employees Involuntarily Separated}}{\text{Number of Employees in Workforce}} = \text{Involuntary Employee Turnover Rate}$$

$$\frac{\text{Number of Employees Voluntarily Separated}}{\text{Number of Employees in Workforce}} = \text{Voluntary Employee Turnover Rate}$$

$$\frac{\text{Cost of Labor}}{\text{Total Sales}} = \text{Labor Cost \%}$$

$$\frac{\text{Total Sales}}{\text{Labor Hours Used}} = \text{Sales per Labor Hour}$$

$$\frac{\text{Cost of Labor}}{\text{Guests Served}} = \text{Labor Dollars per Guest Served}$$

$$\frac{\text{Guests Served}}{\text{Cost of Labor}} = \text{Guests Served per Labor Dollar}$$

$$\frac{\text{Guests Served}}{\text{Labor Hours Used}} = \text{Guests Served per Labor Hour}$$

$$\frac{\text{Number of Estimated Guests Served}}{\text{Guests Served per Labor Dollar}} = \text{Estimated Cost of Labor}$$

$$\text{Forecasted Total Sales} \times \text{Labor Cost \% Standard} = \text{Cost of Labor Budget}$$

$$\frac{\text{Forecasted Number of Guests Served}}{\text{Guests Served per Labor Hour Standard}} = \text{Labor Hours Budget}$$

$$\frac{\text{Actual Amount}}{\text{Budgeted Amount}} = \text{\% of Budget}$$

Chapter 8—Controlling Other Expenses

$$\frac{\text{Other Expense}}{\text{Total Sales}} = \text{Other Expense Cost \%}$$

$$\frac{\text{Other Expense}}{\text{Number of Guests Served}} = \text{Other Expense Cost per Guest}$$

Chapter 9—Analyzing Results Using the Income Statement

$$\frac{\text{Food Category Cost}}{\text{Total Food Sales}} = \text{Food Category Cost \%}$$

$$\frac{\text{Cost of Food Consumed}}{\text{Average Inventory Value}} = \text{Food Inventory Turnover}$$

$$\frac{\text{Beginning Inventory Value} + \text{Ending Inventory Value}}{2}$$
$$= \text{Average Inventory Value}$$

$$\frac{\text{Cost of Beverages Consumed}}{\text{Average Beverage Inventory Value}} = \text{Beverage Inventory Turnover}$$

This Year's Sales × Last Year's Adjusted Labor Cost %
= This Year's Projected Labor Cost

$$\frac{\text{Net Income}}{\text{Total Sales}} = \text{Profit Margin (Return on Sales)}$$

$$\frac{\text{Net Income This Period} - \text{Net Income Last Period}}{\text{Net Income Last Period}} = \text{Profit Variance \%}$$

Chapter 10—Planning for Profit

Selling Price − Product Cost = Contribution Margin per Menu Item

Total Sales − Total Product Costs = Total Contribution Margin

$$\frac{\text{Total Contribution Margin}}{\text{Number of Items Sold}} = \text{Average Contribution Margin per Item}$$

$A \times B \times C \times D = \text{Goal Value}$
where
$A = 1 - \text{Food Cost \%}$
$B = \text{Item Popularity}$
$C = \text{Selling Price}$
$D = 1 - (\text{Variable Cost \%} + \text{Food Cost \%})$

Total Sales − Variable Costs = Contribution Margin

Selling Price − Variable Cost/Unit = Contribution Margin/Unit

SP/Unit − VC/Unit = CM/Unit

SP% − VC% = CM%

100% − VC% = CM%

$$\frac{\text{Fixed Costs}}{\text{Contribution Margin \%}} = \text{Break-Even Point in Sales}$$

$$\frac{\text{Fixed Costs}}{\text{Contribution Margin per Unit (Guest)}}$$
$$= \text{Break-Even Point in Guests Served}$$

$$\frac{\text{After-Tax Profit}}{(1 - \text{Tax Rate})} = \text{Before-Tax Profit}$$

$$\frac{\text{Fixed Costs} + \text{Before-Tax Profit}}{\text{Contribution Margin \%}}$$
$$= \text{Sales Dollars to Achieve Desired After-Tax Profit}$$

$$\frac{\text{Fixed Costs} + \text{Before-Tax Profit}}{\text{Contribution Margin per Unit (Guest)}}$$
$$= \text{Guests to Be Served to Achieve Desired After-Tax Profit}$$

$$\frac{\text{Minimum Labor Cost}}{1 - \text{Minimum Operating Cost}} = \text{MSP}$$

or

$$\frac{\text{Minimum Labor Cost}}{1 - (\text{Food Cost \%} + \text{Variable Cost \%})} = \text{MSP}$$

Budgeted Revenue − Budgeted Expense = Budgeted Profit

$$\frac{\text{Total Sales}}{\text{Available Seats}} = \text{Sales per Seat}$$

Chapter 11—Maintaining and Improving the Revenue Control System

Product Issues = Guest Charges = Sales Receipts = Sales Deposits

Documented Product Requests = Product Issues

Product Issues = Guest Charges

Guest Charges = Sales Receipts

Sales Receipts = Sales Deposits

Appendix C

Management Control Forms

ABC Inventory Analysis

Unit Name: _____

Item	Monthly Usage	Purchase Price	Monthly Value	Category

Attainable Food Cost

Unit Name: _____

Date Prepared: _____   Time Period: _____

Prepared By: _____

Item	Number Sold	Attainable Portion Cost	Total Cost	Menu Price	Total Sales
Total					

Actual Food Cost: _____

Attainable Food Cost: _____

Operational Efficiency Ratio: _____

Attainable Food Cost Percentage: _____

Banquet Event Order/Invoice

Unit Name: _____ Date: _____

Banquet Event Order/Invoice

Day of Event: _____ Date of Event: _____

Time of Event: _____ to _____ Time Ready By: _____

Type of Event: _____ Location: _____

Expected Count: _____ Guaranteed Count: _____ Final Count: _____

Organization Housing Event: _____

Organization Contact Person: _____

Organization Address: _____

Organization Telephone: _____ Fax: _____ E-Mail: _____

Price: _____ Tax: _____ Service Charge: _____ %

Deposit Amount: _____ Deposit Received: _____

Total Amount Due: _____ Payment Due Date: _____

Menu	Setup (Style of Room, A/V)
	Linen
Wines/Liquors	**Decor/Flowers**

Signature of Guest: _____ Date: _____

Signature of Manager: _____ Date: _____

Beverage Consumption Report

Unit Name: _____

Event: _____   Date: _____

Beverage Type	Beginning Amount	Additions	Ending Amount	Total Usage	Unit Cost	Total Cost
Liquor						
1.						
2.						
3.						
4.						
5.						
6.						
Beer						
1.						
2.						
3.						
4.						
Wine						
1.						
2.						
3.						
Other						
1.						
2.						
3.						
Total Product Cost						

Total Product Cost: _____

Guests Served: _____   Cost per Guest: _____

Remarks: _____

Beverage Product Request Log

Unit Name: _____

Date	Item Requested	Entry By

Bid Sheet

Unit Name: _____

Vendor: _____   Buyer: _____

Vendor's Address: _____   Buyer's Address: _____

Vendor's Telephone #: _____   Buyer's Telephone #: _____

Vendor's Fax #: _____   Buyer's Fax #: _____

Vendor's E-Mail: _____   Buyer's E-Mail: _____

Item Description	Unit	Bid Price

Bid Prices Fixed: from (date) to (date)

Salesperson Signature: _____ Date: _____

Bid Card

Product Name: _____   Bottle Size: _____

Balance Brought Forward: _____   Date: _____

Date	In	Out	Total on Hand

Butcher's Yield Test

Unit Name: _____   Item: _____   Date Tested: _____

Specification: _____   Item Description: _____

AP Amount Tested: _____

Price per Pound AP: _____

Loss Detail	Weight	% of Original
AP		
Fat Loss		
Bone Loss		
Cooking Loss		
Carving Loss		
Total Product Loss		

Net Product Yield: _____   EP Cost per Pound: _____

Yield Test Performed By: _____

Contribution Margin Income Statement

Unit Name: _____

		Per Unit (Guest)	Percentage
Total sales		SP	
Variable costs		VC	
Contribution margin		CM	
Fixed costs			
Before-tax profit		Guests served: =	_____
Taxes (40%)			
After-tax profit			

Cost of Beverage Sold

Unit Name: _____

Accounting Period: _____ to _____

Beginning Inventory $_____

PLUS

Purchases $_____

Goods Available for Sale $_____

LESS

Ending Inventory $_____

LESS

Transfers Out $_____

PLUS

Transfers In $_____

Cost of Beverage Sold $_____

Cost of Food Sold

Unit Name: _____

Accounting Period: _____ to _____

Beginning Inventory	$_____	
PLUS		
Purchases	$_____	
Goods Available for Sale		$_____
LESS		
Ending Inventory	$_____	
LESS		
Transfers Out	$_____	
PLUS		
Transfers In	$_____	
Cost of Food Consumed		$_____
LESS		
Employee Meals	$_____	
Cost of Food Sold		$_____

Cost of Food Sold by Food Category

Unit Name: _____

Date: _____

	Meat	Seafood	Dairy	Produce	Other	Total
Beginning Inventory						
Purchases						
Goods Available						
Ending Inventory						
Cost of Food Consumed						
Employee Meals						
Cost of Food Sold						

Credit Memo

Unit Name: _____

Vendor: _____   Delivery Date: _____

Invoice #: _____   Credit Memo #: _____

Correction

Item	Quantity	Short	Refused	Price	Credit Amount
Total					

Original Invoice Total: _____

Less: Credit Memo Total: _____

Adjusted Invoice Total: _____

Additional Information: _____

_____

_____

Vendor Representative: _____

Vendor Representative Telephone #: _____

Operation Representative: _____

Operation Representative Telephone #: _____

Daily Inventory Sheet

Unit Name: _____

Item	Description	Unit	Par Value	On Hand	Special Order	Order Amount

Employee Schedule

Unit Name: _____   Date: _____

Labor Category: _____   Shift: _____   Labor Budget: _____

Employee Name	Schedule	Hours Scheduled	Rate	Total Cost
Total				

Equipment Inspection Report

Unit Name: _____

Time Period:_____

Item Inspected	Inspection Date	Inspected By	Action Recommended
			_____ _____ _____ _____
			_____ _____ _____ _____
			_____ _____ _____ _____
			_____ _____ _____ _____
			_____ _____ _____ _____

Goal Value Analysis Data

Unit Name: _____

Item	Food Cost % (in decimal form)	Number Sold	Selling Price	Variable Cost % (in decimal form)

Goal Value Analysis Results

Unit Name: _____

Rank	Menu Item	A	B	C	D	Goal Value
1						
2						
3						
4						
5						
6						
7						

Guest Check

| Unit Name: _____ | | | | Phone #:_____ |

Date	Table	Server	Guests	Check Number

Items Ordered	Price
Subtotal	
Tax	
Gratuity	
Total	

Guest Receipt

Date	Table	Server	Guests	Check Number	Total

Guest Check Control Form

Unit Name: _____

Date:_____   Shift:_____

Check Numbers
__Issued__

Check Numbers
__Returned__

From	To	Issued To	From	To	Checks Used	Checks Accounted For	Number Missing

Unaccounted Checks:

Check Number	Issued To	Explanation	Manager's Initials

Income Statement (P&L)

Unit Name:_____

Last Year Versus This Year

	Last Year	%	This Year	%
SALES:				
Food				
Beverage				
Total Sales				
COST OF SALES:				
Food				
Beverage				
Total Cost of Sales				
GROSS PROFIT:				
Food				
Beverage				
Total Gross Profit				
OPERATING EXPENSES:				
Salaries and Wages				
Employee Benefits				
Direct Operating Expense				
Music and Entertainment				
Marketing				
Utility Services				
Repairs and Maintenance				
Administrative and General				
Occupancy				
Depreciation				
Total Operating Expenses				
Operating Income				
Interest				
Income Before Income Taxes				
Income Taxes				
Net Income				

Income Statement (P&L) Variance

Unit Name: _____

	Last Year	This Year	Variance	Variance %
SALES:				
Food				
Beverage				
Total Sales				
COST OF SALES:				
Food				
Beverage				
Total Cost of Sales				
GROSS PROFIT:				
Food				
Beverage				
Total Gross Profit				
OPERATING EXPENSES:				
Salaries and Wages				
Employee Benefits				
Direct Operating Expense				
Music and Entertainment				
Marketing				
Utility Services				
Repairs and Maintenance				
Administrative and General				
Occupancy				
Depreciation				
Total Operating Expenses				
Operating Income				
Interest				
Income Before Income Taxes				
Income Taxes				
Net Income				

Inventory Turnover

Unit Name: _____

Inventory Category	Cost of Goods Consumed	Average Inventory	Inventory Turnover
Total			

Inventory Valuation Sheet

Unit Name: _____

Inventory Date: _____

Counted By: _____   Extended By: _____

Item	Unit	Item Amount	Item Value	Inventory Value
			Page Total	

Job Description

Unit Name: _____   Position Title: _____

Primary Tasks:

1. _____   7. _____
_____   _____

2. _____   8. _____
_____   _____

3. _____   9. _____
_____   _____

4. _____   10. _____
_____   _____

5. _____   11. _____
_____   _____

6. _____   12. _____
_____   _____

Special Comments: _____

_____

_____

Salary Range: _____   Signature: _____

Job Specification

Unit Name: _____   Position Title: _____

Personal Characteristics Required:

1. _____

2. _____

3. _____

4. _____

5. _____

6. _____

Special Comments: _____

_____

Job Specification Prepared By: _____

Labor Budget

Unit Name: _____

Time Period	Forecasted Total Sales	Labor Cost % Standard	Cost of Labor Budget
Week 1			
Week 2			
Week 3			
Week 4			
Total			

Labor Cost Analysis—Actual Versus Budgeted

Unit Name: _____

| | Sales | | | Labor Costs | | | Labor Cost % | |
| | Budgeted | Actual | % of Budget | Budgeted | Actual | % of Budget | Budgeted | Actual |
Week								
1								
2								
3								
4								
Total								

Labor Productivity—Guests Served per Labor Dollar

Unit Name: _____

Week	Guests Served	Cost of Labor	Guests Served per Labor Dollar
1			
2			
3			
4			
Total			

Labor Productivity—Guests Served per Labor Dollar

Unit Name: _____

Week	Guests Served	Labor Hours Used	Guests Served per Labor Dollar
1			
2			
3			
4			
Total			

Labor Productivity—Labor Cost %

Unit Name: _____

Week	Cost of Labor	Sales	Labor Cost %
1			
2			
3			
4			
Total			

Labor Productivity—Labor Dollars per Guest Served

Unit Name: _____

Week	Cost of Labor	Guests Served	Labor Dollars per Guest Served
1			
2			
3			
4			
Total			

Labor Productivity—Sales per Labor Hour

Unit Name: _____

Week	Sales	Labor Hours Used	Sales per Labor Hour
1			
2			
3			
4			
Total			

Matrix Analysis

Unit Name: _____

Food Cost Percentage

High Food Cost %
(Above _____)

Low Food Cost %
(Below _____)

Low Popularity
(Below_____) High Popularity
(Above_____)

Contribution Margin

High Contribution Margin
(Above _____)

Low Contribution Margin
(Below _____)

Low Popularity
(Below_____) High Popularity
(Above_____)

Menu Analysis Worksheet

Menu Item	Number Sold	Selling Price	Total Sales	Item Cost	Total Cost	Item Contribution Margin	Total Contribution Margin	Food Cost %
Total								
Weighted Average								

Other Expense Cost %

Unit Name: _____

Sales	Fixed Expense	Variable Expense %	Total Other Expense	Other Expense Cost %

Performance to Budget Summary

Unit Name: _____

Item	Budget	Actual	% of Budget
Meals Served			
Revenue			
Food Expense			
Labor Expense			
Other Expense			
Total Expense			
Profit			

Price Comparison Sheet

Unit Name: _____

Vendors

    A. _____

    B. _____

    C. _____

Category: _____

Date Bid: _____

Item Description	Unit	A	B	C	Best Bid $	Best Company	Last Price Paid

Reviewed By: _____

Product Specification

Unit Name: _____

Product Name: _____   Spec #: _____

Pricing Unit: _____

Standard/Grade: _____

_____

_____

Weight Range: _____

_____

Packaging: _____

_____

_____

Container Size: _____

Intended Use: _____

Other Information: _____

_____

Product Yield: _____

Production Schedule

Unit Name: _____

Date: _____

	Menu Item	Sales Forecast	Prior-Day Carryover	New Production	Total Available	Number Sold	Carry-over
1.							
2.							
3.							
4							
5.							
6.							
7.							
8.							
9.							
10.							
11.							
12.							
13.							
14.							
15.							
16.							
17.							
18.							

Special Instructions: _____

_____

_____

_____

Production Manager: _____

Purchase Order

Unit Name: _____

Vendor: _____   Purchase Order #: _____

Vendor's Address: _____   Delivery Date: _____

Vendor's Telephone #: _____

Vendor's Fax #: _____

Vendor's E-Mail: _____

Item Purchased	Spec #	Quantity Ordered	Quoted Price	Extended Price
1.				
2.				
3.				
4.				
5.				
6.				
7.				
8.				
9.				
10.				
11.				
12.				
13.				
14.				
Total				

Order Date: _____   Comments: _____

Ordered By: _____   _____

Received By: _____   _____

Delivery Instructions: _____   _____

_____   _____

545

Receiving Report

Unit Name: _____

Date: _____

Distribution

Supplier	Invoice #	Item	Unit Price	Number of Units	Total Cost	A	B	C	D	E
Total Units										
Total Cost										

Distribution Key:

A. _____ D. _____

B. _____ E. _____

C. _____

Comments: _____

_____

_____

_____

Requisition–Liquor

Unit Name: _____

Shift: _____   Date: _____

Service Area: _____

Verified by Management

Product	Number of Empties	Bottle Size	Bartender	Management
Total Empties				

Requisition–Storeroom

Unit Name: _____

Requisition #: _____

Date: _____

Item	Storage Unit	Requested Amount	Issued Amount	Unit Cost	Total Cost
Total					

To: Kitchen_____   Requisition Approved By: _____

Bar_____   Requisition Filled By: _____

Salad Bar or Buffet Product Usage

Unit Name: _____

Date: _____

Item	Category	Beginning Amount	Additions	Ending Amount	Total Usage	Unit Cost	Total Cost
Total Product Cost							

Total Product Cost: _____

Guests Served: _____   Cost per Guest: _____

Sales Forecast—Menu Items

Unit Name: _____

Menu Item	Guest Forecast	Popularity Index	Predicted Number to Be Sold
Total			

Sales Forecast—Quarterly

Unit Name: _____

	Total Sales			Guest Counts			
Month	Last Year	% Increase Estimate	Sales Forecast	Last Year	% Increase Estimate	Guest Count Forecast	Average Sales per Guest Forecast
January							
February							
March							
Total							

	Total Sales			Guest Counts			
Month	Last Year	% Increase Estimate	Sales Forecast	Last Year	% Increase Estimate	Guest Count Forecast	Average Sales per Guest Forecast
April							
May							
June							
Total							

	Total Sales			Guest Counts			
Month	Last Year	% Increase Estimate	Sales Forecast	Last Year	% Increase Estimate	Guest Count Forecast	Average Sales per Guest Forecast
July							
August							
September							
Total							

	Total Sales			Guest Counts			
Month	Last Year	% Increase Estimate	Sales Forecast	Last Year	% Increase Estimate	Guest Count Forecast	Average Sales per Guest Forecast
October							
November							
December							
Total							

Sales History—Average Sales per Guest

Unit Name: _____

Sales Period	Date	Sales	Guest Served	Average Sales per Guest
Monday				
Tuesday				
Wednesday				
Thursday				
Friday				
Saturday				
Sunday				
Week's Total				

Sales Period	Date	Sales	Guest Served	Average Sales per Guest
Monday				
Tuesday				
Wednesday				
Thursday				
Friday				
Saturday				
Sunday				
Week's Total				

Sales History—Daily Guests

Unit Name: _____

Guests Served

Serving Period	Mon	Tues	Wed	Thurs	Fri	Sat	Sun	Total

Guests Served

Serving Period	Mon	Tues	Wed	Thurs	Fri	Sat	Sun	Total

Sales History—Menu Items

Unit Name: _____

Date: _____

Menu Item	Mon	Tues	Wed	Thurs	Fri	Total	Week's Average

Sales History—Quarterly Variance

Unit Name: _____

Month	Sales This Year	Sales Last Year	Variance	Percentage Variance
January				
February				
March				
Total				

Month	Sales This Year	Sales Last Year	Variance	Percentage Variance
April				
May				
June				
Total				

Month	Sales This Year	Sales Last Year	Variance	Percentage Variance
July				
August				
September				
Total				

Month	Sales This Year	Sales Last Year	Variance	Percentage Variance
October				
November				
December				
Total				

Sales History—Seven-Day Rolling Average

Unit Name: _____

Seven-Day Period

Date	1–7	2–8	3–9	4–10	5–11	6–12	7–13	8–14
		–						
			–					
				–				
					–			
						–		
							–	
								–
Total								
Seven-Day Rolling Average								

Sales History—Total Sales Record

Unit Name: _____

Date: _____

Item	Number Sold	Selling Price	Total Sales
Total			

Sales History—Weekly Sales

Unit Name: _____

Sales Period	Date	Daily Sales	Sales to Date
Monday			
Tuesday			
Wednesday			
Thursday			
Friday			
Saturday			
Sunday			
Week's Total			

Sales Period	Date	Daily Sales	Sales to Date
Monday			
Tuesday			
Wednesday			
Thursday			
Friday			
Saturday			
Sunday			
Week's Total			

Sales Mix Data

Unit Name: _____

Total Sales: _____   Guests Served: _____

Total Food Cost: _____   Food Cost %: _____

Item	Number Sold	Item Cost	Total Food Cost	Selling Price	Total Sales	Food Cost %
Total						

Sales Receipt Report

Unit Name: _____

Performed By:

Date: _____   Cashier: _____

Shift: _____   Supervisor: _____

Revenue per Guest Checks

Guest check totals   _____

Service charges   _____

Tax   _____

    Total guest check revenue   _____

Receipts

Charge cards

  VISA   _____

  MasterCard   _____

  Discover   _____

  American Express   _____

    Total charge cards receipts   _____

Cash

  Twenties and larger   _____

  Tens   _____

  Five   _____

  Ones   _____

  Change   _____

    Total cash   _____

Less: Bank   _____

      Tip-outs   _____

Net cash receipts   _____

Net total receipts   _____

Variance check revenue to net receipts   _____

561

Six-Column Form

Unit Name: _____

Date: _____

Weekday	Today	To Date	Today	To Date	Today	To Date

Staffing Guide

Unit Name: _____ Date:_____

Number of Guests Anticipated	Number of Employees Needed

Standardized Recipe

Unit Name: _____

Menu Item: _____

Special Instructions: _____   Recipe Yield: _____

_____   Portion Size: _____

_____   Portion Cost: _____

_____

Ingredients	Amount	Method

Standardized Recipe Adjustment

Unit Name: _____ Date: _____

Ingredient	Original Amount	Ounces	% of Total	Total Amount Required	% of Total	New Recipe Amount
Total						

Standardized Recipe Cost Sheet

Unit Name: _____

Menu Item: _____   Recipe Number: _____

Special Notes: _____   Recipe Yield: _____

_____   Portion Size: _____

_____   Portion Cost: _____

_____

Ingredients   Ingredient Cost

Item	Amount	Unit Cost	Total Cost
Total Cost			

Total Recipe Cost: _____   Recipe Type: _____

Portion Cost: _____   Date Costed: _____

Previous Portion Cost: _____   Previous Date Costed: _____

Transfer Record

Unit Name: _____

Date: _____

Product Value

Date	Item	Quantity	To Department	From Department	Issued By	Received By
Total Product Value						

Wine Cellar Issues

Unit Name: _____

Date: _____

	Product	Vintage	Number of Bottles	Guest Check #	Removed By
1.					
2.					
3.					
4.					
5.					
6.					
7.					
8.					
9.					
10.					
11.					
12.					

Remarks: _____

_____

_____

_____

_____

Wine List

Unit Name: _____

	Sparkling Wine and Champagne	$ per Glass/$ per Bottle
101		
102		
103		
104		
105		
	Chardonnay	
201		
202		
203		
204		
205		
	Other White Wines	
206		
207		
208		
209		
210		
	Cabernet Sauvignon	
301		
302		
303		
304		
305		
	Merlot	
306		
307		
308		
309		
	Pinot Noir	
310		
311		
312		
313		

Appendix D

Fun on the Web! Sites

Chapter 1–Managing Revenue and Expense

www.restaurant.org

Chapter 2–Determining Sales Forecasts

www.micros.com   www.datatrakpos.com
www.squirrelsystems.com

Chapter 3–Managing the Cost of Food

www.produceonline.com   www.thomasregister.com
www.namp.com   www.externalharddrive.com
www.seafood.com   www.usda.com

Chapter 4–Managing the Cost of Beverages

Do a Web search! Search for "Alcoholic Beverage Commission" to find regulations on the sale and service of alcohol. When you get a list of sites, just pick a state. Yours might be one of them! (Recommended search engine–MSN)

www.beerweek.com   · www.winespectator.com
www.alestreetnews.com   www.wineculture.com
www.beeerhistory.com   www.wino.net
www.allaboutbeer.com   www.vine2wine.com
www.celebrator.com   www.cocktails.about.com
www.wine.com   www.food.epicurious.com

If you are 21 or over, you can explore numerous sites developed by liquor companies. Go to the MSN search engine and click on "Liquor & Spirits." From there, you will be launched into a world of spirits companies.

Chapter 5–Managing the Food and Beverage Production Process

www.computrition.com www.restaurantplus.com
www.cbord.com www.foodtrak.com
www.foodsoftware.com www.chefdesk.com

Chapter 6–Managing Food and Beverage Pricing

www.zagat.com

Chapter 7–Managing the Cost of Labor

www.alohapos.com www.symbioticsys.com
www.foodsoftware.com www.dol.gov

Chapter 8–Controlling Other Expenses

www.epa.gov/smallbiz www.dinegreen.com
www.cygnus-group.com

Chapter 9–Analyzing Results Using the Income Statement

www.restaurant.org www.clubnet.com
www.ei-ahma.org

Chapter 10–Planning for Profit

Search these sites using key words such as food and beverage, cost control, hospitality accounting, and menu engineering to find resources to add to your book collection.

www.amazon.com www.barnesandnoble.com
www.borders.com

Chapter 11—Maintaining and Improving the Revenue Control System

www.totalmerchant-ca.com   www.visa.com
www.novusnet.com   www.treas.gov/usss
www.americanexpress.com

Chapter 12—Using Technology to Enhance Control Systems

www.micros.com   www.restaurant.org
www.squirrelsystems.com   www.ahma.com
www.datatrakpos.com   www.eatright.com
www.computrition.com   www.dmaonline.org
www.cbord.com   www.acfchefs.org
www.foodsoftware.com   www.cmaa.org
www.restaurantplus.com   www.asfsa.org
www.foodtrak.com   www.ienace.org
www.alohapos.com   www.iaha.org
www.symbioticsys.com   www.ih-ra.com

Glossary

Acceptance hours. The hours of the day in which an operation is willing to accept food and beverage deliveries.

Accounting period. A period of time, that is, hour, day, week, or month, in which an operator wishes to analyze revenue and expenses.

Accounts receivable. The term used to refer to guest charges that have been billed to the guest but not yet collected.

Alcoholic beverages. Those products that are meant for consumption as a beverage and that contain a significant amount of ethyl alcohol. They are classified as beer, wine, or spirits.

Ap required. As purchased amount necessary to yield the desired EP weight. AP required is computed as EP required divided by yield percentage.

As needed. A system of determining the purchase point by using sales forecasts and standardized recipes to decide how much of an item to place in inventory.

As purchased (AP). This term refers to the weight or count of a product as delivered to the foodservice operator.

Attainable food cost. That cost of goods consumed figure that should be achievable given the product sales mix of a particular operation.

Auditors. Those individuals responsible for reviewing and evaluating proper operational procedures.

Average. The value arrived at by adding the quantities in a series and dividing the sum of the quantities by the number of items in the series.

Average sales per guest. the mean amount of money spent per customer during a given financial accounting period. Often referred to as check average.

Back of the house. The kitchen production area of a foodservice establishment.

Beer. A fermented beverage made from grain and flavored with hops.

Beginning inventory. The dollar value of all products on hand at the beginning of the accounting period. This amount is determined by completing a physical inventory.

Best price. The lowest price that meets the requirement of both the foodservice operation and its vendor.

Beverage costs. The costs related to the sale of alcoholic beverages.

Bid sheet. A form used to compare prices among many vendors in order to select the best prices.

Bin card. An index card with both additions to and deletions from inventory of a given product. To facilitate its use, the card is usually affixed to the shelf that holds the given item. Used in a perpetual inventory system.

Bonding. Purchasing an insurance policy to protect the operation in case of employee theft.

Break-even point. The point at which operational expenses are exactly equal to sales revenue.

Broken case. A case of beverage products in which several different brands or products make up the contents of the case.

Budget. A forecast or estimate of projected revenue, expense, and profit for a defined accounting period. Often referred to as plan.

Bundling. The practice of selecting specific menu items and pricing them as a group, in such a manner that the single menu price of the group is lower than if the items comprising the group were purchased individually.

Call-in. A system whereby employees who are off duty are required to check in with management on a daily basis to see if the volume is such that they may be needed.

Call liquors. Those spirits that are requested (called for) by a particular brand name.

Carryover. A menu item prepared for sale during a meal period but carried over for use in a different meal period.

Category food cost percentage. A food cost percentage computed on a portion of total food usage. Categories include meat, seafood, dairy, produce, etc.

Check average. *See* **Average sales per guest.**

Cherry picker. A customer who buys only those items from a supplier that are the lowest in price among the supplier's competition.

COLA. Cost of living adjustment. A term to describe a raise in employee pay.

Comp. Short for the word complimentary, which refers to the practice of management giving a product to a guest without a charge. This can be done for a special customer or as a way of making amends for an operational error.

Contract price. A price mutually agreed upon by supplier and operator. This price is the amount to be paid for a product or products over a prescribed period of time.

Contribution margin. The profit or margin that remains after product cost is subtracted from an item's selling price.

Contribution margin for overall operation. The dollar amount that contributes to covering fixed costs and providing for a profit.

Contribution margin income statement. A financial summary that shows P&L items in terms of sales, variable costs, contribution margin, fixed costs, and profit.

Contribution margin per menu item. The amount that remains after the product cost of the menu item is subtracted from the item's selling price.

Controllable expense. An expense in which the decisions made by the foodservice manager can have the effect of either increasing or reducing the expense.

Cost. *See* **Expense.**

Cost accounting. *See* **Managerial accounting.**

Cost of food consumed. The actual dollar value of all food used, or consumed, by the operation.

Cost of food sold. The dollar amount of all food actually sold, thrown away, wasted, or stolen plus or minus transfers from other units, minus employee meals.

Cost per guest. A method of analyzing costs that uses the total expense and total number of guests served to establish an actual cost of servicing each guest.

Count. Term used to designate size.

Credit memo. An addendum to the vendor's delivery slip (invoice) that reconciles differences between the delivery slip and the purchase order.

Cycle menu. A menu that is in effect for a predetermined length of time such as 7 days or 14 days.

Daily inventory sheet. A form that lists the items in storage, the unit of purchase, and the par value. It also contains the following columns: on hand, special order, and order amount.

Daily menu. A menu that changes every day.

Desired profit. The profit that an owner seeks to achieve on a predicted quantity of revenue.

Draft beer. The term used to identify beer products sold in a keg.

Dramshop laws. The term used to describe a series of legislative acts that, under certain conditions, holds businesses and, in some cases, individuals, personally responsible for the actions of guests who consume excessive amounts of alcoholic beverages. These "laws" shift the liability for acts committed by an individual under the influence of alcohol from that individual to the server or operation that supplied the intoxicating beverage.

Edible portion (EP). This term refers to the weight or count of a product after it has been trimmed, cooked, and portioned.

Embezzlement. The term used to describe theft of a type where the money, although legally possessed by the embezzler, is diverted to the embezzler by his or her fraudulent action.

Ending inventory. The dollar value of all products on hand at the end of the accounting period. This amount is determined by completing a physical inventory.

Ethics. The choices of proper conduct made by an individual in his or her relationships with others.

Expense. The price paid to obtain the items required to operate the business. Often referred to as cost.

Extended price. The price per unit multiplied by the number of units. This refers to a total unit price on a delivery slip or invoice.

FIFO. With the first-in, first-out method of storage, the operator intends to sell his or her oldest product before selling the most recently delivered product.

Fiscal year. Start and stop dates for a 365-day accounting period. This period need not begin in January and end in December.

Fixed average. The average amount of sales or volume over a specific series or time period, for example, first month of the year or second week of the second month.

Fixed expense.   An expense that remains constant despite increases or decreases in sales volume.

Fixed payroll.   Those dollars spent on employees such as managers, receiving clerks, and dietitians whose presence is not generally directly dependent on the number of guests served.

Food cost percentage.   The portion of food sales that was spent on food expenses.

Food costs.   The dollar costs associated with actually producing the menu item(s) a guest selects.

Forecasting.   The process of estimating future revenue or expenses of a hospitality operation.

Franchiser.   The entity responsible for selling and maintaining control over the franchise name. (Alternative spelling: franchisor.)

Free-pouring.   Pouring liquor from a bottle without measuring the poured amount.

Fresh dated.   A food package upon which a date is stamped to indicate the freshness of its contents.

Goal value analysis.   A menu pricing and analysis system that compares goals of the foodservice operation to performance of individual menu items.

Goods available for sale.   The sum of the beginning inventory and purchases. It represents the value of all food that was available for sale during the accounting period.

Guest check.   A written record of what was purchased by the guest and how much the guest was charged for the item(s).

Guest count.   The number of individuals served in a defined time period.

Half-bottle.   A bottle of wine that is approximately one-half the size of the standard 750-ml wine bottle. Typically sold for either room service or dining room consumption. Also known as a split.

Hardware.   The machines and equipment used to operate computer software.

Head size.   The amount of space on the top of a glass of beer that is made up of foam. Thus, a glass of beer with 1 inch of foam on its top is said to have a 1-inch head.

House wine.   The term used to indicate the type of wine to be served in the event a specific brand name product is not requested by the guest.

Hydrometer.   An instrument used to measure the specific gravity of a liquid.

Ideal expense.   Management's view of the correct or appropriate amount of expense necessary to generate a given quantity of sales.

Income.   Net income. *See* **Profit.**

Income statement.   *See* **Profit and loss statement (P&L).**

Ingredient room.   A storeroom or section of a storeroom where ingredients are weighed and measured according to standardized recipes, and then delivered to the appropriate kitchen production area.

Inventory turnover.   The number of times the total value of inventory has been purchased and replaced in an accounting period.

Issuing.   The process of supplying food or beverage products from storage by management for use in an operation.

Jigger.   A bar device used to measure predetermined quantities of alcoholic beverages. Jiggers usually are marked in ounces and portions of an ounce, for example, 1 ounce or 1 1/2 ounces.

Job description.   A listing of the tasks to be performed in a particular position.

Job specification.   A listing of the personal skills and characteristics needed to perform those tasks pertaining to a particular job description.

Labor costs.   *See* **Labor expense.**

Labor expense.   All expenses (costs), including payroll, required to maintain a work force in a foodservice operation.

LIFO.   With the last-in, first-out method of storage, the operator intends to sell his or her most recently delivered product before selling the older product.

Loss leader.   A menu item that is priced very low for the purpose of drawing large numbers of customers to the operation.

Managerial accounting.   The process of documenting and analyzing sales, expenses, and profits. Sometimes referred to as cost accounting.

Minimum order requirement.   The smallest order, usually expressed in dollar value, that can be placed with a vendor who delivers.

Minimum sales point (MSP).   The dollar sales volume required to justify staying open.

Minimum staff.   The term used to designate the least number of employees, or payroll dollars, required to operate a facility or department within the facility.

Mixed expense.   An expense that has properties of both a fixed and a variable expense.

Negligent hiring.   Failure on the part of an employer to exercise reasonable care in the selection of employees.

Net income.   The profit realized after all expenses and appropriate taxes for a business have been paid.

Noncontrollable expense.   An expense that the foodservice manager can neither increase nor decrease.

Occupancy costs.   Expenses related to occupying and paying for the physical facility that houses the foodservice unit.

OJT.   On-the-job training. A method of training in which workers are training while they actually are performing their required tasks.

On-call.   A system whereby selected employees who are off duty can be contacted by management on short notice to cover for other employees who are absent or to come to work if customer demand suddenly increases.

Open bar.   A bar in which no charge for an individual drink is made to the customer, thus establishing an all-you-can-drink environment. Sometimes referred to as a hotel bar.

Opportunity cost.   The cost of foregoing the next best alternative when making a decision. For example, with two choices, A & B, both having potential benefits or returns, if A is chosen, then the potential benefits from choosing B are lost.

Other expenses. The expenses of an operation that are neither food, beverage, nor labor.

Oxidation. A process that occurs when oxygen comes in contact with bottled wine, resulting in a deterioration of the wine product.

Padded inventory. The term used to describe the inappropriate activity of adding a value for nonexisting inventory items to the value of total inventory in an effort to understate actual costs.

Par level. A system of determining the purchase point by using management-established minimum and maximum allowable inventory levels for a given inventory item.

Payroll. Total wages and salaries paid by a foodservice operation to its employees.

Percent. The number "out of each hundred." Thus, 10 percent means 10 out of each 100. This is computed by dividing the part by the whole.

Percent selecting. A formula for determining the proportion of people who will buy a given menu item from a list of menu choices.

Percentage variance. The change in sales, expressed as a percentage, that results from comparing two operating periods.

Perpetual inventory. An inventory control system in which additions to and deletions from total inventory are noted as they occur.

Perpetual inventory card. A bin card that includes the product's price at the top of the card, allowing for continual tracking of the quantity of an item on hand and its price.

Physical inventory. An inventory control system in which an actual or physical count and valuation of all inventory on hand is taken at the close of each accounting period.

Plan. *See* **Budget.**

Point of sales (POS) system. A system for controlling hospitality operations' cash and product usage by using a computer processor and, depending on the size of the operation, additional computer hardware, communication devices, and/or software.

Popularity index. The percentage of total guests choosing a given menu item from a list of menu alternatives.

Predicted number to be sold. A method of determining the number of a given menu item that is likely to be sold if the total number of customers to be served is known.

Premium liquors. Expensive call liquors.

Price blending. The process of assigning prices based on product groups for the purpose of achieving predetermined cost objectives.

Price spread. The difference in price on a menu between the lowest and highest priced item of a similar nature.

Productivity. The amount of work performed by a worker in a set amount of time.

Productivity ratio. This formula refers to the total unit output divided by the total unit input.

Productivity standard. Management's expectation of the productivity ratio of each employee. Also, management's view of what constitutes the appropriate productivity ratio in a given foodservice unit or units.

Product mix. *See* **Sales mix.**

Product specification. A detailed description of an ingredient or menu item.

Profit. The dollars that remain after all expenses have been paid. Often referred to as net income.

Profit and loss statement (P&L). A detailed listing of revenue and expenses for a given accounting period. Also referred to as an income statement.

Projected sales. Sales that may be determined by either dollar sales or customer count. Projected sales are established by using sales histories and other knowledge the operator may have that could impact total volume. They are predictions of future sales volume.

Pull date. Expiration date on beverage products, usually beers, after which they should not be sold.

Purchase order. A listing of products requested by the purchasing agent. The purchase order, or PO, lists various product information, including quantity ordered and price quoted by the vendor.

Purchase point. The point in time when an item held in inventory reaches a level that indicates it should be reordered.

Purchases. The sum cost of all food purchased during the accounting period. Determined by adding all properly tabulated invoices for the accounting period.

Quick-change artist. A guest who, having practiced the routine many times, attempts to confuse the cashier; in his or her confusion, the cashier gives the guest too much change.

Recipe ready. A recipe ingredient that is cleaned, trimmed, cooked, and generally completed, save for its addition to the recipe.

Refusal hours. Those hours of the day in which an operation refuses to accept food and beverage deliveries.

Reporting period. The process of reporting a time period for which records are being maintained. This may be of the same duration as an accounting period.

Requisition. When a food or beverage product is requested from storage by an employee for use in an operation.

Return on sales (ROS). Often referred to as operating profit percentage. ROS can also be stated in whole dollar terms.

Revenue. The term used to indicate the dollars taken in by the business in a defined period of time. Often referred to as sales.

Rolling average. The average amount of sales or volume over a changing time period, for example, the last ten days or the last three weeks.

Safety stock. These are additions to par stock, held as a hedge against the possibility of extra demand for a given product. This helps reduce the risk of being out of stock on a given item.

Salaried employee. An employee who receives the same income per week or month regardless of the number of hours worked.

Sales. *See* **Revenue.**

Sales forecast. A prediction of the number of guests to be served and the revenues they will generate in a defined, future time period.

Sales history. A record of sales achieved by an operator in a given sales outlet during a specifically identified time period.

Sales mix. The series of consumer purchasing decisions that result in a specific food and beverage cost percentage. Sales mix affects overall product cost percentage any time menu items have varying food and beverage cost percentages.

Sales to date. The cumulative sales figures reported during a given financial accounting period.

Sales variance. An increase or decrease from previously experienced or predicted sales levels.

Sales volume. The number of units sold.

Separated. The term used to describe employees who have either quit, been terminated, or in some other manner have left their place of employment.

Shelf life. The period of time an ingredient or menu item maintains its freshness, flavor, and quality.

Shorting. When the vendor is unable to deliver the quantity of item ordered for the appointed delivery date.

Skip. *See* **Walk.**

Software. The set of instructions that control the workings of computer hardware and direct the processing of data.

SOP. Acronym for standard operating procedure.

Source reduction. Working with food manufacturers and wholesalers to reduce product packaging waste.

Spec. *See* **Product specification.**

Spirits. Fermented beverages that are distilled to increase the alcohol content of the product.

Split. *See* **Half-bottle.**

Split shift. A scheduling technique used to match individual employee work shifts with the peaks and valleys of customer demand.

Spotter. An individual employed by management for the purpose of inconspicuously observing bartenders and waitstaff in order to detect any fraudulent or policy violating behavior.

Standard cost. The labor cost needed to meet established productivity standards.

Standardized recipe. The procedures to be used for consistently preparing and serving a given menu item.

Standardized recipe cost sheet. A record of the ingredient costs required to produce an item sold by a foodservice operation.

Standard menu. A printed and otherwise fixed menu that stays the same day after day.

Task training. The training undertaken to ensure an employee has the skills to meet productivity goals.

Two-key system. A system to control access to storage areas.

Uniform systems of accounts. Standardized sets of procedures used for categorizing revenue and expense in a defined industry, for example, uniform system of accounts for restaurants (USAR).

Value pricing. The practice of reducing all or most prices on the menu in the belief that total guest counts will increase to the point that total sales revenue also increases.

Variable expense. An expense that generally increases as sales volume increases and decreases as sales volume decreases.

Variable payroll. Those dollars expended on employees whose presence is directly dependent on the number of guests served. These employees include servers, bartenders, and dishwashers, for example. As the number of guests served increases, the number of these individuals required to do the job also increases. As the number of guests served decreases, variable payroll should decrease.

Vintage. The specific year(s) of production for a wine.

Vintner. Wine producer.

Walk. A term used to describe a customer who has consumed a product, but leaves the foodservice operation without paying the bill. Also known as a skip.

Waste percentage. This formula is defined as product loss divided by AP weight and refers to product lost in the preparation process.

Weighted average. An average that combines data on the number of guests served and how much each has spent during a given financial accounting period.

Well liquors. Those spirits that are served by an operation when the customer does not specify a particular brand name.

Wine. A fermented beverage made from grapes, fruits, or berries.

Wine list. A menu of wine offerings.

Working stock. The quantity of goods from inventory reasonably expected to be used between deliveries.

Yield percentage. This formula is defined as 1 minus waste percentage and refers to the amount of product available for use by the operator after all preparation-related losses have been taken into account.

Yield test. A procedure used to determine actual EP ingredient costs. It is used to help establish actual costs on a product that will experience weight or volume loss in preparation.

Bibliography

Adams, Deborah. *Management Accounting for the Hospitality Industry: A Strategic Approach*. London: Cassell Academic, 1997.

American Hotel and Motel Association. *Uniform System of Accounts for the Lodging Industry*. 9th ed. Orlando: Educational Institute of the American Hotel and Motel Association, 1996.

Chaban, Joel. *Practical Foodservice Spreadsheets With Lotus 1-2-3*. New York: John Wiley & Sons, 1997.

Club Managers Association of America (Editor). *Uniform System of Financial Reporting for Clubs*. Dubuque, IA: Kendall/Hunt Publishing, 1996.

Coltman, Michael M., and Martin G. Jagels. *Hospitality Management Accounting*. 7th ed. New York: John Wiley & Sons, 2000.

Defranco, Agnes L., and Pender B. M. Noriega. *Cost Control in the Hospitality Industry*. Upper Saddle River, NJ: Prentice Hall, 1999.

Deloitte & Touche, LLP. *Uniform System of Accounts for Restaurants*. 7th ed. Washington, DC: National Restaurant Association, 1996.

Dittmer, Paul R., and Gerald G. Griffin. *Principles of Food, Beverage, and Labor Cost Controls for Hotels and Restaurants*. 6th ed. New York: John Wiley & Sons, 1999.

Drysdale, John A. *Profitable Menu Planning*. Upper Saddle River, NJ: Prentice Hall, 1997.

Foster, Dennis L. *Food and Beverage: Operations, Methods, and Cost Controls*. New York: Glencoe/McGraw–Hill, 1994.

Gisslen, Wayne. *Advanced Professional Cooking*. New York: John Wiley & Sons, 1992.

Gisslen, Wayne. *Professional Cooking*. 4th ed. New York: John Wiley & Sons, 1999.

Haines, Robert. *Math Principles for Food Service Occupations*. Albany: Delmar Publishing, 1995.

Harris, Peter. *Managerial Accounting in the Hospitality Industry*. Cheltenham, UK: Stanley Thornes Publications, 1992.

Hug, Richard J., and Marshall C. Warfel. *Menu Planning and Merchandising*. 2d ed. Berkeley, CA: McCutchan Publishing, 1997.

Katsigris, Costas, and Mary Porter. *The Bar and Beverage Book: Basics of Profitable Management*. New York: John Wiley & Sons, 1991.

Keiser, James, and Frederick J. Demicco. *Controlling and Analyzing Costs in Foodservice Operations*. Indianapolis: MacMillan Publishing, 1993.

Keister, Douglas C. *Food and Beverage Control*. Upper Saddle River, NJ: Prentice Hall, 1996.

Knight, John Barton, and Lendal H. Kotschevar. *Quantity Food Production, Planning, and Management.* 3d ed. New York: John Wiley & Sons, 2000.

Kotschevar, Lendal Henry, and Richard Donnelly. *Quantity Food Purchasing.* Upper Saddle River, NJ: Prentice Hall, 1998.

Labensky, Sarah R. *Applied Math for Food Service.* Upper Saddle River, NJ: Prentice Hall, 1997.

Lipinski, Robert A., Kathie Lipinski, and Kathleen Lipinski (Contributor). *Professional Beverage Management.* New York: John Wiley & Sons, 1996.

Lynch, Francis T. *The Book of Yields: Food Facts for Accurate Recipe Costing.* 4th ed. Sonora, CA: ChefDesk, 1998.

Marvin, B. *From Turnover to Teamwork: How to Build and Retain a Customer-Oriented Foodservice Staff.* New York: John Wiley & Sons, 1994.

McVety, Paul J., Bradley J. Ware, and Claudette Levesque. *Fundamentals of Menu Planning.* 2d ed. New York: John Wiley & Sons, 2001.

Messersmith, Ann M., and Judy L. Miller. *Forecasting in Foodservice.* New York: John Wiley & Sons, 1992.

Miller, Jack E., and David V. Pavesic (Contributor). *Menu Pricing & Strategy.* New York: John Wiley & Sons, 1997.

National Restaurant Association. *Menu Analysis: 1997.* Washington, DC: National Restaurant Association, 1998.

Ninemeier, Jack D. *Planning and Control for Food and Beverage Operations.* Orlando: Educational Institute of the American Hotel and Motel Association, 1998.

Ojugo, Clement, and Todd Rymer. *Practical Food and Beverage Cost Control.* Albany: Delmar Publishing, 1998.

Pavesic, David V. *Fundamental Principles of Restaurant Cost Control.* Upper Saddle River, NJ: Prentice Hall, 1997.

Pavesic, David V. *Labor Cost: 25 Keys to Profitable Success (Restaurant Manager's Pocket Handbook Series).* New York: Lebhar–Friedman Books, 1999.

Pavesic, David V. *Purchasing and Inventory: 25 Keys to Profitable Success (Restaurant Manager's Pocket Handbook Series).* New York: Lebhar–Friedman Books, 1999.

Reed, Lewis. Specs: *The Comprehensive Foodservice Purchasing and Specification Manual.* 2d ed. New York: John Wiley & Sons, 1993.

Roberts, Phil, T. J. McDonald, and Jim Sullivan. *Playing Games at Work: 52 Best Incentives, Contests, and Rewards for the Hospitality Industry.* Denver: Pencom, 1994.

Sanders, Edward E., and Timothy H. Hill. *Foodservice Profitability: A Control Approach.* Upper Saddle River, NJ: Prentice Hall, 1997.

Schmidgall, Raymond S. *Hospitality Industry Managerial Accounting.* 4th ed. Orlando: Educational Institute of the American Hotel and Motel Association, 1997.

Schmidt, Arno. *Chef's Book of Formulas, Yields, and Sizes.* New York: John Wiley & Sons, 1995.

Spears, Marion C., and Sharon Morcos. *Foodservice Procurement: Purchasing for Profit.* Upper Saddle River, NJ: Prentice Hall, 1998.

Stefanelli, John M. *Purchasing: Selection and Procurement for the Hospitality Industry.* 4th ed. New York: John Wiley & Sons, 1997.

Sullivan, Jim, Deborah Henckel (Illustrator), and Andrea Steward (Contributor). *Turn the Tables on Turnover: 52 Ways to Find, Hire, and Keep the Best Hospitality Employees.* Denver: Pencom, 1995.

Sullivan, Jim. *Mind Your Own Business: People, Performance, Profits.* New York: Lebhar–Friedman Books, 1999.

Ulm, Robert A. *How Much to Buy: A Foodservice Purchasing Workbook.* Indianapolis: MacMillan Publishing, 1993.

Zaccarelli, Herman E. *Foodservice Management by Checklist: A Handbook of Control Techniques.* New York: John Wiley & Sons, 1991.

Index

CUSTOMER NOTE: IF THIS BOOK IS ACCOMPANIED BY SOFTWARE, PLEASE READ THE FOLLOWING BEFORE OPENING THE PACKAGE.

This software contains files to help you utilize the models described in the accompanying book. By opening the package, you are agreeing to be bound by the following agreement:

This software product is protected by copyright and all rights are reserved by the author, John Wiley & Sons, Inc., or their licensors. You are licensed to use this software as described in the software and the accompanying book. Copying the software for any other purpose may be a violation of the U.S. Copyright Law.

This software product is sold as is without warranty of any kind, either express or implied, including but not limited to the implied warranty of merchantability and fitness for a particular purpose. Neither Wiley nor its dealers or distributors assumes any liability for any alleged or actual damages arising from the use of or the inability to use this software. (Some states do not allow the exclusion of implied warranties, so the exclusion may not apply to you.)

To use this 3.5″ disk, your system must meet the following requirements:

Platform/Processor/Operating System. Windows, Mac, or any system running Microsoft Excel.

RAM. 32MB recommended.

Hard Drive Space. 300KB required to copy all the files to the hard drive. None required to open and print the spreadsheets.

Peripherals. Microsoft Excel and a 3.5″ disk drive.